International Political Economy Series

Series Editor
Timothy M. Shaw, University of Massachusetts Boston, Boston, MA, USA;
Emeritus Professor, University of London, London, UK

The global political economy is in flux as a series of cumulative crises impacts its organization and governance. The IPE series has tracked its development in both analysis and structure over the last three decades. It has always had a concentration on the global South. Now the South increasingly challenges the North as the centre of development, also reflected in a growing number of submissions and publications on indebted Eurozone economies in Southern Europe. An indispensable resource for scholars and researchers, the series examines a variety of capitalisms and connections by focusing on emerging economies, companies and sectors, debates and policies. It informs diverse policy communities as the established trans-Atlantic North declines and 'the rest', especially the BRICS, rise.

NOW INDEXED ON SCOPUS!

Geoffrey Banda · Maureen Mackintosh ·
Mercy Karimi Njeru ·
Fortunata Songora Makene · Smita Srinivas
Editors

Cancer Care in Pandemic Times: Building Inclusive Local Health Security in Africa and India

palgrave
macmillan

Editors
Geoffrey Banda
Edinburgh, UK

Maureen Mackintosh
London, UK

Mercy Karimi Njeru
Nairobi, Kenya

Fortunata Songora Makene
Dar Es Salaam, Tanzania

Smita Srinivas
Bangalore, India

ISSN 2662-2483 ISSN 2662-2491 (electronic)
International Political Economy Series
ISBN 978-3-031-44122-6 ISBN 978-3-031-44123-3 (eBook)
https://doi.org/10.1007/978-3-031-44123-3

This Palgrave Macmillan imprint is published by the registered company Springer Nature Switzerland AG
The registered company address is: Gewerbestrasse 11, 6330 Cham, Switzerland

Paper in this product is recyclable.

Preface and Acknowledgements

This book is a collective product, written and edited in virtual meetings across four countries in 2021/2, as the Covid-19 pandemic shifted and changed while continuing to bite. Most of the research on which the book draws was undertaken for the project *Innovation for Cancer Care in Africa (ICCA)* 2018–2021. That project brought together research teams in Kenya, Tanzania, India, and the UK. When the work began in 2018, there was a relative dearth internationally of published research and active policymaking on cancer care in Africa, and on the potential role of local industrial production for cancer care and local health security. Today, the research attention to cancer in low- and middle-income countries has risen sharply, and the Covid pandemic has urgently refocused attention on the fragility of local health supply chains in Africa, India, and elsewhere. This book is therefore timely in bringing together these two important themes.

The research teams thank the Economic and Social Research Council (ESRC), UK, for grant funding for this project, under the Global Challenges Research Fund initiative (grant reference ES/S000658/1), including financial support for publishing this book in open access form. The authors warmly acknowledge additional funding support from the Open University, UK, and thank the Development and Economic Growth Research Programme (DEGRP) at the Overseas Development Institute, UK, for hosting the webinar cited in Chapter 2. The contents of this book are the sole responsibility of the authors and do not necessarily reflect the views of the UK ESRC or any other funding body.

In both Kenya and Tanzania, the research teams wish to thank all the individuals and organisations who generously shared their time, experience, and knowledge for the purposes of this study including cancer patients, cancer survivors, caregivers, healthcare providers, manufacturers and distributors, policymakers, and regulatory authorities. The research teams are particularly grateful for the time and commitment of those participants living with cancer, many of whom shared their experiences in detail despite serious illness.

The Tanzanian research team wishes to appreciate the commitment and sensitivity of the following interviewers: Samwel Ebenezeri, Teddy Rucho, Nicholas Lusingu, Ikunda Njau, Rehema Paul, Wilfred Massau, Janeth Telekako, and Habambi Habambi. They also thank all participants in three workshops held in Dar es Salaam during 2019–2021. The research team is grateful to the Economic and Social Research Foundation (ESRF) and to its Executive Director Dr. Tausi Mbaga Kida for unwavering guidance and support; thanks also to Aldegunda Ngowi, Principal Accountant, for ensuring sound financial management and compliance, John Kajiba for data management and analysis, and George Temba.

The Kenyan research team particularly thanks the Kenya Medical Research Institute for facilitating in all ways the implementation of the research. Further, we thank the National government (Ministry of Health and State Department for Industrialization), the County governments of Meru, Nairobi, and Mombasa, and the facilities involved, for their support throughout. We also thank the private sector pharmaceutical industry for their participation and all study participants. We specifically thank the research assistants: Dr. Rosemary Gacheri, Fridah Nyaga, Mercy Korir, Joan Kwamboka, Nasra Rashid, Elizabeth Kimeu, Mutheu Ochieng, Maurice Nyakundi, Stella Kathambi, Mercy Kinala, Ronnie Obulomire, and Robert Makori. Without them, this study would not have happened. Thank you also to Fidel Muendo for data analysis and Grace Kuria for financial coordination.

The India team acknowledges the very generous participation of all interviewees across Indian cities, Dr. Pramesh and teams, our great panel for the London Global Cancer Week, Janak Nabar for survey insights, and the survey teams' persistence during the pandemic. ICCA India especially acknowledges the coordination and research efforts of Pritika Rao who participated in several publications and pulled the administrative process together for a small team in difficult times, all with good humour and professional commitment. The India team also acknowledges Abhimanyu Dubey's efforts in two countries and the brief involvement of Rajlaxmi Teli in project management of video and podcast development. The National Centre for Biological Sciences–Tata Institute of Fundamental Research (NCBS–TIFR) and especially Raj Ladher and Satyajit Mayor provided a stable base at a time when the organisation was heavily involved in India's Covid-19 efforts. R. Manikanta's steady, good-natured administrative support and V. Srinidhi's anchoring are especially appreciated.

The UK researchers wish to thank the Open University for administrative support throughout the project, including hosting the inception workshop in 2018 and supporting the project and its Principal Investigator through many pandemic-related challenges. Thank you also to the Innogen Institute and TIBA (Tackling Infections to Benefit Africa) at The University of Edinburgh for support during the project and funding for workshops and conferences on local pharmaceutical manufacturing, health systems strengthening, and collaborative work with supranational organisations. The authors also thank the University of Edinburgh's School of Social and Political Science which availed the Strategic Research Support Fund to support indexing of this book. We are grateful to the webinar contributors for sharing their expertise and time during the pressured times of Covid-19. We also warmly thank Nazeem Mohammed for acting as project adviser from the beginning of the project.

The book editors also thank all our authors for their patience with the collective editing process and for their commitment to the book during very difficult times while working at a distance. At Palgrave we thank our very supportive editor Anca Pusca, and our enthusiastic series editor Professor Tim Shaw. At Springer we thank Aishwarya Balachandar and Nandakini Lahiri for their commitment and copious amounts of patience with us as we finalised the book. We also thank Richard Mutisya Arun for patiently assembling and formatting the manuscript through several iterations and checking referencing details.

We hope this book can make a real contribution to promoting better cancer care and greater local health security alongside industrial development.

Edinburgh, UK — Geoffrey Banda
London, UK — Maureen Mackintosh
Nairobi, Kenya — Mercy Karimi Njeru
Dar Es Salaam, Tanzania — Fortunata Songora Makene
Bangalore, India — Smita Srinivas

Contents

Part I Cancer in Pandemic Times

1 The Cancer Care Challenge in the Light of Pandemic Experience 3
Maureen Mackintosh, Geoffrey Banda, Mercy Karimi Njeru, Smita Srinivas, and Fortunata Songora Makene
Cancer Care Through a Pandemic Lens: African and Indian Perspectives 3
The Cancer Research Focus 5
The Cancer Care Challenge in Low-resource Health Systems 7
Cancer and the Health Industries 9
The State of Health-related Manufacturing Across Africa 10
Researching Cancer Care: Methods and Contexts 14
Perspectives on Cancer Care 14
Health Sector Research Methods 15
Industrial Research Methods 16
Health System Organisation: Key Aspects 17
Book Structure: Evidencing and Reframing the Challenges 19

2 **Broken Supply Chains and Local Manufacturing Innovation: Responses to Covid-19 and Their Implications for Policy** 25
Geoffrey Banda, Cecilia Wanjala, Veronica Manduku, Julius Mugwagwa, and Dinar Kale
Introduction: Warnings Become Reality 25
Covid-19: An Immediate Crisis that Triggered a Wakeup Call for Africa 27
Similar but Unequal Response to Crisis: Proximity and Positionality 29
Sources of Supply Chain Crisis: Cascading Import Dependencies 30
Pandemic Impacts in India 32
Sociotechnical Imaginaries: Imaging and Designing the Future 34
India's Pharmaceutical Industry: Technological and Political Projects 37
African Pandemic Innovation 39
Covid-19-induced Policy Shifts and Need for Long-term Policy Sustainability 41
Regulation 41
Industry Policy 43
Conclusion 44

Part II The Cancer Care Experience in East Africa

3 **The Social Pain of Cancer in East Africa: Understanding Need** 49
Lilian Nyandieka, Charlotte Cross, Mercy Karimi Njeru, and Fortunata Songora Makene
A Carer's Story 49
Understanding Social Pain 51
Despair, Fear and Helplessness 52
Failures of Information and Advice 53
Loss of Social Roles and Relationships 55
Stigma and Rejection 56
Social Isolation 57
The Cost of Cancer as a Source of Social Pain 59

Families' Economic Losses 60
Financial Burden and Social Stigma 62
The Social Pain of Surviving Cancer 63
Recognition of Social Pain in the Health System 64
Conclusion 66

4 **Access to Cancer Care: Navigating the Maze** 69
Mercy Karimi Njeru, Maureen Mackintosh, Richard Ngilangwa, Sharon Mokua, Richard Mutisya Arun, and Jane Mukami
Introduction: Accessing Cancer Care 69
The Access Maze 71
Mapping the Maze 72
Availability and Accessibility in the Cancer Care Maze 75
Unavailable Diagnostic Services Close to Home 75
Travel Challenges 77
Navigation Constraints Within Facilities 79
Unaffordable Care 82
Unaffordability and Delays Within the Maze 82
Insurance and Private Care: Facilitation but High Costs 86
Payment Burdens and Impoverishment 87
Tackling the Maze? 89
Information, Maps and Guides 89
Financial Support and Lower Costs 90
Accessible Capacity for Cancer Care 91
Political and Government Support 91

5 **Beyond "Late Presentation": Explaining Delayed Cancer Diagnosis in East Africa** 93
Charlotte Cross, Sharon Mokua, Richard Ngilangwa, Cristina Santos, Twalib Ngoma, and Phares G. M. Mujinja
Introduction 93
Delayed Diagnosis in Kenya and Tanzania 95
Screening and Early Detection 96
Weak Referral Processes 99
Pathology and Laboratory Capability 103
Cost of Diagnosis 105
Conclusion 111

Part III Local Industry and Cancer Care in India and East Africa

6 **Cupboard Full, Cupboard Empty: The Industrial Building Blocks of Covid-19 and Cancer Systems** 115
Smita Srinivas
Introduction: Generalities About 'Broken Health Systems' Despite Covid-19 Successes 115
Cupboard Full, Cupboard Empty: A Thought Experiment 119
The Building Blocks and Methods Behind a Health-Industry Interface 120
Policy Frames 120
Uncertainty and Demand in the Pandemic 124
Cupboard Full, Cupboard Empty 128
Choosing Wisely for Stocking the Cancer Cupboard 133
Conclusion: a Cancer System's Industrial Building Blocks 134

7 **Manufacturing for Cancer Care in East Africa: Raising the Ambition** 139
Veronica Manduku, Samuel Wangwe, Cecilia Wanjala, Maureen Mackintosh, and Richard Ngilangwa
Building Local Health Industries: Pandemic Lessons 139
The Paradox of Need and Demand 141
Procurement and Market-Consolidation 143
Tackling Market Fragmentation: Involving the Users 143
Consolidating and Refocusing Procurement 145
Innovation and Technological Capability-Building 146
Manufacturing Innovative Capabilities in the Pandemic 146
Systemic Capability-Building for Innovation 148
Technology Transfer and Sources of Finance 149
The Challenge of Sterile Manufacturing 149
Finance, Technology Transfer and Skills 151
Technology, Skills and Learning 154
Strengthening Local Health Industries: Building Collaboration 155
Collaborative Priorities 156
Concluding Reflections: Building Innovation Capability and Ambition 159

8 Oncology Drug Production in Sub-Saharan Africa: The Challenge and Opportunity, with Evidence from India 163
Maureen Mackintosh, Sudip Chaudhuri, Nazeem Mohamed, Samuel Wangwe, Twalib Ngoma, and Veronica Manduku
Introduction 163
Unaffordability of Oncology Drugs 164
Import Reliance and Supply Chain Risk 166
India as Oncology Supplier and Benchmark 169
Competition Failures in Generic Oncology Markets 171
Competition Failures Within India 172
Effective Procurement as Competition Policy 174
The Scope for Local Oncology Manufacturing 175
Local Oncology Manufacturing: Market and Technical Challenges 179
The Role of the Health System in Building Local Oncology Supply Chains 183
Conclusion 186

Part IV Industrial Innovation and Industrial Policy

9 Emerging Business Models in Cancer Diagnostic Startups in India and Lessons for African Countries 191
Dinar Kale, Smita Srinivas, and Geoffrey Banda
Introduction 191
MedTech Startups in Developing Countries and Systemic Scarcities 193
The Business Model in Context 195
Case Studies 197
Sascan 197
AiNDRA 200
Panacea Medical Technologies 204
Analysis and Discussion 206
Catalysts and Gridlocks in Indian MedTech Startups 206
Business Models: Evaluating Value Proposition, Creation and Capture 208
Implications for Startups in LMICs 210
Conclusions 212

10 Realistic Ambitions: Technology Transfer for Biologics Platform Technologies 215
Geoffrey Banda, Cecilia Wanjala, Veronica Manduku, and Dinar Kale
Introduction 215
Why are Biologics, Especially MAbs, Important for African Countries? 217
Incremental Versus Disruptive Innovation and Impact on Business Models 219
African Vaccine Manufacturing Footprint—Where are We Starting from? 222
Planned and New Vaccine Plants Triggered by Covid19 Vaccine Nationalism 226
Biologics as an Incremental Innovation on Vaccines and Molecular Biology Techniques 228
The Market Challenges to Successful Technology Transfer 233
Technology Transfer can be Difficult—The Cipla Biologics Case Study 234
Cipla in South Africa: A Lesson for Policy 236
Conclusion 238

11 Palliation Economics: The Industrial Organisation of Morphine in India 241
Smita Srinivas, Ojasvi Ghai, and Lekhaabra Rajadhyaksha
Introduction: From Health Policy to Industrial Policy 241
Provision of Palliative Morphine 243
An Industrial Organsation Approach: Moving Beyond Price and Availability 245
Differentiating Countries by Industrial Capabilities 246
Insufficient Health Policy Reform 247
Industrial Policy Gaps and Opportunities 251
Capacity Utilization and Technology Used 255
Policy Priorities for India 256
Discussion and Conclusion 259

Part V Tackling Institutional Gaps: Using Scenarios

12 Innovation and Policy in Cancer Pain Management: Systemic Interactions in Tanzania 265
Chux Daniels, Ine Steenmans, Fortunata Songora Makene, Richard Ngilangwa, Twalib Ngoma, Cristina Santos, and Maureen Mackintosh
Introduction 265
Framing the Undertreatment of Pain in Cancer Care 267
Undertreatment of Cancer Pain in Tanzania 270
Experiences of Pain 271
Palliative Care Provision 271
Access to Pain Medication 272
The Need-Demand Gap for Severe Pain Relief 273
Morphine Ordering and Distribution 273
Is Fiscal Constraint the Problem? 275
Measuring the Need-Demand Gap for Morphine: A Comparison with Uganda 278
Addressing the Cancer Pain Management Deficit: Mutually Supportive Innovations 281
The Scope for Local Manufacturing 282
Skills, Training and Management of Medication by Health Workers 284
Conclusion: A Focus on Policies, Regulations, and Licensing 285

13 Using Scenarios to Support Innovation and Mutual Linkages 289
Ine Steenmans, Maimanah Idris, Joanna Chataway, Mercy Karimi Njeru, and Samuel Wangwe
Introduction 289
Tools to Support Innovation and Health-Industry Linkages 291
A Practical Tool: Scenarios 292
Scenarios in Health Policy 294
Developing Scenarios 294
Three-Stage Process for Health System Scenarios 295
Two Scenario Case Studies for Cancer Care Innovation 296
Exploring Innovation Pathways Using Scenarios: A Tanzania Cancer Care Case Study 298
Reflections on Practice 303

Collective Visioning with Scenarios: A Kenya Cancer Care Innovation Case Study 304
Reflections on Practice 308
The Strengths of Scenarios for Cross-Sectoral Innovation Support 309
A Whole System View 309
Synthesis Across Sectors and Professions 310
Usefulness in Research and Evidence 310
Uncertainty and the Absence of Empirical Data 311
Inclusive and Accessible Tools 311
Using Scenarios to Build Cross-Sector Innovation Capability 312

14 Conclusion: Better Cancer Care and Greater Local Health Security: Lessons, Opportunities and Ways Forward 315
Geoffrey Banda, Maureen Mackintosh, Mercy Karimi Njeru, Smita Srinivas, Joanna Chataway, and Fortunata Songora Makene
Core Themes 315
Local Health Security: Pandemic Lessons 317
Need, Demand, Supply, Access: Tackling Institutional Gaps in Cancer Care 319
Scope for Investment in Local Manufacture of Drugs, Vaccines, Biologics and Medical Technologies 321
Interlinking Health Care and Industrial Development: Reframing Policy 322
Concluding Reflection 324

References 327

Index 351

Editors and Contributors

About the Editors

Geoffrey Banda is Senior Lecturer in the Science, Technology, and Innovation Studies group at the University of Edinburgh and Deputy Director of the Innogen Institute. He has a background in natural sciences (Biology and Biotechnology) and social sciences (Finance, Innovation and Industry Development). His industrial experience spans quality assurance and microbial safety of food in the food-manufacturing sector, as well as banking spanning corporate, transactional, and retail banking. His research interests lie in local African pharmaceutical manufacturing, food and health security, innovation and risk management, and health systems strengthening. Geoff is a member of the African Vaccine Manufacturing Initiative (AVMI).

Maureen Mackintosh is Emeritus Professor of Economics at the Open University, UK. She is a development economist specialising in markets in health care and medicines. Her research has focused on local manufacturing of pharmaceuticals and other health-related commodities in Sub-Saharan Africa, and on commercialisation of health care in low- and middle-income countries. She was Principal Investigator for the ICCA project on which this book is based. She was lead editor, with Geoffrey Banda, Paula Tibandebage, and Watu Wamae of the book Making

Medicines in Africa: the Political Economy of Industrializing for Local Health (Palgrave Macmillan Open, 2016).

Mercy Karimi Njeru is a research scientist with the Kenya Medical Research Institute (KEMRI), her research focuses on health systems. She has conducted health research for many years taking the lead in various multi-country, multi-disciplinary, and lately multi-sectorial research projects. She currently leads the ICCA project in Kenya. Mercy was involved in writing a chapter in the 'Making medicines in Africa' book with her published work feted among the top resources in mixed methods research. Additionally, she has mentored students and fellow researchers in the application of mixed methods in research. Dr. Njeru earned her Ph.D. at the University of Bergen, Norway.

Fortunata Songora Makene is a development sociologist and gender expert. Her work is rooted in sociology, but spreads into law and anthropology. She works on research and policy work on social protection and human rights, development, and gender, mainly in Sub-Saharan Africa. Her published work focuses on socio-economic reforms, advancing gender equity, women and girls' economic empowerment, and leadership. Fortunata currently heads the Research and Policy Department at UONGOZI Institute, Tanzania. She also serves as a member of the National Advisory Committee on Generation Equality Forum to promote Economic Justice Rights, in Tanzania. Fortunata has a Ph.D. in Sociology from the University of Minnesota (USA).

Smita Srinivas (Ph.D., Dr./Prof.) (Technological Change Lab) specialises in economic development, innovation, and industrial policy, and served as ICCA India lead at NCBS–TIFR. She is the AFEE 2021 Clarence E. Ayres Scholar in institutional economics, and EAEPE 2015 Joan Robinson Prize awardee for *Market Menagerie: Health and Development in Late Industrial States* (Stanford University Press, 2012). She has held appointments at Columbia University, Harvard University, The Open University UK, the IISc, LSE, UCL, and with several think tanks. She received a Ph.D. from MIT in economic development and technology planning, fellowships from Harvard University, and prior training in mathematics and physics.

Contributors

Richard Mutisya Arun is a senior researcher at the Kenya Medical Research Institute (KEMRI). His research interests and expertise are in health systems, public health, and human nutrition, with keen interests in health systems' organisational culture and local manufacture of healthcare products. Currently, a member of the National Committee on Infant and Young Child Feeding (IYCF) and other technical committees at the Kenya National Bureau of Standards and Ministry of Health, he is also a doctoral candidate at the Open University (UK). His thesis analyses primary healthcare utilisation of medical devices and healthcare systems' technological capabilities in LMICs.

Joanna Chataway is Professor of Science and Innovation Policy at University College London (UCL). She is head of the Science, Technology, Engineering, and Public Policy Department (STEaPP) based in the Faculty of Engineering Sciences. She has led and been part of numerous studies exploring the ways in which science, technology, and innovation align and misalign to social needs in different geographical contexts. Joanna is Fellow of the Academy of Social Sciences.

Sudip Chaudhuri retired as Professor of Economics from the Indian Institute of Management Calcutta after serving there for the last several decades. His research interests include intellectual property rights regime and pharmaceutical industry, industrialisation and economic development in developing countries, and the role of state in economic change. Promoting local production of pharmaceutical products in developing countries has been a major area of his work in recent years. He has written several papers/reports on policies and strategies in general and also specifically on the pharmaceutical industry in Bangladesh, India, Ghana, and Tanzania.

Charlotte Cross is Senior Lecturer in International Development at The Open University. Her research explores the governance and politics of development, with a particular focus on citizens' perceptions and experiences of service delivery and the policing of political and economic change. Her research has been published in journals including *Development and Change* and the *Journal of Modern African Studies*. A recent co-edited volume (2023, Routledge), *Critical Approaches to Heritage for Development*, explores relationships between heritage and development, considering the politics and potential of using the past to build 'better' futures.

Chux Daniels, Ph.D. is Research Fellow in Science, Technology, and Innovation (STI) Policy at the Science Policy Research Unit (SPRU) and Director of the Transformative Innovation Policy Consortium (TIPC) Africa Hub, both at the University of Sussex Business School, UK. He is also Senior Fellow at Future Africa, University of Pretoria, South Africa, where he leads the Transformative Innovation Africa Hub. His research interests and topics include STI, digital, transformation, sustainability and the SDGs, and political economy. Chux is widely published on these topics. Besides his academic activities, he is actively involved in public policies and policymaking.

Ojasvi Ghai has pursued Bachelor of Arts (Economics Honours) from CHRIST (Deemed to be University), Bangalore. She works with Prof. Smita Srinivas in analysing development issues through an evolutionary institutional perspective. She analysed the consumption of palliative morphine in India and in a related project, focused on the first steps to analyse science policy's gaps with industrial regulations for the epigenetic impact of plastics

Maimanah Idris is a doctoral researcher in Science, Technology, Engineering, and Public Policy at University College London. Her research topics are interdisciplinary and systems thinking approaches, monitoring and evidence evaluation, participatory tools, and stakeholder engagement initiatives across different contexts. She holds a BSc (Hons) in Geography & Environmental Management, an MSc in Environmental Technology: Health & Global Environment, and an MRes in Urban Sustainability & Resilience funded by the UCL EPSRC DTP. In the past, she has worked at Imperial College London, at the Faculty of Medicine and has worked as a research assistant on the GCRF-funded ICCA project.

Dinar Kale works in the area of innovation management in healthcare technology industries with extensive research on industrial innovation, industrial-health policy linkages, and health access in developing countries. He is currently Head of the Development Policy and Practice (DPP) group and a director of the Centre for Innovation, Knowledge and Development (IKD), an inter-faculty research centre focused on interdisciplinary international development and innovation research at the Open

University. Prof. Kale has researched and published extensively on issues that influence innovation and development of healthcare industries based in low-middle-income countries.

Veronica Manduku is a medical imaging specialist and Senior Research Scientist in KEMRI where she currently heads the Centre for Clinical Research in KEMRI. She has a Bachelors in Medicine and Surgery from Pune University and a Masters in Medicine (Diagnostic Imaging) from the University of Nairobi. Her broad objectives are enhanced quality of care and health equity in Kenya and globally through early diagnosis and screening for infectious and non-infectious diseases. She works in the health product development ecosystem in particular clinical trials and implementation science where she undertakes clinical trials, health industry research, research governance, and policy and development of tools and interventions for application in health.

Nazeem Mohamed is International Pharmaceutical Consultant with over 40 years of experience in the global pharmaceutical sector. He was the Head of the Pharmaceutical Sector for the Aga Khan Development Network, Chairman of Aga Khan Foundation Regional Committee for East Africa, and CEO at Kampala Pharmaceutical Industries in Uganda. He was VP of Strategic Product Development at Novo Nordisk, in Denmark and then Belgium. Nazeem also worked for Pfizer and GlaxoSmithKline, in international marketing management and strategic product development, in the UK, Belgium, Denmark, and the USA. He is the past Chairman of the Federation of East African Pharmaceutical Manufacturers (FEAPM) and current Vice Chair of the Federation of African Pharmaceutical Manufacturers Association (FAPMA).

Sharon Mokua is Research Scientist who holds an MSc in Global Health and Management from the University of Aberdeen. She is Research Coordinator for the ICCA project in Kenya at the Kenya Medical Research Institute (KEMRI). Over the last 5 years, her research focused on developing sustainable global health solutions for Sub-Saharan Africa's health challenges. Sharon has been proactively engaged in research, design, implementation, and evaluation of various projects such as Innovation for Cancer Care, Universal Health Coverage, Digital Health Solutions for Patient Engagement, and Evaluations within Human Centred Design. Her recent publication is on implementation research for PMTCT.

Julius Mugwagwa is Professor of Health Innovation and Public Policy at University College London, Department of Science, Technology Engineering and Public Policy (UCL STEaPP). He also serves as Global Health Thematic Director for the UCL's Global Governance Institute. He has worked in veterinary research, pharmaceutical R&D, quality assurance, and harmonisation of medicines regulatory systems in Africa. He is an accomplished scholar and published author in the areas of global health, health innovation, and health system strengthening, buttressed by his research and teaching interests in the governance and development implications of technologies and innovations.

Phares G. M. Mujinja is a professor in public health economics at Muhimbili University of Health and Allied Sciences in Dar es Salaam, Tanzania. He holds a Ph.d. in Public Health Economics from Heidelberg University, Germany, MA (Economics), and MPH from Boston University, USA. He has vast experience in research and published in of health systems, reproductive health, communicable and non-communicable diseases, health financing, economic evaluation, pharmaceutical markets, regulatory frameworks, health logistic management, and traditional medicine. He has served as a consultant to various national and international organisations including The World Bank, EU, WHO, UNAIDS, UNDP, UNICEF, UNTAID, and government agencies.

Jane Mukami is an information communication technology expert at the Kenya Medical Research Institute (KEMRI). She has been engaged in various national, multi-disciplinary, and multi-country health research projects and her area of interest is data management. Jane is actively involved in managing and analysing the project findings in the current study of Innovation for Cancer Care in Africa (ICCA) Kenya. Additionally, Jane has been instrumental in various projects including; Response to Accountable Priority setting for Trust in health systems (REACT), Kenya Micronutrient Survey (KMS), Medical Management Systems (MMS), etc., where she has handled both qualitative and quantitative data.

Richard Ngilangwa is Assistant Research Fellow with the Economic and Social Research Foundation (ESRF) a premier policy think tank in Tanzania. He has a background in social sciences, and his policy research has focused on social protection and social service delivery. Mr. Ngilangwa has worked with the ICCA project since 2018, and has co-authored publications on enhancing care and assessing manufacturing capabilities in Tanzania. His experience is in line with the ESRF institutional mandate to undertake research, capacity building in research methods, documentation as part of knowledge management and innovation, and training of stakeholders on policy analysis and advocacy.

Twalib Ngoma currently holds a research chair in the Department of Clinical Oncology at Muhimbili University of Health and Allied Sciences (MUHAS). He is the founder of the Ocean Road Cancer Institute and was the Executive Director of ORCI from 1996 to 2014. He holds an MD from the University of Dar es Salaam and post-graduate training in Radiotherapy and Medical Oncology from Christie Hospital in Manchester, UK. He is a member of the Royal College of Radiologists UK and Fellow of the faculty of Radiology Royal College Surgeons Ireland. He is a member of the American Society of Clinical Oncology (ASCO) and was the President of the Africa Organization for Research and Training in Cancer (AORTIC) from 2007 to 2009.

Lilian Nyandieka is Senior Research Scientist working at the Kenya Medical Research Institute. With a training in Social Sciences, Lilian has undertaken various health research projects to investigate varied issues that affect people's health in communities across Kenya and published some of the work. Lilian is also a trained Counsellor with a passion to alleviate suffering for people who have been through stressful life experiences. Her educational background is M.A. (Sociology), Diploma in Counseling Psychology, and Addiction Counseling and Treatment. Currently she is pursuing her Ph.D. studies in Public Health. She was a co-investigator in the ICCA project.

Lekhaabra Rajadhyaksha is an analyst in Deloitte India. An alumnus of Bombay Scottish School, Mahim, Mumbai and St. Xavier's College, Lekhaabra completed his BMS Degree (Bachelor's In Management Studies) and holds a P. G. Diploma in Economics with a specialisation in Public Policy from Meghnad Desai Academy of Economics, Mumbai. His interests include Public Health and Public Education research, investment, and development impacts.

Cristina Santos is Lecturer in Economics with over 15 years experience of economic evaluation in health, education, and gender. As an academic at the Open University, she also has held consultant posts for international organisations such as World Bank, USAID, and UNDP or was hired by Ministries of Education in Sub-Saharan countries (Angola and Sao

Tome). Some of her research has been funded by bodies such as ESRC, GCRF, the Academy of Medical Sciences, and the European Commission. Within the ICCA project, she was its data manager and supported the development of the patients' instruments and analysis.

Ine Steenmans is Associate Professor in Futures, Analysis, and Policy at the University College London (UCL). Ine's research focuses on future policy competencies and capabilities and asks how their development can be better aligned. She has an special interest in the competencies for integrating knowledge across sectors and time horizons. This includes futures and foresight methods, systems methodologies, and evaluation. All her work takes the same needs-led, transformation-oriented, and partnership-based approach. Before joining UCL, Ine worked as a foresight researcher at the UK Government Office for Science.

Samuel Wangwe holds a Bachelors degree in Economics and Statistics, a Masters degree in Economics, and a Doctoral degree in Economics from the University of Dar es Salaam. He has over 40 years experience as an economist, teacher, policy researcher, policy analyst, and economic advisor to the Government of Tanzania. He has published 16 books and 80 articles in scholarly journals and edited books in various fields of development policy. He has worked at the University of Dar es Salaam where he retired as professor of economics, Executive Director of Economic and Social Research Foundation (ESRF), and REPOA, policy think tanks in Tanzania. Currently, he is a consultant and Chairman at Daima Associates and Principal Research Associate with ESRF and REPOA.

Cecilia Wanjala is Pharmacist with MBA training from the University of Nairobi. She has vast experience in the health industry providing policy advisory services in strategy development to improve service delivery. She has vast knowledge and experience in innovation and research output commercialisation at the Kenya Medical Research Institute, and an extensive network of stakeholders cutting across the public and private sectors in the region. Her major achievements include taking the lead as a technical advisor and team member in the local vaccine and biopharmaceuticals manufacturing initiative. She is passionate about the development of industry-research linkages and local manufacturing in Africa.

Acronyms

AFEE	Association for Evolutionary Economics
AI	Artificial Intelligence
AIDS	Acquired Immune Deficiency Syndrome
AIOCD	All Indian Origin Chemists & Distributors Ltd
AORTIC	Africa Organization for Research and Training in Cancer
API	Active Pharmaceutical Ingredient
ARIPO	African Regional Intellectual Property Organisation
ARV	Anti-retroviral drug
ASCO	American Society of Clinical Oncology
AU	African Union
AUDA	African Union Development Agency
AVMI	African Vaccine Manufacturing Initiative
BARC	Bhabha Atomic Research Centre
BBC	Bangalore Bio-innovation Centre
BCG- vaccine	Bacillus Calmette–Guérin vaccine
BIRAC	Biotechnology Industry Research Assistance Council
BMGF	Bill and Melinda Gates Foundation
BSI	British Standards Institution
CAPEX	Capital Expenditure
CCMP	Centre for Cellular and Molecular Platforms
CDC	Centres for Disease Control and Prevention
CE	Cupboard Empty
CEO	Chief Executive Officer
CF	Cupboard Full
CFCE	Cupboard Full Cupboard Empty
COGS	Cost of Goods Sold

COMESA	Common Market for Eastern and Southern Africa
COVAX	COVID-19 Vaccines Global Access
COVID-19	Coronavirus disease 2019
CPS	Concentrate of Poppy Straw
CRISPR	Clustered Regularly Interspaced Short Palindromic Repeats
CSIR	Council for Scientific and Industrial Research Council
CT-Scan	Computed Tomography Scan
CW – India	Choose Wisely India
DCEA	Drug Control Enforcement Authority
DDD	Defined Daily Doses
DEGRP	Development and Economic Growth Research Programme
DGCI&S	Directorate General of Commercial Intelligence and Statistics
DNA	Deoxyribonucleic acid
DPP	Development Policy and Practice
DRC	Democratic Republic of Congo
DST	Department of Science & Technology
DTI	Department of Trade, Industry and Competition
EAC	East African Community
EBIDTA	Earnings Before Interest, Taxes, Depreciation and Amortization
EBRD	European Bank for Reconstruction and Development
EIB	European Investment Bank
EMA	European Medicines Agency
ENT	Ear, nose and throat
EPZ	Export Processing Zone
ESRC	Economic and Social Research Council
ESRF	Economic and Social Research Foundation
EU	European Union
FAPMA	Federation of African Pharmaceutical Manufacturers Association
FBO	Faith Based Organisation
FDI	Foreign Direct Investment
FEAPMA	Federation of East African Pharmaceutical Manufacturers Association
FERA	Foreign Exchange Regulation Act
FNA	Fine Needle Aspiration
GAVI	Global Alliance for Vaccines and Immunisations
GBS	Group B Streptococcus
GIZ	Deutsche Gesellschaft für Internationale Zusammenarbeit
GMP	Good Manufacturing Practice
GNI	Gross National Income
GOAW	Government Opium and Alkaloid Works
HIV	Human Immunodeficiency Virus

HPV	Human-papillomavirus
IARC	International Agency for Research on Cancer
ICCA	Innovation for Cancer Care in Africa
ICDC	Industrial and Commercial Development Corporation
ICMR	Indian Council of Medical Research
ICU	Intensive Care Unit
IEJ	Institute of Economic Justice
IFC	International Finance Corporation
IITM	Indian Institute of Technology Mandi
IMF	International Monetary Fund
INCB	International Narcotics Control Board
INR	Indian Rupee
IP	Intellectual Property
IPR	Intellectual Property Rights
ISO	International Organisation for Standardisation
IT	Information Technology
IV	Institutional Variety
KEMRI	Kenya Medical Research Institute
KEMSA	Kenya Medical Supplies Authority
KES	Kenyan Shilling
LIMC	Low- and middle-income countries
MCAZ	Medicines Control Authority of Zimbabwe
MEDS	Mission for Essential Drugs & Supplies
MHRA	Medicines and Healthcare Products Regulatory Agency
MMS	Medical Management Systems
MNC	Multinational Corporate
MRC	Medical Research Council
MRI	Magnetic resonance imaging
MSD	Medical Stores Department
MUHAS	Muhimbili University of Health and Allied Sciences
NCBS-TIFR	The National Centre for Biological Sciences-Tata Institute of Fundamental Research
NCCS	National Cancer Control Strategy
NCD	Non-communicable Disease
NDP	New Drug Policy
NDPS	Narcotic Substances and Psychotropic Substances
NEPAD	New Partnership for Africa's Development
NGO	Non-governmental Organisation
NHIF	National Health Insurance Fund
NIDHI	National Initiative for Developing and Harnessing Innovations
NIS	National Innovation System
OECD	Organisation for Economic Co-operation and Development
OOP	Out of Pocket Payment

OPEX	Operating Expenditure
OPML	Oral Potentially Malignant Lesions
ORCI	Ocean Road Cancer Institute
PAGIT	Proportionate and Adaptive Governance of Innovative Technologies
PET Scan	Positron Emission Tomography Scan
PHC	Primary Health Centre
PLI	Production Linked Incentive Scheme
PMPA	Pharmaceutical Manufacturing Plan of Action
PPB	Pharmacy and Poisons Board
PPP	Public Private Partnership
PSA	Prostate-Specific Antigen
QA	Quality Assurance
QC	Quality Control
QCIL	Quality Chemical Industries Ltd
RNA	Ribonucleic Acid
SA	South Africa
SADC	Southern African Development Community
SAMEER	Society for Applied Microwave Electronic Engineering and Research
SCTIMST	Sree Chitra Tirunal Institute for Medical Sciences & Technology
SDG	Sustainable Development Goals
SII	Serum Institute of India
SME	Small to Medium Enterprises
SSA	Sub-Saharan Africa
STI	Science, Technology and Innovation
STS	Science, Technology and Society
TB	Tuberculosis
TIBA	Tackling Infections to Benefit Africa
TMDA	Tanzania Medicine and Medical Devices Authority
TNMSC	Tamil Nadu Medical Services Corporation
TRIPS	Trade-Related Aspects of Intellectual Property Rights
TZS	Tanzanian Shillings
UHC	Universal Health Coverage
UK	United Kingdom
UN	United Nations
UNAIDS	United Nations Programme on HIV and AIDS
UNCTAD	United Nations Conference on Trade and Development
UNDP	United Nations Development Programme
UNIDO	United Nations Industrial Development Organisation
USA	The United States of America
USD	United States Dollar

VIA	Visual Inspection with Lugol Iodine
WHO	The World Health Organisation
WIPO	World Intellectual Property Organisation
ZAR	South African Rand
ZAZIBONA	Zambia, Zimbabwe, Botswana and Namibia

List of Figures

Fig. 1.1	The African pharmaceutical manufacturing footprint as of 2022 (*Source* Author's calculations)	11
Fig. 4.1	Tackling the maze	90
Fig. 11.1	Estimated Indian top 5 opioid requirements (grams) (May 2022) (*Source* Estimated world requirements for narcotic drugs in grams for 2022 (May 2022). Available at: https://www.incb.org/documents/Narcotic-Drugs/Status-of-Estimates/2022/EstMay22.pdf)	254
Fig. 11.2	Opiate raw materials rich in morphine: production in India (in ton) *Sources* International Narcotics Control Board, 2013. Supply for opiate raw materials and demand for opiates for medical and scientific purposes. Available at: https://www.incb.org/documents/Narcotic-Drugs/Technical-Publications/2013/Part_3_supply_E.pdf; International Narcotics Control Board, 2019. Supply for opiate raw materials and demand for opiates for medical and scientific purposes. Available at: International Narcotics Control Board, 2020. Supply for opiate raw materials and demand for opiates for medical and scientific purposes. Available at: Narcotic Drugs — Estimated World Requirements for 2021 — Statistics for 2019 (https://www.incb.org/documents/Narcotic-Drugs/Technical-Publications/2020/8_NAR_2020_Part_III_Supply_and_Demand_E.pdf); Note: A severe drop in the estimates of Morphine production in India was expected due to Covid-19.)	255

Fig. 12.1 Dimensions of cancer care and pain management (*Source* Authors) 270

Fig. 12.2 Understanding the need-demand gap in morphine for cancer pain management (*Source* Authors) 274

Fig. 12.3 Morphine: relationship between procurement and availability levels (*Source* Authors) 276

Fig. 12.4 Median buyers' prices: 2000–2015, morphine sulphate 30 mg tablet and morphine sulphate 15 mg/ml ampoule (USD) (*Source* Drawn by authors from MSH (2015) and previous years (online)) 277

Fig. 12.5 Critical components of cancer pain management (*Source* Authors) 281

Fig. 13.1 Scenarios are tools for exploring how mutual health-industry linkages can shape a wide range of possible health innovation futures (*Source* Authors) 293

Fig. 13.2 A partial view of the systems map of the systemic problem of systemic cancer care pain management and opioid undersupply. It highlights three sub-themes across the driving health-industry linkages discussed 300

Fig. 13.3 Scenario of localised opioid manufacturing 302

Fig. 13.4 A future scenario for local manufacturing of cancer care commodities in Kenya 307

List of Tables

Table 4.1 Levels of entry into the access maze, Kenya and Tanzania (% of all patients) 73
Table 4.2 Cumulative time between milestones (median number of days) Tanzania and Kenya 73
Table 4.3 Household burden of OOP payments: Median cumulative OOP spending from first symptoms to interview date as % of annual income, by income bands 89
Table 6.1 Seven interface uncertainties in the clinical foreground and industrial background of Covid-19 126
Table 6.2 Selected recommendations from Choosing Wisely India, towards a minimum CFCE 135
Table 8.1 Some key oncology medicines for the East African market: main applications 168
Table 8.2 India's exports of oncology medicine to Africa, 2019/20, top country destinations for some key products 170
Table 8.3 Selected anti-cancer drugs: retail market sales in India, 2018–19 173
Table 8.4 The price impact of good procurement in a fragmented oncology medicines market 176
Table 8.5 Challenges for local manufacturing of oncology products 181
Table 9.1 Key tenets of the business model for healthcare innovations in LMICs 196
Table 9.2 Startups under study 197
Table 9.3 Value proposition, creation and capture 209

Table 10.1 Monoclonal antibody therapies and targeted cancers 218
Table 10.2 Impact of disruptive and incremental innovation on business models, value chains and processes 221
Table 10.3 Vaccine and biologics manufacturers and the products manufactured locally as at 2022 223
Table 10.4 Expressed interests in new investments in Covid19 vaccine manufacturing on the continent in 2022 227
Table 10.5 The incremental innovation nature of vaccines types, antigen, production process and skills for incumbent players 231
Table 11.1 Sales of Government Opium and Alkaloid Works (GOAW) in India (kg) 252
Table 11.2 Fragmentation of the industrial organization of palliation 257
Table 12.1 Estimates of the Tanzanian morphine ordering gap 2020, using a Uganda comparison 280
Table 13.1 1 Health systems scenarios process overview 297
Table 13.2 Focus group questions for scenario validation and 'now what?' propositions 303
Table 13.3 Key sectoral and cross-sectoral issues for localised production of commodities 308

PART I

Cancer in Pandemic Times

Health policies and industrial policies will be profoundly influenced from now on by the pandemic experience—or at least, so we hope at the time of writing in late 2022. The research project on ***Innovation for Cancer Care in Africa (ICCA)***, from which this book is largely drawn, was shaped for all the researchers by the impact of the Covid-19 pandemic from early 2020 (Chapter 1). At the same time, the landscape of policy thinking around health security was being dramatically altered, as African countries—and even much more industrialised India—faced the health consequences of the pandemic-induced collapse of trade and travel (Chapter 2). The findings and the debates recorded in this book draw on the experience and the involvement of all the project researchers in both local responses to Covid-19 and continuing research on the emergent crisis of cancer care in Africa and other low- and middle-income countries.

Chapter 1 traces the scale of that emergent cancer crisis, and the rising international recognition of the scale of the health challenge posed by the associated suffering. The chapter also introduces a central theme of the book, built on earlier research, of the importance of local manufacturing of medicines and other health supplies for local health security. The importance of those local industries, already a theme of cancer care research, was dramatically confirmed by the impact of Covid-19, as Chapter 2 documents. The health care resilience of individual low- and middle-income countries in Africa, and of India, in the face of the pandemic was deeply influenced by the depth and breadth of industrial development in those countries and the associated capability for innovation to meet essential need. Chapter 2 sets out the initial case—followed up in the rest of the book—for learning the pandemic lessons about how to build local health security on stronger health-industrial linkages.

CHAPTER 1

The Cancer Care Challenge in the Light of Pandemic Experience

Maureen Mackintosh, Geoffrey Banda, Mercy Karimi Njeru, Smita Srinivas, and Fortunata Songora Makene

Cancer Care Through a Pandemic Lens: African and Indian Perspectives

This is a book about improving cancer care in Africa and India that is a child of its pandemic times. It has been collaboratively researched and written by colleagues in Kenya, Tanzania, India and the UK, working within a cross-country, multidisciplinary research project, *Innovation for*

M. Mackintosh (✉)
The Open University, Milton Keynes, UK
e-mail: maureen.mackintosh@open.ac.uk

G. Banda
University of Edinburgh, Edinburgh, UK
e-mail: Geoffrey.Banda@ed.ac.uk

M. K. Njeru
Kenya Medical Research Institute (KEMRI), Nairobi, Kenya
e-mail: mnjeru@kemri.go.ke

G. Banda et al. (eds.), *Cancer Care in Pandemic Times: Building Inclusive Local Health Security in Africa and India*, International Political Economy Series,
https://doi.org/10.1007/978-3-031-44123-3_1

Cancer Care in Africa (ICCA).[1] We began international meetings and fieldwork in late 2018. We then found ourselves working at a distance and under pandemic restrictions from March 2020 until the time of writing. The project researchers—like so many others across the world—have sustained this research and collaboration through lockdown, personal trauma, illness, bereavement, over-work, frustration, mutual support—and through many virtual international meetings.

Since this was a health-focused research project, ICCA researchers during the pandemic not only continued to work on the cancer research project but were also called upon by their governments to respond to immediate pandemic needs. The variety of those demands to which ICCA researchers responded stretched from supporting and documenting local innovations in African countries, through finding ways to fill supply gaps as international import supply chains collapsed in 2020 (Banda et al., 2021a), to deep involvement of some colleagues in day-to-day management of the pandemic in their respective countries. At the same time, cancer services like other health services were widely undermined by pandemic constraints (Barasa et al., 2021, Martei et al., 2021, Nnaji & Moodley, 2021, Ranganathan et al., 2021).

In combining these two concerns, for improving cancer care and responding to pandemic needs, our original project aims have been challenged, deepened and reworked. ICCA's initial collaborative research focus included—against the grain of most global health literature—the potential role of enhanced local production of essential healthcare supplies for improving cancer care in African countries. That research focus was built on results of sustained earlier work by some of the ICCA researchers into industrial-health linkages in Africa and in India, and their implications for revisiting theory, research methodology and policy (Mackintosh et al., 2016, 2018a; Srinivas, 2012). The pandemic experience has strikingly validated these earlier findings on the importance of industrial development for health care. That experience identified for national governments

S. Srinivas
Bengaluru, India
e-mail: researchtclab@duck.com

F. S. Makene
Economic and Social Research Foundation, Dar Es Salaam, Tanzania
e-mail: fmakene@esrf.or.tz

and multilateral agencies the central importance of deepening and redirecting industrialisation in African countries as well as other continents to improve healthcare inclusion and strengthen local health security. It has also strongly demonstrated the scale of the opportunity for local industrial/health collaboration, its complexities and its substantial potential benefits.

As a result, the pandemic crystallised for researchers and policymakers an often overlooked phenomenon: global health security is built on the foundations of strong local health security. The whole chain is as strong as the weakest link, especially as concerns highly transmissible infections. We argue in this book that new analytical thinking from social scientists and others is required on how to build local health security. We use the "lens" of original research on cancer care in East Africa and India to build up an understanding of the scope for the development of stronger synergies between local health industries and health care, in order to strengthen local health security and develop tools for policy making. The rethinking and reimagining presented here is required for different African countries, for India and the wider world, and this research on cancer care has taught us that this imperative goes much wider than infectious diseases.

The Cancer Research Focus

The growing challenge of non-communicable diseases in Africa was well recognised by the mid-2010s. Kenyan colleagues, in a research workshop in 2017 aiming to build on our earlier work, presented a reasoned argument for tackling cancer specifically, as an emergent, serious and under-studied non-communicable disease challenge that was gaining a high profile in Kenyan public and policy debate. In contrast to the limited international focus on cancer in low- and middle-income countries when we began in 2018, we find ourselves at the time of writing in 2022 contributing to an expanding research literature on cancer in Sub-Saharan Africa.

As a team of multidisciplinary researchers, we are conscious of the multiple ways that cancer care can be framed, especially with our attention focused on different types of innovation, notably those that can lower cost and simplify delivery but are not antagonistic to scientific advances or the latest technologies. The urgent context of the pandemic also made our diverse training and methods lenses even more visible than at the start. Collaborators on this project had different disciplinary, professional, geographic, national and personal responses to the challenges we were facing. The authors include social scientists from a range of disciplines including economics, researchers with science, engineering, finance and business backgrounds, pharmacists, health systems analysts and clinicians. The chapters are all shaped by these disciplinary divides and include efforts at synthesis, attempting the integration of acutely differing perspectives.

The theme and structure of this book reflect this complex experience. Our sustained argument—in some sense, perhaps, a manifesto—is that African countries and India, like other low- and middle-income countries, can enhance their populations' health care and health security, regarding both communicable and non-communicable disease, by bringing much closer together health needs, health systems strengthening, health innovations and improved industrial capabilities within new local (national or regional) collaborations. Cancer care provides a key challenge and research field for this argument, since cancer is a hard case (or "wicked problem") in terms of the number and complexity of cancers and the socio-economic, technical and financial challenges in addressing this complexity.

The book thus argues that tackling the difficult case of cancer care is crucial in itself for human wellbeing and inclusive health care, while the findings and experiences also have much to teach about building better local health security in low- and middle-income contexts with specific reference to Africa and India. Notably, the book advocates for a broader view of cancer care, expanding it beyond the clinic and patient to the supporting social and economic networks and the wider industrial sphere. We bring together industry, health, economic and public policy linkages in new ways, and call for new institutions, infrastructures and processes that can help generate better cancer care. The pandemic can be a turning point towards a greater focus on building local health security in low- and middle-income countries through sustained and purposive linkages of industrial and health capabilities. The book points forward to how that can be achieved.

In a book of this scope, the contributions are several, to improved evidence, more fine-grained analysis, and contributions to theory and methods. This chapter first sets out the motivation for this research, in the scale of the cancer crisis facing low- and middle-income countries and specifically Sub-Saharan Africa and India. We explain why we chose to study cancer care broadly, not initially focusing on specific cancers, and outline our methodologies. This chapter also briefly identifies aspects of the political economy of the health systems in Kenya, Tanzania and India that are relevant for the chapters that follow. It then introduces the industrial context for this research and explains the focus on linkages between industry and health, with reference to the state of the health industries across Africa and in India, and the pandemic context which has brought these linkages to the fore. Finally, we outline the structure of the book.

The Cancer Care Challenge in Low-resource Health Systems

Cancer care is now internationally recognised as an emergent crisis in the health systems of African countries and in other low-resource health systems (WHO, 2020). Since 2017, when the World Health Assembly passed a resolution requesting WHO guidance on cancer prevention and control, there has been a sharp rise in international documentation of the ways in which health systems across the globe are very severely failing cancer patients (Hack et al., 2019; Knaul et al., 2018; Ngwa et al., 2022a; Sullivan et al., 2017). The prevalence of cancers is rising across low- and middle-income countries (WHO, 2020), where evidence of severe suffering and exclusion from cancer care are rightly alarming national and international policymakers.

Sub-Saharan African countries are facing a dual challenge: high and rising levels of non-communicable disease including cancers, and continuing severity of infectious diseases, now sharply worsened by Covid-19. This has put huge pressure on fragile health services. Furthermore, infections and cancers interact: a higher proportion of cancers are linked to infection in Africa than in most other parts of the world (de Martel et al., 2020). The Global Cancer Observatory estimated 1.1 million new cancer cases in Africa (North and Sub-Saharan) in 2020 (Globocan, 2020a). The most commonly reported cancers in Sub-Saharan Africa in 2020 were cervical and breast cancer in women, and prostate cancer in men. Strikingly women's cumulative risk of dying from cancer was higher in Eastern Africa (11.0%) than in North America or Western Europe (Sung et al., 2021). Cervical cancer was the leading cause of cancer death for women in much of Eastern and Southern Africa: countries including Kenya, Uganda and South Africa record rising premature mortality from cervical cancer, a largely preventable illness (Jedy-Agba et al., 2020). Breast cancer incidence is also rising rapidly in Sub-Saharan Africa, where breast cancer mortality rates are now some of the highest in the world (Joko-Fru et al., 2020). Both incidence and mortality rates for prostate cancer have also risen in Eastern and Southern Africa, and this is the leading cause of cancer mortality among Sub-Saharan men (Seraphin et al., 2021).

A major cause of high cancer mortality in Sub-Saharan African countries is late stage diagnosis, and therefore starting treatment at stages 3 or 4. High case fatality rates are closely associated with late stage diagnosis and treatment (WHO, 2020). It is recognised that downstaging cancer diagnosis and treatment can improve outcomes even in low-resource systems. Furthermore, downstaging can be achieved for cancers with external symptom markers, for example breast and cervical cancer, without population-based mammography, and by using trained health aides (Duggan et al., 2021; Ngoma et al., 2015). More broadly, it is recognised that low-resource health systems suffer from a very severe shortage of diagnostic capabilities (Fleming et al., 2021).

Pathology limitations are a major constraint on cancer diagnosis, alongside a failure by high-income country-based funders to focus on pathology requirements (Horton et al., 2018). Other barriers to timely cancer diagnosis include stigma and lack of public awareness of symptoms; misdiagnosis within the health system and financial barriers to diagnostics such as imaging (Brand et al., 2019). There are also documented delays, financial barriers and lack of availability of treatment including chemotherapy and radiography resources (Elmore et al., 2021). Finally, the widespread lack of access to palliation and pain control has been described as an "abyss" (Knaul et al., 2018). All this has been worsened by the pandemic impact on access to cancer care (Mutebi, 2021).

Despite higher levels of resource, India has also long struggled to provide effective cancer care for its population. Incidence has been rising (Mallath et al., 2014; Smith & Mallath, 2019), with an estimated 1.3 million new cancer sufferers in India in 2020 (Globocan, 2020b). Patients face continuing problems of misdiagnosis, late-stage diagnosis and poor treatment outcomes, and inequality in access to care is compounded by the burden of out-of-pocket payments (Pramesh et al., 2014). Covid-19 has had a documented major impact in further impeding access to cancer care in India, from screening to treatment (Ranganathan et al., 2021). Delivering affordable and equitable cancer care in India's complex health system has been described as "one of India's greatest public health challenges" (Pramesh et al., 2014, p. e223).

Across Sub-Saharan Africa, and also in India, governments have recently been giving greater policy attention to cancer care. Public pressure has helped to push cancer care up the political agenda in African countries. Cancer registries and data are improving in quality and scale. In East Africa, some countries have recently added oncology medicines to their essential medicines lists, following WHO essential medicines guidance, and have developed or updated cancer treatment guidelines MoH Kenya (MoH, 2017, 2019). India has had a National Cancer Control Programme since the 1970s.[2] India's ambitious new National Cancer Grid brings together a vast network of cancer centres that work at setting standards for care, providing training and supporting research (Pramesh et al., 2014)[3] North-eastern India which faces a high cancer burden now has several regional cancer centres in Assam, new hospitals and training centres and education efforts serving the region.[4] There is an increasing focus on adapting cancer care to improve access and outcomes in low-resource countries including India (Pramesh et al., 2019; Sullivan et al., 2017).

Cancer and the Health Industries

Industrial organisation is a vital foundation for the study of cancer care innovation and a key contributor to improvements in care. This argument, a core theme of this book, remains rarely reflected in frameworks of analysis of health systems in general and cancer care in particular. The quality of health care self-evidently relies on the timely availability of industrial supplies of essential medicines, medical devices and equipment, diagnostics, laboratory reagents and other essential commodities such as disinfectants. The Covid-19 pandemic has reinforced awareness of the fragility of international supply chains for health care. It is time for the industrial building blocks of health systems to be now integrated into revised frameworks for health analysis and policy as well as interventions.

By "health industries" in this book we mean all these industrial suppliers, and also their upstream reliance on active pharmaceutical ingredients (APIs) and other major inputs from the chemicals, plastics and other industries. And by "local production", we mean all such manufacturing undertaken within a specified country or region, whatever the ownership structure.

In these terms, the contrast between India and Sub-Saharan African countries is sharp, and some aspects of that contrast are explored in this book. India benefits from depth and breadth of industrial scale and capabilities in the health industries developed over many decades. India's pharmaceutical companies, many multinational in operation, are global suppliers of generic medicines and are increasingly innovative. They are the dominant suppliers of essential medicines in Eastern and Southern Africa. India's medical device industries, though less internationally dominant, are extensive, growing and highly innovative. India also displays industrial depth in upstream suppliers and input products from plastics to design consulting services.

While the Indian pharmaceutical and other health industries have been extensively studied, this is not the case for the health industries of Sub-Saharan Africa. We therefore briefly survey here the current state of these industries, as a background to the chapters to follow.

The State of Health-related Manufacturing Across Africa

Many Sub-Saharan African countries have a long history of pharmaceutical production, from the colonial period onwards (Banda et al., 2016b). Some countries, including South Africa, Kenya, Nigeria and Ghana, have substantial industrial clusters of pharmaceutical firms, predominantly locally owned, which have survived the exit of most large US- and Europe-based multinationals in the 1980s and 1990s (Mackintosh et al., 2016).

Figure 1.1 summarises the current footprint of medicines production across Africa.[5] The African continent is home to over 689 pharmaceutical manufacturers, many of which fall in the small to medium enterprise category. North Africa has the greatest number (estimated at 272), followed by West Africa (estimated at 213), Southern Africa (estimated at 139) and East Africa (estimated at 65). The largest industrial clusters of local pharmaceutical manufacturing are in South Africa (122), Egypt (120) and Nigeria (150). Others with 30 or more plants include Algeria, Tunisia and Morocco; Kenya, the East African hub and Ghana. Smaller industrial clusters exist in Sudan, Cameroon, Ethiopia and Uganda.

Most of this production is of basic generics (tablets and capsules including antibiotics; topical preparations and syrups for children). Some firms in Kenya, South Africa and elsewhere can produce injectables under sterile conditions. Product ranges are limited, and few firms can produce more complex generics such as those required for non-communicable diseases, or those embodying slow-release or dual-layer tablets. At the

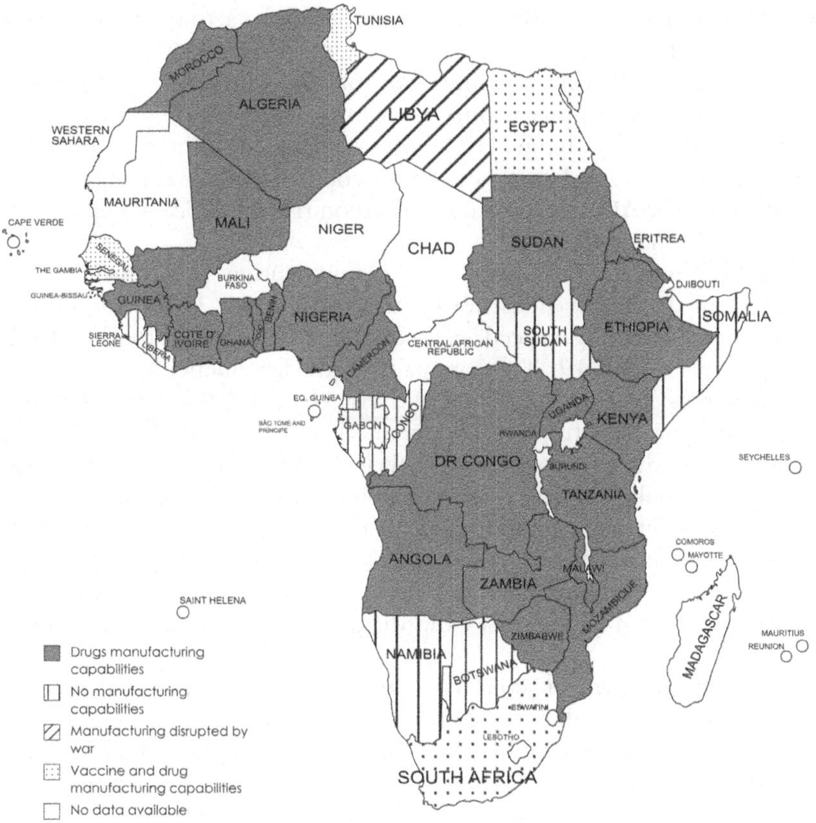

Fig. 1.1 The African pharmaceutical manufacturing footprint as of 2022 (*Source* Author's calculations)

time of writing there is very little oncology drug production in Sub-Saharan Africa.

North Africa is the most vibrant region and Egypt has the most local pharmaceutical manufacturers. North Africa leads in formulations and technological capabilities and has successfully used technology transfer to move upstream in drugs and biologics technologies. The vaccine manufacturing footprint on the continent is much smaller. There are only four countries with vaccine manufacturing plants: Egypt, Senegal, Tunisia and

South Africa (Fig. 1.1). These four countries manufacture drugs, vaccines (hatched pattern in Fig. 1.1), and feature prominently in current efforts for local Covid-19 vaccine manufacture on the continent.

The only API manufacturing companies are in South Africa, with a very limited product range. APIs and excipients are otherwise imported from China, India and some European countries. This very high import dependence for APIs creates a concentration risk for Africa with particular regard to China.

Medical devices and diagnostics manufacturing is a much smaller segment of the health industries in Africa (Mkwashi, 2020). The limited device manufacturing placed the continent on a poor footing to be prepared for Covid-19. There remains high dependence on imports of raw materials from India, China and elsewhere for the medical devices and diagnostic industry, and for chemical reagents, the scale and range of locally produced products is very limited. China is an increasingly important supplier of devices and equipment to African countries' health systems. The lethargic development of the medical device sector may be attributable to a lack of concerted policy efforts to develop the sector by supporting entrepreneurs and providing appropriate regulatory and governance systems for devices and diagnostics (Mkwashi, 2020; WHO, 2016b).

Sub-Saharan African countries' health systems thus remain very heavily import-dependent for manufactured health commodities, in sharp contrast to India's deep industrial capabilities in these health-related industries, and indeed in contrast to the somewhat stronger industrial base of some North African countries such as Egypt and Morocco. This import dependence is in sharp contrast to India's ability to supply a large proportion of its medicines requirements from its highly successful pharmaceutical sector, and India's lively medical device industry.

Even before Covid-19, new national government policy attention was being paid to local pharmaceutical production in a number of African countries, including Tanzania and Kenya. New investors were also coming into the East African pharmaceutical industry from India, Bangladesh and South Africa, and this investment was associated with industrial upgrading and expansion of product range (Wangwe et al., 2021). The pandemic however transformed this policy landscape. As imports dried up, prices of inputs rose vertiginously, and international transport stopped, the limitations of local industrial production became evident (Banda et al., 2021a). Even India, with its far stronger industrial base, reflected more sharply on its dependence on China for bulk imports of active pharmaceutical ingredients (APIs) for its medicines' production (Chatterjee, 2020). And the lack of vaccine manufacturing in SSA was thrown into particularly sharp relief. The shift in thinking within global health debates towards support for more local production of essential health commodities within low- and middle-income countries, including Africa, was sharply illustrated by the WHO's convening of the first World Local Production Forum in June 2021 (WHO, 2021c).

It became clear, as the pandemic developed, that those African countries with a somewhat stronger industrial base were able to respond more effectively to the pressure for import substitution by health industries, from local production of protective equipment and sanitiser to test kits and oxygen supply (Banda et al., 2021a). India, with a large vaccine producer in addition to its other industrial strengths, was able to do much more.

In Africa, furthermore, the crisis added fuel to the local policy debates on routes to greater self-reliance, adaptation of health care to local needs, local industrial-health sector collaboration and arguments for decolonisation of research and policy priorities. African governments, multilateral African institutions and high-income country-based funders have focused attention on localising vaccine production in African countries, and the investment and technology transfer required (Irwin, 2021; Nkengasong et al., 2020). Internationally there are cautions about the industrial and trade strategies to accomplish this (Fransen et al., 2021).

A Kenyan clinician also recorded a pandemic-induced upsurge of virtual networks and clinical knowledge sharing that has helped to "democratise" access to learning resources, including an East African weekly medical education event in oncology (Mutebi, 2021). She argued for more global attention to local solutions to tackling complex systemic problems, citing "Choosing Wisely Africa" (Rubagumya et al., 2020) as a practical exercise in identifying locally appropriate clinical approaches in cancer care. A contrast is often drawn in East Africa between the international financial and infrastructural support for HIV and TB treatments versus the lack of such support for cancer treatment. However, there are warning voices that high-income country-based support for expanding cancer treatment needs to avoid "onco-colonialism" by building collaborative partnerships that meet rather than override national priorities, and that strengthen local health system integration (Hack et al., 2019).

Researching Cancer Care: Methods and Contexts

"Cancer is a deeply personal disease". Tedros Adhanom Ghebreyesus, Director-General, World Health Organization. (WHO, 2020)

While most writing on cancer is clinically focused, cancer is, as the WHO Director-General noted, "personal": a disease that affects us all, and generates huge levels of "physical, emotional and financial strain on individuals, families, communities, health systems, and countries" (WHO, 2020, p. 12). A key argument in this book is that cancer is deeply social in its impact on patients, families, carers, communities and economies. The research on cancer care in this book is therefore rooted in social science methodologies appropriate for tracing these effects, though the research teams also included expert clinicians. We aim to explore and present in this book a range of predominantly African and Indian perspectives on cancer care, including the perspectives of those who have experienced the disease as well as their carers, health professionals, policymakers and industrialists in Eastern and Southern Africa and India. A variety of robust research methodologies were applied across the three countries, mixing quantitative and qualitative study design and drawing on a range of analytical frameworks.

Perspectives on Cancer Care

The ICCA project of which this book is an outcome took the decision at the start not to focus on specific cancers, but to seek experiences of cancer care in general and the scope for policy responses. We are aware that "cancer" refers to a wide and complex range of illnesses. But we recognised, and have seen it confirmed, that policymakers and patients do also think about cancer as a general category of disease, despite the complex range and diversity of interventions needed, which makes private sector involvements unpredictable and difficult to regulate (Srinivas, 2021b). We identified across the cancer care spectrum shared issues for cancer patients and for all those impacted by the disease, from diagnostic costs and cost of treatment, through fear and stigma, and access to pain control, to industrial production and trade in essential supplies such as oncology drugs.

We also refer to experiences of distinct cancers where appropriate, especially those that are most prevalent and those for which earlier diagnosis would be both possible and life-sustaining.

While the literature on cancer in Africa and India is expanding rapidly, it largely continues to operate in a health system research "silo", within which the industrial and distributive institutional structures that shape the supply of essential commodities are not considered. Yet improving cancer care centrally includes effective industrial supply chains and the innovation required to provide essential medicines, devices and other commodities at manageable prices, a lesson the pandemic has hammered home.

It is our contention in this book therefore, for the important and challenging case of cancer care, that building local health security while moving towards Universal Health Coverage (UHC), in East Africa and India as elsewhere, must include close attention to building the linkages and mutual interactions of investment and innovation in industry, regulation, market management, health system demand and procurement, as well as health system organisation. We locate our research findings within the perspective of strengthening local health systems partly through reinforcing linkages with local industrialisation efforts. We identify major challenges for cancer care that can be addressed through cross-sectoral, multidisciplinary collaborations within resource-constrained systems and demonstrate practical broad-spectrum approaches to policy making for this purpose.

The development of our argument in this book is mainly narratival. We draw on some quantitative survey results and secondary data analysis where appropriate, using them as elements of our arguments from the extensive qualitative primary interviews. Our aim as a multidisciplinary team is to reflect and convey, through the use of narrative cases and summary evidence, the perspectives of the hundreds of stakeholders in cancer care, who gave their time in difficult circumstances, on the current functioning of cancer care and the scope for improvement through innovations that link industry and health. We describe the research methods below.

Health Sector Research Methods

Extensive fieldwork was carried out for the ICCA project on the experience of cancer care in Tanzania and Kenya, from the perspectives of patients, carers, cancer survivors, health professionals and other stakeholders including procurement agents and policymakers. The research included a survey of 467 cancer patients' experiences (405 in Kenya and 62 in Tanzania). The interviews invited patients to narrate their "pathways", using a structured questionnaire. Patients were asked to start from first recognising worrying symptoms and to recount their experience to date as a series of self-defined events. For each event, patients were asked what they did, when, where, what happened as a result, what they paid and how they paid; also how they travelled if required. Background information on gender, hometown or village, economic activity and estimated household income was included, and patients were finally asked for comments, including missed requirements and aspects that could be improved. This interview structure, innovative in this field at the time, allowed us to combine gathering narratives in which the steps reflected patients' perspectives on events and hurdles. Later, the analysis could identify clinical hurdles such as diagnosis and analyse patients' experiences for aspects such as length of delays before diagnosis and amounts expended in relation to self-estimated household income.

A parallel set of in-depth interviews in Tanzania and Kenya sought the perspectives of health professionals (doctors, nurses, clinical officers, pharmacists and community health workers) and also caregivers and policymakers (43 interviews in total). Focus groups with cancer survivors and health workers added to qualitative understanding, allowing discussion of perspectives. The study participants were recruited in three Kenyan counties and three regions in Tanzania.

Industrial Research Methods

In the most innovative aspect of this project's methodology, in addition to the health data, in-depth interviews were conducted with health-related industrialists in both East Africa and India. In Tanzania and Kenya, we interviewed local manufacturers (16 in total in East Africa including also one Ugandan manufacturer), plus public and private importers/distributors (3) and regulators and policymakers (5). The interviews explored manufacturers' product range, their interest in expanding into cancer-related production, and their understanding of local market demand for cancer-related items in short supply or unavailable to respond to need. The range of manufacturing organisations included firms producing pharmaceuticals and other health-related products such as medical devices, chemicals and plastics.

In India, with its large and innovative industrial base, the initial research focus was exclusively on the industrial organisation of firms and the "cancer industry" of diverse products and services. A central concern was Indian industrial and technological innovations relevant to cancer care in resource-constrained health services. However, early interviewing rapidly expanded the research focus to investigate the interconnections (and lack of connections) between healthcare provision and industrial change, including interviews with clinicians, scientists and industrialists working on this interface. It became clear, in part through pandemic experience, that the Indian team needed to explore the often disconnected but often separately analysed productive ecosystem of economics, surgery, entrepreneurship, regional care hospitals and laboratory science. Findings from 25 in-depth interviews and discussions, many with follow-up discussions and emails, are drawn on in this book, alongside innovative open-resource podcasts and video materials,[6] created by the Indian team as a dividend of the new at-distance world we were inhabiting, and a necessary action to identify and create public dialogues between disparate actors.

The chapters in this book draw extensively on this large data resource, collected both before and during the pandemic. In addition, the chapters draw on wider interviewing of industrialists in the context of related work on pandemic responses and pandemic-incentivised investment initiatives, notably in vaccines,[7] as well as secondary sources and literature review as indicated in the chapters that follow.

Health System Organisation: Key Aspects

The Tanzanian and Kenyan health systems share a number of characteristics relevant to tackling cancer care. Each has a public health system under constant stress from funding constraints and high levels of need and demand; in each country the bulk of the population survive on low incomes and rely on public health care. In both countries, most health facility visits require payment out-of-pocket in cash. Efforts to mitigate the impact of these charges on access to care include insurance initiatives and exemptions from payment for certain categories of patients or types of care, but out-of-pocket payments remain a major impediment to patients' access to care.

In both countries the public health system is hierarchically structured. In this book, we refer to primary levels of care including community health workers, dispensaries and health centres; first-line or local hospitals including district hospitals in Tanzania and sub-County hospitals in Kenya, that is, the general hospitals most accessible to most patients; and referral hospitals including those offering different levels of specialist care, typically including diagnostic testing and cancer treatment centres. Patients are typically envisaged to start at lower levels and be referred upwards as needed; as will be seen, cancer patients' experiences are however rather different.

In addition, both Tanzania and Kenya have a private sector in health care, with the Kenyan private sector markedly larger. The private facilities vary greatly, but include private dispensaries and maternity homes, private diagnostic laboratories and higher-end private hospitals. The pattern of public and private provision can have a marked effect on the experience of cancer patients, including access to timely diagnosis.

In India, healthcare structure and performance vary sharply between states. However, both not-for-profit organisations and the businesses of the private sector are acknowledged to be central to health service performance across the country, even those often seen to be "public" or "community health". There is now an emerging debate on the relative roles of public and private cancer care, in Africa and more broadly in LMICs including India. In East Africa, Indian private sector cancer care is also known as a resource for African cancer patients with comprehensive insurance or high incomes, who pre-pandemic travelled to Indian hospitals such as the Apollo chain for diagnosis, treatments and follow-up. This can provide a misleading impression in Africa of Indian cancer care which however suffers, more broadly, from many problems familiar in African contexts, including public sector cancer treatment centres overwhelmed by high demand (Pramesh et al., 2014; Sirohi et al., 2018) and widespread failures of timely diagnosis.

On both continents, the evolving role of the private sector and private funding in cancer care therefore poses policy challenges for moving towards UHC. Public and non-profit hospitals may rely on international philanthropic support for diagnostic equipment, training and staffing and struggle when that support is reduced. The concentration of expertise in a small number of cancer centres, while supporting the retention of expertise and research development can force patients to travel very long distances in search of care. Challenges for policymakers include finding and applying models that bring aspects of cancer care much closer to patients, and creating stronger links between private and public sector care. India's Cancer Grid, Kenya's external partnerships such as AMPATH, and Uganda's success in bringing pain control closer to patients are some of the many current responses to these challenges.

Book Structure: Evidencing and Reframing the Challenges

This book begins by locating the research on cancer within the pandemic context that has shaped our work since 2020. Chapter 2 surveys the pandemic context in both Africa and India within which this research has been done. It documents the immense scale of the resultant healthcare supply crisis, especially in Sub-Saharan Africa, and identifies the extent to which a stronger industrial base allowed India, and some African countries, to better tackle the pandemic supply gaps. The scale of the rethinking forced on governments by Covid-19 can be understood, the chapter argues, as a shift in socio-technical imaginaries: new manageable, social and technical, shared visions of what is possible and important in addressing local health security. The pandemic also confirmed the widespread pre-pandemic African predictions that in a major crisis, African countries would find themselves at the back of the queue, while wealthier countries first looked after their own. Recognition of that truth and its implications are driving the new view of industrialisation's role in local health security. This book applies this new imaginary to the huge challenge of cancer care in Africa.

The next section of the book, "The cancer care experience in East Africa" (Chapters 3–5) explores key aspects of how the "cancer explosion" in Africa (Ngwa et al., 2022, p. e252) is experienced in Kenya and Tanzania, drawing on the health system fieldwork. Each chapter argues for a specific reframing of the understanding of the cancer care challenge in these countries. Chapter 3 reframes the scale of cancer crisis through the concept of "social pain". This concept, used by the interviewees themselves, understands cancer as a whole-society problem, with psychological, social, economic and spiritual impacts much wider than the sufferer. The chapter argues for much more attention to survivability and human dignity in policies, practices and provision.

Chapter 4 turns to the experience of individual sufferers and creates an image of how cancer care appears to them in the narratives they shared. The image frames their experience as being confronted by a "maze", through which they grope largely on their own initiative. Too often, patients lacked maps or guides to aid their search for information, diagnosis and treatment. The chapter presents patterns of experience within the maze and implications for access to care. Chapter 5 then steps back from that maze and examines it from the perspective of health system professionals aiming to create a smooth, managed pathway to and through cancer care. The chapter reframes the challenge of late diagnosis, a key cause of poor patient outcomes. Instead of the familiar frame of "late presentation", a concept tending to focus attention on patients' behaviour as a source of delay, the chapter identifies core bottlenecks once patients come to the health services and points of leverage for improvement.

The next section, "Local industry and cancer care in India and Africa" (Chapters 6–8), examines the disjunctions and gaps between cancer care and industrial production in both India and East Africa. Chapter 6 is written from the Indian perspective of a country with a much stronger local industrial base and innovative capabilities, yet struggling to build on that advantage to sharply improve access to timely cancer diagnosis and treatment. The framing of the chapter challenges the reader to understand the complexity of responsibility in designing viable policy, the linkages and gaps between the economic basis for the industrial "building blocks" of cancer care and the health system that uses the products. The chapter draws directly on the author's Covid-19 experiences of working across health/industrial boundaries under pressure and forces attention to conceptual frames and gaps in policy that block effective translation of need into secure supply.

Chapters 7 and 8 then explore the current state of the health industries in East Africa, the failure to address cancer-related requirements and the scope for investment and innovation. Chapter 7 surveys the current state of development of the health industries in Kenya and Tanzania. It frames this, perhaps controversially, as a lack of ambition on the part of the entire local industrial/innovation ecosystem, including manufacturers, entrepreneurs, regulators and policymakers. The pharmaceutical firms were failing to upgrade, expand product ranges and develop new markets, though that was starting to change before the pandemic. The chapter identifies market disorganisation and fragmentation as one of a number of key constraints on improving cancer-related manufacturing and points to the scope for institutional change to link industrial incentives to health needs. Chapter 8 then focuses on the scope for local production of oncology medication, drawing on local clinical needs in East Africa, on Indian data on markets for generic oncology medication, and on industrial and regulatory experience.

The next section, "Industrial innovation and industrial policy" (Chapters 9–11), examines three areas where industrial innovation and investment have high potential for health-linked industrial development and health improvement: medical devices, vaccines and biologics and medication for severe pain. Chapter 9 describes and discusses several Indian medical device start-ups with potential for improving cancer care in low-resource health systems. It explains the emerging business models of these firms in India's innovative medical devices sector, identifying regulatory and policy successes and failures and the adaptations of innovative start-ups to the complexity of cancer care markets in India. It identifies innovative ways in which India supports entrepreneurship through incubators and funding in the medical devices sector and draws some lessons for African policy actors on how to structure innovation ecosystems that can support emerging local health-industry complexes.

Chapter 10 then turns to the high-profile topic of vaccines. Charting the explosion of international interest and investment in vaccine production in Africa, the chapter argues for a rethinking of the scope for investment. The chapter argues that better cancer care entails the expansion of technological capabilities in biologics manufacture. The current vaccine manufacturers are the possible candidates to transition into the biologics sector because this is an incremental innovation for them. It argues that the current interests in vaccine manufacture can be seized by national policymakers as an opportunity to develop broader biotechnology manufacturing capabilities.

Chapter 11 is the first of two chapters to explore the local specificities of a broad cancer care crisis that crosses countries and types of cancer: pain management. There is a well-acknowledged failure to provide effective strong pain medication for late-stage cancer sufferers in Sub-Saharan Africa and India and elsewhere outside high-income countries (Knaul et al., 2018). Chapter 11 tackles this problem in the first of two sharply contrasting contexts: India, where the entire supply chain of industrial production of morphine is within the country, yet the need remains unmet. It shows that cost is *not* the main constraint on access to pain relief and explores the systemic institutional gaps between clinical training, decentralised care, ambition and scope of supply chain management and ability to carve out national autonomy on palliation needs that prevent resolution of this crisis. In India, the complexity is increased by the state-level responsibility for most areas of health policy.

The final section of the book, "Tackling institutional gaps: using scenarios" (Chapters 12–14) looks forward. Chapter 12 picks up the analysis of the crisis in access to pain medication in Tanzania, where all opiate medication is imported and needs are also largely unmet. The chapter analyses the complex sources of this cancer care failure and contrasts the Tanzanian situation to the Ugandan approach to providing more widespread access to opiate medication for severe pain. It reports the findings of multi-sectoral and multidisciplinary workshops in Tanzania aiming to find a way forward.

Chapter 13 then builds on the evidence in Chapter 12, as part of an exploration of a practical tool for addressing complex social and economic challenges of this type: scenario building. The interviews in Kenya and Tanzania had identified a number of serious unmet needs for cancer patients that could in principle be met without unmanageable requirements for additional funding. In addition to the lack of control of severe pain, cancer patients and cancer survivors were eloquent about the difficulty of obtaining, at all or at manageable prices, commodities that are essential for living with cancer productively and with dignity, including colostomy bags and prostheses. Chapter 13 describes in practical terms the use of collaborative scenario building with stakeholders from industry and healthcare, including clinicians, policymakers and regulators to identify interlocking constraints and scope for intervention to create virtuous circles of improvement.

The concluding Chapter 14 pulls together analytical themes and practical lessons from the book as a whole.

Notes

1. See Acknowledgements for details: the authors are grateful to the Economic and Social Research Council, UK for research funding; the authors are solely responsible for the book content.
2. https://main.mohfw.gov.in/Organisation/Departments-of-Health-and-Family-Welfare/national-cancer-control-programme. Accessed 23/03/22.
3. See also https://tmc.gov.in/ncg/. Accessed 23/03/22.

4. See https://www.tatatrusts.org/media/press-releases/pm-inaugurates-multi-level-cancer-care-network-in-assam; https://theprint.in/india/ayushman-bharat-scheme-helped-in-early-detection-of-cancer-pm-modi/934803/. Last accessed 18-10-2022.
5. These data were updated with funding support from the Open Society Foundation for a project at the Institute of Economic Justice, Johannesburg. Research collaboration including data collection and analysis by Andrew Mkwashi and Julius Mugwagwa is gratefully acknowledged. The content of this chapter is the sole responsibility of the authors.
6. ICCA India podcast series 2021 https://www.youtube.com/watch?v=03T3pFKufHQ. See also https://www.lgcw.org.uk/event/economics-and-updating-the-war-on-cancer-hosted-by-the-open-unversity/.
7. One of the authors is a member of the African Vaccine Manufacturing Initiative (AVMI). AVMI is an association composed of current and aspiring African vaccine manufacturers, and its remit is promoting local vaccine manufacture through advocacy, technology transfer and industrial development.

CHAPTER 2

Broken Supply Chains and Local Manufacturing Innovation: Responses to Covid-19 and Their Implications for Policy

Geoffrey Banda, Cecilia Wanjala, Veronica Manduku, Julius Mugwagwa, and Dinar Kale

Introduction: Warnings Become Reality

For decades, industrialists, industry associations, supranational organisations such as AU (African Union) and AUDA/NEPAD (African Union Development Agency/New Partnership for Africa's Development), development agents such as GIZ and UNIDO (United Nations

G. Banda (✉)
University of Edinburgh, Edinburgh, UK
e-mail: Geoffrey.Banda@ed.ac.uk

C. Wanjala · V. Manduku
Kenya Medical Research Institute (KEMRI), Nairobi, Kenya

J. Mugwagwa
University College London, London, UK

G. Banda et al. (eds.), *Cancer Care in Pandemic Times: Building Inclusive Local Health Security in Africa and India*, International Political Economy Series,
https://doi.org/10.1007/978-3-031-44123-3_2

Industrial Development Organisation) and academic researchers have been advocating localisation of medicines production in Sub-Saharan African countries. However, governments had responded that they were juggling multiple intractable development problems. Consequently, the local health industries have struggled to gain attention and policy priority.

Then Covid-19 laid bare Africa's state of unpreparedness for pandemics. Faced with an impatient public, governments that had traditionally not prioritised support for local health industries suddenly turned to them for urgent help. Covid-19 changed the policy and innovation dynamics. Faced with an existential threat, African governments suddenly paid attention to local medicines production. The results, discussed in this chapter, have been striking. The pandemic crisis opened up innovation spaces and scope for collaborations among local agents, some of whom, such as local entrepreneurs, had been ignored for a long time. Governments facilitated collaborative innovation.

What caused this sudden volte-face? Covid-19 caused African policymakers to wake up to the implications of broken supply chains for medicines and other key health-related commodities, both for Covid-19 and for the wider health system (Banda et al., 2021a). Crises typically have these effects, discrediting conventional ways of doing things: the bigger the crisis, the bigger the policy and practice impact (Nohrstedt & Weible, 2010, p. 3). African health stakeholders had been well aware before the pandemic of the risks implied by extreme import dependence and the imperative on governments to protect their own populations first. Hence, their central expressed concern when asked about pandemic preparedness was to build local scientific competence and production capacity (Mackintosh et al., 2018a, p. 603). The pandemic demonstrated the relevance of these concerns and forced a re-evaluation of accepted wisdom, norms, policies and institutions.

This chapter surveys these experiences and argues that they hold important lessons for building stronger health security in Africa and even in the much stronger industrial context of India. The rest of the book builds on this understanding of the pandemic achievements of coordination and collaboration across multiple policy and industrial sectors, and the agency, urgency and legitimacy of action achieved in that period. It

D. Kale
The Open University, Milton Keynes, UK

argues that the cancer care crisis requires and enables a similar response. Themes identified here that run through the book include: the importance of demand for health inputs and how that structures supply and industrial capabilities; the interconnections between local production and local health security; and how local capabilities imbue health systemic resilience against sudden exogenous shocks. We thus use the impact of the Covid-19 pandemic on health-related manufacturing in India and African countries to understand the induced scale of shift in thinking and re-evaluation of public policy required.

Covid-19: An Immediate Crisis that Triggered a Wakeup Call for Africa

Covid-19 started in China, Europe and Africa at different times; however, public health policy responses on lockdowns, clinical approaches and dependence on local industrial capabilities were largely similar. What was different was the extremely inequitable access to vaccines, drugs and Personal Protective Equipment (PPE) for medical personnel and the public. African populations lost out because of weak local industrial capabilities. In addition, African countries with low purchasing power failed to benefit from global supply chains that served Europe and North America first.

In order to understand how Covid-19 generated an immediate crisis for Africa, we briefly describe the sequence of events to show how global supply chains were broken and Africa was left vulnerable.

On 31st December 2019, the WHO Country Office in China was notified of the incidence of viral pneumonia in Wuhan, caused by severe acute respiratory syndrome coronavirus 2 (SARS-CoV-2). The genomic sequence of this new coronavirus was released shortly afterwards on 10th January 2020, and the WHO announced on 11 February 2020 that the new disease would be called Covid-19.[1] In about a month, on 14th February 2020, the first case of Covid-19 on the African continent was confirmed in Egypt. In Sub-Saharan Africa, the first country to confirm the disease was Nigeria at the end of February 2020. Two years later, by 28th February 2022, the African Centres for Disease Control (CDC) had reported 249 000 deaths, 11.2 million total cases and total recoveries of 10.4 million. Tests administered to 28th February 2022 totalled 99.6 million.[2]

From early in the pandemic, major producing countries for vaccines, drugs, medical devices and diagnostics prioritised their own populations, and governments imposed export controls. Elsewhere, imports of essential finished items dried up, and supplies of key inputs to local manufacturing were cut off by competition from large-scale buyers with deeper pockets. The sharp financial squeeze on firms was aggravated by other sources of financial loss: private debtors and governments were slower to pay, while input suppliers required pre-payment. This collapse in supply chains caused serious shortages of raw materials and finished goods in African countries. At a webinar organised in October 2020, a Southern African industrialist crystallised the impact of total dependence on pharmaceutical imports as follows: "Africa found itself inevitably at the back of the queue for *all* product supplies" (Banda et al., 2021a).

Flight cancellations and shortage of cargo carriers caused freight charges to skyrocket and historical orders' prices were revised upwards. A facemask-producing company in Ghana saw their key input prices—for meltblown fabric—rise 20-fold. An East African pharmaceutical manufacturer who was waiting for a delivery of bulk chloroquine, ordered from an Indian company before the pandemic and delayed in delivery for months, saw an 800% price increase from USD 32 per Kg to USD 260 per Kg. The company had no option but to cancel the already delayed order (Banda et al., 2021a). These broken input supply chains reduced local manufacturers' capacity utilisation just at the moment when local demand was rising and local buyers turned to local suppliers. Those manufacturers without large stocks in their warehouses had to grapple with lower quality and more expensive inputs, especially for the production of diagnostics and PPE products.

This local production crisis was worsened by shortages of APIs and excipients. There is an absence of API producers in Sub-Saharan Africa except for South Africa where a few APIs are produced. South Africa is making efforts through the Department of Trade, Industry and Competition (DTI) to localise API production. In Ghana, La Gray Pharmaceuticals had progressed through the API development phases for the antibiotic azithromycin, however after working with a technical partner and due to other challenges, this highly innovative company is currently closed. The behaviour by leading producers of medicines, medical devices and diagnostics caused Africa's policymakers to stop and revaluate their reliance on global supply chains, which at a time of crisis had failed them. Suddenly local medicine production became a national security issue.

Similar but Unequal Response to Crisis: Proximity and Positionality

African industrialists, scholars and promoters of local medicines production have long sounded the alarm that in the event of a pandemic or epidemic, African countries would be left extremely vulnerable. This occurred when African countries could not import Covid-19 medicines or place orders for vaccines when they became available. The vaccine nationalism that gripped high-income countries and dominated access to early vaccine supplies, with devastating destructiveness elsewhere, reflected purchasing power, technological capabilities and willingness to use these assets for national benefit to the detriment of others.

While the severely detrimental impact of monopolising behaviour by high income countries was rightly excoriated, a focus by national governments on their own populations was a general pandemic response. Global collaborations and global supply chains rapidly disintegrated, while responses to the crisis were strongly structured by proximity and accountability to local populations.

Prior to the pandemic, we predicted, reflecting the widespread views of African stakeholders, that in the event of a medical disaster, Africa would be left in a lurch as all countries would look after their own citizens first (Mackintosh et al., 2017, p. 6). We argued for close attention to the implications of proximity and positionality in understanding the importance of local health industries in Africa and their direct link to local health security (Mackintosh et al., 2018a). Proximity, we argued, has several facets. Geographical proximity can generate benefits of shared knowledge, resource pools and short supply lines. Relational proximity recognises shared culture and economic spillovers of knowledge. The values assigned to proximity reflect the scope for mutual understanding, legitimation and trust. These benefits of co-location, however riven by other sources of division, can be economic and social assets in times of crisis. Meanwhile positionality, defined by the extent of local power, agency and responsibility, generates distinctive local priorities and sharply differentiated capabilities to use these assets for national benefit.

The interconnected pressures of proximity and positionality played out strongly in the pandemic. They structured the form and shape of responses to the pandemic. Countries with strong industrial capabilities and deep pockets exploited the strengths of proximity to secure the health of their citizens first, using forward contracts on vaccines, and export bans of APIs and finished products. Other countries benefitting from local manufacturing close to local populations could also generate greater health security in the face of the pandemic. Geographic proximity of manufacturing and technological capability to local populations was shown to be critical in building agile responses to medical health emergencies (Banda et al., 2021a; Mackintosh et al., 2018a). As we show below, the confluence of geographic and public policy proximity allowed a rapid re-purposing of industrial capabilities in some countries, including India, to meet public health policy objectives. An inability to use strong local manufacturing capabilities to support public health objectives drove the crisis for African policymakers elsewhere.

Sources of Supply Chain Crisis: Cascading Import Dependencies

The Indian domestic pharmaceutical sector has 3000 companies and 10,500 manufacturing units. It is the largest global supplier of generic medicines. It met approximately 60% of global demand for vaccines as of 2021, over 40% of generic demand in the USA and 25% of all medicines in the UK (India Brand Equity Foundation, 2022). The pharmaceutical industry is expected to be valued at USD 130 billion by 2030, and is currently ranked third by volume and 14th by value globally (*ibid.*). Sub-Saharan African countries are particularly highly dependent on India for imports of essential medicines (Chaudhuri, 2016). Chaudhuri et al. (2010) had earlier warned that the African reliance on Indian suppliers was based on the unexamined assumption that provision of low-cost generics from Indian manufacturers was sustainable. Reviewing Indian firms' strategies, the authors warned of the risk that African countries faced a reduction in reliable low-cost Indian suppliers, identifying the risk that a change in market strategy would see the Indian suppliers targeting more lucrative higher margin products, and markets in higher-income countries. Shifting from low margin generics to higher margin products could be an astute business strategy for Indian companies, since businesses are driven by profit motives and not philanthropy. Thus, a large-scale strategy shift to wealthier markets would have huge implications for African health systems. Hence, they argued, that it was important to enhance African local manufacturing capabilities to improve access to local populations (ibid).

Africa however was not the only area that had built up supply chain risks. Not only India and Africa but the whole world is highly dependent on China for APIs and other technologies. India, renowned for its generic medicines production capabilities over the last two decades has become highly dependent on China for APIs. According to the Trade Promotion Councils India imports about 85% of its APIs from China.[3] When in the pandemic China imposed lockdowns that led to factory closures, it triggered a domino effect and cascaded global supply shortages. First China then India imposed exports controls on PPE, medical devices and APIs, reserving what they had in stock for their countries. As the pandemic rolled out, a number of potential antiretroviral and anti-inflammatory agents were trialled for effectiveness against Covid-19 (Carvalho et al., 2021). However, shortages of these medicines, and of oxygen, quickly became common (Stein et al., 2020) and these gaps were exacerbated by disruptions to global cargo movement. The African continent then bore the brunt of these logistics and export controls.

The dominance of China in medical health technology production results from national initiative. China has over the last five decades rapidly built up technological capabilities through reverse engineering, and at the same time making in-roads in creating new-to-the-world technologies. As a result, China overtook India to become the world's largest API and excipient producer, covering 40% of global APIs production. Its pharmaceutical market value grew from USD 158 billion in 2016 to a projected USD 315 billion in 2020 (Medicines and Healthcare products Regulatory Agency, 2017). In addition, China has become an important medical device exporter, including into Africa. This context shows the scale of the impact of China's 1st April 2020 imposition of export controls on five classes of Covid-19-related products namely "Covid-19 detection reagents, medical masks, medical protective clothing, ventilators and infrared thermometers".[4] Reuters reported that the move was triggered by highly publicised reports from some governments and hospitals who alleged they had received faulty goods.[5] However, in a time of crisis, this fuelled export embargoes by producers, and panic and price increases for import dependent countries.

Export controls that started in China spread to Asia, Europe and the Middle East as well as the USA (Federation of German Industries, 2020). India on the 3rd of March 2020, imposed export restrictions on some vitamins and APIs, and medicines which included paracetamol, antiviral agents and antibiotics (*ibid.*). In March 2021, facing a devastating second

Covid-19 wave, India imposed a de facto export ban on Covid vaccines produced by the Serum Institute of India (SII), diverting the vaccines to local needs. The SII is the largest manufacturer of vaccines in the world and was at the time the biggest supplier to the international Covax programme on which many African countries relied for vaccine access.[6] In June 2021 the Indian Finance Minister allocated USD 26.578 billion to the pharmaceutical Production Linked Incentive Scheme (PLI scheme)[7] covering 13 sectors that include APIs and excipients, drug intermediaries and starting materials (India Brand Equity Foundation, 2022). The PLI scheme targeted the enhancement of India's manufacturing capabilities and investment in the productive sector to enable diversification and transition to high-value pharmaceutical goods. Another key target for the scheme was to develop global champions out of India that would participate in cutting-edge technology value chains (Ministry of Chemicals and Fertilizers, 2021). The PLI Schemes also covered domestic manufacturing of medical devices, and there were other schemes to promote bulk drug and medical device parks.

In September 2021, India restarted vaccine deliveries from SII to Covax.[8] At the same time, access to the highly innovative and more expensive mRNA vaccine BNT162 (Carvalho et al., 2021) was difficult for African nations to achieve. The African continent therefore had by far the lowest vaccine rates. By late August/September 2022, Tunisia and Morocco had the highest percentage of the population having received at least one dose, at 72.5% and 68%. In Sub-Saharan Africa, rates remained low: countries where at least 30% of the population had received one dose included South Africa, Uganda, Ghana and Tanzania; large countries with very poor vaccination rates included the Democratic Republic of Congo (DRC) (4.4%) and Nigeria (19%)[9] (see also [Mathieu et al., 2021]). By contrast the figures for India and China, both with vaccine industrial capability, were 73% and 91%.

Pandemic Impacts in India

In India, the first Covid-19 case was reported in Kerala on 27th of January 2020. This patient zero had returned from Wuhan city on 23rd of January 2020, because of the outbreak in that city (Andrews et al., 2020). Early treatment in India consisted of azithromycin (500mg), cetirizine (10mg) and saline gargle. On referral to the Government Medical College, patient zero was put on oseltamivir (brand name Tamiflu), an antiviral used to treat influenza A and B, viruses that cause flu. The patient recovered and was released on 20th of February 2020 (ibid.). All the drugs used to treat patient zero are manufactured in India as generics, thus India leveraged its deep industrial capabilities in responding to the pandemic. India used its broad pharmaceutical and biopharmaceutical capabilities to achieve a higher vaccination rate compared to African countries with limited industrial capabilities. India's Serum Institute of India produced the Covishield (Astra Zeneca) vaccine for worldwide low-cost distribution. In addition, Bharat Biotech, an Indian company, developed and produced Covaxin (BBV152) a whole inactivated vaccine.

Nevertheless, India suffered from supply chain problems during the pandemic. Chinese factory closures in the first quarter of 2020 had a ripple effect in India. Ordinarily, the raw material stockholding capacity for many producers is two to three months, as companies try to avoid holding costs by locking-in money in raw materials. Order lead times after factory closures in China rose to as much as three months which disrupted the continuity of raw material supplies for local producers (UNAIDS, 2022). In a webinar discussion (Banda et al., 2021a), Indian industrialists and academics acknowledged that India had made a mistake in allowing such a high API concentration risk arising from reliance on Chinese suppliers. They reported that Covid-19 served as a warning to reconsider the wisdom of off-shoring such an important production activity.

Shortages of packaging in India were also acute as producers generally keep low stock levels. The lockdowns, border closures, export controls and bans triggered by Covid-19 restrictions did not only affect Covid-19 medicines but included other lifesaving drugs such as ARVs for HIV/AIDS. In a press release in June 2020, UNAIDS highlighted lockdowns negatively affecting supply and distribution chains for HIV medicines as manufacturers faced logistical challenges that could last for months (UNAIDS, 2022). Eight Indian generic manufacturers that collectively supply 80% of generic ARVs globally faced these logistical challenges. India exports generic ARV drugs valued between USD 850 million and USD 900 million per annum. The other affected countries with domestic ARV producers were Brazil, Indonesia, Kenya, South Africa and Thailand.

Compounding these input challenges was operating capacity. Local companies in India were forced to operate at 50% of normal workforce levels, because of movement restrictions. In addition, finished goods piled up at factories, as they could not be transferred to ports. Indian manufacturers' sea freight of finished products faced three logistical issues. Goods movements at ports significantly slowed down due to customs workforce shortages. The shortage extended to the cargo handling staff, and third, road distribution links were disrupted because of lack of road transport, which made transporting goods to and from the port problematic. Air freight also faced three challenges: it suddenly had to undergo multiple customs and clearance processes; only a few cargo planes were flying; and even passenger planes that handle a significant amount of cargo were cancelled (UNAIDS, 2022).

The impact on India therefore created coordination challenges for both productive activities and logistics that policymakers may not have thought through clearly at the beginning of the pandemic. As inputs for production including APIs and packaging ran low, local small stockpiles were rapidly used up. Temporary halts on exports of vaccines and other products were compounded by the huge logistics challenges. However, because of the broad industrial and technology bases of India, the country bounced back fast, and even at the height of the pandemic the local industry quickly adapted, for example to produce needed oxygen supplies for the hospitals.

Sociotechnical Imaginaries: Imaging and Designing the Future

These glaring concentration and technology risks have exposed the need for more proximate manufacturing of generic medicines in Africa. Local production needs to cover a wider range of off-patent drugs as well as gradually moving to include more innovative drugs, APIs, excipients, vaccines and other biologicals (see Chapters 7–9). This shift requires concerted efforts to support industrial development and transition. The science and technologies required are not new. However, the shift calls for investment and technology transfer as well as incentives that cover issues such as upstream inputs, waste treatment plants, logistics and affordable energy. We use the notion of sociotechnical imaginaries to explore how envisaged technological futures can be created and at the same time have the legitimacy critical for such long-term projects.

Sociotechnical imaginaries and proximity are useful notions to frame what generates government agency, urgency and provides legitimacy with the public. We combine science, technology and society (STS) and innovation systems literature in this chapter. There is merit in using theory as a sense-making tool, no matter how sub-optimal, to solve time-sensitive problems. Sociotechnical imaginaries have been defined as "collectively held, institutionally stabilised, and publicly performed visions of a desirable future, animated and shared understandings of forms of social life and social order attainable through, and supportive of, advances in science and technology" (Jasanoff & Kim, 2015, p. 6). Critical to the argument in this chapter, these authors assert that sociotechnical imaginaries are important in shaping technological design and hence technological futures, as well as legitimating the channelling of public resources to projects based on the deemed benefits that will accrue to society from the technological advancement.

The attraction of the sociotechnical imaginaries concept is that it helps to make sense of how political actors, innovators and the public can generate shared "visions of desirable technological futures" emanating from science and technology advances. Covid-19 demonstrated the urgent need for Africa to leverage science and technology to prepare for not only pandemics but economic development as well. Investment in pharmaceutical sector development and upgrading is critical for enhancing local health security.

However, because sociotechnical imaginaries arise from deliberate choices, they can be contested. In addition, multiple sociotechnical imaginaries can exist, depending on the actors driving them. These could be private or institutional actors (Mager & Katzenbach, 2021). Thus, conflict or contestations can arise on which particular sociotechnical imaginary to pursue. This could be more problematic in resource-constrained settings with multiple intractable development objectives. Conflict arises if for example, the sociotechnical imaginaries driven by the private sector differ from those held by the state. On the other hand, different sociotechnical imaginaries can co-exist (Mager & Katzenbach, 2021). For resource-constrained settings, collaborative approaches are preferable that support aligned visions of the future and efficiently use available public resources.

The notion of sociotechnical imaginaries has been applied in emerging sectors such as new energy systems (Jasanoff & Kim, 2013) governance of digital technologies (Mager & Katzenbach, 2021), public security (Gerhold & Brandes, 2021) and the defence industry (Martins & Mawdsley, 2021). Sociotechnical imaginaries are particularly applicable to new or emerging technologies because they are potent "cultural resources that help shape social responses to innovation" (Jasanoff & Kim, 2013, p. 190). These cultural responses are inherently linked to politics, public mood and scarce resource allocation, the remit of the political economy of technological development and advances. Covid-19 changed the public mood and shaped pro-technology intervention public policy responses in African countries. This drove sudden political imagination, agency and urgency to prepare the continent for future pandemic threats. This crisis-driven shift and questioning of conventional wisdom still requires shared sociotechnical imaginaries co-generated and sustained by not only technocrats, but also political leaders and the public.

These visions of the future entail science, technology, innovation and social transitions/change. Thus, who creates and sustains sociotechnical imaginaries matters a great deal. Over the last twelve years development agents such as UNIDO, GIZ, WHO and UNCTAD, supranational organisations such as (AUDA/NEPAD), and local industry associations have been driving the sociotechnical imaginary of a future vibrant innovative African pharmaceutical sector. The Pharmaceutical Manufacturing Plan for Africa (PMPA) is one encapsulation of this imaginary. However, national governments, except for a few and even the public have not engaged in shaping these technological futures. Covid-19 placed governments under siege from an impatient public, which demanded government do something about the pandemic, and news about investments in vaccine manufacturing plants was met with public approval. The success of such projects depends on patient investment and support for the local health industries. Covid-19 forced disparate but geographically proximate African private and public professional networks and actors to stop, regroup and collaborate, and this momentum needs to be sustained. India on the other hand, which has developed technological capabilities and skills still faced challenges during Covid-19 with collaboration, multidisciplinary working and coordination between health and industry (see Chapter 6).

Historically promoters of African local manufacturing and roadmaps lacked sufficient patient capital, political reach, urgency and agency to successfully execute what are essentially politico-technological projects. Shaping new technological trajectories and industrial transitions generates commercial and political resistance from incumbents whose economic competitiveness or market dominance is threatened. Mager and Katzenbach (2021, p. 1) while focusing on digital technologies highlighted that sociotechnical imaginaries have elements of "function, power and performativity" which can be used to shape and govern new technologies. Consequently, the state is a key actor because of its political power and reach, legitimacy, access to resources and latitude to use public policy to shape technological transitions of the magnitude required for this sector—hence our calling them politico-technical projects.

However, the state cannot do it on its own. It has to work with both the private and public sectors and other organisations important for the sector. Our argument is that localisation of the medical health technology industry requires sustained technological skills development, value chain upgrading and development of new business models. The only actor possessing the legitimacy to galvanise the development of technological futures is the state. In addition, through policy and incentive structures, the state can reward good behaviour and punish errant behaviour through penalties.

The state similarly played an important role in restructuring the pharmaceutical sector in India and Bangladesh (Chaudhuri, 2021; Lall & Bibile, 1978) and these examples clearly show that it was a socio-political process that drove technological transitions observed in these countries today. We briefly describe below how India developed its pharmaceutical sector. When India and Bangladesh changed public policy and incumbents felt threated, those incumbents resisted the change and even roped in health professionals to discredit local manufacturing, claiming quality would be compromised. Thus, significant reforms depend on political conditions within and outside the country (Reich, 1994). However, Covid-19 has generated a window for African governments to cite vaccine nationalism as a significant threat to their local health security. We argue that this window should be used to shift public policy and generate local medical health technology production sociotechnical imaginaries that improve the local health outcomes for local populations, and in particular for this book for cancer care.

India's Pharmaceutical Industry: Technological and Political Projects

The Indian pharmaceutical industry's journey from importers in 1947 to imitators by 1990 and finally innovators represents a story of technological upgrading and self-reliant development influenced by protective public policy instruments, processes of contestation and local entrepreneurship (Kale, 2019a; Watkins et al., 2015). The Indian pharmaceutical industry developed in several stages across different political administrations that adopted and sustained industrial policies to address three key objectives/sociotechnical imaginaries: achieving self-reliance in the supply of medical products; improving the local healthcare sector and securing access to the industry's global research and development (R&D) knowledge through selective compliance with international intellectual property rights (IPR) laws. These were national politico-technical projects that developed because of purposive political support in policy design and execution in addition to incentives to support the growth of the nascent sector.

At independence, the Indian industry and market was dominated by European-based MNC subsidiaries that focused on sales with little local R&D or manufacturing. Post-independence, the Indian government, led by Nehru, adopted state intervention economic policies and set up public sector units to encourage the domestic development and manufacturing of pharmaceuticals. However, the real boost to the development of the Indian pharmaceutical industry happened under the leadership of the Indira Gandhi government. It initiated effective industrial protection policies such as the Patents Act 1970, the Foreign Exchange Regulation Act (FERA) 1973 and New Drug Policy (NDP) 1978 that helped the Indian industry to achieve remarkable success from the 1970s.

Economic liberalisation initiated in 1991 by the Rao government later brought significant changes to the operation of the Indian pharmaceutical industry, by abolishing industrial licensing and encouraging foreign capital. Economic liberalisation proved a contentious issue among industry associations, political groups, civil society organisations and industry leaders (Kale et al., 2015). However, the Indian pharmaceutical industry responded positively by performing well in export markets. For example, the export of bulk drugs increased by 14% and formulations by 18% from 1991 to 2000 (James et al., 2021). The Vajpayee government further extended the era of economic liberalisation by negotiating and signing the TRIPS (Trade-Related Intellectual Property Rights) agreement that made all pharmaceutical products and processes eligible for 20-year patent protection aligning with international IPR laws. This government disinvested from most Public Sector Units and further amended domestic investment and FDI regulations (James et al., 2021).

The Indian government, led by different political leaders with roots in diverse ideologies, managed to transform the country from an economic laggard to one of the most dynamic economies in the world (Srinivas, 2012). The Indian economic and industrial policies adopted under different political administrations helped build solid technological capabilities in local healthcare technology industries. Comparably, in very different political contexts, China also provided manufacturing incentives, and over 20 years built API manufacturing capabilities. Using the incentives of building waste treatment plants, industrial parks and subsidised energy costs, China wooed partners for joint ventures and successfully transferred the technology for API production (WHO, 2017). What are the lessons for industrialisation leadership in the expanding markets of large African countries and regions?

African Pandemic Innovation

African countries' responses to being locked out of global health supply chains caused a re-thinking of innovators' roles. Scarcity-induced innovation was triggered. Local industries, universities and research institutes which had operated in the background and in the words of a respondent, were "denied the opportunity, space and latitude to innovate" all of a sudden were thrust into urgently producing ventilators, diagnostic kits and reagents, among others. For a moment public policy was sharpened to focus on supporting local innovation ecosystems (Banda et al., 2021a, 2021b). African governments, like others across the world, focused on their own populations.

Some of the innovations included local production of sanitisers, face shields, medical scrubs, and PPE and there was also an acceleration of local production of Covid-related medicines such as dexamethasone, paracetamol and azithromycin. Kenya provides a number of examples of innovative African responses to the pandemic emergency. The Kenyan Medical Research Institute (KEMRI) worked closely with government ministries and local manufacturers, to scale up existing products, including hand sanitiser and viral transport medium, switching to local input suppliers where possible. KEMRI collaborated with local manufacturers to design and produce swabs for Covid-19 testing and redesign and scale up production of appropriate bottles for sanitiser when inputs such as pump caps from China were blocked. These responses leveraged the technological capabilities that had been developed and sustained in KEMRI for years. They also tested both the depth and limitations of Kenya's local industry. A key challenge raised was the dearth of local testing laboratories and notified bodies for medical devices among the local Standards Bodies (Banda et al., 2021a).

It remains to be seen if the reliance on the local innovative capabilities will be sustained. A test case may be Kenya's vaccine manufacturing ambitions. Kenya had announced plans to construct a vaccine manufacturing plant before Covid-19. Work by a multidisciplinary team on plans for Biovax started in 2015, reviewing the feasibility of vaccine manufacture in Kenya; in 2019, attention focused on human vaccines. Again, the progenitor institution was the KEMRI Production Unit. The 2015 concept note proposed the establishment of a biomedical manufacturing facility in Kenya through a public–private partnership. The pandemic accelerated the plans, and it became a government project. At the time of writing, an appointed CEO has begun global recruitment for staff. The shortages of vaccines and urgency of the situation have forced nationalisation of the project.

The initial focus was the production of childhood vaccines targeting primary vaccination programmes in the East African Community market. Kenya was exiting the GAVI vaccine procurement programme, hence the supply concern. Covid-19 broadened the scope and ambition, with participation in African Union vaccination meetings. A key consideration was whether it was cheaper for Kenya to continue relying on importing vaccines, or should they bite the bullet now and set up manufacturing capacity for the longer run? In line with our discussion on sociotechnical imaginaries Kenya has a "big four" policy agenda for economic development and local manufacturing features in that agenda (see Chapter 7). Biovax is using the resources allocation from government and political goodwill to progress the setting up of the manufacturing plant.

Procurement will be key for vaccines as for other local production initiatives in Africa. Manufacturers repeatedly identify procurement commitments as a key signal for investment and a key determinant of survival. In Kenya, the longstanding animal vaccine manufacturing is a commercial enterprise, since farmers pay for the vaccines. Human vaccines on the other hand are more of a public good, largely procured through public health programmes to ensure wide uptake. Hence, investors require government procurement commitment that had not been assured in Kenya at the time of writing. The industrial capabilities development in vaccines will also need to be accompanied by commensurate local vaccine and biological regulatory skills development.

Covid-19-induced Policy Shifts and Need for Long-term Policy Sustainability

Covid-19 triggered a huge shift in public policy towards the development of local health industries. However, internationally, there was a biased focus on vaccine production at the expense of APIs, drugs, medical devices and diagnostics. The WHO backed a technology transfer hub in South Africa to manufacture an mRNA vaccine (see Chapter 10); South Africa and Senegal, with existing vaccine manufacturing capabilities, were nominated as centres of excellence for technology transfer, while Ghana, Kenya and Uganda announced plans to set up new vaccine production facilities.

These plans for increased local manufacture are commendable, since state policy for domestic manufacturing and technology sectors is critical for technological transitions (Lall & Bibile, 1978). However, planners and development coordinators must carefully think through the right policy mixes required to meet the short, medium and long-term industrial structure, health systems funding, procurement and localisation policies. In particular, the pandemic has demonstrated the importance of industrial depth and breadth as well as scientific and research capability, in generating innovation under pressure. Important considerations for achieving sustained localisation of medicines manufacture include the following. What should the government, public, innovators and the private sector envision as the science and technology futures they want? What type of industrial policy should come out of the Covid-19 pandemic? What type of collaborations and linkages within and outside the country are required? How can pragmatic industrial policy seek to learn from those doing well, create new opportunities for technological upgrading and connect with health policy?

Regulation

Covid-19 demonstrated the need for policy shifts in regulation and regulatory capabilities. Regulatory capabilities are an important component of local industrial mix of sociotechnical imaginaries, in the quest to mend broken supply chains and develop and sustain manufacturing innovation for health. Colleagues have argued in allied work that health sector regulatory authorities in African countries not only face challenges regarding their own capabilities, but have to grapple with heterogeneous levels of technological and innovation capabilities within firms (Mkwashi & Brass, 2022). The rapid pace of change in technologies and other regulatory requirements necessitated by the Covid-19 pandemic presents both challenges and opportunities for African regulators.

In Kenya, pandemic innovators in a university and a manufacturing company encountered a regulatory maze. A private firm and a university had designed ventilators. University students after designing their ventilators had no knowledge of what to do next to get regulatory approval. The private company that developed a ventilator had no idea of the science and rigour that goes into governing medical devices. In addition, both needed to comply with regulations overseen by the Pharmacy and Poisons Boards as well as the Kenya Bureau of Standards. These challenges led to the ministry setting up a sectoral task force composed of different regulators to resolve these regulatory traffic jams during the pandemic. What was apparent was although innovators could produce technologies rapidly, there were no attendant regulatory, funding and production support mechanisms.

The advent of many new manufacturers, including those traditionally not involved in manufacturing for health is both a challenge and an opportunity to stress-test the systems and mechanisms of national drug regulatory agencies, medicines control agencies and other regulators. It is also both a challenge and an opportunity to put to test some of the aspirations of some supranational activities, such as AUDA/NEPAD's African Medicines Regulatory Harmonisation. The pandemic gave traction to arguments we made in earlier work on standards (Banda et al., 2016a) making a case for mutability in some of the standards as a way of removing some of the bottlenecks in the progression to high levels of manufacturing capability for African countries. The pandemic opened up the space for using appropriate, adaptive and agile governance systems that balanced safety and supply security needs. Some of the sub-optimal responses seen not just in Africa but globally in regulating technologies during the pandemic are a result of working in silos and a lack of cross-sectoral coordination. Co-evolution of technological and regulatory capabilities, including close collaboration between researchers, industrialists and regulators will be important in building new institutions for regulation on the continent.

Industry Policy

Establishing and sustaining a future vibrant local pharmaceutical industry can take up to twenty-five years. It takes time to set up local, regional and international value chains, create backward and forward linkages and establish relationships of trust. Training personnel and generating institutional memory as well as passing on tacit knowledge gained through learning by doing and through making mistakes also takes time. Covid-19-induced industrial policy shifts need to take into consideration these and other factors, such as bridging value chain gaps, absence of critical actors and institutions as well as the business environment.

At industry level, we have found serious disjunctures in sectoral policies. The pharmaceutical industry is linked to other industrial sectors such as plastics and packaging, engineering, energy, water reticulation and treatment and transport and logistics for example. Inter-sectoral policies need to be aligned to support the co-evolution of mutually reinforcing capabilities and innovations.

Covid-19 demonstrated that those countries that were quick to re-purpose local industrial capabilities to supply drugs and other commodities were those with these deep and broad industrial capabilities (Banda et al., 2021a). Local pharmaceutical industrial policy needs to support the development of these deep and broad industrial capabilities and linkages across different sectors. This calls for a broad systemic industrial capabilities development approach, which entails identifying existing and future collaborative industrial structures critical for the medical health technologies sector emergence and upgrading.

Evidence of this scope for collaboration can be seen in the medical devices manufacturing sector where an emerging medical devices company in South Africa collaborated with a plastics manufacturing company to start producing medical grade products (Banda et al., 2022). The medical devices company approached the local plastic manufacturing company and they agreed on risk sharing with the medical devices company incurring the development costs for a new to that country medical device. However, for a set time the medical devices company would enjoy a preferential price from the plastic company because they had been involved in the development work with the plastics company thereby giving it additional revenue streams. There was recognition that once the plastics company had developed medical grade plastics manufacturing they could expand their portfolio of products. The development of these local company collaborations that broaden and deepen local manufacturing capabilities and expand product portfolios and markets are critical planning and coordination roles that industrial policy needs drive.

Crises act as pivotal points for questioning conventional wisdom and generally accepted principles and policies. Covid-19 amply demonstrated that public policy and active state intervention for emerging or fledgling industries is a legitimate exercise. Building institutions of technological capabilities learning, regulation and governance, as well as acting as an innovation brokers, are functions that the state is best placed to take. From our discussion, it is evident that the state is currently the only institution with the agency, legitimacy, reach and resources to lead local industry development, technological capabilities upgrading, entrepreneurial activity, knowledge development, knowledge diffusion, resource mobilisation, market formation and legitimation. Crises such as Covid-19 generate the urgency and legitimacy needed to create new sociotechnical imaginaries.

Conclusion

Covid-19 amply demonstrated productive and logistics coordination problems, the consequences of API, raw material and component concentration risk, and the sharp limitations of not having a broad industrial and technological base. The current status of technological and industrial unpreparedness for future epidemics and pandemics is not sustainable for African countries. One of the lessons learnt from the Covid-19 crisis is that global health systems literature that sees medical health technologies as easily accessible commodities available from global health value chains is problematic. The system is vulnerable and will be subverted by governments with money and those proximate to technology producers focusing on their own citizens. African governments need to generate new sociotechnical imaginaries that place their citizens at the centre of their preparedness for pandemics and epidemics by having geographically proximate industrial and technological capabilities.

The story of India developing pharmaceutical capabilities demonstrates how such projects are politico-technical projects that require continuity across different political regimes. China demonstrated that with the right incentives given by the state and through joint ventures, it is feasible to come from behind and overtake the leaders in API production to the extent of the forerunners becoming dependent on the latecomer. When the right actor with legitimacy, access to resources, agency and urgency is placed at the right locus for designing sociotechnical imaginaries, legitimating political decisions and resource allocation, then huge politico-technical projects can be achieved. Our discussion points to the importance of generating political currency and sustaining sociotechnical imaginaries across different political administrations. The actors in government with longevity and permanency to be able to carry these projects are the permanent secretaries in ministries. Industrial and health policies can be harnessed to produce successful sectoral policies if astute collaboration and coordination are achieved. Urgency plus agency are drivers of change that need to be reflected on and used as a springboard for urgent policy shifts for future pandemic preparedness to avoid broken supply chains that expose African countries to the scale of risk that occurred during Covid-19.

Notes

1. https://www.who.int/docs/default-source/coronaviruse/situation-reports/20200211-sitrep-22-ncov.pdf?sfvrsn=fb6d49b1_2. Accessed on 20/02/2022.
2. https://africacdc.org/covid-19/. Accessed 28/02/2022.
3. https://www.worldpharmatoday.com/news/to-be-the-global-pharmacy-india-must-detach-from-china-first/. Accessed on 28/02/2022.
4. https://www.twobirds.com/en/insights/2020/china/china-imposes-new-export-restrictions-for-covid-19-medical-products#:~:text=Taking%20effect%20from%201%20April,clothing%2C%20ventilators%20and%20infrared%20thermometers. Accessed on 28/02/2022.
5. https://www.reuters.com/article/us-health-coronavirus-china-masks-idUSKCN21S141. Accessed on 28/02/2022.

6. Financial Times 23/3/2021 https://www.ft.com/content/5349389c-8313-41e0-9a67-58274e24a01. Accessed on 28/02/2022.
7. https://pharmaceuticals.gov.in/schemes#:~:text=Production%20Linked%20Incentive%20(PLI)%20Scheme%20for%20Promotion%20of%20Domestic%20Manufacturing,(APIs)%20in%20the%20Country. Accessed on 28/02/2022.
8. Serum Institute Of India. Press Release—26 November 2021. Accessed on 28/02/2022.
9. Coronavirus (COVID-19) Vaccinations—Our World in Data.

PART II

The Cancer Care Experience in East Africa

The book now steps back from the pandemic and international context, and refocuses on the cancer challenge in East Africa, drawing extensively on ICCA field research. Cancer is, too often, seen as an individual physical crisis, a painful experience for a sufferer from one of the many forms of this category of non-communicable disease. Chapter 3 shows that, on the contrary, cancer needs to be understood as a cause of deep *social* pain. This is a disease that spreads its tentacles through families and friends, social groups and the wider economy, generating stigma, financial destruction, social and psychological damage. We make the case for a very broad social understanding of cancer need, drawing on a wide range of testimony from patients, carers, health professionals and cancer survivors.

Chapter 4 then returns to the individual perspective of cancer patients in Kenya and Tanzania. The participants had received a wide range of cancer diagnoses. We analyse their narratives to understand what their cancer "journeys" have felt like from their own perspectives. We characterise these experiences as too often find themselves in a "maze". Rather than a smooth clinical pathway from symptoms to diagnosis, too many patients had found themselves struggling to find money to move through a confusing health system maze, largely without maps or guides.

Chapter 5, then reflects on these experiences from the perspective of health professionals in Tanzania and Kenya. The chapter identifies key areas where the speed of diagnosis—key to survival chances—could be improved. Its central argument is that the wider cancer literature's concept of "late presentation" as the core problem is misleading: it tends to direct attention to delays by patients in presenting symptoms. However, most of the diagnostic delays faced by the ICCA participants occurred *after* presenting their symptoms to a facility. Chapter 5 considers, from health professionals' perspectives, what can be done.

CHAPTER 3

The Social Pain of Cancer in East Africa: Understanding Need

Lilian Nyandieka, Charlotte Cross, Mercy Karimi Njeru, and Fortunata Songora Makene

A Carer's Story

We start this chapter with the story of a man we will call Mr. Maneno. Maneno's wife had been receiving treatment for breast cancer for 6 years by the time he was interviewed at a referral hospital in Kenya in 2019. Although some of the costs of care had been funded by the National Health Insurance Fund (NHIF), its coverage was only partial, and the current regimen of Herceptin, following multiple rounds of chemotherapy that had not prevented the cancer from metastasizing, was

L. Nyandieka · M. K. Njeru
Kenya Medical Research Institute (KEMRI), Nairobi, Kenya

C. Cross (✉)
The Open University, Milton Keynes, UK
e-mail: charlotte.cross@open.ac.uk

F. S. Makene
Economic and Social Research Foundation (ESRF), Dar es Salaam, Tanzania

G. Banda et al. (eds.), *Cancer Care in Pandemic Times: Building Inclusive Local Health Security in Africa and India*, International Political Economy Series,
https://doi.org/10.1007/978-3-031-44123-3_3

particularly expensive. Thus, Maneno and his wife had been obliged to "hustle for money" at points, holding a ***harambee*** (community fundraiser) to fund chemotherapy and accessing support from an NGO to pay for a mastectomy. Maneno explained that "...the big challenge with this thing is the finances". He did his best not to allow his wife to be affected by the stress of finding money, meaning that as a caregiver "you have to carry that burden...you have to make sure she is psychologically well, and then you struggle looking for money".

While facing the significant costs associated with treatment, household income had suffered after Maneno's wife stopped work when he was concerned it was making her illness worse, and his caring responsibilities affected his capacity to run their business, which was now less successful than previously. In part this was due to the psychological difficulties he faced in coping with his wife's illness, and he explained that for those caring for loved ones, "you cannot settle at work". Caring for his wife was also time consuming for Maneno, as "you can't leave her to come to the hospital alone, so it takes a lot of your time, such that it is hard to concentrate.... She can't stay home without a help because she can't do many things on her own".

In addition to day-to-day challenges, the cost of care impacted the potential for Maneno, his wife, and their two children to imagine and realize future aspirations. Maneno had become used to "the stress" of managing ongoing essential expenditure on medicine, food and school fees, and no longer considered how they might invest in future plans. He noted, "you can't, because when you think of investing, she relapses", meaning further costs for hospitalization and medicine and more time spent away from the business.

Although the household had drawn on networks of friends and family to finance care, and for general social support, cancer had a difficult impact on these relationships. Maneno's brothers had helped, but he acknowledged, "you know everyone has their own responsibilities... You can't fully depend on them". The high costs and multiple rounds of treatment involved in cancer care also meant that "sometimes it reaches a time they view you as a burden. When you call somebody they tell you that they will get back to you. It is difficult". Friends too sometimes broke off relationships due to cancer. Maneno was grateful that his friends in the church had continued to be extremely supportive, "even when things are really bad", and welcomed participation in a support group for those who had undergone cancer treatment and their carers. However, this was not the case with his older friends and Maneno explained, "now you know you have to get new friends...the older ones feel that you have become a burden...those that we used to have a good time with ran away because there is a huge burden".

Maneno described the stigma associated with a cancer diagnosis and recognized that his wife was fortunate to have been able to purchase a woven breast prosthesis, not available to many, for a relatively affordable price. This helped to "remove her stigma", which was essential as from Maneno's perspective, "it is the stigma that makes people sicker than the disease". In discussing stigma, Maneno made clear the close relationship between limited awareness about cancer and cancer treatment and the unaffordable cost of care, which means patients forced to rely on friends and family risk undermining social relationships, saying:

> Some people – when you mention cancer [they think of] the *harambees* that have been held... [when the patient] dies even before they treat the patient. Let us reduce the stigma. I actually was talking to someone else and I told him it is better to have AIDS, you know, because of that pain. Because, like for this chemo I have had to sell land too ... so the problem is that cost of medicine.

Understanding Social Pain

The interrelated challenges associated with emotional distress, stigma, loss of social relationships, and the financial burden associated with accessing care described by Maneno echo those experienced by many cancer patients and their loved ones whom we interviewed in Kenya and Tanzania (see Chapter 1). That the suffering caused by cancer could not be understood only in physical and individualized terms was often recognized by healthcare workers, who referred to pain as "psychological", "spiritual", and, importantly, "social". We thus argue for the importance of a holistic understanding of cancer pain, which acknowledges the impact of cancer beyond the individual patient, positioning them within wider social networks that are often essential to initiating and sustaining care.

The experiences and understandings of cancer and cancer care explored in this chapter illustrate the extent to which suffering is social (Kleinman, 1997). Existing literature exploring cancer care in Africa has considered the social construction of physical pain, which shapes how it is expressed and understood (Livingston, 2012). Here, we emphasize how cancer pain is experienced socially, affecting valued relationships and undermining the agency and dignity of patients and caregivers, with implications for how they see themselves in society. Social pain is thus an experience arising from interpersonal rejection or loss, entailing relational devaluation or threats to social belongingness (Hudd & Moscovitch, 2021).

Maneno's story also illustrates the extent to which the pain he and others described is intimately connected to wider socioeconomic inequalities and structural vulnerability (Quesada, 2019). Thus, understanding the pain caused by cancer as social "points to structural configurations of power in the many institutional contexts people living with cancer move through" (Burke et al., 2019, p. 6) such as hospitals, insurance schemes and communities. At the same time, the challenges faced by cancer patients and their families have an important social impact, with "staggering" economic consequences for society as a whole (Ministry of Health, 2017, p. 8).

The next sections explore in more detail these aspects of the social and economic pain generated by cancer. At the end of the chapter, and in subsequent chapters, we consider some of the implications of this revisioning of cancer as a social and economic as well as an individual crisis.

Despair, Fear and Helplessness

Being diagnosed with cancer was often hugely challenging for patients, many of whom shared widespread understandings of cancer as an untreatable disease that would result in their death. In addition to fear of the disease itself, misconceptions about how cancer was treated and the anticipation of treatment in itself (considered harmful and even deadly) caused distress for some. Feelings of despair were compounded by helplessness arising from an inability to perform expected social roles, which affected patients' and caregivers' relationships with others, and their sense of agency.

Having seen others undergo treatment or die from cancer, patients sometimes found that it could feel futile to continue or simply too difficult to bear. One woman described her own thoughts of killing herself, saying:

> But now, you have been told you have breast cancer. You are devastated. You feel lost. You don't want to fight anymore. You have seen, like me, I look at how my mum was languishing in pain and I thought, I will commit suicide. (survivor, Kenya)

A cancer diagnosis was also difficult for those patients who understood their illness as having a non-biomedical cause. Some patients and caregivers described their own prior assumption, and that of their neighbours and relatives, that cancer resulted from being cursed or being a victim of witchcraft. One man described his difficulty in reconciling himself with his own diagnosis, saying he went to his church:

> ...to tell them that I have cancer and the cancer is not mine. I gave myself courage, and people even wondered why does this person have cancer? I told them cancer is not mine, it is a disease of the evil. (survivor, Kenya)

Limited understanding of cancer as a disease that could be treated generated fear for many, such that "some even fear mentioning the word cancer" (survivor, Kenya). In addition to fear of the disease, a widespread belief that treatment for cancer itself resulted in death was reported in Kenya and Tanzania. In the words of one survivor, "there are many myths and misconceptions in the general public...chemo itself is associated with death" (survivor, Kenya). One former patient from a rural area of Kenya explained how such fears had contributed to their own reluctance to seek treatment, explaining:

> The message in my home village was that if you have cancer, you are being treated in a coffin...I think that person got the message wrong because what he was telling you about as a coffin is what you lie on in an MRI or CT scan machine...so that was my biggest challenge. And believe me, I got myself stigma for six years. I just kept the symptoms to myself, I tried everything, how can you go to be treated in a coffin? (survivor, Kenya)

Radiotherapy was described as particularly frightening for many. One doctor in Tanzania noted that some patients prescribed radiotherapy decided it was "better to remain with the disease and wait for the mercy of God" (health worker, Tanzania).

Failures of Information and Advice

Survivors described their despair as being compounded by the way they were treated by medical professionals, and particularly a sense they were not adequately informed about what their diagnosis meant and the likely implications, often relying instead on seeking guidance from friends and family. One person who had been diagnosed with leukaemia recalled having received no further information at the time about what the disease was, prognosis, or possible treatment, instead being told by a family member that they had cancer of the blood and could not be healed. They explained:

> So for me that is the time my world got shattered, but later after some time…when I went to this doctor, for him to tell me what I am supposed to do, he actually told me, 'we are looking at six months, there is nothing we can do.' So he didn't give me information, so he already killed me at that particular moment. So I think close to like nine months after, that is when I got someone to remove that stigma and tell me I can do treatment, even if I won't survive I can be managed for some —but it was not from him.

Indeed, incomplete or insufficient disclosure of the likely outcomes of treatment and of ways of mitigating them was a common complaint from those who had undergone treatment (see also Mulemi, 2010). One survivor described his shock upon having awoken from a colostomy, which had not been fully explained to him:

> …I wake up from theatre and find my intestine hanging out, and I am like 'what! How can the doctor do this? An intestine is an organ that should be in the body. How come mine has been left out and I am already from theatre?' You know, it is so traumatizing. (survivor, Kenya)

Others outlined their uncertainty regarding sex and fertility following treatment for cervical cancer and the extent to which they felt they were not sufficiently prepared to experience side effects of chemotherapy, such as hair loss, and the lasting effects of their cancer, which included hearing loss for one participant. For many this marked a continuation of a pattern that had characterized their pathway to and through treatment. Health workers and survivors shared stories of patients who remained unaware of their diagnosis after having been referred for oncology, and even, in one case, having been treated for two years (health worker, Kenya; survivors, Kenya). Limited understanding of their condition and the treatment required was discussed as a source of anxiety for patients. In the words of one Kenyan survivor:

> Sometimes [a] cancer patient doesn't die of the disease. They die of the lack of information, the stigma, the trauma that they are taken through. That is what is killing patients most of the times.

In addition to the individual psychological and emotional toll of cancer, being ill could generate a sense of helplessness, and of an inability to fulfil meaningful social roles. Some patients spoke of the impact of their illness and side effects of the medications on their ability to provide their spouse with their "conjugal rights" (patient, Kenya). As one woman being treated for cervical cancer explained, "I cannot do some wife duties because of pain. I have been forced to live with my husband just like a brother" (patient, Kenya).

Loss of Social Roles and Relationships

Patients were also unable to undertake other important familial roles. One caregiver in Tanzania whose father was undergoing treatment shared:

> My father is everything to our family. He is a mentor, provider and good advisor, so to be honest our family has been affected a lot - not only financially, but socially as well.

Like Maneno's wife, many patients were also forced to give up or reduce paid labour following their diagnosis, and the impact of resulting financial difficulties on the ability of these individuals and family members to maintain social relationships and pursue their aspirations is discussed further below.

Informal caregivers are usually regarded as fellow sufferers alongside the patients they are caring for. The unmet needs of patients can intensify the level of caregiver burden. Many caregivers put their own needs and feelings aside to focus on the person with cancer. This can be difficult to maintain for a long time and undermines caregivers' health as well as compromising patient care. Many informal caregivers, including those who do not regard caregiving as a burden, suffer from a wide range of problems, such as sleep disturbance, anxiety, depression and practical and financial difficulties (Wang et al., 2018).

As Maneno described, caregivers sometimes tried to protect patients from the challenges they faced in providing care, bearing a significant psychological burden themselves. One Kenyan caregiver explained:

> I have no happiness at all, even if you were to give me anything, I would not be happy. If you go into that room you will feel a lot of pain, I always tell other women that it's better to be sick than to look after the sick. Because you don't know if they appreciate the work you are doing for them. So you stay with a lot of pain in the heart.

The financial sacrifices caregivers made and the impact of caring responsibilities on their ability to work are discussed further below. In other ways, caring for a cancer patient could affect social life quite fundamentally. As one man, who had moved his family in with his mother to provide care explained, "we are missing a sense of being a family, such as privacy and togetherness" (caregiver, Tanzania).

Stigma and Rejection

Maneno's account of the impact of his wife's cancer on their social relationships was echoed by many patients and caregivers, who described experiences of rejection by partners, friends, or relatives, as well as sometimes a more general sense of alienation within the wider community. This social exclusion was often very difficult for patients and carers, contributing to feelings of despair and generating practical challenges in accessing care, both within public sector facilities and in patients' daily lives.

Unlike Maneno's wife, not all patients could rely upon the support of partners and close family. Patients and survivors described examples of spousal abandonment. One survivor suggested this was not uncommon, noting "some leave immediately, some go [and] come back after chemo to see how your reaction is" (survivor, Kenya). Patients and caregivers also told of examples of limited support from adult children, who were "tired of [the patient's] phone calls" (patient, Kenya), and from siblings who were "showing signs of giving up" on them (patient, Kenya). Others, like Maneno, described losing friends, who "left because they felt I was a burden" (patient, Kenya).

A range of reasons were described as contributing to the severing of social relationships. The symptoms that can accompany cancer and cancer treatment, such as odour or visible wounds, were sometimes difficult for others to tolerate and led to avoidance and reluctance to provide support (caregivers, Tanzania). One patient reported that his wife had left him after he had undergone surgery in part "because of the disease and the smell" (patient, Kenya). The side effects of treatment could also affect the willingness of others to spend time with the patient. One survivor who had had chemotherapy described visitors' response to finding she had lost her hair, saying "they say this is AIDS definitely, so you are isolated" (survivor, Kenya). Indeed, (Mulemi, 2010, p. 148) also notes that the similarity between some symptoms associated with cancer and cancer treatment, such as hair and weight loss, and those of HIV and AIDS generated anxiety for Kenyan cancer patients, who feared the moral judgement of others.

Misunderstandings about how cancer was spread were also identified as leading to avoidance and isolation. One caregiver, for example, explained that a belief cancer was communicable by touch caused others to "stay away from patients as much as possible" (caregiver, Tanzania). The misconception that cancer was communicable could be particularly challenging for spousal relationships, attributed by one survivor to a mistaken conflation of cancer with HIV (survivor, Kenya). Another described her husband leaving when she started treatment as "he didn't want to be infected", only wanting to return now she had recovered (survivor, Kenya) (see also (Mulemi, 2010, p. 152).

Social Isolation

Fear of the disease and how it was treated and the assumption that the patient would die also led others to socially and physically distance themselves from those with cancer. Stigma associated with a terminal prognosis is observed in other studies of cancer care in Africa (Livingston, 2012; Mulemi, 2010). In the words of one survivor, "once people know that cancer has no cure, even marriages break, men go underground. So the information in the community is that cancer has no cure, and then there is stigma" (survivor, Kenya).

A doctor compared cancer to HIV to illustrate the importance of the potential for effective treatment in reducing stigma, noting:

> With HIV we see at least they say they have found treatment. That is why people say they are okay with it. But you know they are spreading the gospel that cancer there is no treatment, so somebody knows that now I am just going to die. (health care worker, Kenya)

This sentiment was echoed by one survivor, who outlined their belief that "when you take someone and ask them to choose between cancer and AIDS they will pick AIDS [rather] than cancer...people are fearful" (survivor, Kenya).

Such challenges could be compounded when patients underwent treatment for a long time without evident improvement, as "sometimes if relatives take care of the patient for a long time without any hope, they start to discriminate against them" (caregiver, Tanzania). Reluctance to support a patient deemed unlikely to recover was closely linked to the financial burden associated with cancer care, discussed further in the following section.

Lacking social support was very difficult for patients and their primary carers. Firstly, it could be challenging to manage day to day care without support. One female caregiver, for example, whose husband was bed ridden, resorted to asking passers by for help to take the patient out for air and back inside, "because the children were refusing [to provide support] so I would sit and wait for young men passing by the road and ask them to remove him from bed since he cannot step down, his legs shake" (caregiver, Kenya). Those patients who travelled for treatment alone were pitied by survivors, who recognized how challenging it would be to navigate treatment alone. One described having offered space in his home to a fellow patient, a young man whose family were not supporting him, saying "you know when you are ill, you don't have the strength to stand in queues, if you have a partner or a relative [they can help you], but someone is sick and is queuing!" (survivor, Kenya).

Outside of health facilities, unsupported patients could face significant challenges in managing everyday life, particularly if they themselves had caring responsibilities. A survivor in Kenya told the following story about a woman with the same cancer for which she had been treated:

> There was a husband who used to visit his wife at the hospital and has young children and he said "I cannot stay with a person who has cancer and is dying" ... so he ran away. So when we went to visit them, we found that mum was very sick, and her breast was cut and she could not cook, she doesn't have food. And her first born is in form one [first year in high school] and the one who remains with her in the house is in standard four (junior primary school) and is nursing the mum. I cried because that is a kid who is in class four and is nursing the mother and bathes her and dresses her and you wonder, even the neighbours neglected her. So the

> neighbours ran away because maybe they saw she is going to die. So we went all along from here and we bought food for them, and we found her and that is why we are telling you it makes people languish in poverty.

Social rejection was also very emotionally difficult for patients and their carers. Echoing Maneno's assertion that stigma made people sicker than cancer itself, one survivor, reflecting on her own difficult experiences, felt "sometimes [a] cancer patient doesn't die of the disease, they die of the lack of information, the stigma, the trauma that they are taken through. That is what is killing patients most of the times" (survivor, Kenya). As the accounts described above demonstrate, survivors particularly recognized support from loved ones as essential, and often did what they could to help others with whom they empathized, through providing informal counselling and advice about treatment expectations or symptoms management, or sometimes practical assistance with managing the disease and day to day needs and responsibilities. They placed significant value on peer support, in light of the misunderstanding of lack of respect they often encountered in the wider community and in their interactions with medical professionals.

The Cost of Cancer as a Source of Social Pain

Cancer can impose a significant financial burden on patients and their families and friends. The cost of care, and of travel and accommodation to access it, reduced opportunities to generate income. Illness, caring responsibilities, travel to access care, and sale of assets to fund care, all generated stress for participants in the research, and impacted their social relationships.

The cost of care as a contributing factor in generating social pain in African countries has been explored in relation to HIV. In his account of the HIV epidemic in Burkina Faso and Cote D'Ivoire in the 1990s, Nguyen (2010, p. 78) quotes a research participant who described diagnosis as "knowing you are condemned to a slow death and most probably to being abandoned by your family and friends - not because they don't love you anymore, but because they can't afford to look after you and won't be able to bear looking you in the eye because of that". Since the expansion in access to antiretroviral therapies (ARVs), the development of a large donor-funded NGO sector focused on HIV and AIDS in Kenya and Tanzania, and provision of free treatment in both countries, such challenges are now less common for patients testing positive for HIV and indeed HIV-dedicated clinics can be relatively privileged spaces within public health facilities (Prince & Otieno, 2014; Sullivan, 2012). In contrast, cancer care, as described in greater detail in the following chapters, is often extremely expensive, even in Tanzania where many public sector treatment charges are waived after diagnosis with cancer. Indeed, survivors and health workers in Kenya, where there is no free treatment policy, sometimes explicitly compared cancer to HIV, calling for cancer to be declared a "national disaster", as HIV was in 1999, and for provision of free treatment and counselling and support for peer support groups on the same scale.

In contrasting the experience of cancer patients and their families with those diagnosed with HIV, survivors and health workers illustrated the extent to which suffering resulting from cancer is not something that can be resolved only through interventions addressing the individual physical and psychological health, but will also require action to address the barriers to care explored further in Chapters 4 and 5, which mean that those with cancer must rely heavily on social relationships in order to fund and manage their care.

Families' Economic Losses

Families in Tanzania and Kenya had been obliged to sell a range of assets to meet the costs of treatment, costs of travelling with the patient, and to cover family expenses over sometimes very long periods of time. Some of the sacrifices made related to future aspirations and are thus difficult to quantify but were felt to be very significant by caregivers and survivors in explaining the impact of the disease on their family. One caregiver in Tanzania explained that his sister had been unable to study medicine as course fees were too high "because 70 percent of our income was used for [our father's] treatment" (caregiver, Tanzania). Others had delayed or abandoned plans to invest in business opportunities or had been obliged to stop sending their children to school. The "psychological stress" (health worker, Kenya) associated with becoming "poor" due to paying for care was closely associated for some with the impact on family, as "if we sell our property, even our children will not have anything" (survivor, Kenya). A Kenyan health worker reflecting on the challenges facing patients noted that "the whole family gets drained and when the family is drained, maybe the client was paying school fees. Children cannot go to school because the sickness eats up the whole family" (health worker, Kenya). Being seen to fail to provide for family could also expose patients to stigma. As one survivor described someone with cancer, "buys the drugs with school fees and they look for other ways to pay fees for their children, so that it does not look like this one has cancer" (survivor, Kenya).

The illness also had an impact on opportunities to generate income, for patients and caregivers. Like Maneno's wife, the vast majority of patients interviewed (94% in Tanzania and 97% in Kenya) had experienced an impact on their working life following their diagnosis, either becoming unable to work or having to reduce their working hours and thus earning capacity. Close to half of those interviewed in both countries (48% in Tanzania and 53% in Kenya) reported having had to cease paid work entirely. The impact on household income could be very significant, to the extent that "you become very poor, even food at home becomes a challenge" (survivor, Kenya). In addition to this, patients could become vulnerable once they were no longer able to contribute to their households. Some female patients were sent away from their matrimonial homes after the condition made them poor. As one recounted: "I separated with my husband, I stopped being a bread winner, [I] drained family resources" (patient, Kenya).

Like those for whom they cared, many primary caregivers reported the impact supporting patients had on their ability to work and generate income due to time spent accompanying patients as they received treatment at distant hospitals. One woman, who had travelled approximately 600 kilometres to Ocean Road Cancer Institute in Dar es Salaam explained "everything I do for my personal living has stopped. Like last week my neighbour from the village called me to tell me all my paddy has been destroyed because there is nobody to harvest it" (caregiver, Tanzania). In addition to the impact on livelihoods, caregivers often described a less tangible impact on their potential to realise future aspirations, whether, for example, to own a milling machine or to attend medical school. As articulated by one woman supporting her mother, "whatever I had in my plan about my personal development was totally changed, because it's better to forgo everything in order to keep your mother safe" (caregiver, Tanzania).

Financial Burden and Social Stigma

Many in Kenya and Tanzania are obliged to seek financial support from friends and family in order to access cancer care. This could have a difficult impact on patients' and carers' social relationships. As one Tanzanian patient's daughter explained, "between us relatives we are sometimes not on good terms because not everyone is willing to help my mother" (caregiver, Tanzania). Several caregivers felt that this was particularly challenging because the treatment did not always seem to be helping, and many believed cancer was not curable. One recalled:

> ...a relative called my brother [the patient] on the phone and told him "you will not be healed as cancer is incurable." Unfortunately this relative then refused to give financial support for [my brother's] treatment. Others didn't answer the phone when we called to ask for support or hung up. (caregiver, Tanzania)

Sometimes even when people did contribute, it was evident to patients that they were doing so reluctantly and with little hope it would make a difference. One survivor in Kenya described his experience of being "discriminated" against by relatives, saying:

> When you ask for 200 shillings, they will give you the money but [they] know that you will not last three days before you ask again. When I wanted to go to Nairobi for treatment I organized for a *harambee*, but it was painful. People contributed, but at the back of their minds they knew that I would not make it. Some called me to find out how I was doing and disclosed that their contribution was not going to help, that I was going to die. As we speak, I have never gone [since] to my home. People think I am dead.

The challenges associated with accessing support when an illness was assumed to be terminal are also documented by Benson Mulemi (2010) in his ethnography of the cancer ward at Kenya's Kenyatta National Hospital, which documents the extent to which cancer can undermine relations of mutual reciprocity. He observes that as a patient's illness progressed, relatives and friends "tended to reduce their support as they expected less in return from terminally ill patients" (Mulemi, 2010, p. 143).

Difficulty in accessing financial support could be compounded by co-morbidity with HIV, which is common in the case of cervical cancer and other cancers including Kaposi's Sarcoma. One doctor at a regional hospital explained that HIV-positive people with suspected cervical cancer sometimes did not get diagnosed as their HIV status made family members less willing to contribute to support travel and treatment costs (health worker, Tanzania).

Inability to access financial support through social networks, could lead to feelings of isolation when family "run away"' due to the financial burden (health worker, Kenya) and when contacting friends felt "like it is just disturbing them...Even if they know it is very difficult, the problem is yours and your family" (health worker, Kenya). One Kenyan survivor described having concealed her illness due to the anticipated cost of treatment, recalling:

> I got sick and made a plan on how to lie to my mother because of the drugs. It was 22,000 [Shillings] and the drugs were not there, so I lied to my mum that I have been told not to take any medicine because I might die, and it is because I did not have money. (survivor, Kenya)

Caregivers too suffered when unable to afford to provide what they believed to be meaningful care for their loved ones, as described by Maneno. Beyond expensive hospital bills, patients often had other needs which were difficult to provide for. The cost of appropriate food in Nairobi, where Kenyan patients had to travel to receive radiotherapy as well as other treatments, was frequently raised by survivors. One caregiver explained they felt "psychologically tortured", because "the patient is not eating, and things like fruits and vegetables, [in] the dry season they are expensive and not available...so it is also challenging, both financially and psychologically" (caregiver, Kenya).

The Social Pain of Surviving Cancer

Those who had been successfully treated for cancer also described ongoing experiences of social pain. Their accounts of the difficulty they faced in living with dignity and affording continuing care needs have important implications for how high quality cancer care is conceptualized and provided.

Those who have been treated for cancer may experience subsequent disability that further affects social relationships and generates psychological distress. Mulemi (2010) discusses the trauma experienced by Kenyan cancer patients who had undergone amputations, mastectomy or skin grafts. Described by some as "being half-dead" (*ibid.*, 136), the after-effects of treatment compromised patients' sense of personhood, making them "an incomplete physical and social being" (*ibid.*, 137).

Survivors described the difficulties they faced in mitigating such challenges and regaining full participation in social life. Rehabilitative commodities were often difficult to obtain due to availability and affordability constraints. In the case of some items, such as colostomy bags, this has a significant impact on a person's ability to conduct daily activities and to interact with others. As one Kenyan who had been treated for bowel cancer explained, "you can't live in dignity without a colostomy bag. I could not be seated here with you if I was not wearing one" (survivor, Kenya).

Cancer survivors may face many ongoing care needs that may not be well understood by others. As described by one Kenyan survivor: "they say, hasn't she already healed?... when you are sick they can fundraise for you, they can take you to hospital, but the moment the disease is not there, you sort yourself". For many, the costs associated with survivorship remain significant, and some described a difficulty in seeking help when they were considered to be recovered. One survivor who was part of a group of young cancer survivors, mostly in their early 20s, outlined the struggles they and their peers faced, having finished school but lacking employment:

> ...Your parents have let you go, because you are now a person. They paid school fees, they are done with you...You are sick... there are some bills. You have called home until now... You just have to take care of yourself...Every time [you have to go for a check-up in the clinic] you are calling home, 'send me money for the clinic'. They reach a point they tell you they don't have any either (survivor, Kenya)

Recognition of Social Pain in the Health System

Healthcare professionals working with cancer patients often recognized these complex psychosocial aspects of pain. Understandings of social pain reflected the entanglement of the financial burden of cancer care and its impact on social relationships as well as the need for psychosocial support. One healthcare professional at the national specialist cancer hospital in Tanzania described the provision of palliative care at the facility as follows:

> It depends...if it is social or physical pain. One pain can cause another pain. So we do a holistic assessment and integrate the findings into a plan. So for physical pain we use morphine. For social pain we coordinate with spiritual leaders and they conduct guidance sessions. In certain cases we coordinate with the social worker(s), whereby they then link with the finance department if the issue concerns money... for example if the patient is thinking about costs of tests. (health worker, Tanzania)

Thus, practical support to address financial issues was an important aspect of palliation, as well as counselling from spiritual leaders. As one health professional noted, "palliative care consists of many caregivers: nurses, psychologists, doctors, religious leaders, social workers and Sheikhs. After assessment you will know the area to focus the intervention on" (health worker, Tanzania).

Health workers in Kenya discussed the role of their own faith in the care they provided to cancer patients. One nurse described one of the first stages of her working day as entailing spiritual preparation, saying: "there are so many challenges which we usually meet, so first of all before you start working you have to prepare yourself spiritually, you tell God to guide you" (health worker, Kenya). Spiritual dimensions were evident in both the pain experienced by patients, who were "not only...sick physically; mentally, spiritually they are also sick" (health worker, Kenya), and in the kind of care they required. When asked about responsibilities for patient care, one nurse explained:

> This cancer patient is like in the centre of [the] whole world where there are the health care providers, the relatives, the nutritionist, the spiritual worker. So because of the aspects that will make you to be what you are, they are diverse, ranging from spiritual, psychological, physical - you need to eat, you need love - so it is like everybody [who cares for the patient]. (health worker, Kenya)

The importance of faith in supporting provision of cancer care, for both patients and staff, has been observed in relation to palliation (Esmaili et al., 2018; Hartwig et al., 2014) and more generally (Mulemi, 2010, pp. 155–156) at health facilities in Kenya and Tanzania. However, health workers also recognized the importance of connecting patients and their families to hospital social workers who could sometimes exempt them from treatment costs or support them to find ways to pay, and they were acutely aware of the impact of the financial burden of care on patients and their families. Thus, the extent to which sympathetic health workers can meaningfully relieve the suffering of cancer patients is constrained by the wider policy framework within which cancer care is provided, and the barriers to access it produces.

Conclusion

This chapter has explored the value of understanding the pain that results from cancer as social, illustrating the importance of social relationships in financing and providing care, and the often-devastating impact of illness on the ability to maintain them. That suffering is not experienced only as physical and individual was recognized by many health workers, who used terms such as "social pain" to describe the experiences of cancer patients they cared for, and by patients and carers who emphasised the impact of stigma and rejection on their wellbeing, even in some cases describing this as worse than the disease itself.

Crucially, experiences of social pain are shaped by the wider socio-economic and institutional context in which patients and their loved ones seek care, and create further economic and social damage. Maneno's story and the others explored here offer compelling insights into the consequences of barriers to accessing care explored in later chapters in this volume, illuminating the devastating everyday realities that the growing cancer burden in Tanzania, Kenya and other African countries often entail. Addressing these challenges may involve greater recognition of the emotional challenges associated with cancer, and greater attention to psychosocial support within cancer care. The scale of the misinformation about cancer documented here, and its association with stigma and despair, require to be tackled through a major public health information effort.

However, those who participated in the research also called for much broader and more fundamental changes, involving improving the affordability of care improving the ability of patients and their families to rely upon a safety net in times of crisis and enabling those who suffer, and those who survive cancer, to live with dignity. This chapter has documented the broad economic and social losses engendered by cancer, including destruction of social relationships and loss of ability to work and support the family. This research project has thrown into sharp relief the need for much more attention to survivorship and has identified the social benefits that would result from support for carers' and survivors' ability to work and rebuild lives. Cancer patients, and their families and social networks, can as shown become trapped in a downward spiral of social isolation and economic and financial loss that damages whole families' futures. Cancer, in this sense, is a whole-society crisis and needs to be tackled as such.

CHAPTER 4

Access to Cancer Care: Navigating the Maze

Mercy Karimi Njeru, Maureen Mackintosh, Richard Ngilangwa, Sharon Mokua, Richard Mutisya Arun, and Jane Mukami

Introduction: Accessing Cancer Care

How is access to care experienced by cancer patients in East Africa? Interviews with 467 patients in Kenya and Tanzania showed many ways in which patients struggle to access care, including diagnostic tests, treatment and follow-up. Other participants including health workers and care givers supported patients' accounts. Here is one example of patients' often lengthy and frustrating experiences (Box 4.1).

M. K. Njeru (✉) · S. Mokua · R. M. Arun · J. Mukami
Kenya Medical Research Institute (KEMRI), Nairobi, Kenya
e-mail: mnjeru@kemri.go.ke

M. Mackintosh
The Open University, Milton Keynes, UK

R. Ngilangwa
Economic and Social Research Foundation (ESRF), Dar Es Salaam, Tanzania

G. Banda et al. (eds.), *Cancer Care in Pandemic Times: Building Inclusive Local Health Security in Africa and India*, International Political Economy Series,
https://doi.org/10.1007/978-3-031-44123-3_4

Box 4.1: Accessing Care for Colon Cancer

A Kenyan woman of 68 had first experienced bloating of the abdomen and discomfort in mid-2016. At a public health facility, she was told she had amoeba and typhoid, and bought medication. Her symptoms worsened over several months, with constipation, loose stools, pain and failure to relieve herself fully. She became afraid to eat. Worried, she went to a private facility where they suspected cancer of the rectum but could not do a colonoscopy because the only doctor able to do it was away.

At a later visit, she found that doctor was still away. Now in severe pain she went to a faith-based hospital, but they also could not do a colonoscopy. She then travelled to a private hospital in Nairobi (about 130 kilometres away): here she was admitted immediately and sedated for severe pain. A CT-scan and surgery found a large tumour in the colon.

After surgery and four days in the intensive care unit, she was discharged with a colostomy stoma bag, and referred to a mission hospital (MH) about 50 kilometres from Nairobi. While admitted, after a wait elsewhere for a bed, her stoma became infected, requiring emergency surgery and a two-month stay. She was then told to go to a private hospital, again in Nairobi, where she stayed with relatives and underwent chemotherapy and radiotherapy.

Back at the MH, a CT scan showed no tumour, and she refused a third surgery to remove the tumour site, thinking she would die. She went several times for private clinic check-ups at her own initiative. Then in October 2018, she experienced renewed symptoms; a self-referral for a CT scan at the MH found metastases. Referred back to a Nairobi private hospital, she underwent second line chemotherapy. After an MRI scan at a private clinic, she returned with her MRI results to find that her doctor had relocated to Meru. Unwilling to change at a critical time, she referred herself to the Meru specialist cancer hospital (about 230 km from Nairobi), where she was happy to find her doctor. When interviewed in May 2019, she was about to start her second radiotherapy treatment.

This patient declared a monthly household income of KES 20,000 (USD 196). She could not remember all her treatment costs, but the sums she recalled totalled KES 1,841,000, or USD 18,000. She stated that she had raised around KES 1 million (USD 9800) through fundraising. Some payments had been made by the National Health Insurance Fund (NHIF) and some other private insurance; other payments were out of pocket.

This patient's experience illustrates many familiar dimensions of the access challenges faced by cancer patients. She was initially wrongly reassured. She found some services (colonoscopy) widely unavailable, especially close to home. She had to wait for a bed, and to follow a doctor for continuity of care, then travelled repeatedly to find care, an expensive process, and worse for those with no relatives or friends close to the small number of major cancer treatment centres to host them. She was sent to private diagnostic centres, and treated at times in the private sector, as are many in Kenya. Charges were very high in relation to income, and she used a mix of funding including out-of -pocket spending, fundraising and insurance to access care. Fear and exhaustion made some proposed treatment unacceptable. While waiting for a bed, she felt despairingly that people "wanted me dead"; at another point she "lost hope", "there was too much suffering".

Access to health care is a complex notion (European Patients Forum, 2016; Levesque et al., 2013; Shengelia et al., 2003). Different dimensions interact and reinforce each other, including challenges of accessibility and availability of services, and also their (un)affordability. Tiring, tormenting, impoverishing and sometimes hopeless: as a recently bereaved carer said of the cancer experience: "it is a journey that is majorly made up of losses". People lose their own and family savings, properties and more, yet in the end, "they lose the very life that they protected so much".

The Access Maze

As we read patients' narratives of their experiences in seeking care, the image of a 'maze' sharpened in our minds. Patients had frequently faced a confusing, 'unmapped' route through a maze of facilities and other providers such as pharmacies, laboratories and traditional healers. Some patients had started with self-medication; most had gone directly to a health facility in search of competent advice, timely diagnosis and essential treatment. In both countries, what followed that first facility visit was experienced by many patients as groping through a maze without maps or guides.

In the process patients faced dead ends, such as being sent away with inappropriate medication or false reassurance. They often returned repeatedly to particular facilities as their symptoms worsened, or they self-referred on their own initiative, sometimes multiple times, to different facilities. As they moved around, costs rose and patients had to search for funds, creating cumulative delays. Lack of information, unavailable services, long waits for diagnostic results, lack of clear referral pathways, the need for individual initiative and determination to find help, all these combined to create an experience of the health system as a 'maze'.

This 'access maze' is an image or metaphor, strongly reflecting patients' descriptions of their experience in groping through a health system with little control and only sporadic guidance. The image and experiences contrast with the smooth continuum for patients that cancer clinicians would aim for. As one clinician explained:

> When you think of cancer control, it has to be a continuum of care. So you have to address all of it from prevention, to screening, to early diagnosis, to treatment, palliative care, survivorship, all the way. (Health worker, Kenya)

Mapping the Maze

How was the maze experienced by patients? We highlight four aspects: where patients entered the maze; how long it took to move through it; how winding their paths were; and how much help patients received on their winding journey.

The maze had many points of entrance. While a minority of patients, faced with worrying symptoms, stayed home initially, or self-medicated at a pharmacy or drug shop, most (66% in Tanzania, 64% in Kenya) had gone directly to a health facility. Patients had to decide for themselves where to go with their symptoms. There was no systematic population-based cancer screening in either country at the time. Just one patient in Tanzania and seven in Kenya had entered the cancer care maze by being picked up in one-off community screening events such as a screening camp.

A majority of patients had used a public sector portal to the maze. A minority had entered at public sector primary care level: through screening, dispensary or health centre attendance (Table 4.1). In both countries, around one-third had gone directly to their local hospital: a district hospital in Tanzania; a sub-county hospital or other Level 4 hospital in Kenya. A slightly larger share of patients in Kenya than in Tanzania had started at a private facility (Table 4.1). In both countries, just over 20% had taken their symptoms directly to more specialist referral hospitals (Table 4.1). This behaviour is consistent with other evidence that patients often "'by-pass" lower-level facilities, aiming to

Table 4.1 Levels of entry into the access maze, Kenya and Tanzania (% of all patients)

*Level of entry**	*Tanzania*	*Kenya*
Primary: screening, public dispensary/health centre	28	17
First line local hospitals**	30	34
Referral hospitals ***	21	22
Private sector / other FBO facility	21	27
All respondents	**100**	**100**

* Participants for whom level of entry is available; 3 Kenyan patients started their journey abroad
** Tanzanian district hospital/ Kenyan public, FBO or NGO hospital level 4
*** Tanzanian national, regional or zonal hospital/ Kenyan public or FBO hospital level 5 & 6

Table 4.2 Cumulative time between milestones (median number of days) Tanzania and Kenya

Between milestones:	*Tanzania*	*Kenya*
From first symptoms to approaching a facility	0	0
From first facility visit to diagnosis	194	77
From diagnosis to first treatment	58	28
From first symptoms to first treatment	535	184

spend limited funds in facilities they believe to be best able to respond to their needs (Kanté et al., 2016).

Once in the maze, patients relied on health care staff to pick up symptoms and advise whether they might be at risk. Many had then suffered delays and setbacks. In Tanzania, the median time taken, from first experiencing the symptoms that were later found to indicate cancer, to starting treatment, was a year and a half; in Kenya it was six months (Table 4.2). Worryingly, there was a wide spectrum of delays in both countries: a quarter of patients in Tanzania waited well over two years from first symptoms to starting treatment, while a quarter in Kenya waited over 1.4 years. Since cancer survival rates are negatively influenced by diagnostic and treatment delay, such delays are potentially damaging to patients' outcomes (WHO, 2020).

Most hurdles recorded by the colon cancer patient were faced by others too. We tracked participants through the maze, observing their experiences between several "milestones": when they first noticed symptoms, first approached a facility, received a diagnosis and first entered treatment. Most patients had accessed treatment when interviewed; a few had left the maze as survivors. The longest delays within the maze were between first entry and diagnosis (Table 4.2), with little time expended before entry. The delays between diagnosis and treatment were generally shorter in both countries (Table 4.2), but again there was worrying variation.

Once in the maze, patients had moved between facilities, sometimes returning repeatedly to the same facility in search of help (Box 4.1). We call this stressful experience 'churning' (Makene et al., 2022): multiple visits that generated cost burden for patients and their families, even as their symptoms worsened. A majority of the moves in both countries were so-called 'self-referrals': patients' failing to find the care they needed, hence, trying another facility. From entry to first treatment, a quarter of patients had visited seven or more facilities in Tanzania, and eight or more in Kenya. Many patients had used their own knowledge, advice from friends and family or just tried other places in their search for help.

Clinicians interviewed in both countries acknowledged that referral systems were failing to provide patients with an effective guide through the maze. One commented:

> Referral patterns ... need to be improved in our country ... we need to be able to have a proper referral, not just to send a patient to a higher level of hospital without communicating to the doctors there. (Health worker, Kenya)

As a result, the cancer care access maze included many dead ends, where patients turned away and tried another route, with increasing frustration and pain. Navigation was difficult: each individual pathway through the maze reflected a patient's fears, information, actions, responses, emotions, thoughts and considerations of family needs, and worries as they interacted with health care providers.

Did the different points of entry influence experience in the maze? Patients who entered the maze at referral hospital level might be expected to have received more rapid diagnosis. But strikingly in Tanzania that was *not* the case, raising questions about diagnostic capabilities in the regional hospitals (Makene et al., 2022). In Kenya however, those starting at primary level did spend more time in the maze before diagnosis (median 3.3 months) than those starting at hospital level (median 2.4 months).

Yet some patients did find a more rapid route through, avoiding blind alleys. In Kenya, starting at a private facility speeded diagnosis a little. In Tanzania, many of those starting in the private sector found a more rapid path: their median delay between first facility visit and entering treatment was just over 5 months, much faster than 16.5 months for all patients. A Tanzanian breast cancer survivor explained how that could work (Box 4.2).

Box 4.2: A Private Sector Access Pathway for Breast Cancer
A Tanzanian woman cancer survivor, aged about 40, a professional with higher education, felt pain in her left breast. She was unwilling to do anything, but a work colleague informed her employer, who insisted she seek care. She held private health insurance, and went directly to the leading private hospital, also a cancer centre, in Dar es Salaam. Ten days after a mammogram and biopsy she was told she had breast cancer and required surgery. She resisted at first, and sought a second opinion from a specialist private clinic, who counselled her and sent her back for treatment at the initial hospital. The time from first approaching the hospital to starting treatment was just two months. The key facilitating factors were insurance, entering at a cancer centre, rapid turnaround and good advice.

Why was access to cancer care experienced by many as a maze? Two key reasons stand out from patients' stories. First, a malign interaction between availability—whether services exist—and accessibility—whether patients can get to them. And second, the closely linked unaffordability of care, that delayed and diverted patients as they searched for funds.

Availability and Accessibility in the Cancer Care Maze

Unavailable Diagnostic Services Close to Home

For diagnosis to be accurate and fast, essential services need to be close to patients. The Kenyan colon cancer patient (Box 4.1) found the diagnostic services she needed unavailable close to home. Later, having travelled, she found colonoscopy still unavailable. Meanwhile the Tanzanian breast cancer patient (Box 4.2) had unusually benefitted from diagnosis and treatment available in the same private facility in her home town. An absence of diagnostic capability close to home was a widespread experience among patients interviewed in both countries.

Unavailable services often included lack of recognition and rapid response to early symptoms that could indicate cancer, resulting in false reassurance. Patients had often experienced these failures when going initially to lower-level facilities such as dispensaries and private clinics that might be close to home. They also met delays at hospital level, when health personnel treated patients' symptoms without a detailed search for their underlying cause. It often took persistence and repeated visits before cancer was suspected. Once there was suspicion, local facilities often lacked key diagnostic capabilities, as one breast cancer survivor described:

> I was breastfeeding, then my breast started swelling. I went to the dispensary and I was told that it was just milk. I was given painkillers and other medication to use, but they were not working. I went back and was sent to take a mammogram, and then it was found out that there was a mass-like substance, which needed further investigation. I was then sent to do a biopsy, that is when they found out I had cancer. (Cancer survivor, Kenya)

The capabilities patients identified as unavailable included diagnostic equipment, laboratory capabilities and staff with the relevant expertise.

The primary public facilities and local public hospitals, along with some private clinics, were generally the closest facilities to people's homes. Most patients in both countries had started there (Table 4.1). However, the experienced diagnostic limitations—in both staffing and equipment—meant that most patients had to move on as their symptoms worsened. A majority in both countries had been diagnosed at public referral hospitals (61% in Tanzania and 55% in Kenya), while a substantial minority had accessed diagnosis in private facilities, including private laboratories, that offered diagnostic tests and interpretation (22% in Tanzania and 20% in Kenya). Only 3% of patients in Tanzania, but a much larger 23% in Kenya, had been diagnosed in local public or lower level FBO hospitals (mainly district hospitals in Tanzania and sub-county hospitals in Kenya). The winding route to accessing facilities with staffing and equipment available for diagnosis made up much of patients' maze-like experience of searching for care, as Box 4.3 illustrates.

Box 4.3: Accessibility Struggles for Prostate Cancer

A 74-year-old Kenyan farmer and small businessman with a declared household income of USD 20 per month saw a TV advert urging people in his age group to go for cancer screening. Encouraged, he went in February 2018 to a private clinic for a check-up of testicular swelling he was experiencing. The clinic did blood tests, suspected abnormality, and sent him to a referral hospital in Meru town for imaging; the results were sent back to the private clinic for interpretation. There, he was given medication (antibiotics and analgesics) and reassured. His symptoms worsened and two months later he self-referred, on a friend's advice, to a Meru hospital with a cancer centre. After blood tests, he was again reassured. Frustrated by worsening symptoms, he went to another private clinic, receiving more reassurance and medication while his suggestion of surgery was rejected. In worsening pain, he self-referred back to the first referral hospital where a PSA test[1] gave the same result.

He then went to a mission hospital (MH) in another town (about 260 km from Meru), where after another PSA test, they finally booked him for surgery. A month later he was told he had cancer. Shocked, he self-referred to a private cancer treatment centre in Nairobi, which sent him straight back to the MH to get the medical report. Back in Nairobi, the hospital required X-rays, CT scan and MRI which he could not afford, so he went home. Later, he went to a private radiology facility for the imaging, but they had no MRI. Sent to a different Meru hospital for the MRI, he found the required staff member was absent. After discussion with his children, he went to a private clinic in Nairobi where the MRI was done. He took the results to the private hospital cancer centre in Nairobi. That hospital referred him to a hospice in Meru. (He commented that he did not understand why.) The hospice sent him back to the Meru public hospital cancer centre, where he paid for yet another CT scan, and was enrolled in oncology treatment in May 2019. The patient commented when interviewed that he was relieved to be now receiving care near his home, which he felt was affordable. Up to that point, before starting treatment, he had spent KES 104,750 (USD 1027). He did not mention any access to insurance.

Travel Challenges

Both the prostate cancer patient (Box 4.3) and the colon cancer patient (Box 4.1) had to travel from home to specialist cancer centres and other facilities with diagnostic capabilities, located in the major towns or cities away from patients' homes. A cancer survivor shared similar experiences:

> ...as we talk about the distance, for instance I have gone to the dispensary, and I have done some tests. Later I am referred to the sub-county hospital, and I am told that the tests that I require cannot be done in that facility, so that is a challenge. (Cancer survivor, Kenya)

These accessibility challenges were a very common experience. Cancer is a complex disease, and once it is initially diagnosed, more tests are required before treatment can be decided. The prostate cancer patient had faced delays because of inability initially to pay for those further tests, and like many others, he had moved between facilities looking for more affordable tests and, later, treatment options.

A Kenyan health professional in a specialist cancer centre pointed to the range of tests available nationally which patients may not realise they require before and after treatment:

> Key diagnostic tests we have are imaging, ranging from PET scan ... to CT scan, MRI, ultrasound and X- rays ... to see the extent of the disease, to be able to stage the patient. We also do laboratory tests of patients which [are] quite available like seeing how the organs work like liver function, kidney function tests. And sometimes just to see that the full haemogram .... this enables us to make decisions regarding whether they need chemotherapy. (Health worker, Kenya)

In some cases, patients had to travel to another town or city to deliver their biopsy sample to a laboratory. Even when the hospital sent the sample, it could be slow: one caregiver noted that two months later, the patient still did not have the result of a biopsy sent to Nairobi.

All this travel between facilities, and number of payments to facilities, imposed costs on patients. Disparities among patients emerged as patients struggled to raise funds to continue to navigate the cancer care maze. When patients had to travel long distances, they also had to find the means to cater for accommodation and food.

Travel to access diagnostic procedures and treatment emerged as a key reason for delayed diagnosis, sometimes leading patients to abandon their search before diagnosis (see Chapter 5). Health workers in both countries were aware of patients' responses to these accessibility constraints. One health professional working far from the main cancer centres commented:

> Sometimes you might know that this patient will go home with no follow-up and finally they die. Because you identify a problem [abnormal cervical cells] and refer, but they can't afford to go financially… (Health worker, Tanzania)

In Kenya, the same travel constraint was noted as regards treatment:

> When you send a patient, the patient is not able to follow up for radiotherapy sessions all the way to Nairobi, so it is our wish that these services are at the point where the patient may be in Meru, are well taken care of, rather than going all the way to Nairobi. (Health worker, Kenya)

Navigation Constraints Within Facilities

Once patients arrived at higher level facilities expecting available services, accessibility of timely care was still not guaranteed. Access was impeded by familiar navigation challenges that included no clear guides on where to start, long queues and capacity constraints. Navigating very large hospitals not solely dedicated to providing cancer services becomes difficult for patients. It may take a lot of time to get to know where to start, as a patient's caregiver explained:

> So, when they talked of [a national referral hospital], we went there and we stayed for like two months. Just looking for ways of entering the place. Since this facility normally has so many people, we were told that we will be called and to follow the line [queue], as was compulsory. I wanted it to be faster. (Caregiver, Kenya)

The long queues to book appointments were familiar to many:

> You come to [a referral hospital], and then you are given a booking and then you are told, "Come the next two weeks, this Tuesday is [fully booked]". And then you come again, you are told again the clinic is fully booked, "We will give you [an appointment] another two weeks" … while your cancer is growing. (Cancer survivor, Kenya)

Another said:

> I used to be given appointment[s] but every time I would come, the doctors were busy because they were few and client[s] many and so I decided not to come any more. (Patient, Kenya)

The patient is thus smacked with the reality of the health systems' challenges even at high level hospitals, including shortages of staff and equipment. Cancer as a disease is complex, and there are many types of cancer, making care and management varied and difficult. Cancer care requires patients to interact with different departments, facilities and health personnel, who in most cases are not well linked up. Different professionals with different expertise have to be accessed to reach a milestone such as diagnosis. Patients' stories show how the disease demands great resources from them and their families, and the winding path can be disheartening.

As the cancer burden has risen, specialist cancer centres in both countries have multiplied and improved (see Chapter 5). In Kenya, a clinician commented:

> We do all types of treatment for cancers here, all kinds of cancers, both liquid and solid cancers, we are managing here. (Health worker, Kenya)

In Tanzania, recent improvements in availability of oncology medicines and also equipment, for example for radiotherapy at the specialist national cancer hospital, were mentioned.

> Currently about 80% of medicines are available at the hospital. This situation is not like it was before.[2] At that time patients prescribed three consecutive rounds of treatment often could not get the drugs on time as the hospital used to run out of stock, forcing patients to look for other alternative drug stores. (Health worker, Tanzania)

Increasingly, these facilities were drawing patients for chemotherapy and radiotherapy treatment from all areas of both countries, exacerbating pressure on available services in the major towns and cities. Like diagnosis, patients had to travel long distances and repeatedly in order to access multiple treatment sessions for cancer management, in facilities based mainly in the major cities:

> We are treating people from as far as Western [Kenya] …From Ukambani [Eastern Kenya], they have been coming here. (Health worker, Kenya)

Access to required blood transfusions had been experienced by many patients as a source of treatment delay, experiences health workers confirmed:

> A patient can be in the ward and stay for almost one month chasing blood, the patient doesn't get and the patient gets worse and worse...then the next day you hear your patient is gone just because of waiting for blood. (Health worker, Kenya)

Transfers and movement of key staff also posed accessibility challenges for patients. Trust is an important value in health care and one of its key aspects is loyalty to particular doctors or facilities (Gopichandran and Chetlapalli, 2013). The colon cancer patient's experience (Box 4.1) of following their doctor's transfer worked out well in the end, but for others, care might stop if personnel changed. Drug stock-outs that truncate treatment continued to be experienced by patients: another angle of unavailability:

> You had started a treatment…and you are told you have to go for 18 sessions but after 10 sessions you are told that the drug is not available… they knew you are supposed to take it continuously, and then you are told to come back the next month. When you do, the drug is not available…and you don't know the consequences [of not finishing the treatment]. (Cancer survivor, Kenya)

Furthermore, even at specialist public health facilities, targeted cancer therapies were generally unavailable:

> Yes, we do have the main regimens, I would classify them as first line, and we have like at least 80% or 90% first line regimens. The only challenge we have is targeted therapy, which can still be included in and give very good outcome especially with breast cancer patients… We currently are not able to access most of the regimens. (Health worker, Kenya)

Finally, counselling remains largely unavailable for patients groping through the maze, despite the scale of spiritual and psychosocial pain associated with cancer by patients and their carers (Chapter 3).

> Most patients with cancer need counselling generally…like every patient has her own issues she is undergoing…from social, financial all the way up to fear of death, because once somebody gets cancer, she feels like this is a death sentence. (Health worker, Kenya)

Unaffordable Care

Cancer is *expensive*, in terms of money, resources and time. Payments by patients were a heavy financial burden on the low-income families who made up most of those interviewed. Health professionals saw the need to reduce costs:

> … because it is expensive …the screening, the treatment, the investigation, the diagnosis, everything is expensive to them, and these people are poor. (Health worker, Kenya)

Unsurprisingly, some participants felt that seeking cancer care becomes a narrative by only those who could afford it. Many managed to pay large sums, but the amounts families had raised should *not* therefore be characterised as 'affordable'. Rather, these families had lost assets, foregone other essential expenditures and lost future opportunities (Chapter 3). In truth, cancer care was *un*affordable and impoverishing for most patients interviewed, concurring with other recent findings (Kizub et al., 2022). Hence, we cannot know what happened to those excluded for inability to pay: are they the forgotten?

Three aspects of unaffordability are discussed here: how unaffordable payment demands interact with unavailability and inaccessibility to worsen delays within the maze; the effect of the private sector in raising costs for patients even while facilitating access for some; and the regressive and impoverishing impact of payments on family incomes.

Unaffordability and Delays Within the Maze

Why are cancer costs so high? Some elements of cancer care are inherently expensive: chemotherapy uses expensive medication; radiography uses expensive machinery. Scanning and laboratory investigations add to costs: cancers are complex illnesses and good diagnostic testing is key to both diagnosis and effective treatment.

However, the maze experiences add severely to the financial burden on patients ***and*** the health system. Every time patients moved around, or returned to a facility, in search of care more payments were accumulated. Most were paid out-of-pocket (OOP), especially before diagnosis. Difficulty in finding money caused delays and frustrations, causing more "'churning"' between facilities hence further financial costs. The next narrative (Box 4.4), from a patient undergoing treatment for metastasized cancer, illustrates how unaffordability, distance, locally unavailable services, and delays in diagnosis and treatment interacted.

Box 4.4: Unaffordability and the Costs of Delay
A female Tanzanian farmer, with primary education and a household income of USD 43 per month, first experienced pelvic pain and fever in 2017. After treatment for malaria had no effect, a dispensary ultrasound found a suspected lump in her uterus. She was referred to a district hospital, who repeated the ultrasound, did blood tests, and diagnosed a urinary tract infection. Antibiotics did not relieve her symptoms. In mid-2018, with pain and heavy bleeding, she returned to the district hospital which repeated the ultrasound, found a lump in her uterus, and referred her to the national referral hospital for surgery, a road trip of at least 200 kilometres. She did not go. Two months later, with more severe symptoms, she went to a regional referral hospital where the lump was found again, and she was again referred to the national hospital as the only place for a surgical biopsy. She could not pay the TZS 150,000 (USD 65) biopsy cost, so she was discharged. At the end of 2018, now very weak, she returned to the district hospital and again was referred to the national hospital for surgery. She did not go. Two months later however she went directly to the national cancer hospital where she was admitted and diagnostic tests repeated, this time without charge.

Two months' later the results showed advanced cervical cancer that had spread. Surgery at the national referral hospital also diagnosed inoperable ovarian cancer. The patient returned to the national cancer hospital for six cycles of chemotherapy. After three cycles she was asked to go back to the national hospital for a biopsy to check the impact, but again she could neither pay TZS 150,000 (USD 65), nor afford to go home and come back, so she continued with the last three cycles at the cancer hospital, where we met her in mid-2019. She calculated OOP spending by then of over TZS 1.1 million (USD 482), more than seven times her declared monthly household income. She had raised this through considerable financial support from her mosque, some help from other local organisations including local government, and USD 155 from personal funds. We cannot know what her prognosis would have been if she had undergone a biopsy when a dispensary first picked up a suspected lump, two years before we met her.

This upsetting story illustrates several key aspects of the maze as experienced by patients: a hospital failure to follow up on an early suspicion of cancer (showing that it was not always at lowest levels that cancer symptoms were missed); inability to pay for surgical biopsies delaying diagnosis and preventing diagnostic investigations important in fine-tuning chemotherapy; the costs and difficulty of travel also delaying diagnosis; and the sheer burden of accumulating payments causing reliance on religious communities and local forms of solidarity just to reach a diagnosis. Conversely, chemotherapy without charge at the specialist hospital facilitated access to treatment.

Diagnostic failures generated cumulative payments by patients which could quickly become unmanageable. Payment for diagnostic tests was often preceded by a history of other payments: charges for medication, tests and surgery, using up scarce family financial resources as well as delaying treatment. Patients had spent money on multiple consultations and inappropriate or unnecessary treatment. Each visit of this type generated payments and used up precious savings. Even screening in response to public health information—as the prostate cancer patient had undertaken—could be prohibitive:

> People are encouraged to go for screening, but when they start enquiring you are told you have to pay x amount or y amount and a lot of them just shy away from it because of the cost. I can do a lot more with that money. I have children to feed, I have this and other costs. (Cancer survivor, Kenya)

Diagnostic charges had repeatedly caused delays as patients searched for funds. For example, a Tanzanian patient with a breast lump paid for an ultrasound and X-ray at a faith-based referral hospital. However, the hospital also "wanted to take sample from my breast, but I didn't have extra money". This caused a further five months' delay until money was found, and earlier tests had to be repeated: her total OOP cost including the later biopsy after the patient found more money was TZS 190,000 (USD 83).

The costs of travel for consultations, tests and treatment could be prohibitive, as the cervical cancer patient's story (Box 4.4) illustrated. Even when more accessible hospitals could take biopsies, patients in both countries frequently had to travel to take their biopsy samples to a higher-level hospital laboratory for analysis (see Chapter 5). Lack of accessible services close to home, and long distances and costs of travel to a specialist hospital meant that some patients gave up, as a health worker in a geographically remote Tanzanian hospital noted above. A Kenyan health worker concurred:

> …those who are coming are the ones who can actually afford to have that fare to come to the hospital. There are others who want to come but they don't have the fare. (Health worker, Kenya)

Just fear of these costs could derail care. A Tanzanian female patient, and farmer, recounted that she had waited more than six months after diagnosis before travelling to the national cancer hospital, because she did not have the bus fare, and because people had said it was so expensive that she initially decided not to go at all.

That fear was based on experience. The highest charges faced by patients were for surgery and treatment. Chemotherapy medicines are unaffordable for most patients. In the Tanzanian specialist public cancer hospital where free treatment depended on availability of drugs, supply was good in 2019, but patients in earlier years had experienced stock-outs. In Kenya, those who had paid OOP for chemotherapy drugs reported delays and drop-out:

> I had bladder cancer stage 1 …. I was told to start on chemotherapy. I was booked for the therapy. But I stayed [waited] for two months as I was looking for money. (Patient, Kenya)
>
> It reached a point I had no money to continue with chemotherapy treatment. I used to buy the drugs. (Patient, Kenya)

Insurance and Private Care: Facilitation but High Costs

Each of the patients' stories, except the cervical cancer patient (Box 4.4), had included use of the private sector. Resort to private, independent faith-based and NGO facilities had been greater in Kenya than in Tanzania: 27% of Kenyan patients had started there (Table 4.1), and 36% had been diagnosed there. The figures for Tanzania were 21% and 22%, reflecting greater private sector availability in Kenya.

Private facilities in both countries focused on offering diagnostic services. Multiple tests were sometimes proposed, and charges could be prohibitive. A patient recounted a visit for urinary pain to a private doctor, for a second opinion after medication had not resolved his symptoms:

> The surgeon asked me to do some tests including ultrasound of the prostate, colonoscopy, blood tests, rectal examination. I went home to look for money. (Patient, Kenya)

The payment for those tests at a private hospital was KES 24,000 (USD 235). Kenyan patients in particular were aware that private facilities imposing these high charges were benefitting from limited testing availability within the public sector:

> When I go elsewhere and talk about my cancer status, people become afraid. They also say that cancer has become a business, because of the many tests that one has to undergo, and therefore someone becomes overwhelmed because of financial [demands]. (Cancer survivor, Kenya)

The private facilities and laboratories had increased availability of care while exacerbating the serious affordability challenges.

Insurance, conversely, was a key facilitator of access to cancer treatment, as the breast cancer patient's story illustrates. The National Health Insurance Funds of Tanzania and Kenya (NHIF in both) covered public employees, some other employees, and individuals who paid for the cover. In Tanzania, 31% of patients interviewed held NHIF, private insurance or both, far higher than the national population coverage of 9% estimated for NHIF in 2019.[3] In Kenya patients arriving at cancer treatment centres without insurance were encouraged to take up NHIF insurance, though it covered only part of cancer care costs:

> If you come and you are diagnosed with cancer, the first thing we tell them is to have an NHIF card, because we do educate them that the process is long and it is expensive, and you cannot always be paying cash. You can pay for six months, but we educate them so that when they start on radiotherapy and chemotherapy, they can be using NHIF so that by second session it would have matured. It matures in a very short time. (Health worker, Kenya)

This advice had clearly been facilitative for patients in Kenya. Strikingly, only 20.5% of the patients interviewed in Kenya had *not* had recourse to NHIF funding at some point. However, 88% had paid part or all of their first treatment costs in cash. Treatment exclusion is likely for those who cannot reach hospitals where treatment is free in Tanzania, or fail to gain NHIF membership in Kenya.

Payment Burdens and Impoverishment

> Many people have sold a lot of things at home. When you get cancer, you and your family will get poor. (Health worker, Kenya)
> Cancer treatments should be at low cost in order to be manageable by low-income people. (Patient, Tanzania)

Patients could not afford these cost-related delays, which reduce survival, nor the impoverishment and financial stress the payments implied. Most were on low incomes, and almost all were interviewed within the public health system (all in Kenya, 80% in Tanzania). Of the public sector cancer patients, 25% in each country declared household incomes of below one dollar a day; half declared less than 3 dollars a day. Payments that impoverish families can never be called "affordable" even if, somehow, people have managed to pay.

Patients' strategies to find money had brought much collateral family damage (see also Chapter 3). Many payments had been far beyond the limit of what was truly affordable while continuing to support families' basic needs. Furthermore, these were patients who had succeeded in *finding* the resources to continue through the cancer care maze, despite delays. Their struggles strongly suggest that there will be many people living with cancer in Kenya and Tanzania whom we could not interview because they had been unable to meet the financial demands and had dropped out of the maze. There exists no database in either country of people living with cancer excluded from diagnosis and treatment because of inability to pay.

Cancer had leached family resources in multiple ways, as patients explained:

> When you get this cancer, you leave your work, and you become so poor. And when you become very poor even food at home becomes a challenge. (Cancer survivor, Kenya)

> I needed money to pay for treatment. All I had, pigs and cows, were sold to access treatment at [a private] medical centre. By the time I came to [the cancer centre at a public hospital], I had nothing to sell. (Patient, Kenya)

Many had lost family assets that would otherwise produce income. In Tanzania, one patient sold a plot of land to finance a CT scan (USD 173); the husband of another sold chickens to fund an ultrasound, X-ray and surgery (USD 78); a third sold a cow to fund a biopsy (USD 65); another sold 4 hectares of land worth TZS 1.2 million (USD 522) to fund six chemotherapy cycles costing USD 417 at a time when the national cancer hospital had suffered severe shortages of oncology medication.

Worse still, this impoverishing effect was greatest at the lowest income levels. Table 4.3 compares total reported out-of-pocket spending on consultations, tests and treatment, from first symptoms to our interview, to patients' reported household income levels. It shows that, at the lowest of three income bands, median cumulative OOP spending had reached 72% of patients' declared annual income in Tanzania, and 155% in Kenya. A quarter of patients in Tanzania in the lowest income band furthermore had spent over 1.5 times their annual income; in Kenya the figure was 4.5 times. The burden of OOP spending was sharply lower at higher income levels in both countries.

These participants were at different stages in their cancer journey, so spending had necessarily varied. But the finding of regressive impact of OOP spending is robust.[4] OOP spending by these cancer patients in both countries was unjustly distributed, falling most heavily on the poorer households. Cancer is unaffordable.

Table 4.3 Household burden of OOP payments: Median cumulative OOP spending from first symptoms to interview date as % of annual income, by income bands

Income bands	*N**	*Median OOP spending % annual household income*
Tanzania: Bands of declared household monthly income (TZS)		
Up to 150,000 [Up to USD 65]	12	72%
160,000–390,000 [USD 70–170]	13	9%
400,000 upwards [USD 175 upwards]	13	9%
All respondents	38	17%
Kenya: Bands of declared household monthly income (KES)		
Less than 5000 [less than USD 49]	116	155%
5000–10,500 [USD 49–107]	138	45%
11,000 upwards [USD 108 upwards]	134	17%
All respondents	354	43%

*Number of patients able to recall 70% or more of payments. Currency conversion equivalence established according to the exchange rate at the time of interview

Tackling the Maze?

Access to cancer care, as patients described, formed a 'maze' experience that was often frustrating, frightening, slow, confusing, expensive, exclusionary and debilitating. What would it take to straighten patients' pathways and dismantle the walls of the 'maze' (Fig. 4.1)?

Information, Maps and Guides

Patients' experiences of the maze were often lonely. Many repeatedly 'self-referred', a phrase that does not do justice to an unguided search for help, relying on advice from family, friends and neighbours. So one big gap for patients was *information*. Many interviewees asked for more information about cancer symptoms, diagnosis and prognosis, care and treatment. There was a widespread lack of information on screening, on key symptoms and on what to do if symptoms were experienced. Public information campaigns would help, explaining symptoms and also providing reassurance that cancer diagnoses are not an inevitable 'death sentence'.

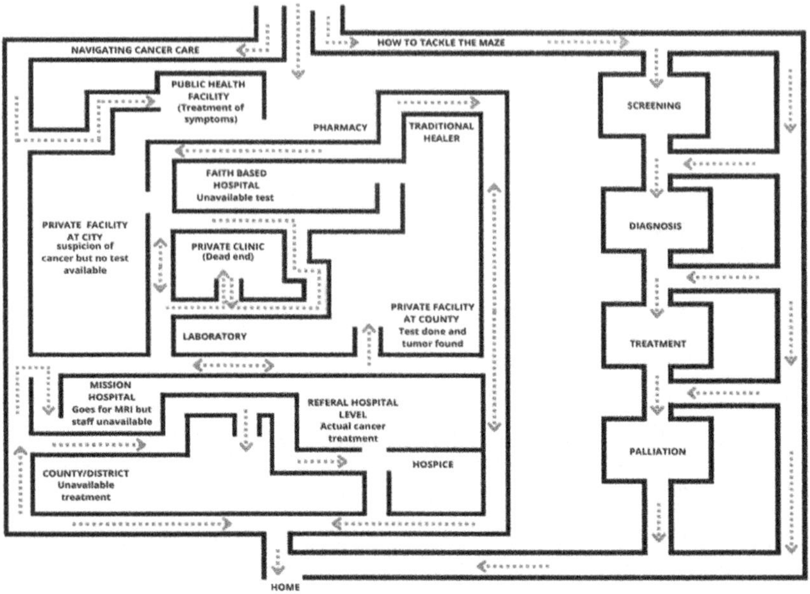

Fig. 4.1 Tackling the maze

Even when a patient was formally referred, suspicion of cancer was often not followed up at a higher-level. Many health facilities' staff lacked information and index of suspicion about symptoms that could indicate cancer, repeatedly treating patients for other illnesses even as the symptoms recurred. Appropriate referral with relevant data for the receiving facility is essential, as is better support for patients navigating to cancer care services within facilities.

Financial Support and Lower Costs

Maps and guides are no help if a patient cannot afford to turn the next corner in the maze. 'Affordability' is a demanding ambition in the context of cancer care. Affordable care requires charging that does not leave families impoverished, nor force patients to delay or drop out of care. Charges remain prohibitive for lower income patients. The more people can be brought into adequate insurance, covering all cancer treatment costs, the less impoverishing the access maze will become. Insurance in turn must be affordable. Extending social insurance, and subsidising premia for those of lower incomes, would reduce cost barriers. So would subsidy or waiver for diagnostic tests once cancer is suspected. Finally, lowering diagnostic and treatment costs from the supply side facilitates these efforts (see also Chapters 7–9).

Accessible Capacity for Cancer Care

Much public sector cancer care capacity in the maze was inaccessible for many patients from their homes and families. Improvements in diagnostic capability in health facilities accessible at district or sub-County level would reduce travel costs, speed up diagnosis and treatment initiation, and help to reduce OOP spending through less reliance on expensive private services. The more that diagnostic, treatment and palliation facilities can be spread outwards from the larger cities in both countries, the more the inequitable disparities in accessibility can be reduced.

Political and Government Support

Political will to support cancer care initiatives at the counties was reported in both countries, with counties in Kenya, where health planning is devolved, taking the matter seriously. Financing from the County administration in Kenya, and from the national government in Tanzania, was credited by participants with having increased availability of cancer drugs and specialist equipment. Current efforts in both countries to improve availability and affordability can be built upon, including strengthening insurance and fee waivers.

Chapter 5 picks up from these points, and makes a deeper dive, from the point of view of health system professionals and policy makers, into one of the most serious aspects of the access 'maze': the delays before diagnosis.

Notes

1. A prostate-specific antigen (PSA) test is a blood test that can help to identify early stage early-stage cancer.
2. That is, before the current government administration at the time of interview.

3. https://www.nhif.or.tz/pages/profile#gsc.tab=0 consulted 22/07/21.
4. The OOP spending is also regressive for other categories, such as spending from entry into the maze to diagnosis, and it is regressive across the spending distributions.

CHAPTER 5

Beyond "Late Presentation": Explaining Delayed Cancer Diagnosis in East Africa

Charlotte Cross, Sharon Mokua, Richard Ngilangwa, Cristina Santos, Twalib Ngoma, and Phares G. M. Mujinja

Introduction

> [Diagnosis] is like the basis of everything. If I am diagnosed early, I have a chance to survive. (Survivor, Kenya)

In Tanzania and Kenya, as in many other low- and middle-income countries (LMICs), the majority of cancer patients are diagnosed when their cancer is at a late stage, with negative implications for treatment options

C. Cross (✉) · C. Santos
The Open University, Milton Keynes, UK
e-mail: charlotte.cross@open.ac.uk

S. Mokua
Kenya Medical Research Institute (KEMRI), Nairobi, Kenya

R. Ngilangwa
Economic and Social Research Foundation (ESRF), Dar es Salaam, Tanzania

G. Banda et al. (eds.), *Cancer Care in Pandemic Times: Building Inclusive Local Health Security in Africa and India*, International Political Economy Series,
https://doi.org/10.1007/978-3-031-44123-3_5

and efficacy, the cost of care, and rates of survival (Lehmann et al., 2020; Makau-Barasa et al., 2018; Mlange et al., 2016; Ngoma et al., 2015). Reducing delays to diagnosis, and increasing the number of patients diagnosed, is a policy priority in both countries (Ministry of Health, 2017; Ministry of Health and Social Services, 2013) and internationally (WHO, 2020). Enabling earlier diagnosis is critical not only for patient outcomes but also for its potential to reduce the cost of care for patients and healthcare providers (Espina et al., 2017, Moodley et al., 2018). However, research regarding factors influencing the timeliness of diagnosis of cancers in LMICs remains limited (Nnaji et al., 2022).

Delayed diagnosis is often framed as a challenge of "late presentation" by patients at health facilities, to be explained by patient behaviour and characteristics, and prompting calls for public education about cancer symptoms and treatment and the importance of prompt facility attendance (Kassaman et al., 2022; Mlange et al., 2016, Mwaka et al., 2021). Indeed, interventions aimed at addressing barriers to timely diagnosis in LMICs tend to emphasise improving patient, community, and to a lesser extent health provider knowledge, rather than addressing structural issues such as the financial costs associated with care (Qu et al., 2020).

It is certainly the case, as explored in Chapter 3, that limited knowledge and understanding of cancer and cancer treatment among patients, caregivers, and their communities contribute to fear and experiences of stigma, influencing whether and how patients seek care. However, this chapter builds on Chapter 4's demonstration, from the accounts of patients, caregivers, and survivors, of the limitations of "late presentation" in explaining delays to diagnosis. We shift here to a more "professional" health system perspective, drawing largely on interviews with health professionals and policymakers in Kenya and Tanzania. These interviews identified key challenges, including access to screening, weak referral systems, the very limited availability of diagnostic pathology, and the direct and indirect costs of obtaining a cancer diagnosis, to which feasible responses could speed diagnosis. We argue that policy aimed at increasing early diagnosis must go well beyond improving population knowledge to

T. Ngoma · P. G. M. Mujinja
Muhimbili University of Health and Allied Sciences (MUHAS), Dar es Salaam, Tanzania

address wider health system issues such as referral procedures, availability and accessibility of diagnostic tests, and the affordability of care.

Delayed Diagnosis in Kenya and Tanzania

Late diagnosis of cancer is a significant problem in Kenya and Tanzania. Health workers providing specialised cancer treatment in both countries described the challenges associated with "late presentation" of cancer patients at specialist hospital level and the implications for treatment and outcomes. As one Kenyan policymaker explained:

> ...people are just presenting... to hospitals and being diagnosed with cancer when it is too late...when you present with cervical cancer, for example, and it is stage 1, you might be lucky, maybe you will only need surgery. But when you present with stage 4, you will need surgery, chemotherapy, radiotherapy, I don't know [immunotherapy]... they will be so many treatments and the outcomes may not be that good.

They estimated that 80% of patients "present late, so that means in stage 3 or 4, when it is already too late". In Tanzania too, a health worker at the national cancer hospital reported that 80% of patients arrived at that hospital "when their disease is at a late stage. Only 10 or 20 percent come at an early stage when their cancer might be curable". Much of the treatment provided thus involved palliation. A Kenyan nurse working in oncology claimed they had "never seen a patient who [is] stage 2, as in early stages", meaning "we just try to control and try to prolong life", something they found "just devastating", and that meant "it calls for God's grace" to do their job.

Some health workers did attribute late diagnosis to patients' lack of knowledge of cancer and cancer treatment, and their preference for alternative healing:

> You know some people think [their illness is] witchcraft and we have to take them from that thinking... I know in Kenya 95% of people believe in witchcraft... I have seen some dying of cancer when they are saying it is witchcraft...there are others in the interior. Those people remain on traditional things. They just use their...what we call traditional medicine, and they don't go to the hospital. (Health worker, Kenya)

The use of alternative healers was described as causing patients to delay reporting to health facilities, meaning that "when they figure out it is not working, they present themselves and by then it is a little bit too late in terms of curative options" (health worker, Kenya). By that time, "they have lost most of their income and the situation has worsened to an advanced stage" (health worker, Tanzania).

However, health workers also often acknowledged that patients were not solely responsible for their late diagnosis. As one Kenyan nurse put it, "by the time they land there [in the hospital] they came from somewhere; they have a story in between". This story involved difficult attempts to navigate the "maze" described in Chapter 4. Indeed, the majority of delays for patients in both Kenya and Tanzania, occurred *after* their first visit to a health facility, so these patients' delays cannot solely or primarily be attributed to patient attitudes, knowledge or behaviour. This chapter explores the systemic health system factors causing delay, demonstrating that attempts to speed up diagnosis must go beyond efforts to increase patient awareness or discourage the use of alternative healers.

Screening and Early Detection

For some cancers, screening offers a significant opportunity to increase early detection. Consider cervical cancer, which represents a significant burden in Kenya and Tanzania, and which can be screened for using low-cost methods with potential for early preventative treatment. Both Kenya and Tanzania have adopted cervical screening policies, involving a combination of visual inspection of the cervix with acetic acid (VIA) and/or Lugol's iodine (VILI), cytology-based screening (e.g. a pap smear), and testing for human-papillomavirus (HPV). However, in neither country is screening provided as a comprehensive population-based, regular service for at-risk populations. Instead, screening is largely provided through ad hoc "outreach" events run by specialised public facilities or non-governmental organisations or is sought or undertaken in response to potential symptoms.

One health worker in Tanzania explained: "only women who suspect they have a problem attend the [cervical screening] clinic…[by which time] it is difficult to help them… Some women come here telling you, 'I just accompanied my friend', while at the same time they also need to be screened. So education hasn't reached many". These views were echoed by cancer survivors in Kenya, who explained: "Not many people know where you can get these services, especially people in the rural areas, they don't know which hospital to go to, they don't have information". In addition to education and awareness deficits, research participants in both countries attributed low levels of screening to the absence of a "culture" of attending health facilities in the absence of illness. According to a senior policymaker in Kenya, "[t]he major challenge we have currently in cancer as a society [is] we have never embraced the idea of wellness checks or screening, so ...people are just presenting to hospitals and being diagnosed with cancer when it is too late". Thus, one health worker in Tanzania concluded "we need to develop a culture of checking our health often".

Limited *demand* for cervical screening, however, is only part of the challenge. While outreach events in both countries were described as popular, with attendances of approximately 1000 reported at events run by national cancer hospitals, their reach is inevitably limited. One Tanzanian health worker noted, "when we take screening to the community people respond positively. The problem is that it doesn't reach them a lot." Another health worker confirmed that "'all these efforts aren't enough because the programmes reach a very small population" (health worker, Tanzania). In regions outside of major cities, screening is not widely and routinely available in lower tier facilities. Where it is offered, staff shortages and high workloads constrain the ability of staff to provide an effective and consistent service. In Tanzania, staff at one regional hospital, located in a region with very limited other screening provision, noted that the four people trained to perform screening using VIA struggled to do so alongside their other roles. As one nurse explained, "we are not sufficient. Sometimes women go back home without accessing a [screening] service because we might be dealing with other responsibilities". Indeed, elsewhere, if demand for screening were to increase, it was anticipated it would be difficult to retain existing levels of provision (health worker, Tanzania).

There are also barriers to attending screening programmes where they are available. In Kenya, one survivor articulated the difficulty people faced in spending money on routine and preventative health care when there was no urgent need for treatment, saying:

> People are encouraged to go for screening but when they start enquiring you are told you have to pay x amount or y amount and a lot of them

just shy away from it because of the cost. "I can do a lot more with that money. I have children to feed, I have this, and I have other costs".

Although in Tanzania VIA is available free of charge, the limited geographic coverage meant many people faced travel costs to reach a facility (Chapter 4). Without running events to provide screening closer to people's homes, health workers realised it could be difficult for people to attend. As one doctor at a facility which only conducted screening at the hospital described, only those who can afford transport are able to attend, meaning "when we are looking for big numbers, we don't get those numbers, we just get some numbers" (health worker, Kenya).

International and local NGOs play a big role in cervical screening provision in Kenya and Tanzania, including the provision of training to health workers, funding of clinics and equipment, and organisation of outreach events. For some health workers, this model raised concerns about its likely sustainability and ability to cope with greater numbers of patients. In Tanzania, where a different international NGO supported screening in each region in which research was carried out, some funders had indicated that cost-sharing might be required in the future, suggesting providers "need to be independent because in the future they might not be able to supply us with the necessary equipment" (health worker, Tanzania). In Kenya, a health worker described attempts to encourage people to attend screening, and to incur the travel costs associated with doing so, by offering lunch, but "the sponsors ran short of it and they just had to go away".

A more general difficulty associated with maintaining donor-sponsored initiatives also posed a potential challenge to the sustainability of cervical screening, as described by one Tanzanian health worker:

> The problem is that this training is part of vertical programmes... for example, people come to a place for research and diagnose many women etc. and incentives are made available. But when they leave, despite the fact they built capacity, when the programme ends those who are left don't continue...I have seen this in [my previous posting]. You realise [the work has stopped] after you see the number of people who visit the centre going down. Their argument is that they don't have money to keep it going...these vertical programmes make our health providers lazy because they think this is the way of doing things that should continue while in reality these are their responsibilities... The problem arises when it comes to sustainability. When they [the sponsored projects] leave is when we see

gaps. You made this guy feel comfortable with the programme, when you ask them to start walking by themselves they start going backwards.

Others highlighted the importance of donors in shaping priorities within the health system, comparing the relative lack of support for cancer to that available for HIV or for maternal and child health, which indeed were largely the primary focus of those international NGOs supporting cervical screening. One pharmacist concluded, "we only prioritize things that will be supported by our partners" (health worker, Tanzania).

Weak Referral Processes

In order to access diagnostic imaging and laboratory tests, patients who entered the health system at lower tiers generally had to be referred, or to self-refer, to a referral hospital (levels 5 or 6 in Kenya; regional, zonal or national hospital in Tanzania), or to access procedures in the private sector. As described in Chapter 4, referrals were a challenging aspect of the maze. The "churning" (Makene et al., 2022) described there also affected patients prior to diagnosis, contributing to delay. In both countries, national cancer treatment guidelines and cancer control strategies emphasise the importance of effective referral systems, while also acknowledging challenges faced by patients in obtaining timely referrals at present (Ministry of Health, 2017; Ministry of Health and Social Services, 2013). Indeed, Tanzania's National Cancer Control Strategy notes that the current referral system is "long and leads to late detection of cancer and delays in treatment" (Ministry of Health and Social Services, 2013, p. 8).

Health workers, survivors, and patients recalled examples, and sometimes their own experiences, of mis- or partial diagnosis over extended periods and multiple visits to health facilities, which led to costs and delayed the start of appropriate treatment. One survivor in Kenya who was a member of a support group for those with cancer of the colon, for example, reported that many of their peers had been "treated for typhoid, amoeba, ulcers, h-pylori, for a very long time. Some even for years". Limited capacity to identify potential cancer symptoms at lower tiers of the health system was part of the problem, as a senior policy maker in Kenya described: "health workers, especially at the primary care level, may not really have a high index of suspicion. So the patient may be treated for the wrong condition even many times before they are found to have cancer". One health worker in Tanzania explained, "the bad thing is that when people [at lower tiers] can't detect [cancer] early, in most cases they just offer medication and give [patients] prescriptions to use them for three weeks and come back for a check up again".

A health worker at a facility providing cancer treatment agreed that sometimes "it is our fault" (health worker, Kenya). They recalled a patient who had arrived at the facility with breast cancer so advanced that:

> Her breast is...just like a wound until the necrosed flesh is falling off until the chest becomes flat...So the client will start telling me, 'I went to this clinic and they were dressing me with different solutions, the wound was not improving. Now after the breast worsened I came to [national hospital]'...Now this clinician in a dispensary could have suspected... there was low suspicion index in this health care provider at that level because he or she had this information to suspect this patient is having cancer, could have taken an initiative, this patient maybe right now could be having a different stage of illness, not the metastasized stage. So...I think...we as the health care providers, we contribute in delaying the diagnosis.

Even when given a referral for suspected cancer, patients face challenges and delay. It was not always possible for patients to move directly from lower tiers to a facility at which they could be treated. One health worker at Tanzania's national cancer hospital, which does not have its own pathology lab, explained:

> You cannot open a file if the documents are not signed to indicate [prior investigations are complete]... If they are not signed it means there is a problem and a patient requires further investigative procedures... If a patient has been referred by a general practitioner, we will have to send them to [another national hospital] if we think what has been done is not sufficient, but if there is adequate information you can admit them.

Diagnosing cancer often involves multiple types of diagnostic procedure, often not available in the same place, generating delays when patients have to raise funds for travel or to wait for appointments or results (Chapter 4). Health workers in Kenya and Tanzania recognised the burden imposed by the requirement to move for care and identified the value of having tests and treatment available in one place for increasing speed of access to treatment. A health worker in Kenya reflected on the tumour boards they convened at their hospital, at which staff discuss the patient's pathway to diagnosis. This helped them to understand the extent to which patients "are taken up and down: go to surgical clinic, they are delayed; they [perform a] biopsy, the results get lost. So you are delaying the patient care". They noted this was even a problem when patients were required to attend different departments within the same hospital and explained the aspiration for the oncology unit to be a 'one stop shop', with the ability to provide screening, symptom assessment, and to perform and analyse biopsies, "because it will prevent so many people coming when they are late". With the current system, "sometimes when we go for tumour board we discover that some patients have... [had a] biopsy, but after the surgery nobody referred them to oncology for review and for treatment. So we need to pull our socks up on that bit".

Experiences of long waiting times, broken equipment, or absent staff made it even harder and more expensive to negotiate referrals for many, and increased delays. One health worker in Kenya described challenges that could arise when referring patients with possible cancer to an already busy minor surgery unit in the emergency department for a biopsy: "sometimes emergency is also busy, they are delayed a bit, many activities—it is busy, there are accidents coming in—so sometimes you find a patient went for a biopsy and by the time he is coming with the result [it has been] like 3 months. It takes long actually".

The weaknesses of the referral system meant patients often had to try to navigate the system themselves, self-referring up and down the tiers in search of a diagnosis and relief from their symptoms. Indeed, as explained in Chapter 4, a majority of moves by patients between facilities were self-referrals, which could involve moves up and down the tiered health system, and between the public and private sectors. Former patients described their own attempts to navigate the health system to obtain a diagnosis, often relying on advice from family and friends. This account, from a survivor in Kenya who had been treated for what they were told was "just a sinus problem" at ten different facilities over a six-month period is illustrative of the extent to which patients sometimes had to struggle to be heard and obtain a diagnosis:

> I kept telling [health professionals] 'no, I have been treated for this twice, it has not gone away.' They tell me 'take this antibiotic' or 'take this particular medicine – in two weeks it should be okay.' And even when you are telling the doctor that 'I have been treated for this thing twice, this is not what it is, it is something else', he still prescribes the same things. So

> even when you challenge them, they assume that you are a lay person, you don't understand these medical things. It is only when I started talking to friends and family and saying, 'look I have been going to [these] places they have been treating me for this I don't know what is going on because they keep treating and it is not going [away]'. And then I started talking to people and someone said, 'maybe you should see an [Ear, nose and throat (ENT)] specialist'. I went to see two or three, same thing, then somebody actually referred me to a specialist: 'I know this is a very good ENT go and see him, he might be able to sort you out'. But it is just that process of going back and forth and even when you challenge, they assume you are not a medical professional, your opinion does not matter: 'I know what I am doing this is a sinus problem'. And that is why it took six months to diagnose (survivor, Kenya).

Thus, contrary to some analysis that suggests a "lack of personal initiative" on the part of patients who are diagnosed late (Mlange et al., 2016, p. 1), one survivor in Kenya, who had undergone tests in three public and private facilities before being advised to see a specialist who diagnosed them with breast cancer, observed, "if I didn't insist, I don't know where I would be, I would be six feet under". Persistence on the part of the patient was important in speeding up diagnosis but was often dependent on the ability to bear the costs associated with moving between facilities, and access to advice about how best to do so.

Moving between facilities, whether due to a formal referral or self-referral, was a major contributor to delay, with patients in Tanzania who moved more times waiting longer to be diagnosed (Makene et al., 2022). In addition to the time spent pursuing inappropriate treatment or waiting for appointments, moving between facilities involved additional costs for patients without insurance or who needed to travel away from their homes to access care. It could therefore be challenging to persuade patients to follow a referral, due to the cost and inconvenience it represented. One health worker in Tanzania described the response of patients to news they were being referred as follows:

> ...the big issue is that when you ask a patient to go for a referral they become resistant....[for two reasons] one is education and another is distance, because if a patient came from far away and had already spent a lot to come here thinking that they will get everything from here and you then ask them to go for a referral...they resist.. [they give] you excuses, even if

> they have money they get argumentative thinking they can be treated from here.

Improving the speed of referral for those with suspected cancer could therefore play a key role in reducing delays. However, the necessity for referral and the difficulties patients face in navigating moves between facilities are closely linked to the availability of diagnostic tests at different levels of the health system, and the cost of care and of travel required to reach it.

Pathology and Laboratory Capability

A key factor necessitating referral to higher tiers of the health system, and consequently generating delay, is availability of pathology. This challenge was particularly acute in Tanzania, where regional referral hospitals cannot provide pathology. While some regional facilities can extract a biopsy, patients are still required to transport the sample themselves to a zonal or national hospital for analysis. Even at the highest tiers and in the private sector, pathologists are few. A leading private hospital had only one pathologist at the time the research was conducted, meaning that when this individual was on leave, they had to refer cases to a public national hospital (health worker, Tanzania). Although pathology services were available at the Kenyan level 5 facilities included in the study, capacity remains concentrated in Nairobi (Lehmann et al., 2020), and health workers described other challenges that caused delays for patients, meant they had to be referred elsewhere, or led them to use the private sector.

Limited access to pathology in the lower tiers of the public health sector means patients with a visible mass or other visually identifiable symptoms are likely to be referred upwards for further investigation (Schroeder et al., 2018; Stefan et al., 2015). While possible indicators of some cancers can be identified through a physical examination at lower tiers of the health system where pathology and imaging are not available, such as cervical, breast, skin, and advanced oesophageal cancers, others, such as blood cancers, are "very difficult to identify because it needs laboratory diagnosis" (health worker, Tanzania). As one Tanzanian health worker located a long distance away from specialised cancer care explained:

> We only provide physical examination services to patients suspected to have cancer. For example, a woman who comes with a history of vaginal bleeding who reached the menopause three years ago and reports pain during sex with her husband; a man who is coughing up blood – we suspect these people have cancer and they are referred to referral hospitals.

In Tanzania, health workers at regional facilities without pathology capability identified expanding pathology as a key way in which their provision of cancer care could be improved. At one facility located over 340 kilometres away from the nearest public hospitals where a biopsy could be performed, the inability to carry out diagnostic tests meant staff were sometimes unable to provide surgical treatment despite its availability at the hospital. A doctor gave the following example regarding prostate cancer:

> …you cannot plan to start treatment before you know whether it [prostate swelling] is benign or malignant. There is a very small tool we use called a tru-cut needle. It's something we insert to take a flesh sample to take to the laboratory. But our laboratory isn't equipped to do such a test which is very basic. If we could get such a tool and get a pathology lab… At least in every regional hospital there must be a small pathology unit so that small operations like that can be carried out. We wouldn't need to make a large number of referrals, because sometimes you get a patient with an enlarged prostate. We can remove it, but we aren't allowed to do this before confirming the type. So you have to send people to [zonal hospital over 340 km away] or [national hospital over 800 km away] or [zonal hospital over 400km away] just for a biopsy so that they can bring back the results as a go ahead. But if regional hospitals could be empowered in terms of supplies and equipment, as well as personnel, and have the capacity to do all those basic cytological investigations, I think we would have made a very big step within cancer care… If we have a pathologist in every regional hospital and good laboratory infrastructure we will move forward.

This was particularly pressing because health workers knew of cases when people had abandoned treatment prior to being diagnosed due to the cost imposed by a referral for diagnostic tests, as described in the following section.

Although the facilities outside of Nairobi at which research was conducted in Kenya could perform some pathology, interviewees identified challenges that could delay diagnosis. Delays in receiving biopsy results due to congestion in surgery were described above, and health workers at one facility also discussed delays that arose due to relying on the general laboratory, rather than one dedicated to cancer. Shortages of reagents and equipment could also delay patient access to procedures. One health worker explained "in the side of diagnosis, we are lacking, because most of the patients you are given a request form and you are told to do the tru-cut [biopsy] or the FNA [fine needle aspiration] and you can wait as long as two weeks, three weeks, and a month, waiting to be booked". They attributed this to reagents not being available, also noting that sometimes patients were asked to purchase biopsy needles to undergo a procedure, which meant that some patients chose to wait until the facility could provide this.

When certain tests were not available in public facilities, patients had to use the private sector, which could have significant cost implications, or were sometimes required to travel or faced a delay while samples were sent away to Nairobi. As one health worker at a facility which offered some pathology, but not histology, noted, "human resources is a problem, infrastructure is a problem, equipment is a problem. If we could get a better MRI machine and other things in processing like histology in the lab [that would be an improvement], because that runs around the cost of the patient". Indeed, in Kenya, 27% of first visits to a health facility made by patients who participated in the research, all of whom were being treated in a *public* hospital at the time they were interviewed, were to a private sector facility (Chapter 4). Private clinics and laboratories played an important role in providing diagnostic tests for many, even as they continued to seek care in the public sector. Indeed, almost a fifth (18%) of all health facility visits reported by patients in Kenya since they developed cancer symptoms were to private facilities. This may be due to the wider availability of diagnostic tests in the private sector, which provides the majority of medical laboratory services in Nairobi, as well as perceptions of greater quality, convenience, and anticipation of a faster result for those who are able to afford such services (Bahati et al., 2021).

Cost of Diagnosis

Delays associated with navigating referrals and the limited availability of diagnostic tests at lower tiers of the system were exacerbated by the costs associated with diagnostic procedures and moves between facilities. Patients and their families often delayed while they sought funds.

Although this research could not capture the experiences of those who abandoned the formal health system prior to being diagnosed, the number of undiagnosed cancer sufferers is significant (Gesink et al., 2020; Olson et al., 2020; Severance et al., 2022; URT, 2017). Interviews with health workers and survivors suggest that costs incurred prior to diagnosis and anticipated further costs are an important factor in causing patients to exit the formal healthcare system before diagnosis, or to delay seeking further care (see also Ariga & Mujinja, 2017). Facilitators of access discussed in Chapter 4, and particularly the National Health Insurance Fund (NHIF) in Kenya and the provision of free treatment for cancer patients in Tanzania, did not benefit patients to the same extent prior to diagnosis.

In Kenya, the NHIF covers most diagnostic tests, such as CT scans, MRIs, and some biopsies. However, health workers described encouraging patients to join the scheme *after* a cancer diagnosis. One caregiver described the limited protective potential of NHIF for new joiners prior to diagnosis, noting:

> You must have money to do the tests because if you rely on NHIF, yes they will pay for you, but it will take some time. So it makes the process of diagnosis slow even to start on treatment. So you have to look for cash if you really want to get the diagnosis on time and to be started on treatment. So I had to pay for all those tests - it was expensive.

Some procedures, which were not available in public facilities, could not be paid for using NHIF, such as lymph node biopsies, which must be taken to the private sector for analysis, meaning "for the biopsy, they [are] deep in their pockets, the relatives" (health worker, Kenya).

In Tanzania although free treatment is available in the public sector for patients who have been diagnosed with cancer, many incur significant costs prior to diagnosis. One health worker explained:

> Cancer patients receive free medical treatment from dispensary level up to referral level, including palliative care. However, anybody who hasn't been diagnosed with cancer would find it almost impossible to get free treatment, even if they have all the symptoms of cancer.

As another health worker in a different region summed up: "treatment is free, but people pay".

Challenges linked to poor referral systems and low capacity to diagnose outside of specialised cancer treatment centres, described above, meant some patients incurred costs from attending multiple consultations and receiving inappropriate or unnecessary treatment before cancer was suspected see also (Kohi et al., 2019). A survivor in Kenya described his story of treatment prior to diagnosis with prostate cancer:

> In 2009, I could not go for a short call. Our family doctor advised me to take him a sample. It was very painful to pee. So he took it for examination. He did not tell me anything – he told me that it was normal for people my age.... He injected me and half an hour later I could now urinate normally. Then after a while... after intercourse with my wife I felt pain. I went back to the same doctor and he did not tell me anything. He told me to go to Doctors Plaza to do physiotherapy, but every day I had to pay 1000 Shillings (8 USD) and I am a retired person. He then told me to go to [public referral hospital]. So the physiotherapy continued here for three good years – 2009, 2010, 2011 – and then [cancer] was discovered early 2012. I spent a lot. The doctor told me to go and do an MRI. I did not know what it meant. I went to [private hospital] and it was costing 46,000 [386 USD] ...biopsy was done and it was discovered that I had stage 4 prostate cancer. PSA [prostate-specific antigen] was 100.... I don't know if my doctor knew that I had cancer, maybe he wanted to mint money off me before he made the right diagnosis.

As illustrated by the account above, when cancer is suspected, diagnostic tests can be expensive, and patients often required multiple types of test or for these to be repeated on multiple occasions. In Tanzania, patients had spent a median of 150,000 TZS (65 USD) on diagnostic imaging. Reported costs for imaging varied considerably in Kenya, but patients' median reported charge for CT scans for example was 8000 KES (66 USD). Meeting these costs could be very challenging for patients, as described in Chapter 4, where a Kenyan survivor argued that cancer testing had become "a business" there. Indeed, as another survivor reflected, it could feel like "diagnosis is a money minting affair" (survivor, Kenya).

Both patients and clinicians sometimes had to make decisions about care based on the financial circumstances of the patient. A survivor in Kenya described their experience of attending a public referral hospital with symptoms of pain and being told by the doctor that they suspected cancer:

> So I asked where to start. He told me if I had 20,000 [168 USD] you can be tested further. I asked if he wanted cash and I told him I could not afford. I went back home, I stayed for 3 days, and my friends called me and advised me to go to [another public hospital]. I went [there] and stayed there for 9 days as they did their own investigations. They [performed a biopsy], and it was cheaper than [the original hospital]. After the operation I was given the mass to take to labs and then they told me that it was cancer and they referred me [back to the referral hospital], because they said that they did not have a cancer hospital.

Thus the patient self-referred, following advice from friends, to seek care that was affordable, delaying their eventual diagnosis and the start of treatment. Although this patient was able to access the tests they needed, sometimes this was not possible. One Kenyan health worker at a facility outside of Nairobi explained, "even if we have done their biopsies, they are sometimes needed to go to Nairobi for histology and [to] do staging investigations because…they cannot afford the CT scans or…we are not able to do tumour markers. So many of the times you will find the socio-economic status of the patient actually limit[s] us, because sometimes we cannot make a clinical decision or a way forward for this patient".

This meant that patients had spent large amounts on health care, such as consultation fees, medication and diagnostic tests, prior to being diagnosed, representing a significant burden for many households. In both Kenya and Tanzania, the burden of costs relative to household income was much worse for the poorest patients prior to diagnosis, as well as over the course of treatment (Chapter 4). In Tanzania over a quarter of participants in the lowest income band had faced costs prior to diagnosis that exceeded their annual household income (Makene et al., 2022). In Kenya, a quarter of those with the lowest declared incomes had spent at least double their annual income before they were diagnosed.

In addition to the direct costs of care, patients also incurred travel costs when referred or self-referring between facilities, as well as costs of accommodation and subsistence away from home. As noted above, many patients moved multiple times between facilities in search of a diagnosis, which increased the costs they faced. These challenges are compounded when there is high demand for procedures, such as biopsy extraction, meaning that patients may be asked to return to the hospital on multiple dates, which can be prohibitively expensive for patients residing at significant distances from the facility. These costs were not insignificant for many. Reported travel costs are likely to be underestimated, due to the assistance many received from family or friends with accommodation and subsistence and difficulty in recalling every day-to-day cost incurred. However, the reported median travel costs of 36 USD in Tanzania and 21 USD in Kenya represented a high proportion of annual income for some participants. Indeed, in Kenya, a quarter of those in the lowest income band had spent almost 30% of their declared annual income on transport.

These challenges were particularly acute for those who lived at a considerable distance from referral hospitals. In Tanzania, staff at a regional hospital located approximately 350km from the nearest public hospital with a CT scan and MRI and with the capacity to perform a biopsy, and over 800 km from the specialist national cancer facility, were very aware of the difficulties meeting travel costs could generate for patients. Indeed, they reported that this could cause patients to abandon seeking care entirely, prior to being diagnosed, even when cancer was suspected. A health worker quoted in Chapter 4 explained that after cervical screening found signs of cancer, some patients did not follow up on recommended tests because of unaffordability, and so went home and would die. They continued

> If we could manage to take a biopsy here we could send it ourselves and get the results sent here, but when you ask them to go to [zonal hospital over 340 km away] or [national hospital over 800 km away] you know they will not go and you just write the referral.

Travelling even over relatively short distances is unmanageable for some, particularly when combined with the costs of accommodation and subsistence. As one doctor at a hospital in a region neighbouring Dar es Salaam explained, lack of access to histology and cytology services at a regional level, "can lead to a patient not going to the hospital because of financial problems, because once they think about going to [a national hospital] for tests they become scared and you find they delay, but if tests could be done from here, at least people from [this region] could come here because they know they can just come here and get treatment, rather than thinking about going to [a national hospital] where they expect expenses to be high" (health worker, Tanzania).

Costs contributed to delays for many patients, who had to seek financial support from friends and family prior to undertaking recommended procedures, or to sell assets. In Tanzania, one patient who was subsequently diagnosed with breast cancer, for example, had spent over a year seeking a diagnosis and relief of her symptoms before being referred for a biopsy (her third), which she could not afford. After another five months and following advice from a neighbour who was married to a doctor, she was able to return and pay for the biopsy and further examinations and was diagnosed with cancer. This patient calculated they had spent 160 USD on care at public and faith-based facilities, in addition to a further 176 USD on alternative healing, which she had sought out only after four months of inconclusive investigations in the formal sector, prior to being diagnosed, in addition to at least 42 USD on transport to access care. With a monthly household income of only 26 USD, this represented a huge financial burden, before she became eligible for free treatment.

In Kenya, even those with NHIF coverage could find it challenging to afford diagnostic tests, as insurance did not always cover the entire cost. One survivor recalled: "sometimes there are tests that you go for, for instance MRI, when you go to a private facility…They tell you it is [298 USD] and NHIF pays for you [128 USD] so [the rest] has to come out of your pocket. Getting that money is a challenge, and that is why there is a delay…" (survivor, Kenya). Even when tests are available in the public sector at a reasonable distance from the patient, it is sometimes necessary to delay in order to seek funds. One health worker who had described the availability of diagnostic procedures at County level for breast cancer nevertheless highlighted affordability challenges, which meant that "you can get a patient who has come to the hospital with a breast lump; you send them for a mammogram; they come with the results after a month, later" (health worker, Kenya).

A Kenyan survivor gave an example that echoes many of the experiences shared by patients, carers, health workers and survivors:

> …for instance, I have gone to the dispensary and I have done some tests. Later I am referred to the sub-county hospital, and I am told that the tests that I require cannot be done in that facility – so that is a challenge. They refer you to another facility, for instance [public referral hospital], [private hospital], [elite private hospital] depending on your ability [to pay]. So when you get to the facility, you are told the cost of the tests and often they are expensive. So you are forced to go back home and wait until you have more money.

The psycho-social challenges associated with obtaining that money, or being unable to do so, were discussed in Chapter 3.

Conclusion

This chapter has reviewed key factors contributing to delayed diagnosis of cancer in Kenya and Tanzania. We argue that rather than framing the challenge as one of *late presentation*, which places responsibility for delay on the patient, research and policy analysis should instead consider the central problem as one of *late diagnosis*, which is caused by multiple interrelated factors, including characteristics of the health system. Thus, although increasing public awareness of cancer, and its symptoms and treatment, may play a role in reducing delays to diagnosis, the health system-related problems explored here must also be addressed. The challenges identified in this chapter echo the relationship between experiences of cancer and cancer care and wider socio-economic inequalities discussed in Chapters 3 and 4. The WHO (2020) identifies the three primary issues hindering early diagnosis in LMICs as the inability of primary care providers to identify symptoms, challenges with referral systems, and limited availability of pathology and diagnostic imaging (WHO, 2020, pp. 78–79). This list overlaps with our interviewees' identification of key aspects of the system requiring intervention. However it should be expanded to include more routine screening, more affordable diagnostic tests, especially in the public sector, greater availability of diagnostic testing at lower levels of the health system, and reducing the need for "self-referral", in order to have a meaningful impact.

PART III

Local Industry and Cancer Care in India and East Africa

This section returns to the industrial and supply chain issues introduced in Part 1. Given the cancer care situation in Kenya and Tanzania charted in Part 2, and the pandemic learning experience concerning the fragility of extreme import dependence for health system inputs (Chapter 2), what can be done? Can industrial development and innovation in health-industry linkages support improvement in cancer care in East Africa—and also in the industrially more developed context of India?

Chapter 6 creates a bridge between health and industrial concerns. India—with its deeper manufacturing capabilities—struggled to sustain supply chains for health care but also saw many successes during the pandemic. Chapter 6 builds on the author's personal experience and responses to the pandemic challenges. It urges a deliberate move to bring health policy, industrial organisation, and economics researchers closer together, in the interests of better health care and industrial development.

Chapter 7 considers what this might mean for cancer-related manufacturing in East Africa. Starting from the paradox of unmet need for cancer supplies alongside unmet market demand, the chapter sets out, drawing on pre-pandemic and pandemic experience, what it will take to raise the ambition of local manufacturers and generate more sustainable manufacturing investment and innovation in health-related industries in East Africa.

Chapter 8 then focuses on a key requirement for cancer care: essential oncology drugs. Import-dependence in oncology is almost complete across Sub-Saharan Africa, while India is a key exporter. The chapter documents competition failures in generic oncology markets and the huge affordability impact of effective procurement within India. Challenges for local oncology manufacturing are identified. The chapter argues that active health-industrial-research linkages can build a local African oncology industry.

CHAPTER 6

Cupboard Full, Cupboard Empty: The Industrial Building Blocks of Covid-19 and Cancer Systems

Smita Srinivas

Introduction: Generalities About 'Broken Health Systems' Despite Covid-19 Successes

A large number of detailed and candid conversations with scientists, clinicians, public health specialists, and industrialists were underway in India well before the pandemic was upon us. Although the world went awry in 2020 with Covid-19, I realised how awry it was in 2018. What everyone kept saying in their own distinct way was that India's 'health system was broken'. Each expert described this problem in their own professional language. Doctors often said 'we can't get supplies when we need them', or 'those big companies are just making profits'; public health researchers said 'it's about inequalities and health equities', 'patients are marginalised'; scientists said 'we need to talk more with industry',

S. Srinivas (✉)
Bengaluru, India
e-mail: researchtclab@duck.com

G. Banda et al. (eds.), *Cancer Care in Pandemic Times: Building Inclusive Local Health Security in Africa and India*, International Political Economy Series,
https://doi.org/10.1007/978-3-031-44123-3_6

or 'start-up culture is helping' (some said it was hurting). The overall impression I had, was that despite considerable brilliance and professional credibility arrayed before me, and plenty of good-heartedness and hard work, people were speaking in strange generalities about health as if the problem was so complex or diffuse that it was an utter mystery. This was especially intriguing because India has, over the years, many health successes to its credit and emerged during Covid-19 with substantial technology, industrial, and health system gains.

Despite over two decades on these issues in the context of industrial policies and economic development, I was finding that even sincere senior scientists and clinicians and many bureaucrats who oversee important policies, philanthropies, or grant-making, were still speaking in peculiar hand-wringing generalities about major policy gaps. Cynicism, depression, or apathy? Lack of training in social sciences and policy analysis? I had a strong feeling that the generalities reflected their perception that this *implementation* of science or health technology, or ensuring the availability of therapeutic products, was/should be someone else's problem (perhaps even those irrational patients!). Perhaps because some scientists and engineers considered that making policies more effective was somehow trivial, we just had to get someone to put their minds to it? A problem below their pay grade, as we say. After all, they were solving the world's most complex problems in the lab or becoming Directors, senior ministry officials, CEOs, wasn't that sufficient?

One exercise I recall initiating with a clinical co-author, first on a napkin, then a clear sheet of paper, then a whiteboard, was a map of gaps from first arrival of a patient to a doctor. This in a social context when many people, especially women, postpone visiting a healthcare practitioner. We wanted to think through the delay in arrival, then the hit-or-miss process of diagnosis, then referral which itself reflects serious delays and misdiagnoses, and then the patient returning (if at all) for treatment(s). I focused not on the complexity of cancers but on 'simpler' dengue.

Furthermore, my concerns were that these technological capabilities had to serve either the patient or national economic goals and ideally, both. These meant real attention to the combination of skills, new knowledge, techniques, equipment, service, and delivery quality or location. Groups that more notably engaged in these realistic terms about gaps and hurdles in practical, non-utopian, language were family physicians, surgeon-engineers, or surgeon-entrepreneurs. As with many innovators-by-necessity, they understood the importance of iterative work, the limits of instrument availability or breakdown, and importance of instinct and skills, the materials and location challenges of prototyping, the practical issues of technical design in the real world. Surgeons in particular were also conscious of extensive procedural bottlenecks in working within hospitals, such as dealing with tissue samples or varied techniques for tumour removal which had to fit with approved protocols but needed to be inventive. Similarly, companies in commodity manufacturing or distribution understood the practical challenges well and spoke in specifics because they had created routinised systems of rules to work by. Still, by and large, the claim that the 'health system was broken' was as imprecise and unsatisfying in 2018 as it had been when I first entered the field myself over two decades ago, and so I spent my time listening and making notes to extend the earlier work.

Days passed as I thought about the dengue discussion and late referrals, where the *Cupboard* question started emerging, asking doctors and others in informal conversations how they knew what to use when a patient walked in and what if they didn't have items such as drugs or diagnostic tests when they needed them. It was evident that the industrial background was getting little conceptual attention. Worse, *industry* was being referred to in terms of private industry, which misled one to think that corporate R&D was the solution to all problems.

Covid-19 was suddenly upon us. I had entered a gruelling two years of work that had only abated as I wrote in mid-2022: advisory boards, technical meetings, an avalanche of data, and suddenly people shouting themselves hoarse over the same issues, but now in confined expert rooms, spitting distance as it were, that 'the health system is broken!'. Where I was asked to intervene in meetings, there was a serious breakdown in training, of disciplines and professionals establishing hierarchies, of differentiating which professions or methods should speak, but unable to speak to each other. At the same time, a practical set of professionals and new teams were trying very hard to build gadgets, and new science, and do the much-needed field work to assess the urgency of treatment, plus the urgent treatment protocols required for Covid-19 patients. In some of the major problems of routine healthcare, science per se was not at the heart of every problem. I was repeatedly invited to global health meetings, but most discussions ignored the economics of industrial organisation or focused on discussing diagnostic kits or vaccines primarily in mechanistic 'technology-push' or 'supply-driven' terms as if assuming that in any emergency, an entire industry 'behind the Cupboard' (see below) would resolve itself. Many in the science and engineering professions were ignoring how demand and delivery had to consider a dynamic uncertainty about consumers shaping the longevity of their business models or delivery systems.

Here too, several opportunities to build long-term economic development were being sidelined. This was the case even in multilateral forums on the specifics of technology transfer where precise economic development goals could be set for technology acquisition in the short or long term. Strangely, many experts assumed that national production capabilities would resolve demand and delivery, and those countries without technological capabilities should somehow await global health management systems or advanced market commitment mechanisms (such as COVAX or other global coordination). This global health role, as the world was witnessing in real time, was not working particularly well in a context of export bottlenecks and supply chain breakdowns. It was witnessing industrial chaos, but only slowly recognizing how the health systems were built atop it.

I was committed almost 18–20 hours/day in advisory roles, pro bono teams, and round-the-clock data debates on social media, email, phone, and in policy groups. With my clinical colleague who was an infectious disease specialist, and with frequent debates, we finally wrote a working paper to make sense of what we were seeing at the time, to frame the problem of responding to dramatic shifts occurring in the design and manufacture of Covid-19 diagnostic kits. Despite all the handwringing, India has had considerable successes in this area and many others, generating critical services and manufacturing in a highly truncated period.[1] Yet, the same uncertainty of Covid-19 had derailed stronger health systems and richer economies than India.

In part this success was because the Indian central and state governments were able to, in a variety of ways, manage a centralised, yet coordinated system of action. They converted from plans, protocols, emergency production shifts, and new procurement rules. New organizations and innovations emerged. In short, at least for a time, a new set of norms and rules was being attempted with substantial national and sometimes municipal, or district-level experimentation, and open partnerships with the private sector. Likewise, the acknowledged strengths of India's community health workers were evident during Covid-19 at significant personal and social costs, raising questions of how decentralised industrial decision-making would respond to this agile community expertise. Questions that were critical in my mind seemed to be getting little or no explicit debate in meetings. Who is the user? Who is the consumer? Doctors, hospitals, individuals, or other firms? What are the error margins in estimating Covid-19 demand? How will the demand be sustained? Will superfluous product variety and competition be resolved among these firms once the pandemic is over?

Cupboard Full, Cupboard Empty: A Thought Experiment

While there have been attempts in the health policy world to define minimum service baskets, there is arguably little bridge to the dynamic domain of technology development, investment, or practical choices of ensuring availability of product A or B. This chapter is thus focused on shifting from the imprecise complaint that 'the health system is broken' towards a more precise discussion of the interface between health policies and industrial capabilities. The 'Cupboard Full, Cupboard Empty' (CFCE) thought experiment fills in some of the too-quickly glossed over conceptual and methods questions in health systems. The introduction of the CFCE is offered as one step to future methodologies that can more effectively bridge industrial and health policies in public health design. While the early chapters have identified critical health gaps, this chapter pushes towards clarifying how we then bridge to what is an 'appropriately full' cupboard of products, procedures, techniques, and services.

India of course had some luxury of choice developed over decades of building technological capabilities in the health industry. Many countries, however, had no choice except to import under severe domestic constraints and global export curbs. Although each country context is different, the India case is relevant for other industrialising countries and those traditionally offered unsolicited or generic international development advice. India's private sector is now immense: numbers of firms whatever their size, clinics, hospitals, medical and nursing colleges, private research labs, some private venture capital, and diversified industrial capabilities relevant to healthcare from plastics to robotics. This volume, variety, and number of firms, from micro-level service and product providers to large corporate firms, is both a curse and a boon. It makes policy goal-setting and regulation noisy and complex, but it also makes much public health ideology economically archaic and notably mismatched to the technology dynamism and the diversity of service and customisation options.

Significantly furthermore, within health and in related industries, public sector investments drove private sector growth, making for a rich tapestry in the evolution of institutions, from norms and customs to technical standards, market varieties, and regulation. In this sense, India has much to offer the world as a unique case but also provides useful policy framing and cautions about global health and international development one-size-fits-all generic prescriptions. In some respects, India's similarities are with the US rather than with UK, much farther from Cuba and distant from China, and closer to some features of Germany, Nigeria or South Africa.

The following sections provide an abstract sketch of the practical aspects of uncertainty and possible conceptual building blocks behind investment decisions, required knowledge and technologies, skills and learning, and local administrative context—whether for community workers, nurses, and doctors, or district procurement agencies. The Choosing Wisely India initiative, discussed later, promisingly identifies policy and product mixes for Indian cancer patients. The preliminary 'Cupboard Full, Cupboard Empty' (CFCE) framework introduced in this chapter can extend Choosing Wisely further into the industrial policy domain.

The Building Blocks and Methods Behind a Health-Industry Interface

Policy Frames

Health policy scholars, including clinicians and social scientists, see that health delivery has many moving parts. However, new insights have emerged about institutions and evolution in several domains of economics, especially those concerned with how knowledge is generated, and technological change occurs. Industrial history has focused disproportionately on production capabilities and especially on manufacturing. In contrast, public health arguably has focused on service delivery. Scholarship of industrial development and of health both recognize that technological capabilities matter, but the first is more acutely focused on when and how they matter.

A newer institutional and evolutionary economics argues that to recognise systemic behaviour is to recognise health as a natural domain of study with unique dynamics (Hodgson, 2007). Specifically, we have known for some time that an *institutional triad* (Srinivas, 2012, p. 8) of three different co-evolving institutional domains of production, demand, and delivery *all* reveal industrial features that can be studied in snapshots of time and can usefully contrast countries. Each of the institutional domains co-evolves with the other; involves private and public actors, some mix of new organisation types; or contributes to distinctive types of technological capabilities. Analysing the uneven fits and starts of building these technological capabilities is an essential element of scientific argument in national comparison, where institutional variety (IV)—including the norms and regulations of firms, universities, corporate R&D, or new technical standards—must be studied more explicitly (Srinivas, 2020). For cancer, these dynamic features and the uncertain identification, categorization, and progression of the disease make the metaphor of a 'War on Cancer' outdated and misleading (Srinivas, 2021b). Updating economic frameworks for cancer is also tightly linked to prevention concerns and the rise in carcinogens, making cross-industry regulation concerns more urgent to combine ecology, health, and industrial development (Srinivas, 2021a).

Some medical specialists do recognise that economics and structural issues shape cancer's systemic problems, but these are framed in response to global health priorities:

> Following the UN High Level Summit, the global call to embed all non-communicable diseases, including cancer, in the post-2015 development agenda has been followed rapidly by a plethora of indicators and targets ... Unfortunately, there is little insight into the complex economic and structural issues that emerging economies such as India have to deal with to deliver an affordable cancer care and control system. The provision of affordable cancer care in India needs a deep understanding of the substantial differences between spending on health across individual states and union territories, and the gaps in basic health indicators and outcomes (eg, infant mortality rates, health resources, numbers of clinical staff, and physical infrastructure). (Pramesh et al., 2019)

The quote above well recognises the autonomy and specificity of context and allows a useful bridge to building specific long-term technological capabilities. National context matters in shaping indicators and targets. Probing the institutional context of the triad may identify the scope for greater autonomy for industrialising countries to develop their technological capabilities and health policy choices, and to recognise their national differences. However, *over-engaging* with the global health straitjacket of national health and spending comparisons is one policy challenge; another is *under-engaging* with the analytical differences between the subset of countries that possess or are aggressively investing in greater technological and industrial depth. This special sub-set of countries not only supports the global supplies of essential medicines, vaccines, diagnostics, and devices but ironically may still have some distance to solving their own problems. Those countries with democratic pressures struggle in their own peculiar ways with both the framing of health as well as industrial and other policies. India is one of these countries, which for many reasons therefore may have inspirational as well as cautionary lessons for other countries.

In the policy analysis world, this type of detailed unmasking of different perspectives on institutions and organisations involves a deliberate 'frame reflection' which accommodates different experiential or professional perspectives on the same problem (Rein & Schön, 1994). This unmasking can make the framing process an essential part of design, whether of policy design or engineering design. Some policy challenges persist because their policy frames are different and involve both epistemic and ontological challenges of language in plans, with conflicting normative assumptions of how plans and their methods are developed. Here heuristics such as the 'institutional triad' can open a conversation about methodologies (and generative metaphors [Schön, 1979]). Policy disagreements may continue to occur within seemingly mutual policy frames, and controversies exist because different policy frames are applied but not communicated. Notably, 'more data', a favourite among scientists of all stripes and policy-makers, will not dispel such controversy (Rein & Schön, 1994).

In my own research I have argued that where technology issues are central, policy frames can only be more rigorous if we first debate which technological capabilities are more relevant for health or could be put to better use in public terms. Such articulation of our existing knowledge and technological capabilities should make for a more rigorous process of comparison of long-term health outcomes and greater clarity on which types of translation are required. Such systematic comparisons can still satisfy the routine investment and accountability imperatives that make up the everyday decisions of start-ups, spin-offs, large firms, firm clusters, or decisions on competition, IP, price regulation, and other industrial policy concerns. Countries can approach policy framing as a multi-technology, evolutionary process, where new science may be required only for some problems, and could decide to coordinate multiple knowledge systems that co-exist to solve the same problem. From a health policy or clinical standpoint, co-existing intervention choices or multi-technology interventions provide policy framing because they do not easily reduce to simple cause and effect (e.g. Greenhalgh & Papoutsi, 2018) nor as being substitutes or complements of each other.

In the absence of appreciating this institutional variety, 'innovation' cannot be specified in a systematic way, nor any credible commitment made to healthcare quality. In terms of microeconomics, firms and even hybrid consortia must know both *how* and *how much* to produce. The 'institutional triad' ties between production, demand, and delivery, can be combined in many different ways across time. This type of heuristic establishes a policy framing and helps view the industrial organisation as it changes, identifying countries by their technological capabilities and forcing differentiation among industrialising LMICs. Import and export shutdowns started the pandemic domestic clock, and isolated countries in terms of needed inputs. Only some emerged capable of amassing existing resources to work towards finished products. Notably, not all health problems required either new science or new manufacturing.

Therefore, uncertainty and demand remain untended in the institutional gaps between health policy and industrial policy. What is the cupboard that is proverbially empty and why is it? Doctors ask firms, why didn't you give me what I need when I needed it? Firms turn around and say, you didn't clarify what you needed. Clinicians are not able to articulate what they need to industry: the exception may be clinician engineers such as surgeons who experiment with devices, or some types of family physicians who see patterns across patients and failure modes in diagnosis and treatment.

The hand-wringing claim that 'the health system is broken' was imprecise because it could not explain the more optimistic policy reality, that many parts of the system were surprisingly agile under high uncertainty, unevenness and fragmentation. From an economics standpoint, this was far more than a pricing and market clearing policy frame. Rather, it exhibits evolving, institutional features of how demand becomes solidified through new norms of collaboration, standards and rules.

Uncertainty and Demand in the Pandemic

Covid-19 pointed to a rapid escalation of conflicting needs but uncertain demand. The public policy and administrative response was to consolidate supply (where many countries failed badly) and somehow anticipate needs and institutional shifts (norms, customs, guidelines, rules) to quickly convert this under high biological uncertainty into more certain demand. Market design was fluid but required any firm or public research centre with substantial capabilities to step up. India's response could be seen reflecting a decades-long investment (however uneven or unsubstantial) in science, engineering and technology development, combined with public research and private sector first-mover practice. Rather than ideological lenses on the pandemic, the Indian response was pragmatic: all hands on deck. While too many lost their lives and many parts of the health-care system were revealed as pulled together with duct tape, the country emerged surprisingly robust relative to wealthier, more technologically and industrially superior countries.

It should be emphasised therefore that the 'frame' was *not* global inequality of access in a vacuum of possibilities, although this argument has been made by many; it was inequality of access precisely because only some countries had industrial production capabilities built over decades before Covid-19 arrived. Neither were the countries with such capabilities and Cupboard Full cases only wealthier ones.

This unevenness across countries has not been well explained through equilibrium economics or even the claim that all health breakthroughs came from the biological sciences. During Covid-19 the clinical-industrial interface demonstrated a wide variety of ways that countries responded to Covid-19 diagnostics production, but also several different ways in which policy intervention could be sanctioned based on what was available when trade was impossible, and what was domestically possible to produce. In that instance, starting conditions under trade stoppages defined and separated those countries with distinct domestic capabilities from others and forced a reconfiguration of institutional variety (IV).

A mixed economics and clinical collaboration, begun early in the pandemic, argued for the urgency of generating a first conceptual bridge between health realities and different windows on industrial uncertainty (Srinivas et al., 2020). We specified seven types of observable uncertainties visible in field conditions for Covid-19, with experts acting on patchy data, and decisions in boardrooms, labs, and university offices where different disciplines were speaking past each other. We took as given the following clinical procedures: (a) screening during asymptomatic/pre-symptomatic phase; (b) diagnosis of symptomatic disease; (c) determination of viral shedding in the convalescence phase for decision-making on de-isolation; and (d) epidemiologic surveillance. Uncertainty arises not only because a suitable test may not be available, but given the availability of a suitable test, a clear clinical decision may not follow. We argued that clinical indecision draws from and compounds these uncertainties, leading to marked challenges of industrial supply and demand and the logistical bottlenecks of viable delivery. Table 6.1 describes clinical foreground and industrial background uncertainties we identified to make sense (as a policy frame) of how diagnostic tools, firms, and clinics were operating on the ground. Importantly, many industrialised wealthier countries had little clarity of their own.

The policy frame should help us translate between clinical challenges, biological uncertainties, and economic and policy fundamentals of what the industry was facing. The industrial policy frame better emerges only once the uncertainties are explicitly discussed, and the inherent institutional variety is catalogued and its dynamics studied. These seven uncertainties thus required clear enunciation of a type of policy frame with several types of decisions from plan-making to strategy with a changing biological context: dynamic changes of organisations testing under uncertainty; agnosticism about public and private sector technological capability; push to coordinate and consolidate scale-up in response to centralised orders on building demand. These seven uncertainties observed under fast-moving conditions are more useful framing responses to the WHO's generic policy prescription of 'test, test, test'. They demonstrate the importance of heuristics and theoretical working frameworks to probe the simplistic, despairing idea that 'the health system is broken', because many uncertainties were in fact surprisingly well-managed during Covid-19 through new institutional variety.

The reason this requires intermediate frameworks and discussion is that *uncertainty's twin is risk*. The uncertainties once articulated and appreciated, as opposed to fixed theory blind to local changes, suggest taxonomies and heuristics to sift through the institutional variety (IV). This IV reflects accommodations in the economy and its culture through which a society changes. Any study can then generate real-world hypotheses of how the 'institutional triad' domains of production, consumption (demand), and delivery evolved during the pandemic since

Table 6.1 Seven interface uncertainties in the clinical foreground and industrial background of Covid-19

	Clinical foreground	*Industrial background*
1	Clinicians struggle to determine the extent of medical need ('signal vs. noise').	Covid-19 testing practice: how reliable is the test; the choice of which test; priority of whom to test; the impact of subsequent decision-making on equitably and effectively making the test available; ease of administration; biological uncertainty about comparability across populations and viral strains.
2	Multiple co-circulating pathogens such as H1N1 influenza, and dengue make it difficult to determine priorities for Covid-19 itself and effective technology and testing design.	Other pathogens and also morbidities indicate that co-infection and greater health burden is likely. This cannot be solved by infectious disease specialists or engineers alone because demand and delivery become critical challenges not only for public sector supply but also for business, national fiscal, and industrial development models.
3	Each country has to determine its own national scale of testing.	Covid-19's specific asymptomatic transmission challenges made testing strategies imprecise and ineffective: isolation strategies, whom to test, budgets for testing and cost/kit, trained technicians, or logistical challenges in transportation of tests. The level of uncertainty of spread made sub-national testing and cross-jurisdiction asymptomatic transmission an administrative hurdle.

(continued)

Table 6.1 (continued)

	Clinical foreground	*Industrial background*
4	Technology, industrial scale, and investment uncertainties persist. Biological uncertainty such as 'window period' may give negative test results despite infection, and virus strains keep evolving, viral shedding on test results occurs, sample collection technique has to adapt.	At least in the early stages of the epidemic, and without clear estimates of demand or extent of competition during the pandemic, firms are unlikely to invest in building kits. Existing or better technology is pursued if the scale of investment can be estimated with some margins of error and firms or governments can bear the risk. The public sector role becomes critical. Precise features of the test such as sensitivity and specificity influence which tests among many to use (assuming more than one is available). Furthermore, both governments and firms must consider sunk costs in collection and storage technologies, training of laboratory technicians, reliability of batching collected samples and kits alike, and acceptability throughout which can only be determined through the actual pandemic and which affects the turnaround time of the tests, and in turn affects demand for tests.
5	Norms and customs about disease and ill-health create a stigma of who tests, design of the associated testing process, and demand.	Routinised testing especially at the early stages of the pandemic can generate high stigma and low privacy. Widespread testing faces stigma hurdles. Yet, worries about illness can prompt greater demand for tests. In turn, this may de-prioritise those for whom it is urgent.

(continued)

Table 6.1 (continued)

	Clinical foreground	*Industrial background*
6	'Single disease' health management and testing regimens do not reflect multiple health challenges.	Demand for test kits, vaccines, medicines, and other supplies may spike if policy gives priority to emergency contexts versus chronic health priorities. Thus demand for Covid-19 technologies has arguably derailed for some time routine supply of HIV, TB, and malaria treatment supplies. As in 2, this affects both 'emergency' demand, and also how test kits are designed, as single-disease kits versus multiple and chronic health strategies.
7	Uncertainty affects disciplines and professions unevenly.	From epidemiology, and virology, to clinical diagnosis, each professional differs in training and practice in defining error margins and decision-making under uncertainties.

Source Adapted from Srinivas et al. (2020, pp. 4–5)

only some countries had technological capabilities and experience managing risk through their public management capabilities. Technological capabilities in the private sector, while independently surging ahead, relied on enormous public administration spread across many services, organisations, and regions not only for industrial coordination but for every signal of wider institutional change—from how to reward health workers, to individual health responsibility, to 'acceptable' profits and pricing, to media and 'expert' information and misinformation. Such institutional variety, with some common features, is nationally defined.

Cupboard Full, Cupboard Empty

Framing why and how the national context matters is crucial to understanding the social appetite and public and private capabilities to manage uncertainties and risk. These situate the specific investments for building long-term technological capabilities while establishing national autonomy in decision-making. The Cupboard Full, Cupboard Empty (CFCE) approach in this section is a closer scrutiny of the clinical-industrial interface to frame the seven uncertainties in relationships between production, demand, and delivery (the 'institutional triad'). Not all industrial and economic contexts are the same in making medicines, diagnostic kits, therapies, medical equipment, and vaccines, nor are supplier countries and democracies the same as other 'developing' countries when it comes to health technologies and the health industry.

I began speaking about a 'cupboard' to describe what I thought people were discussing without being explicit about 'products they needed'. When I tested this idea in coffee-led discussions, people often picked it up and responded with phrases such as 'yes, we need to know what's in the cupboard', 'how can we be effective if the cupboard is empty?', or 'why should we care what's behind the cupboard?'. So the metaphor seemed to resonate.

The proverbial cupboard (outside pandemic times) is supposedly filled with products such as antibiotics, analgesics, and possibly a diagnostic kit for routine analysis, from inexplicable fevers to skin cultures. Let us for the moment say that the Cupboard is located in a publicly funded Primary Health Centre (PHC) in rural India or even underserved parts of municipal areas. This does not rule out private sector coordination or partnership which occur in many PHCs.[2] Essential medicines, universal immunisation and other guidelines inform what is stocked at the PHC. The Cupboard is a conceptual building block. In reality, some of the products are stored in a refrigerator, or may even be outsourced, such as some pathology diagnostics, to private labs down the road. But at its bare conceptual minimum, the Cupboard is refrigerated or temperature controlled and everything is stocked in one place. The problem frame (CFCE) is what determines the conditions under which the Cupboard is full or empty? Countries which import their CFCE supplies are particularly vulnerable to logistics bottlenecks, but they nevertheless have to decide what to stock.

An industrial economics standpoint has *evolving, dynamic* features: industries and their investments re-organise and change. They also have an *institutional* perspective since decisions within uncertainty still must prioritise health problems through norms, customs, guidelines, standards, regulations, and laws. The CFCE can thus be stated as a microeconomics problem at the outset about unspecified consumers and producers but also unspecified minimum institutional and organizational units of analysis to judge what product is essential and how that system changes to become more responsive to new technologies. Unlike more generic systems analysis or operations research problems, the CFCE cannot be technology-neutral. Because only some countries have the technological capabilities or the industrial policy priority for building them to scale, *the CFCE is framed within the context of existing and near horizon technological capabilities*. Again, this ties in with minimal but reliable production and delivery for a given (albeit uncertain) demand. The CFCE can thus be considered to act as a policy frame towards questioning both industrial and health methodology, a way of observing the daily interface, for localising ambiguity about decisions and public responsibility.

Let's begin with the intermediate situation of a cupboard of one product, say an antibiotic, and a cupboard that is partially full, neither full nor empty. The person who discovers that the cupboard needs restocking is an attendant, nurse, or doctor. This could be analysed as a routine stock-flow problem taught in basic logistics, engineering, economics, or management. The system is the PHC plus a pharmacy and the joint personnel of the two. However, even in this simple one-product small system, further microeconomics and industrial organization problems emerge. For example, antibiotics availability can be further analysed in a wider system of firms' closures or firms switching out of antibiotics to more profitable pastures, or the messier problem of antibiotics and antimicrobial resistance. Even with the simpler problem of an existing supply chain of PHC to pharmacy and beyond, health administrators and clinicians recognise and bemoan such gaps in health access to minimum required medicines. But the problem is usually unsolved because of upstream challenges, despite recognition here too that the health and industrial systems are interlinked. As noted in Table 6.1, several types of uncertainty including those of systematically building demand, already begin to be visible here.

Alternately, the Cupboard Empty case is the extreme case of a single product missing where no stocks exist at the PHC. In reality, there are multiple CE*i*, CE*ii*, CE*iii*,....C*n* of products *i* to *n*, where one or more is unavailable at any time to a patient at the PHC. These arise from various levels of uncertainty in Table 6.1 and generate corresponding uncertainties for patients, usually in stocking uncertainties and repeat, costly, visits. Simply put, loss in time, money, increased stigma, or even future likelihood of seeking care at all. Either the *n* includes the basic Essentials list deemed by national or state health policy to be available at every PHC, else the patient is told to buy it at the closest pharmacy, at market rate or subsidised price with prescription, such as with the new Jan Aushadi Kendras where a limited set of products is stocked but at vastly subsidised prices. Nevertheless, each uncertainty diminishes the better healthcare outcome.

Note, CFCE problems of the kind above exist even for the simplest of illnesses and treatments that can be fully and appropriately diagnosed and treated. The more difficult the diagnosis and treatment (where personnel skills become important, such as in Covid-19), the less obvious it is that *n* medicines are needed, or that *i* to *n* should not also include basic medical equipment or diagnostics. The several uncertainties 1–7 even in the simplest of cases can thus be compounded when a single product is missing, making it far less likely that reliable demand can be built for the PHC or wider health system.

Thus, the PHC faces policy translation confusion. Medical training to malpractice enforcement determines the range of how a doctor makes do or improvises when something is unavailable. Staff often have limited autonomy and many rules to follow. They must, with existing training and reliability, determine what is an essential minimum product quantity to decide whether a Cupboard is Empty or Full. They report upward through a state-level health bureaucracy, and have no direct links to firms, to a market of products, or services. Arguably, this building block is the first instance where an explicit industrial and health systemic linkage begins to go awry. First, it is unclear about the bare minimum product, service, or combination needed to satisfy a positive health outcome. Second, even with good intentions, the health and industrial suppliers are deliberately kept apart so there are no conflicts of interest from procurement routines to prescription biases. This separation is understandable in that only selective discretion is provided to medical personnel for addressing health challenges. The first feature, however, of ignoring *how* we know whether the Cupboard is appropriately Full or Empty is dependent not merely on a stocking list but on a diffuse policy goal and measurable outcomes which are handed down to the PHC to resolve with the tools at hand. As health is a predominantly state subject in India, state governments do have some autonomy to decide what and how to stock.

Thus, any diagnosis and treatment would include a straightforward process of better stocking of known items in the Full Cupboard, but it would not solve the bigger challenge of how to assure patients that should they come to the PHC at all. The CF situation when a product or service is reliably available is unusual and a true victory would be reliable test results and follow-up diagnosis the same day with easy access to medicines if needed. The commitment to ensure availability of personnel and CF diagnostics and rapid turnaround test results would be one problem framed and solved. With some diseases, this might make associated debates about vaccines either optional or unnecessary. For instance, one study indicates that if such a Cupboard is stocked with simple low-cost and low-technology approaches for cervical cancer, a 31% mortality reduction is achieved (Poli et al., 2015).[3] The absence of such stocks (CE, or partially empty) even in the case of a non-infectious disease, makes it much less likely that the patient will return at all, a sizable demand collapse and knock-on clinical and industrial uncertainties to later stages of healthcare delivery.

It could be argued that for many developing countries, the health policy paradigm (the 'frame') has often been one of inequality or lack of resources and this chapter has argued that from an industrial and technological standpoint, this can be debated. Some 'developing' countries have industrial supplier capabilities and choices to make and they do so under specific institutional and organisational combinations. As discussed earlier, once institutional variety (IV) is explicitly recognised as a specific confounding feature of economic explanation, it becomes easier to see how misleading inferences may be made. While many paths are in principle possible, only some are actually demonstrated in real life, and fewer still are explicit policy priorities. Health knowledge of some types (e.g. how rural Indian women use scanning services) should deliberately be converted into an industrial system of production or into skill sets that are relevant to small firms or employment opportunities. This translation can generate both agile market and non-market strategies for affordable, reliable, high-quality, health services.

Ideally, procurement reform such as underway in India across many sectors will change the 'low-cost vendor' approach to 'high-quality vendor', where quality refers not to product quality but to a product and service *combination* of reliability and speed, since the uncertainties are highly costly to the patient and yet new business models may be slow to emerge. When we consider the technological capability spectrum in a location, rather than a global health paradigm of a one-size-fits-all approach to cancer which is often technology-neutral, there are minimum CF issues to be resolved of a minimum 'technology basket'. Framed as such, the institutional variety (IV) visible locally and the institutional triad's combinations that reflect its technological priorities, provide policy menus and catalogues. These practical administrative tools convert the CFCE methodology into routine policy training and public health practices.

There are consequently deeper philosophical problems that can excite economic and policy debate. After all, uncertainty and lost time exact a heavy toll on health prevention as well as for diagnosis and treatment. Should PHCs or equipment vendors be assessed by combined business or tendering criteria that requires both product and service packages to be made available, and should the patient be the end consumer and judge of care quality? Why are R&D grants or subsidies being offered to new technologies, or new investment markets growing, but not easily translated to PHC 'cupboards'? In the past, such criteria have often been split too neatly into contentious debates about the relevance of PHCs themselves or of privatization threats. However, heavy private sector presence already exists in many public health systems, even in perceived 'public' or 'community' systems in the Indian states of Tamil Nadu or Kerala. At the same time, the sharp growth of more government-funded regional cancer centres, telemedicine, and private sector partnerships have grown in Uttar Pradesh, and more remote areas such as Assam, where traditionally patients have been dissuaded by distance, rugged terrain, Empty Cupboards or unreliable care.

Choosing Wisely for Stocking the Cancer Cupboard

The CFCE is therefore a localised 'institutional triad' of production, demand, and delivery whose abstraction can aid health policy design. Precisely because no long-term policy commitment on production is made, delivery problems persist (or else demand would rise sharply). Likewise, as no existing commitment to reliable delivery is made, no minimum CF 'basket' is possible. Thus the national context can be seen to define specific *minimum* and *maximum frames* (*min CFCE* and *max CFCE*) in which particular clinical interventions are decided. For economists and industrial organization specialists, the consequences are that minimum and maximum CFCE frames require translation into specific industrial policy strategies from the essential medicine and equipment products, the subsidies or other incentives offered for their production, price controls if relevant, procurement guidelines and product quality, competition from suppliers if any, and consistency of large volume suppliers. At a later point, where more stable demand is predicted, other industrial policy interventions may be needed such as competition policy, anti-trust, or IP protections.

Choosing Wisely India (Pramesh et al., 2019) is one practical way in which overall cancer care can map onto a CFCE scenario. The Choosing Wisely India initiative offers guidelines from cancer specialists for deciding on a priority phasing for cancer diagnosis and treatments, in which domestic cancer types and their clinical approach are prioritised. Table 6.2 shows differences between two Canadian/US recommendations accepted for India as adapted, and four new Indian recommendations. The last column begins the process of translation to industrial policy design.

Given the Choosing Wisely Indian suggestions that a break with UK, US, or Canadian cancer strategies is needed to suit the country, one can ask for a first-step refinement of the CFCE strategy for cancer. For instance, radiotherapy is a good case for future study as an industrial and health priority (Samiei, 2013). A traditional health economics metric such as 25 million people per radiotherapy machine in India vs. 250,000 in higher income countries is more effective only when combined with the fact that radiotherapy should, by Choosing Wisely India guidelines, be placed much higher on the list of equipment priorities. However, it will require industrial policy priority in concert, with attention to prototyping, industrial design, development, and procurement priority into a minimum CFCE list, along with higher standards, innovation criteria, and business models for better patient experience. Pricing, competition, or other considerations follow from, not lead, this perspective.

Conclusion: A Cancer System's Industrial Building Blocks

'Cancer policy' will need more clarity. It is currently poorly defined because of its arguably outdated economics and policy frames (Srinivas, 2021b). Not all countries have the same industrial organization nor existing technological capabilities. The variety of environmental and biological processes behind the clinical symptoms also represent diverse cancer diseases under progression and many potential technology or service interventions (including education) that can identify disease early or prevent most cancers. Therefore, CFCE minimums can be debated per disease ('cancer', which is multiple diseases) or by industrial capabilities. Problem-framing, theory, and methodological clarity on 'cancer policy' is certainly needed.

Table 6.2 Selected recommendations from Choosing Wisely India, towards a minimum CFCE

Health challenge	*Recommendations by Choosing Wisely India*	*Min CFCE requirement = industrial policy priority*
Palliation Palliative drugs Chemotherapy	Do not delay or avoid palliative care for a patient with metastatic cancer because they are pursuing disease-directed treatment. Avoid chemotherapy and instead focus on symptom relief and palliative care in patients with advanced cancer who are unlikely to benefit from chemotherapy.	Palliative drugs, especially morphine sulfate
Equipment PET/CT scans Radiation techniques	Do not order PET/CT scans to monitor response to palliative chemotherapy. Do not use advanced radiation techniques where conventional radiation can be just as effective.	Conventional radiation techniques highly customised for Indian settings and mass manufacture.
Multidisciplinary oncology team	Treatment to be resolved with multidisciplinary teams.[4]	Equipment, drugs, surgical procedures, and off-site follow-up built into standardised procurement and simultaneously resolved. Predictable iterations and vendor bids and competition guidelines clarified.
Treatment environment ICU (over)-use	Do not treat patients with advanced metastatic cancer in the intensive care unit unless there is an acutely reversible event.	ICU, non-ICU, and out-patient purchases estimated and prioritized by CW guidelines.

Source Adapted from Pramesh et al. (2019, e220)
Note First row recommendations adapted from CW US/Canada; others are new Indian CW recommendations.

As discussed, the CFCE approach offers a localised abstraction of institutional variety, the evolving, institutional details of production, demand, and delivery of the 'institutional triad' that is often left unspecified in health policy, and an essential preliminary step towards more integrated policy methods. Moreover, the pandemic has helped clarify at least seven practical uncertainties arising at the clinical-industrial interface and underscores the institutional variety through which societies manage this risk. The CFCE forces the uncomfortable conversations of minimum product-service mixes in policy design towards better decisions of public organisations, rather than vague normative maximums.[5] Ideals of equality or all-public systems may not necessarily lead to long-term gains for patients.

Encouragingly, pandemic-induced improvements can now be converted into viable industrial guidelines. But we can only determine how to fill a cupboard if we openly debate questions such as: should we make it at home; can we import it instead? Should this be short or long term and why? What is a good mix for the foreseeable future of local manufacture and imports of specific priority products? Is cancer growing from polluting national industries themselves, with degenerated nature, products and services and what would that CFCE method entail? Can industrial policy goals circumscribe, prevent disease, or enhance health policy and vice versa?

At the very least governments must support and regulate their own health goals and industries. The CFCE thought experiment can underscore this national autonomy, clarity on minimum priorities, and commitments to integrated industrial capabilities.

Notes

1. Global praise for India's manufacture and administration of over 1 billion vaccine doses (over 2 billion first, second, and precautionary doses by August 2022) https://health.economictimes.indiatimes.com/news/pharma/us-lawmakers-say-indias-success-will-help-world-defeat-covid-19-as-it-achieves-100-crore-jabs-milestone/87216337, last accessed June 4 2022.
2. A rich literature exists on PHCs and public sector health delivery systems around the world. The abstraction here will not do it justice but offers a first step to analyse the interface and the institutional design of the proverbial 'Cupboard' and decision-making.
3. Similarly Indian gains for breast cancer examination, https://www.bmj.com/content/372/bmj.n256.
4. National Cancer Grid and tumour boards are now being built into Indian regional cancer centres with standardised multi-specialty

recommendations to lower uncertainty for patients and improve health outcomes.

5. A similar point in Srinivas (2016) that Indian regulation design is idealistic and often satisfies neither the practical minimum nor maximum requirements of better care goals.

CHAPTER 7

Manufacturing for Cancer Care in East Africa: Raising the Ambition

Veronica Manduku, Samuel Wangwe, Cecilia Wanjala, Maureen Mackintosh, and Richard Ngilangwa

Building Local Health Industries: Pandemic Lessons

Health systems are heavily reliant on manufactured commodities, including medicines, vaccines, medical devices, equipment and consumables. East Africa's health industries have been built through a history reaching back to the 1960s' post-Independence industrialisation (Banda et al., 2016b). Kenya is the dominant regional producer of pharmaceuticals and has one successful medical device manufacturer. Yet interviews

V. Manduku (✉) · C. Wanjala
Kenya Medical Research Institute (KEMRI), Nairobi, Kenya
e-mail: vmanduku@kemri.go.ke

S. Wangwe · R. Ngilangwa
Economic and Social Research Foundation (ESRF), Dar es Salaam, Tanzania

M. Mackintosh
The Open University, Milton Keynes, UK

G. Banda et al. (eds.), *Cancer Care in Pandemic Times: Building Inclusive Local Health Security in Africa and India*, International Political Economy Series,
https://doi.org/10.1007/978-3-031-44123-3_7

with local health-related manufacturers over the last decade had picked up some signs of regional industrial stagnation and decline.

Business strategies in the regional pharmaceutical manufacturing industries have until recently lacked ambition to expand and move up to higher value and more complex products. Pre-pandemic, few firms interviewed had ventured into producing medicines for demanding markets such as donor-funded programmes for malaria and HIV/AIDS, where stringent regulatory standards required high capital investments with no guaranteed markets. Furthermore, under severe external competitive pressure, some locally based companies had pulled out of less profitable lines, focusing on core products and limiting their investment plans. Firms with higher technical capability, such as those in Kenya producing injectables, had struggled to maintain profitability. As a result, the vast majority of inputs to East African health systems, including specialised medicines and other essentials for cancer care, continued to be imported.

The 2020 pandemic, with its dramatic fracturing of international supply chains (Chapter 2) broke the conventional wisdom that very high import-dependence for health care was sustainable. In both Tanzania and Kenya, some new direct foreign industrial investment in pharmaceuticals had been coming through shortly before 2020. However, the pandemic brought two notable lessons. First, there existed unexploited local industrial capabilities that could be and were repurposed in an emergency. Second, achieving new productive capabilities imposed complex demands for cross-sectoral and cross-Ministry collaborations that were shown to be achievable.

Intravenous (IV) fluids and oxygen supplies were identified early in the pandemic as key local supply gaps, alongside testing kits and hand sanitiser. To tackle these gaps, linkages between innovation, research and development (R&D), regulatory actors, and manufacturing firms were rapidly built. One participant described the experience:

> I recall the excitement among employees in [a research institution in Kenya], on the production floor. Work had suddenly increased, courtesy of a recent product launch. The staff had worked through a gruelling period of production, re-purposing the production line following a request to find a solution to the lack of viral transport media to facilitate Covid-19 testing in the country. The sales team was also overwhelmed by the calls and flow of customers seeking to buy hand sanitizer. The management was holed up in a crisis meeting to ensure that there was a steady supply of inputs

> which had suddenly gone off the shelves. An urgent trip was underway to ensure that all available materials for the sanitiser, that is, ethanol, bottles and caps and spray pumps were secured. At that moment, the only focus was to ensure that any required production process is facilitated. Applying special procurement procedures was the order of the day, and the result, products were ready for sale in record timing.

Across the region, the pandemic has greatly strengthened government commitments to health-related industrial development while widening perceptions of what is possible, and these developments have considerable potential to support improved cancer care. This chapter draws on interviews with manufacturers (5 in Tanzania, 10 in Kenya) in pharmaceuticals, chemicals, plastics and medical devices, as well as distributors, regulators, policy makers and other stakeholders, before and during the pandemic. It teases out key lessons for building stronger industrial capabilities to support local health systems, and specifically to strengthen cancer care. We argue that building and sustaining collaboration capabilities across health, industry and other agencies while generating and supporting rising ambition on the part of manufacturers and industrial innovators, are essential for greater local health security.

The Paradox of Need and Demand

Cancer care in East Africa presents an acute paradox, made worse by the pandemic: large-scale unmet need sits alongside considerable unfulfilled demand. Yet lack of demand is identified as a key constraint on investment by manufacturers.

The scale of unmet need for medicines, commodities and devices emerged sharply from the research with patients, health professionals and policy makers (Chapters 3–5). In Kenya, 30% of patients interviewed indicated that something they needed was unavailable (whether because of lack of the item, unaffordability, or distance). The missing items included medication, tests, treatment therapies, pain relief and essential commodities. Health professionals supported these claims, adding that oncology and laboratory equipment and supplies were also insufficient. In addition to oncology medication and diagnostic tests, other important cancer care requirements noted to be in short supply included anti-emetics, IV fluids and effective informatics for use in diagnosis, treatment and follow-up.

Particularly notable were patients' and cancer survivors' reported difficulties in acquiring commodities needed for day-to-day dignity and ability to work, including colostomy bags and prostheses (Chapter 3).

In Tanzania, 29% of patients and survivors said they had found something unavailable. The most commonly missed items were medication and diagnostics including biopsies. Health professionals confirmed that oncology medication was not always available, and when any item was missing, patients could find the cost of private purchase unaffordable. Key diagnostic items, such as biopsy needles, were also in short supply.

Almost 100% of all those cancer supplies were imported. The pandemic crisis threw into relief the local health system's reliance on imports of basic items including IV fluids, standard medicines including steroids, antibiotics and pain control, and widely used equipment including syringes, swabs and bandages. Basic commodities such as colostomy bags and breast prostheses, hard to find in the market and expensive, were also imported, as were all oncology medicines and diagnostic and laboratory equipment including basics such as disposable speculums for cervical cancer screening.

Manufacturers interviewed, with one exception, did not plan to introduce production of any commodities or medicines for cancer. Some felt that demand was unknown. Yet needs were great, so why was demand (perceived to be) lacking? A Kenyan policy maker commented:

> I think what we need to do amongst ourselves is to bridge the information gap. Does the industry even know what is required? ... that there are so many patients who yearn to get these kind of products?

Some manufacturers thought the potential market was too small to warrant investment. However, while recognising the rising cancer burden, none had analysed the likely market demand. A pharmaceutical manufacturer in Kenya expressed a widely shared view:

> In East Africa ... there is a small market for cancer treatment today. It's growing, but today it's really small.

Procurement and Market-Consolidation

Expanding demand was thus seen by manufacturers as key to local production. In both Kenya and Tanzania, local manufacturers indicated that new investment to produce cancer care requirements, whether diagnostics, medicines or other essential commodities, required market access and assurance of the potential demand. This was particularly emphasised for more technologically demanding products, as a Kenyan manufacturer explained:

> Now if you put [up] a sterile plant and you switch on, you can't switch off. So whether you are producing anything or not, you will incur expenses daily and that expense is in millions of shillings a day just because of making the sterile [environment]. So, *if the demand is not there,* I think it's not the right time to set a cancer plant in this country at this time." (Our emphasis)

Tackling Market Fragmentation: Involving the Users

Part of the gap between need and demand resulted from funding limitations for public procurement and the unaffordability of commodities and medicines on the private market (Chapter 4). However, the perception of low demand also resulted from market fragmentation in cancer products, as Kenyan interviews demonstrated. In Kenya's decentralised health system, County governments undertake local public procurement, channelling much of their demand through KEMSA (Kenya Medical Supplies Authority), the national health procurement agency. Faith-based facilities can procure through the Mission for Essential Drugs & Supplies (MEDS), a large faith-based procurement body, and from private distributors, as well as through KEMSA. Private facilities generally buy from private distributors. KEMSA and MEDS in turn buy through tenders locally and overseas; private distributors may supply tenders through imports.

Cancer treatment is divided between public and private cancer care centres, resulting in fragmented and poorly documented purchasing of supplies. An interviewee with experience of tendering and distribution commented: "Quantification has been an issue; we don't really know how much [is required]". A forum convened in 2017 under the National Cancer Institute brought together facilities and institutions concerned with cancer care, to try to quantify current usage and needs for oncology drugs and other treatment requirements. The Kenya Essential Medicines List now includes cancer medicines. However, some professionals including pharmacists, as well as manufacturers, stated that they were not aware of the national cancer treatment guidelines, indicating the need for further dissemination and implementation.

Fragmented health system funding and distribution channels continue to complicate the market. KEMSA aims to stock 52 essential oncology drugs mainly purchased through tenders, though biologics may be bought directly from manufacturers. However, there are still gaps in supply. One interviewee commented that quantification for these drugs is still incomplete, so "something [some supply] comes and after three months it is gone". Patients rely on a mix of out-of-pocket payments, the National Health Insurance Fund (NHIF) and private insurance as they struggle to cover their costs (Chapter 4).

The market for other cancer-related requirements, such as commodities for rehabilitation and living with dignity, is also fragmented. Private pharmacies, buying from private importers, may be the only recourse for patients. One local manufacturer when asked why they do not produce colostomy bags, replied that colostomy bags are needed by cancer patients and others too, "'but despite that, there is still no demand for that kind of product"'. That firm could produce the bags but had no enquiries, and their only source of market information was their own marketing people. Another firm, asked the same question, also identified a lack of market information: "this person has the stock, and he doesn't know where to sell it; this person wants it and doesn't know where to buy it". So the patient loses out. This market information gap for the manufacturing sector is an opportunity for research to supply market intelligence.

A final example of the fragmented and information-poor market for Kenyan health commodities is Lugol's iodine, used for cervical cancer screening. This is manufactured locally, but there is no organised purchase for the health service. The manufacturer commented that they were keen to supply local health needs but "we don't know which chemicals are required. Maybe if we knew, then we will focus on that more closely. But for now, we just knew it when people came to buy and said they were going to use for screening, that is, Lugol's iodine."

As the Kenyan National Cancer Institute forum indicated, market consolidation and improving market information mean involving all market participants including end users of the products. The product users are a complex group in health care (Chapter 6) including public and private health facilities, organisations and individuals. One key lesson from this research is the importance of involving patients, survivors and carers in generating market information and contributing to prioritising funding requirements for cancer. We were unaware for example, before the research, of the scale of unmet need for personal commodities such as colostomy bags.

Consolidating and Refocusing Procurement

The Tanzanian market for health products is somewhat more dominated by the national public procurement agency, Medical Stores Department (MSD), alongside private importer/distributors. In both Tanzania and Kenya however, national public procurement processes were not seen by manufacturers and distributors as generally favouring local manufacturing. While both KEMSA and MSD gave price preferences for local supply, these were seen as too small to allow local firms to compete with imports that received export subsidies at source in South and East Asia.

Manufacturers also argued that to incentivise investment in new products, procurement would need to offer market access guarantees for a number of years. A Kenyan public official commented on policy inconsistency: “You know, you have been told to Buy Kenya. On the other hand, procurement rules say, you buy from the lowest bidder”. Manufacturers also noted that trade credit rules favoured imports. In Tanzania a manufacturer said that MSD “is giving local manufacturers tenders, but are not ready to issue letters of credit so that firms can import raw materials and smoothly continue with production.” Yet, he pointed out, when MSD was importing pharmaceutical products from India, China and Singapore, they did extend letters of credit.

Manufacturers strongly perceived market size as an investment constraint for cancer-related products. National procurement bodies can help by contributing to regional market opening and consolidation. Tanzanian policy makers noted that MSD had started to undertake procurement for the SADCC regional market, creating an opportunity for larger orders for cancer-related supplies. There was no similar pooled procurement process at the time of the interviews within the East African Community (EAC). Kenyan manufacturers identified continuing constraints on market integration within the EAC, notably high costs and delays in gaining and retaining regulatory approval for sales in individual countries, given a lack of mutual regulatory recognition within the EAC.

Access to wider markets was also reported to be constrained by the high costs of achieving WHO prequalification for sales to donor-funded markets. The absence of export incentives was also noted: one Kenyan manufacturer stated that "In 1976 to 1980 we used to have export compensation" to incentivise exports and claimed that these had been scrapped at the behest of the IMF and World Bank. He argued that these should now be re-established, to support local manufacturers in expanding their market. Just one health-related manufacturer in Kenya stated that they were exporting a WHO-prequalified product. This firm worked in an export processing zone (EPZ), benefitting from a number of tax and duty waivers. To change these incentive structures would require collaboration among procurement, regulatory and finance authorities.

Innovation and Technological Capability-Building

In addition to the perceived lack of demand, the technological complexity of cancer medication including quality and safety requirements was frequently identified as a challenge holding back cancer-related manufacturing (see also Chapter 8). However, many of the other imported cancer essentials in short supply were not technologically challenging. Many medical devices (including syringes), essential medicines such as anti-emetics, and commodities such as colostomy bags and stents, were well within the technical competence of local manufacturers. Some, such as large-volume intravenous fluids, were felt by local firms to require a scale of production that was out of their reach for local firms. Most upstream inputs to existing health industrial production were also imported, including items such as specialised packaging that were well within local technical competences.

Manufacturing Innovative Capabilities in the Pandemic

The pandemic emergency, however, demonstrated the scope for using the latent capabilities of local manufacturers for product and process innovation. Product innovations occur when a manufacturer introduces an item not previously produced: new to the firm, not usually new to the world. Process innovations involve finding new ways of working that enhance output, productivity or other goals (Lundvall, 2016, p. 26) such as wider access to medicines. Kenya displayed capabilities for both types of innovation during the pandemic, when manufacturers worked with researchers and other stakeholders to fill gaps in essential supplies.

High-volume intravenous (IV) fluids provide an example. The reliance of East Africa on imported IV fluids has long been decried as irrational: it constitutes large-scale import of water. During the pandemic, the loss of these imports fuelled the health care crisis. There was an urgent need for a large volume water-for-injection package for use with mechanical ventilators. A recently established locally owned manufacturer had started producing small volume injectables. Discussions with this firm established that they could produce large-volume IV fluids, including in-house production of the bags. This new manufacturer was able to quickly formulate, obtain authorisation and package the new product, collaborating with local research expertise, and with the Pharmacy and Poisons Board (the regulatory body) to ensure fast registration. The firm's rapid innovation addressed an important gap in items being procured for emergency needs. IV fluids are also an important requirement for cancer treatment, and this firm adapts its IV bags to the needs of oncology treatment on special request.[1]

Pre-pandemic, local firms had not necessarily been using the full capabilities of their plant and equipment to produce a wide range of goods. Another manufacturer in Kenya described repurposing equipment for Covid needs:

> In the start of Covid we never had a lot of the items that we are currently manufacturing right now such as the PPE kits, surgical gowns, surgical facemask ... we sat down together as a team, we said what existing machinery do we have and how can we convert those machinery to start manufacturing other products. So ... the blood collection tube machine ... we identified that we can use the same packaging system to make the Covid test kits.

Other examples of rapid incremental investment and innovation to replace imports included blister strips for tablets and plastic bottles for syrups. One firm in Kenya had already been working with local packaging suppliers to upgrade their capabilities so that, for example, they could import rolls of blister packaging for tablets, and print and supply them locally, and then aimed to move on to other packaging such as for IV sets. After the pandemic cut off supplies, engineering students and specialists in

Kenya worked with local firms to produce missing packaging. Innovations during the pandemic have indeed foregrounded a previous relative lack of encouragement for local innovation and entrepreneurship, given what could be achieved once there was more support and identified demand (Banda et al., 2021a).

Systemic Capability-Building for Innovation

The extent of cross-institution, multi-sectoral and multi-disciplinary involvement required to support this rapid innovation illustrates a key finding of the innovation literature more generally: effective and sustained innovation at the firm level requires a network of supportive institutions, sometimes called an innovation eco-system. The literature links innovation closely to learning and competence-building within the firm and between actors including industrial and health service producers, regulators, policy makers, researchers and civil society organisations. Technological change is determined within firms, research organisations and wider societal structures that frame policy, institutions, and networks of interactive learning and collaboration (Lundvall, 2016).

An industrial sector contains heterogeneous firms in terms of size and product, and as those firms change and evolve over time, so do the institutions that influence them (Malerba, 2002). In the health industries, despite a very wide range of products, there are shared sector characteristics such as technologies and the knowledge base, key upstream producers of inputs, the funding and competitive characteristics of the product markets, and the regulatory institutions for producers and users of the products (Wangwe et al., 2021).

Before the pandemic, the pharmaceutical product range manufactured in Kenya and Tanzania had been narrowing somewhat under pressure from imports. Technological complexity was limited: tablets and capsules, syrups, powders and topical preparations. Several firms were producing antibiotics, including the penicillins (beta-lactams) which required separate plants with excellent air handling. However, in Tanzania, the number of firms producing antibiotics had been falling, since the largest firm, now owned by Aspen, the South Africa-based multinational, had closed its penicillins plant by 2014, and other firms were finding antibiotics increasingly unprofitable (Wangwe et al., 2021). In Kenya, some firms were producing more complex products, notably injectables. However, there was evidence of some historic knowledge depreciation, with producers of injectables reported to be struggling for profitability, and a stated lack of ambition by other firms to move into more technologically complex areas. Very few medical devices were being produced locally.

However, there was also emerging evidence of new industrial ambitions for the health industries in both countries before the pandemic improved incentives, notably from new investors, local and overseas, but also by some existing producers. Some innovations had implications for cancer care. In Kenya, one producer with clean room technology to produce intravenous products, including bags for IV fluids, was planning in 2019 to close temporarily for a major upgrade. Their objectives included production of an additional type of bag that was suitable for administering oncology medication: unlike their current product, the new bags would carry no risk of cross-contamination between the bag and the oncology drug. More broadly, as concern with non-communicable diseases moved up the policy agenda, implying expanding markets, new investors in both countries were planning when interviewed to produce medication—previously all imported—for hypertension and diabetes.

Technology Transfer and Sources of Finance

The Challenge of Sterile Manufacturing

A major concern expressed by firms considering cancer-related product manufacture was the costs of upgrading to, and sustaining, clean room and sterile technology. There was a shared perception that investment funding was hard to raise locally for this scale of investment. As a Kenyan pharmaceutical manufacturer commented:

> There is a big opportunity for local manufacturing. But you see, our investors here, they like to go for quick returns. That's why you see everyone investing in real estate. The people with money don't seem to know this area. And even if they know, they are not willing to wait for 5 years to get returns.

However, two new locally owned firms have recently tackled, in different ways, the challenge of financing investment in clean room technology, one of the essential technology upgrades required for manufacturing for cancer care.

The first is the firm mentioned above as the producer of large-volume IV fluids during the pandemic in Kenya. This firm is wholly owned by two

Kenyan pharmacists, part of a new generation group of Kenyan industrialists of Asian origin. After schooling in Kenya, both trained at universities in the UK. They went on to gain working experience in established firms abroad, then created a business start-up in the UK. They developed the formula for a rapid fever-relief syrup and sold the patent rights to a bigger firm. After exploring opportunities to establish a pharmaceutical manufacturing plant in the United States, they returned to Kenya where, since 2017, they have developed a new dedicated sterile manufacturing facility.

This firm is an example of the Kenyan business and professional diaspora bringing technology and finance raised from overseas businesses to establishing more advanced pharmaceutical manufacturing in East Africa. The firm currently manufactures sterile pharmaceuticals in the form of ampoules and collapsible infusion (IV) bags, and the owners put forward a strong vision of producing quality, efficacious and affordable medicines. They showcase stringent process controls throughout their operations and a commitment to consistent manufacturing in a cGMP facility, aiming to meet WHO guidelines, and to undertake R&D for sterile products to meet customer needs.

A second firm, in Tanzania, is also a recent start-up producing intravenous fluids, showing this is a wider regional trend. This firm is also locally owned and started construction before the pandemic on a site near Dar es Salaam. At the time of writing in 2022, it had recently started production. This is a differently innovative start-up in financial and institutional terms. The firm is owned by a social enterprise that also owns a private hospital in Dar es Salaam and medical and nursing training schools. The manufacturing firm is set up as a separate enterprise, limited by shares, so that it is open to shareholdings, partnerships and stock exchange listings, in other words, to give it financial and institutional flexibility.

Like the Kenyan firm, this company showcases a high-quality sterile manufacturing plant, with stringent quality and environmental controls, including a high-grade water distillation system and automated filling. The plant was built by a turn-key operation. The firm aims to produce solution-based generics plus a large range of small volume parenterals. This is Tanzania's first factory-scale production of intravenous products, and like the Kenyan firm, it is aiming for WHO-GMP compliance and access to export markets.

These two local firms offer evidence of rising ambition within the East African regional pharmaceutical sector, started at a time when other interviewees feared that sterile production could not be undertaken profitably. As they move into a post-pandemic era, the new firms may face challenges in sustaining competitive production within more open markets.

Finance, Technology Transfer and Skills

When substantial investment was required for new products, manufacturers identified technology transfer as a key challenge. Resolving the challenge required access to suitable finance. This often involved funding as well as technology from an overseas partner, who might require a change in the institutional ownership structure of existing firms (Wangwe et al., 2021). In order to innovate, firms rely on a network of market and non-market relationships: with input suppliers, key buyers such as procurement agencies and large donors, financial institutions, research institutes, technical consultants, market researchers and government policy makers and regulators. The ability to use these networks effectively to learn, to transmit information, and to invest effectively, has been called "linkage capability" (Lall, 1992, p. 168). Where these linkage capabilities are weak, knowledge development and diffusion become inadequate, entrepreneurial initiatives can be stifled, and active market development by firms themselves is limited. This section surveys more of the reported linkages firms were building.

Just one pharmaceutical firm interviewed in Kenya in 2019 said their firm was contemplating early production of an anti-cancer medication. They aimed to license the product from an overseas partner who would support its introduction. Also in Kenya, a medical device manufacturer was producing auto-disable syringes, which cannot be reused. This product was developed, and the firm's production line built, with support from the Bill and Melinda Gates Foundation (BMGF). In 2021 the Kenyan firm received further support from the BMGF to sharply increase output.[2] Their financial and technological support allowed the firm to acquire WHO-prequalification for the syringes, and hence to supply donor-funded tenders; the firm was exporting across Africa and to wider markets.

Manufacturers in Tanzania agreed that finding international partners was a key potential route to upgrading technology. A joint venture with a foreign firm was proposed by several interviewees as a route to enhancing technological capabilities. External partners could bring both access to technology and funding for upgrading plants and processes: the challenge was to ensure effective technology transfer to Tanzania through training and shared ownership. The required capabilities included identifying, funding, accessing, installing and using improved technology effectively; improving plant, production machinery, air and waste handling and laboratory equipment; finding or training more skilled labour; and sharply improving process documentation.

In Kenya too, another green-field investment was being undertaken before the pandemic through wholly owned foreign direct investment by a South Asian pharmaceutical firm. This investor was opening its first African plant in Kenya, working closely with an affiliated local Kenyan distributor. Most funding had come from the overseas corporation. Other finance came from the International Finance Corporation (IFC) and local banks. The firm was planning to produce a wide range of generics, including treatments for non-communicable disease, though not for cancer. This firm was aiming for WHO-GMP accreditation from the start, to ensure capability to export widely. For this ambition, they were bringing in wholly new machinery for the start-up.

Another Kenyan firm had a contractual agreement with a UK firm for technology transfer: both North–South and South-South collaborations with partner companies were observed. A variety of arrangements offered experience, technical know-how, finance and technology transfer for new manufacturing capacity in Kenya.

Costs and finance were particularly a challenge for local firms aiming to upgrade. An existing locally owned Kenyan company argued that good second-hand machinery could help to break cost constraints:

> You know, most of the new equipment are out of bounds in terms of costs for SMEs like us. Yes, we have, I would say, 2% new equipment, but a majority of our equipment are actually used. But they are well maintained, and we have technicians locally who are very competent who service them.

Two other local firms interviewed had also bought and used equipment from a plant closure or renovation, as a way to reduce the financial costs of expansion or upgrading.

Locally sourced finance was widely identified as a constraint. One firm noted that bank loan interest costs had reduced somewhat in Kenya, but banks' terms were more stringent in requiring security: loans had become cheaper but harder to get. One firm explained:

> If you get a dollar loan it is seven and a half to 8 per cent and they don't finance you 95 percent, they will say you invest 50 percent and I will give you 50 percent.

Another Kenyan pharmaceutical manufacturer explained that bank finance was particularly hard to find for a major new undertaking:

> For everybody to buy an idea, they want to see what you have done. If somebody wants to make anti-cancers and you are the first ones to make in Kenya, they will first rule [it] out. They want us to draw back, they are wondering, how are you going to get the first one?

The same firm commented that government should help, and added:

> I think the government is trying ... they have tried with ICDC ... ICDC is a government arm, which funds manufacturing industries. And they do not treat you the way banks treat [you].

The ICDC can offer lower interest rates, longer term loans and a mix of equity and debt. However, the interviewee noted that few people know the ICDC.[3]

Financial sources mentioned for upgrading included in-house funding (generally found insufficient for major developments except by overseas investors) and working capital from input suppliers. Large buyers might also supply funding, for example, for making a specialised mould for a plastic syringe or other containers. A plastics firm explained that if a mould was financed by the business customer, then it was then owned by them and used by the supplier for their business. Alternatively production of a new mould might be funded 50/50 buyer/supplier.

Pessimism about funding for cancer products remained widespread before the pandemic. One Kenyan pharmaceutical manufacturer stated that for cancer:

> There is no funding, government doesn't set aside any funds neither does any donor fund it.

This pessimistic assessment may however be beginning to change. Kenyan interviewees noted that the government's push for Universal Health Coverage was expanding health insurance and health funding, potentially generating more access to investment funds as the potential demand for health products rose.

Technology, Skills and Learning

Effective technology transfer also centrally includes upgrading skills. Kenyan manufacturers expressed confidence that staff could be trained, given relatively high levels of education in Kenya. Machinery suppliers generally trained local staff, an example of leveraging linkage capabilities. Expatriate staff may also be needed for initial setup and learning-by-doing for local staff, though one firm emphasised the importance of setting time limits for expatriate involvement. In both countries, manufacturers emphasised the importance of access to skilled expatriate staff when required. As a local partner of an overseas pharmaceutical investor noted:

> Kenya has got fair number of educated people who can be trained. Pharmacists, engineers and so forth. ... [the overseas firm will] just bring the top people who will train. ... Because finally if we have skilled people who are local, it's cheaper than importing.

One pharmaceutical manager explained that the skills and commitment demanded for sterile production are particularly great:

> The personnel have to be highly skilled, they have to demonstrate that they are actually able to do it, to manufacture sterile products. And [that] those products are consistently sterile .... And sometimes you can also add in the attitude because sometimes some people are in a hurry. They don't check very well the processes.

The importance of training people to do quality control (QC) and continuous quality assurance (QA) was repeatedly emphasised by interviewees.

One producer told a cautionary tale about the importance of constant in-house learning. They had the ambition to make rapid test kits for Hepatitis B:

> We started the process, and you know, we were really determined to do that. And then we bought materials and everything, but we had ... not actually known that ... they require a super de-humidified environment.

So they packed kits worth a million Kenyan shillings and lost the whole batch. They then got some training, supported by the Japanese, and learned to do the process well. The story illustrates, the interviewee said, both the importance of basic technical knowledge, but also of learning by doing: "once you start the process, the process must teach you something"; even simple products require continuous learning and improvement. Leveraging the skills and tacit knowledge gained, this producer then launched a locally manufactured rapid diagnostic test kit for malaria and was looking ahead to starting a new venture in biosimilar production.

Strengthening Local Health Industries: Building Collaboration

Even before the pandemic, governments in Tanzania and Kenya were already increasing their commitment to industrial development of the health industries, and to improving cancer care (Chapter 1). There was already recognition of the economic importance of the health sector including industrial suppliers.[4] Policy makers were also working on moves towards universal health coverage. In Tanzania, pharmaceutical industries were identified as a priority industrial sector within the Second Five Year Development Plan (Ministry of Finance and Planning, 2016). Two pillars of Kenya's "Big 4" policy agenda[5] are enhanced manufacturing and affordable universal health coverage (UHC). At a roundtable for the Kenyan National Chamber of Commerce and Industry, a senior Kenyan government official was reported clearly explaining the link between the two[6]:

> In manufacturing of pharmaceuticals we have established that the Universal Health Coverage pillar that we have as part of the Big 4 agenda can help provide a market for locally manufactured medicines as well as those from the COMESA region.

African manufacturers interviewed were well aware of their wider local economic impact and felt this should be a factor in policy making.

One Kenyan manufacturer explained that local wages and purchases of inputs from local suppliers feed money back into the economy, creating further demand (a process economists call the multiplier). He added an observation more characteristic of feminist economists:

> Women tend to take their finances back home, as opposed to men they tend to take the finances to places other than home, that is why we prefer hiring 80 percent women here.

These arguments feed into a pandemic-generated recognition of the importance of shorter and robust health supply chains and combine with a recognition of the importance of government policy leadership. This is a moment of opportunity for industrial innovation and growth in East Africa. The challenge is to develop the health industries in a form that can support better access to health care (Urias, 2019).

These industrial opportunities extend to cancer care. Governments are taking initiatives to improve cancer supplies. Manufacturers are noting the rising health policy priority given to cancer. One Kenyan manufacturer said:

> The government has now started thinking about cancer. No one has been thinking about it, it has been completely neglected. As you can see, all these years since independence, there was no budget for cancer drugs and they were not in the essential drug list. It speaks volumes.

In both countries, investment is going into infrastructure and equipment for cancer care. In Kenya one national hospital has now been declared as a centre of excellence in cancer care and gone ahead to establish the first public integrated molecular imaging facility. In Tanzania, the national cancer hospital, Ocean Road Cancer Institute, has installed a PET scanner and is constructing an associated plant to produce radio isotopes: the intention is to generate revenue by treating paying patients travelling from abroad.

Collaborative Priorities

How to ensure that the health industries grow and contribute to cancer care needs? What policies, and what forms of collaboration, are needed to support expanding and competitive local manufacturing?

First, much more active engagement by the health system is needed in industrial development. The commitment to Universal Health Coverage is a major opportunity since UHC is only achievable with a reliable and responsive supply chain of essential medicines, devices and other essential supplies. In the words of one participant, the health system will have to move away from being "comfortable importing everything", and actively engage in promoting procurement locally for key needs. This in turn involves effective quantification of needs, and also collaboration across the system between public, faith-based and private providers to identify priorities, share objectives in terms of cost reduction and quality standards, and collaborate on effective local procurement. Health care is financed through many funding streams—individuals, insurance, philanthropic and official donations, and government funding; yet collaboration among institutional funders—even data sharing—remains a challenge. As Kenya has moved into the lower middle-income bracket, donor funding for health is reducing, requiring urgent government response.

Health care thus needs to shift away from a rather passive approach of ordering requirements and waiting for their arrival, to a much more active role in ensuring security and availability of appropriate supplies at competitive costs (Chapter 6). Key tools are information and procurement, and both require health system actors to develop their own linkage capabilities.

Market information was repeatedly identified as lacking for industrial business planning. Clarification of health needs and identification of the likely extent of demand expansion are required from health policy makers, including medicines, medical devices and commodities for cancer care. Once information is consolidated, demand fragmentation also needs to be reduced, to provide a core market to incentivise local investment. This is key both for major initiatives, such as producing oncology medication (see Chapter 8), and also for items requiring only incremental investment, such as colostomy bags, where the industrial capability is available but unused, so that need is not translating into private demand, and public procurement is not supporting access.

In both Kenya and Tanzania there were moves towards more preferential procurement for local manufacturers, for example through identifying items for local tenders and developing local content policies. These can be built on to ensure key cancer care items—many of which have wider health system uses—are increasingly available. In Kenya, mechanisms to support local manufacturers include a directive to agencies to procure

40% of their goods and services locally, in line with the Buy Kenya Build Kenya strategy (Ministry of Industry Trade and Cooperatives, 2017). Ensuring these initiatives work together to support local suppliers requires continuing collaboration between health, procurement, regulatory and industrial actors: collaboration that can easily be undermined by institutional barriers and mutual misunderstandings.

Second, the need to increase market size and improve incentives to invest also requires collaboration, among industrial, tax, trade, manufacturing and procurement actors. Government initiatives for regional market consolidation were high on manufacturers' wish lists, alongside a measure of industrial protection against (often subsidised) import competition. Trade duties and taxes that favour importers need reviewing and revising (UNIDO, 2019) Regional initiatives could include pooled public procurement for the EAC (perhaps on the SADCC model). Tackling cost barriers and slow country-based product registration, while speeding up regional regulatory harmonisation can greatly improve cross-border trade and competition. This requires active international collaboration, as an industry policy maker explained:

> We play a very active role in regional integration and the initiative is to create market access for Kenyan exports. We play a very active role in EAC integration and retention … .we are [in] this African continental free trade area; we are active in trying to find room in that. And also, we are engaging the EU for market access.

Other methods to improve incentives for local firms include adapting local procurement preferences to include for example extra points for proximity and short supply times. Trade credit for local firms to match the credit for overseas suppliers; longer contracts to incentivise investment; and reduction in payment delays were all highlighted. Local firms, in response, need to engage with wider concepts of their potential market.

Third, the links between technology upgrading and sources of investment finance need strengthening. Strengthened development banking, and other sources of long-term funds are needed to facilitate innovation. Technical support is required to ensure effective technology transfer from partners and joint venture investors; also advice on business models, finding finance, and help with searching for business partners. Active support for local entrepreneurship and local innovators, including university-firm-government linkages, is needed to build on policy learning during pandemic about the scale of potential local initiative. Several interviewees mentioned the importance of support for local R&D and innovation including building on and developing local informatics.

Fourth, support for skills improvement was high on Tanzanian interviewees' lists. In both countries facilitation of appropriate external work permits was mentioned, alongside adaptation of local training provision more closely to industrial needs, initiatives requiring education-industrial linkages to be improved.

Fifth, export support needs identified included supporting local firms' market access, and support for reaching WHO prequalification and WHO-GMP certification. Interviewees' experiences of being blocked from public tendering by donor funding requirements imply that governments can do more to ensure that donor funding supports local suppliers, without undermining essential quality control. Low-cost (necessarily temporary) philanthropic imports, for example of cancer products, while welcome, should be designed to ensure they do not unintentionally block the market for investors in local production of the same items, an approach requiring ongoing health-industrial collaboration.

Concluding Reflections: Building Innovation Capability and Ambition

Local industrial researchers in Kenya and Tanzania identified the demonstration effect of the pandemic as showing that it is possible to align local resources to facilitate an intended transition from a technology-importing economy to a technology-generating economy. They see the moment as an opportunity to embrace innovation, R&D and entrepreneurship and to foster research organisation/industry linkages to that end. A central lesson has been the ambitious collaboration required, across disciplines and institutions, to achieve rapid product innovation and distribution. The local pharmaceutical manufacturing sector received political goodwill and support for their engagement in the pandemic response. However, an interviewee in a research institute deeply involved in those processes felt there was still fragmentation of efforts and argued that product development must be supported as a process all the way from the innovator to commercialisation. Can complex collaboration be sustained outside emergencies?

There are instances where researchers can act effectively as champions and advocates for manufacturing. One researcher described many meetings and negotiations to try to convince pharma to initiate and invest in vaccine production (Chapter 10):

> And then I remember calling with them, because initially they were not willing to set up a vaccine filling facility.., they wanted to test if the business is viable, but I said, "in this country if we are not going to have the filling, even our anti-cancers once we develop them, where are we going to do the filling?". So we are pushing, that is one area we know we are pushing the manufacturer.

In order to enhance the growth of the local entrepreneurial culture, R&D is needed to support innovation. Most manufacturers had no research departments. Some had joint ventures, with R&D embedded within the agreement, where research was done offshore. A Kenyan interviewee said:

> We know we do not have that kind of full capacity, because we do not have a proper R&D... we do not have our own R&D... so we will even outsource ... the R&D from outside where we are so sure.

Research institutions and universities can and should serve as a platform where innovators are trained, mentored and further linked to industry to support R&D. However, the frameworks for such arrangements are largely lacking, and legal protections for the intellectual property of local innovators could be enhanced and implemented, for example through strengthening roles in WIPO (World Intellectual Property Organization) and ARIPO (African Regional Intellectual Property Organization). One institution interviewed has used trademarks to support commercialisation of their products but recognised the need to explore other available channels of innovation commercialisation such as patents and spin-outs and strengthening research organisation—industry collaboration.

Coordination across sectoral boundaries will remain hard. Discussions with stakeholders showed how disjointed the health, industry and education sectors really were. Various problems were understood in principle to have homegrown solutions. However, it was difficult to narrow down to resolving the core hurdles. Experience suggests that learning and sustaining collaboration for ambitious ends—in this case, growing the health industries to benefit health care in general and cancer care in particular—involves two very different aspects. On the one hand, instituting high-level leadership, generating impetus and incentives to resolve problems and achieve results. On the other hand, growing the very different skills of day-to-day problem solving and implementation across traditional boundaries.

Raising the ambition for local manufacturing for health requires a coordination framework with high-level oversight, to ensure cancer care products are eventually delivered to the patient in a timely and cost-effective manner. It may be that a multi-agency/ multi-sectoral team with a long-term vision is required to lead the process. For leading practical coordination across boundaries, the pandemic experience identifies two candidates: researchers able to analyse requirements and pull together solutions; and those professionals traditionally and uniquely working on the health/industry boundary: regulators and procurement officers, often pharmacists by training. These groups need to be able to pull in: manufacturers who show an inherent ambition and resilience in building their businesses; health professionals interested in learning capabilities to work with suppliers; and—a core lesson of this whole project—also "users", that is the patients, carers and survivors for whose benefit the collaborations are built, and among whom we have met many who were anxious to engage. Their agency is essential: as Calestous Juma (2016, p. 301) a Kenyan innovation scholar, argued forcefully: "It is not sufficient that policies are inclusive; their formulation and the design of new technologies also need to include potential beneficiaries".

Notes

1. https://tasapharma.com/special-requests.
2. https://www.gatesfoundation.org/ideas/articles/syringe-vaccine-distribution-in-africa, consulted 17/01/22.
3. The website does not appear very active, and the last annual report available was 2016-17 https://icdc.co.ke/, consulted 17/01/22.
4. Mackintosh and Tibandebage (2016) provided evidence for this debate in Tanzania.
5. Big-Four-Agenda-Report-2018_19.pdf (planning.go.ke), consulted 20/09/22.
6. https://www.africansv.com/five-ways-kenyan-government-bets-will-boost-manufacturing-sector-2/.

CHAPTER 8

Oncology Drug Production in Sub-Saharan Africa: The Challenge and Opportunity, with Evidence from India

Maureen Mackintosh, Sudip Chaudhuri, Nazeem Mohamed, Samuel Wangwe, Twalib Ngoma, and Veronica Manduku

Introduction

Cancer is expensive for all concerned, as Chapters 3–5 confirmed. One core reason for its unaffordability is the price of chemotherapy. Chemotherapy is lengthy, physically demanding with difficult side effects,

M. Mackintosh (✉)
The Open University, Milton Keynes, UK
e-mail: maureen.mackintosh@open.ac.uk

S. Chaudhuri
Indian Institute of Management Calcutta, Kolkata, India

N. Mohamed
International Pharmaceutical Consultant, Cheltenham, UK

S. Wangwe
Economic and Social Research Foundation (ESRF), Dar es Salaam, Tanzania

G. Banda et al. (eds.), *Cancer Care in Pandemic Times: Building Inclusive Local Health Security in Africa and India*, International Political Economy Series,
https://doi.org/10.1007/978-3-031-44123-3_8

and emotionally and financially draining. The oncology medicines required are expensive for cash-strapped individuals and health systems, and in Sub-Saharan African countries those medicines are almost all imported. This chapter argues that the current context provides a major opportunity for Sub-Saharan African countries to invest in local production of some key oncology medicines. The chapter traces the most important contextual factors facilitating local investment including the rising need for these drugs; the structure of their international production, marketing and pricing that is sustaining higher than necessary prices; and the current post-pandemic trends and policies that are encouraging new investment and growth in local health industries in Eastern and Southern Africa including those needed for cancer care, in order to strength local health security (Chapter 7).

This chapter establishes the unaffordability of these medicines and identifies the import gap and supply chain challenges. It then uses research on the Indian and international market structure for generic oncology medication to evidence over-pricing and lack of effective competition to drive prices down. The chapter then assesses the emergent business opportunity for local production in East Africa and associated challenges faced by potential investors, drawing on discussions with local manufacturers and distributors. Finally, the chapter argues that there is an opening for a combination of ambition and initiative from an interest coalition of local stakeholders including policy makers to generate investment in oncology production in Eastern and Southern Africa, to benefit both patients and industrial development.

Unaffordability of Oncology Drugs

Access to oncology medication remains problematic for cancer patients in both countries where patients were interviewed. In Tanzania, oncology treatment is free of charge to uninsured patients in the public sector, but

V. Manduku
Kenya Medical Research Institute (KEMRI), Nairobi, Kenya

T. Ngoma
Muhimbili University of Health and Allied Sciences (MUHAS), Dar es Salaam, Tanzania

the availability of these essential medicines has fluctuated in recent years, and some patients recounted past struggles to buy some of the medication privately. One farmer, with an annual household income equivalent to USD 400 had found his required chemotherapy drugs unavailable and had paid a sum roughly equal to his annual income to buy them privately. He had funded this by selling family farming land. Another Tanzanian patient recounted that she could not afford the recommended drugs for her kidney cancer, which she would have had to purchase for approximately USD 2000 (two-thirds of the household annual income); she was therefore prescribed other available cancer medication.

In Kenya, we found that access to chemotherapy relied on insurance funding or private payment. The cost of a cycle of oncology medication could be very challenging for Kenyan patients, even those with some insurance coverage. Here are some examples of out-of-pocket payments for chemotherapy at public hospital cancer centres in Kenya. A young man, 35 years, self-employed, with cancer of the jaw, had paid out of pocket KES 40,000 (USD 392) for his first chemotherapy sessions. This came on top of tests and surgery costing USD 1340 equivalent, all paid out of pocket, totalling in all 1.5 times the household's annual income. A prostate cancer patient, 51 years old and self-employed, in a very low-income household, had National Health Insurance Fund (NHIF) coverage but it was incomplete. He had topped up KES 78,000 to complete five chemotherapy cycles, a sum roughly twice the household's annual income. A 76-year-old breast cancer sufferer had paid 49,000 shillings (USD 480) for nine cycles of chemotherapy, equivalent to 13% of her household's annual income. A 58-year-old woman with breast cancer who did not wish to declare her household income stated that the NHIF had covered payments of KES 80,000 (USD 784) for eight sessions of chemotherapy, and commented, "the medication is very expensive when it is not available at the hospital [i.e. has to be purchased privately]". A retired professional woman, a breast cancer sufferer, recorded a total NHIF payment of KES 105,000 (USD 1030) for eight chemotherapy sessions.

A complete chemotherapy cycle will thus cost at least several hundred dollars if paid out of pocket or by a national health insurance fund, and the price may run into thousands. The financial demands may rise to multiples of household income, and they come on top of other payments for tests and surgery (Chapters 4 and 5). These are very large sums for low-income populations: in Kenya, the median consumption expenditure per head in 2015/16, three years before our interviews, was 1.8 dollars a day (KNBS, 2018, p. 60); in Tanzania, the figure in 2017/18 was equivalent to USD 1 per day (MoFP- PED and NBS, 2019, p. 93).[1]

This unaffordability and financial toxicity for patients and families is replicated across Sub-Saharan Africa. In South Africa, it was recently calculated that the private price for a course of treatment for colorectal cancer was equivalent to 325 days of the minimum wage (Mattila et al., 2021). In 2018 the WHO calculated that a standard treatment for early-stage HER2-positive breast cancer would cost about 10 years of average annual wages in India and South Africa (WHO, 2018c).

The unaffordability of chemotherapy is also national, and not only concerns new patented treatments. Access to essential chemotherapy medicines remains poor across Sub-Saharan Africa. However, even standard, long off-patent oncology medications, if made available to all those in need, create a substantial burden on government and social insurance health funding systems (Gelband et al., 2016; Ngwa et al., 2022b). Rising cancer need will increase that burden on national health insurance systems, especially where, as in Kenya, many patients are persuaded to pay into insurance only once they become ill. While fully including cancer patients within financially fragile systems of universal health coverage will remain a huge challenge, there are nevertheless areas where costs could be reduced for national benefit. This chapter considers one such area: the scope for local production initiatives to produce essential oncology drugs to help reduce some of the identified costs and tackle some supply gaps, and the facilitative policy changes that would be required.

Import Reliance and Supply Chain Risk

Sub-Saharan Africa is almost completely reliant on imports for its access to essential oncology medication. The pandemic, as Chapter 2 has shown, focused minds on the supply chain risks inherent in extreme import dependency. The pandemic impact on cancer care in African contexts remains to be fully investigated but is likely to have been profound (Martei et al., 2021; Nnaji & Moodley, 2021). Even before the pandemic, however, the authorities in Tanzania and Kenya were well aware of supply chain gaps, and the risks and uncertainties of extreme import reliance for oncology medicine procurement. Kenyan interviewees noted that Kenya had developed an essential medicines list for cancer medication, alongside new treatment guidelines (Chapter 7). These exercises had identified an initial list of 52 essential cancer products for an invitation to tender. However, that tendering exercise had resulted in purchases of only 38 of the required 52 items. None of these essential items were high-priced biologic medications. The procurement problems encountered by the Kenyan public sector buyers included a lack of registrations since some potential suppliers abroad had not registered the products in Kenya. However, the more challenging problem cited was that "the quantities were not lucrative": that is, the Kenyan orders were too small to interest external suppliers. Some of these items were later successfully sourced, but the supply constraints remain. We return to the implications for procurement policy below.

For East African cancer care, which oncology products are currently the most important for ensuring continuous high-quality supply at low cost? This question can feel invidious since all products are important to particular patients when that is what they need. However, some oncology products are "workhorses" with many applications. The WHO has developed, and regularly updates, a list of essential cancer medication (WHO, 2021b). For analysis of trade and pricing in this chapter, we have selected a subset of these, drawn from two East African expert sources (Table 8.1). In Table 8.1, the first column lists the "top ten" required medications identified by an experienced local oncologist. The second column list was developed by a local pharmaceutical manufacturer who had been investigating, with expert support, which oncology medicines were of particular local market importance in East Africa and had local production potential.

These medicines are all off-patent and are regarded by local and other clinical experts as key inputs to first line and continuing cancer treatment appropriate for lower income contexts. Furthermore, these medicines are predicted to continue in widespread use in the near future. We have added to this list one biological medicine, Trastuzumab, also off-patent, which is included, in originator and biosimilar formulations, in the WHO's priority list for the treatment of HER2+ breast cancer (WHO, 2021b). These medicines, widely produced in generic formulations, have as the final column shows a wide range of applications for highly prevalent cancers.

East Africa is 100% reliant on imports of these products. There is currently very little local production of oncology drugs in Sub-Saharan Africa as a whole. In South Africa, Fine Chemicals, an Aspen subsidiary, produces the API for Vincristine, a drug with a spectrum of uses in oncology.[2] Aspen also opened in 2018 a sterile facility for the production of cytotoxic medication in Port Elizabeth.[3] The initial production plans

Table 8.1 Some key oncology medicines for the East African market: main applications

Generic name: active ingredient	*Local oncologist's priority list (2019)*	*Local manufacturer's potential product list (2019)*	*Main application(s)*
Cyclophosphamide	X	X	Numerous
Methotrexate	X		Numerous
Fluoro Uracil (5FU)	X	X	Cervical, Breast, Colorectal
Doxorubicin	X	X	Numerous
Docetaxel	X	X	Numerous
Paclitaxel	X	X	Numerous
Gemcitabine	X	X	Numerous
Etoposide	X		Numerous
Cisplatin	X	X	Numerous
Goserelin		X	Breast, prostate
Bicalutamide		X	Prostate
Oxaliplatin		X	Colo-Rectal
Carboplatin		X	Ovarian
Tamoxifen		X	Breast
Anastrozole/Letrazole		X	Breast
Temozolamide		X	Brain
Vincristine		X	Numerous
Epirubicin		X	Numerous
Capecitabin		X	Numerous
Trastuzumab			Breast

Source Interviews

included Melphalan (under Aspen's brand name Alkeran), an anti-cancer agent with a number of applications. Aspen, a large South African-based multinational pharmaceutical company, has cancer APIs capability also in the Netherlands, allowing it to envisage an expanded and vertically integrated cancer portfolio.[4]

Otherwise, reliance by Sub-Saharan African governments on imported oncology medicines is complete. However, data on the current sources of imports of cancer medication into Eastern and Southern Africa remain poor. Available international trade data[5] do not provide a breakdown of international trade by cancer products: oncology medicines are included in a residual category,[6] after major medicine categories including antibiotics and anti-malarials are separately classified. The value of imports in this residual category in 2019 was large: USD 410 million for Kenya;

USD 219 million for Tanzania; USD 226 million for Uganda; and USD 1.4 billion for South Africa, but we cannot separately identify oncology drugs.

India as Oncology Supplier and Benchmark

India is an important supplier of essential oncology medicines to Eastern Africa. Indian exports, as a historically cheaper source of generic medicines, have dominated medicines imports into East Africa more generally (Chaudhuri et al., 2010; Mackintosh et al., 2018b). This dominance appears to be reflected in oncology medicine imports, benefitting from lower Indian prices,[7] even though data are incomplete. Detailed Indian export data can therefore provide some insight into the current import cost of essential cancer drugs for East Africa.

India is a major global exporter of anti-cancer medicines, with an export value of USD 757.34 million in 2019/20.[8] These exports reflect the pattern of cancer medicines access globally: 80% went to Europe and the Americas; just 6.1% (USD 46.1 million) went to the whole of Africa. The value of oncology imports from India into Kenya in 2019/20 (that is, largely before the Covid-19 emergency constrained the trade) was USD 1.67 million; into Tanzania USD 1.12 million; into Uganda USD 0.24 million; and into South Africa USD 10.07 million[9]: small shares of total medicines imports.

India's oncology drug exports to Africa were furthermore quite concentrated in a few countries: Table 8.2 evidences these concentrated export links for the medicines listed in Table 8.1, showing that India exports these medicines largely to East Africa, South Africa and some countries in North Africa.

Furthermore, these Indian export data confirm the market importance of some of the medicines listed in Table 8.1. In 2019/20 for example, 57% of Tanzania's oncology drug imports from India consisted of these categories: paclitaxel and docetaxel; actinomycin, dactinomycin and doxorubicin; and L-asparaginase, cisplatin and carboplatin. That share for Kenya was 24%, Uganda 29% and for South Africa just 23%. Furthermore, the values of these oncology imports from India, while showing erratic movement over time, have been growing between 2011/12 and 2020/21 at an annual rate of 16.5% in Kenya, 18.7% in South Africa and 2.4% in Tanzania.

Table 8.2 India's exports of oncology medicine to Africa, 2019/20, top country destinations for some key products

Product	*No of receiving countries*	*Top 5 recipient countries*	*Share of top 5 countries*
Cyclophosphamide	3	Ethiopia, Kenya, Tanzania	100
Methotrexate, 5-fluorouracil(5-fu) and ftorafur	10	Ethiopia, Sudan, South Africa, Kenya, Angola	89
Bincristine and vinblastine	7	Morocco, Ethiopia, South Africa, Botswana, Kenya	87
Paclitaxel and docetaxel	23	Morocco, South Africa, Tanzania, Egypt, Ethiopia	80
Etoposide	9	Ethiopia, Djibouti, Angola, Kenya, Mozambique	73
Actinomycin d (dactinomycin) and doxorubicin	16	South Africa, Tanzania, Nigeria, Egypt, Kenya	87
L-asparaginase, cisplatin and carboplatin	20	Algeria, Ethiopia, Egypt, South Africa, Tanzania	73
Tamoxifen	2	Angola, Mozambique	100
Other anti-cancer drugs	31	Algeria, South Africa, Morocco, Kenya, Ethiopia	88

Source Calculated from the DGCI&S database (from: https://tradedx.cmie.com/, June 2022)

We have no comparative data on oncology imports into East Africa and South Africa from other exporters including those from high-income countries. However, since India is generally a low-cost medicines exporter, it would be the key competitor for local oncology manufacturing. It is also a potential source of direct overseas investment in oncology manufacturing in East Africa. As such India provides a useful benchmark for local production debate. What can we learn from Indian experience about the scope for local manufacturing to help to address supply constraints in oncology? We argue below that Indian and other international evidence suggests substantial scope, within current international markets for oncology medicines, for competitive local production in African countries.

Competition Failures in Generic Oncology Markets

Most oncology drugs on the essential medicines lists in East Africa and at the WHO are chemical not biological products which are long off-patent, and their production is well understood. Furthermore, those products are widely produced globally, by generics companies in South Asia, Europe and elsewhere. The technology is widely available, and many of the required products can be produced and used in tablet form as well as intravenous products. The focus of this chapter on these widely produced generics contrasts with much of the international debate on access to cancer medication which has focused quite strongly, as reflected in several of our interviews, on legal constraints such as the TRIPS agreement to accessing innovator medicines under patent. While this latter concern reflects a serious issue for some categories of cancer patients, it should not displace a wider focus on continuing access constraints for cancer patients to the wide range of off-patent essential oncology medicines.

The international market for most essential oncology medicines is a market for branded generics: different manufacturers sell each medicine on private markets under their own brand name for that item. This international market is known to exhibit patchy competitive conditions and disorganisation. Prices have not been effectively driven down, as many expected, by the entry of many generic suppliers, and some key essential drugs still have only a few producers (WHO, 2018b). Furthermore, import prices paid for generic cancer medicines have historically varied very sharply by country, with lower income countries often paying above the best market price (Cuomo et al., 2017; WHO, 2018b). This evidence of market fragmentation suggests there is scope for collusive behaviour in the context of poor market information, poor regulation and disorganised public procurement processes.

These problems of high-priced generic oncology drugs are also experienced by high-income countries, which are starting to address the competition problems. In February 2021, after an investigation, the European Commission agreed a binding commitment by Aspen, the large South Africa-based generics multinational, to reduce the prices of six of its cancer medicines by an average of 73%.[10] All six had been off-patent for around 50 years. Sold under various brand names, they contain the active ingredients melphalan, mercaptopurine, chlorambucil, tioguanine and busulfan, with a wide range of uses. Aspen has also committed to continue to supply these medicines, some of which are for small patient groups, having previously been accused of threatening to withdraw them from some European markets.[11] This investigation illustrates the continuing competition failures in the market for oncology generics, and also the potential role of both competition policy and effective procurement initiatives in addressing these market problems.

Competition Failures Within India

Market data for India confirm that, for the subset of drugs studied in this chapter, these competition failures occur also within the large and complex Indian medicines market. Within India, there are huge local disparities in the prices of key oncology medicines (Natarajan et al., 2020). The subset of oncology drugs studied in this chapter are all long-established in the Indian market. Table 8.3 demonstrates that many of these medicines have been available in the Indian private retail market for 20 or 30 years (Table 8.3 column 3). For almost all these medicines, there are many competing Indian and overseas firms selling into the Indian private market (Table 8.3 column 2). Note that the sales data (column 4) are for drugs sold by stockists primarily in the private retail market in India. The data do not include sales in the Indian institutional markets where drug products are purchased by procurement agents through a competitive bidding process (see further below).

None of these drugs in Table 8.3 are patent-protected in India, and seven were launched before the TRIPS agreement came into force. Only one drug—Trastuzumab—was introduced after India re-introduced product patent protection in pharmaceuticals in 2005, but this biological medicine is also not under patent in India. The importance of this subset of drugs is confirmed by Indian data since the listed drugs contributed about a third of the total Indian anti-cancer drugs retail market of Rs. 28,552.85 million (USD 408.3 million) in 2018–2019.

There is a large number of suppliers for almost all of these medicines in the Indian market (Table 8.3 Column 2). Competition is missing only for Goserelin: of two suppliers, AstraZeneca (European MNC) and an Indian firm (Bharat Serums & Vaccines), only AstraZeneca sold it in 2018/19. Only three other medicines have fewer than ten brands in the market (Table 8.3). Given this large number of sellers and the well-established technology for producing these drugs, the expectation might be these drugs should benefit from competitive pricing, with competition between

Table 8.3 Selected anti-cancer drugs: retail market sales in India, 2018–19

Drug	*No. of brands*	*Launch date in India*	*Retail sales 2018–19 (USD million)*[a]
Anastrozole	27	Apr-03	3.57
Bicalutamide	20	Jan-02	4.27
Capecitabine	30	Apr-04	6.50
Carboplatin	18	Feb-97	8.92
Cisplatin	22	Apr-90	1.50
Cyclophosphamide	14	Sep-00	1.82
Docetaxel	32	Mar-00	6.57
Doxorubicin	24	May-91	1.64
Epirubicin	23	Feb-98	1.82
Etoposide	11	May-91	0.28
Fluorouracil	7	Jul-81	0.16
Gemcitabine	28	Aug-00	6.37
Goserelin	1	Feb-97	2.95
Letrozole	64	Jul-01	11.42
Methotrexate	35	Dec-80	10.83
Oxaliplatin	27	Apr-00	5.53
Paclitaxel	45	Sep-98	19.99
Tamoxifen	17	Feb-86	1.01
Temozolomide	25	Jan-02	3.58
Trastuzumab	12	Jan-10	35.05
Vincristine	9	Feb-88	0.16
Total (these medicines)			133.93

Source Sales Audit Data, PharmaTrac of AIOCD Pharmasofttech AWACS Pvt Ltd (henceforth AIOCD-AWACS)
[a]INR/USD exchange rate 2018–19 average: Rs. 69.9229

sellers driving falling and convergent pricing. However, recent research in India has shown that oncology medication prices have not fallen, as a result of generic production and market competition, as far as would be expected from comparisons with other types of medication (Chaudhuri, 2019a, 2019b).

Detailed price data for the medicines in Table 8.3 confirm that these competitive effects on prices are not working in the Indian retail market. Prices for each of these medicines, for each particular formulation (e.g. a tablet of a certain strength), display vast variation. The median differential between the maximum and minimum retail price for the Table 8.3 medicines was 142%. These differentials varied hugely and were above

1500% for five medicines. The median differential between the retail price charged by the market-leading firm in each case and the minimum retail price was large at 117%, with five differentials over 500%. These differentials were not negatively correlated to the number of sellers; they are likely to reflect greater trust in some firms' brands than in others. An extreme case of price differentials in this sample of medicines is Anastrozole 1 mg tablet: the maximum price was Rs. 7718.75 (USD 108.87) compared to the minimum price of Rs. 27.20 (USD 0.38) (differential 28,277%). In this case, an innovator firm (AstraZeneca) has not been willing to reduce prices in India to match that of its generic competitors despite losing sales: the Indian market share of the product sold by AstraZeneca was only 3% in 2018–2019. These price differentials reflect competition failure, compounded by a failure of Indian government policies to reduce oncology market prices.

Effective Procurement as Competition Policy

What therefore can Indian experience teach about building more effective oncology markets and ensuring that competition does help to drive down prices? The key role of effective procurement in reducing prices and undercutting potential retail market collusion can be illustrated by the striking impact on prices achieved through effective public procurement in India.

A good example is provided by price data for the Tamil Nadu Medical Services Corporation (TNMSC). TNMSC is an agency of the Tamil Nadu state government for procuring and distributing medicines to different government organisations providing health services. It has earned a reputation as a successful and efficient medicine procurement agency. It procures medicines through a competitive bidding process, but the bids are restricted to those manufacturers who have the capacity and capability to supply quality medicines.

This is where the real market competition occurs. Table 8.4 shows the price impact. The table compares prices of selected like-for-like formulations between the private Indian retail market and the TNMSC achieved prices. The table shows that the price reductions achieved by the TNMSC are huge and consistent as compared to retail market prices. The median differential for this sample between the *minimum* retail price and the TNMSC price was 300%; between the market leader price and the TNMSC price the differential was 552%. In only two cases did the

TNMSC price exceed the minimum retail price despite strong quality standards.

These striking reductions show how competitive bidding for procurement orders, associated with the presence of several sellers, can make oncology medicines affordable. This evidence holds important lessons for East Africa. In the current situation of import dependence, fragmented procurement is further reducing the limited market leverage public buyers can exercise, helping to keep import prices high and reduce access. With few bidders for small procurement orders, a Kenyan interviewee with procurement experience noted the lack of leverage they experience:

> Few manufacturers for these commodities, it is the biggest challenge ... it is like you need to do a lot of negotiation; if they were ten [suppliers bidding], you see you could even bring the price down.

Furthermore, in these circumstances of fragmented procurement, local importers in African countries may find scope to combine to keep prices high. In 2017, the South African Competition Commission opened an investigation of Aspen, Roche and Pfizer for suspected "excessive pricing" of six imported cancer drugs.[12] It was noted by the Commission that Aspen did not have any local competitors in this market, raising the scope for collaboration among importers. We return to local procurement strategies below. First, we consider whether the local manufacturers could find market space in a consolidating and growing East African oncology market.

The Scope for Local Oncology Manufacturing

The potential market in East Africa is growing as cancer cases rise. Prices are known to be a constraint on access to care (see above). Could local production of some of these medicines help to reduce prices in East Africa and increase the regularity of supply? There are reasons to think this might be possible, since the sheer lack of effective private competition, just documented for a key supplying country, is keeping generic cancer medicine prices high. This in turn suggests the existence of market space for local manufacturers to combine lower prices with sustainable profitability, once established.

Recent international initiatives to try to increase access to cancer medicines in Sub-Saharan Africa have not, to date, gone down this

Table 8.4 The price impact of good procurement in a fragmented oncology medicines market

Drug name	*Unit*	*TNMSC Price (USD)[b] (March 2019)*	*Retail Price of Market leader (USD) (Mid-2019)[b]*	*Price differential: retail market leader and TNMSC (%)[b]*	*Price differential: minimum retail and TNMSC (%)[b]*
Anastrozole	1 mg tablet	0.02	3.46	17,426	1843
Bicalutamide	50 mg tablet	0.06	0.69	1060	386
Capecitabine	500 mg tablet	0.20	1.87	817	−31
Carboplatin[a]	450 mg, 45 ml injection	5.15	35.51		
Cisplatin	10 mg injection 10 ml	0.62	1.02	64	46
Cyclophosphamide	200 mg injection	0.22	0.68	210	105
Cyclophosphamide	50 mg tablet	0.04	0.06	35	5
Docetaxel[a]	120 mg injection 3 ml	8.18	216.91		
Doxorubicin (Plain)	10 mg injection 5 ml	0.45	3.02	572	440
Epirubicin	10 mg injection	1.39	8.08	481	147
Etoposide	50 mg capsule	0.89	0.81	−10	-23
Fluorouracil	500 mg injection 10 ml	0.19	0.33	71	59
Gemcitabine	1000 mg injection	4.63	78.66	1600	624
Goserelin	3.6 mg injection	N/A	137.58		
Letrozole	2.5 mg tablet	0.02	0.55	2877	149

(continued)

Table 8.4 (continued)

Drug name	*Unit*	*TNMSC Price (USD)[b] (March 2019)*	*Retail Price of Market leader (USD) (Mid-2019)[b]*	*Price differential: retail market leader and TNMSC (%)[b]*	*Price differential: minimum retail and TNMSC (%)[b]*
Methotrexate	50 mg injection 2 ml	0.21	1.34	532	160
Methotrexate	10 mg tablet	0.10	0.17	68	60
Oxaliplatin[a]	50 mg injection 25 ml	5.19	66.84		
Paclitaxel	100 mg injection	3.17	70.52	2122	908
Paclitaxel	260 mg injection 43.4 ml	7.76	129.16	1565	679
Tamoxifen	10 mg tablet	0.01	0.04	219	86
Temozolomide	100 mg capsule	0.58	28.43	4781	566
Temozolomide	250 mg capsule	1.17	53.74	4512	326
Trastuzumab	440 mg injection	200.15	829.65	315	152
Vincristine	1 mg injection 1 ml	N/A	0.72		

Sources

1. For TNMSC prices, TNMSC website as follows. "Essential Drug 1 Year Rate Contract Details from March 2019" (https://tnmsc.tn.gov.in/user_pages/drugtender.php?drugcat=T18028) and "Essential Drug 1 Year Rate Contract Details from March 2019" (https://tnmsc.tn.gov.in/user_pages/drugtender.php?drugcat=T18028), accessed 11 November 2020
2. For Retail prices, AIOCD-AWACS database (see source Table 8.3)

Notes [a]For these products, the units are not exactly the same. For TNMSC prices, the units are: Carboplatin—10 mg, 45 ml injection; Docetaxel: 120 mg injection; Oxaliplatin: 2mg/ml

[b]INR/USD exchange rate 2019–20 average: Rs. 70.8970

route of supporting local production. As with previous global disease-focused initiatives, the focus has been on reducing the price of imported medicines, with philanthropic support. In 2017 the BMJ reported (Dyer, 2017, cited also in WHO, 2018b, p. 36) on an agreement negotiated by the American Cancer Society and the Clinton Health Access Initiative with Pfizer and Cipla to provide "at or near production cost price" to Ethiopia, Kenya, Nigeria, Rwanda, Uganda and Tanzania the following cancer drugs: docetaxel, doxorubicin, epirubicin, fluorouracil, gemcitabine, leucovorin, methotrexate, and paclitaxel (Pfizer); anastrozole, bleomycin, capecitabine, cytarabine, and vinblastine (Cipla); and carboplatin, cisplatin, and oxaliplatin (both). This was described as "a sustainable model of philanthropy" (Dyer, 2017). Cipla appears to have later dropped out of this initiative.

In 2021, an expanded "Cancer Access Initiative" was announced,[13] with four companies: Biocon Biologics (an Indian biotech), Novartis and Pfizer (innovator companies), and Viatris. The last is now the largest generics multinational, headquartered in the USA, formed by merging the generic arm of Pfizer with Mylan, a large US pharmaceutical company, which subsequently became a large API generic player by taking over an Indian firm, Matrix. The stated aim of the initiative is to generate savings of 60% on the purchase by low- and middle-income countries' governments of chemotherapy and hormonal medication for 30 cancers including a range of breast cancer regimens. The proposed reductions—very welcome in themselves—do indeed illustrate the scope for sustainable price cutting in generic oncology medication.[14]

These initiatives, which involve no technology transfer to African producers, also raise questions about sustainability, and the extent to which they could help to address health security concerns in crises including the recent pandemic and the next (Chapter 2). It is also an open question whether the initiatives, if effective, could undermine the market for local producers of oncology medicines, as has occurred through vertical programmes in the past (Mackintosh et al., 2018a). Some recent writers have characterised this issue as the need to avoid "onco-colonialism" when addressing access to cancer medicines (Hack et al., 2019).

The problem of high private market prices in India, noted above, appears furthermore, to be multiplied for those products when imported into East Africa. One interviewee in Kenya told a personal story. They had recently taken a friend with cancer for treatment in India. On return, they spent KES 45,000 (around USD 400 at current exchange rates), for chemotherapy medication for three months' treatment. He commented:

> While that of course will cost him here around hundred and fifty thousand shillings [USD 1,325] to buy the same medicines. So it is cheaper to go, getting checked, buy medicine and come back.

This story aligns with other evidence of high import and procurement prices for oncology medication in Africa (Ngwa et al., 2022a; WHO, 2018b). If the cost of the imported medicine—by implication in this story, when prescribed in the private sector—was more than three times as high locally as when prescribed in India, then there is market space for local firms to both compete and lower prices.

Local Oncology Manufacturing: Market and Technical Challenges

In interviews with pharmaceutical producers in Tanzania, Kenya and also Uganda, respondents were asked whether they were planning to invest in the production of oncology medication. Just one manufacturer in Kenya stated that they had future plans to produce one anti-cancer medicine. All others said no. All firms saw oncology production as risky, both in practical and financial terms.

One manufacturer emphasised the physical risks:

> Cancer products are cytotoxic, so cancer products are actually killing your cells. ... Because they are cytotoxic compounds, the whole aspect of handling the compounds, preventing cross-contamination, becomes a major critical issue and that's why no regulatory authority will allow you to make cancer products in the same facility where you're making, let's say, paracetamol. So if anybody is serious about manufacturing cancer products, they will have to think of putting up a new facility.

Another experienced manufacturer agreed about the risks involved:

> Cancer is not something that you are going to rush and start taking chances. It's a matter of life and death.

Many manufacturers' concerns focused on technical challenges and the implied scale of new investment. Oncology medication, they noted, required specialist plant and equipment to ensure sterile production of (mainly) intravenous medication. This in turn required very substantial investment, including modularity and partial automation to help keep staff safe, given the toxicity of the products. Greatly enhanced training and quality assurance—major changes in the culture of production processes—were required to achieve this upgrading, including major improvement of waste management capabilities:

> For cytotoxins … [you have] to make sure that they are decontaminated and that the waste is then stored and destroyed in a very specific manner.

One manufacturer in Kenya listed the key challenges for his firm for such a move: identification of the products (tablets, injectables); technology and machinery and the required production environment; methods, technical know-how and sources of inputs. This was a firm that had previously produced injectables but had then stopped; the interviewee also had experience of sterile production elsewhere. He reflected on his experience:

> Sterility is the issue and the requirements for sterile. … I know the challenges that are there. The kind of capital outlay you need to maintain the sterile environment is really huge and it requires a lot of discipline for you to be able to maintain the standard. So, the environment and the personnel are the main issue … the regulators … understand the seriousness … I would not allow anybody to set up the sterile plant unless they are sure they will maintain the standards.

Another manufacturer in Kenya noted that the infrastructure cost drivers, especially power, were particularly problematic for intravenous (IV) products:

> The main cost comes from two things, the power and the plastic. … plastic uses a lot of power. … if you are paying five times more on power how will you be competitive?

A manufacturer in Tanzania stated that oncology medicines production was possible with an international partner but still constrained by limited local production capabilities. These technical challenges all raised the need for technology transfer and learning from abroad. Table 8.5 lists systematically the challenges identified.

Table 8.5 Challenges for local manufacturing of oncology products

Challenge category	*Detail*
Technological	• Specialist equipment to manage toxic materials • Special plant configuration and contained use • Sources of API • Modularity as a key step in investing in oncology production • Automation as a key risk management approach to minimising contact with toxic raw materials • Cost of automation—and link to return on investment as key trigger for investors
Strategic	• Product portfolio choice and drivers, based on market intelligence • Information on acceptable cost of goods (COGS) and profitability parameters
Environmental Management	• Managing toxicity of production facilities • Waste management
Skills upgrading	• Management and documentation of sterile production • Staff training in handling sterile toxic products • Quality control and assurance • Laboratory skills
Markets or market signalling for investment	• Market intelligence • Market organisation, innovative procurement • Pre-orders, procurement contracts
Platform technologies	• Leveraging certain industry platforms, e.g. biosimilars (see Chapter 10)

(continued)

Table 8.5 (continued)

Challenge category	*Detail*
Government industry and trade policy	• Support for accreditation and export success • Commitment to local purchasing in practice • Trade policy that does not disadvantage local manufacturing against importing • Inter-government collaboration to guarantee regional procurement, to ensure sufficient market size for a local facility • Active problem-solving support for new investment and upgrading
Finance	• Affordable long-term finance for CAPEX (capital expenditure) for building new cGMP-compliant plants or upgrading existing plant • Affordable short-term finance for OPEX (operating expenditure) for day-to-day operations • Early-stage finance (grants, etc.) for technology incubation and maturation • Incentives for local manufacture and export (tax credit schemes, export guarantees, export pay-outs)

Source Authors

This is a formidable list. However, the challenges are not unfamiliar, and in most cases, the technical and managerial capabilities to address these challenges already exist in East African manufacturing. Technology transfer will require overseas partner firms, using a variety of potential institutional forms including new investors, joint ventures or licensing relationships. Long-term patient capital and government facilitation of the technology transfer are essential.

The list also includes challenges of market organisation and integration also addressed in Chapter 7. A new facility for intravenous oncology medication might cost, it was estimated by one interviewee, USD 20–25 million. Hence, the scale of demand, and the need to consolidate demand and overcome market fragmentation, were seen as key to estimating profitability and return on investment. Manufacturers told us that they lacked knowledge of the choice of portfolio of products to produce, notably because both quantification of current use, and knowledge of treatment guidelines, were still limited among industrialists. This brings us back to the key role of procurement. More broadly, the formidable list of risks and challenges suggests a need for a major initiative from African governments to change the local market and—as it turns out—the international policy "weather" for local oncology manufacturing.

The Role of the Health System in Building Local Oncology Supply Chains

If health system policymakers and clinicians in East Africa are looking for scope to build more robust oncology medicines supply chains, including potentially local producers, then the health system needs to be an active player in building the local oncology market and industrial options. There are two strands to the initiative required: one international, one local.

The international aspect is clearly illustrated by the experience of one local manufacturer. Interested in investigating the scope for local oncology production, pre-Covid-19, he recounted a discussion with WHO health experts in which he was strongly counselled against the initiative. Their argument went, he recalled, that African countries should first learn to manage these drugs well within their health systems before moving on to local manufacture. A list of the required improvements in health system oncology capability included handling of drugs, staff safety in using toxic chemicals, avoiding cross-contamination during treatment, and managing waste.

In this, the WHO experts were reflecting a wider international viewpoint. For example, speaking in 2016, Pascal Soriot, head of AstraZeneca, is recorded as arguing that "there is no point giving free cancer drugs to Africa...[because]...it is not only a question of medicine, it is a question of infrastructure" (Lancet Oncology Editorial, 2017).

These are undoubted challenges in local cancer services, of which East African health professionals are keenly aware. An interviewee in one Kenyan cancer centre noted that many nurses were afraid of mixing and handling oncology drugs, being aware of their toxicity, and finding the protective clothing alarming, commenting: "There is a lot of stigma, when it comes to the preparation and administration of chemotherapy". That oncology clinic had initially improvised a filtration and extraction system with a chimney and ventilation. Recently they had received a donated biosafety cabinet for mixing medication but had found that the filters needed very frequent changing because the lack of air conditioning required open windows, hence dusty air. They have requested an air conditioner but, the interviewee reflected:

> Things happen very slowly at the County level, so we are still waiting. So at the moment we still use the filter and the extractor, and I think if we still had the biosafety cabinet [i.e. it was functioning] we would still need to utilize the chimney because we are getting more and more patients for chemo, so we need to mix more and more chemos and the biosafety cabinet is such that one person can mix.

This discussion shows a clear local awareness of the need for secure handling, and the pressures that can undermine safety as patient numbers increase. It also reflects the importance of attention to the full range of requirements—including spare parts and working environment—needed to support equipment donation.

The interviews with health professionals attest to commitment to improving care at the facility level, and there are a number of initiatives underway in both Tanzania and Kenya to improve oncology management. The health facilities are treating rising numbers of cancer patients and expanding their capabilities, despite pandemic constraints. The number and range of cancer treatment centres are rising, and continuing weaknesses in the health system are being addressed, in some cases through external clinical partnerships. More generally, there has been push-back from African clinicians in recent years against these negative international views of local health system capability, emphasising local knowledge, training and skills to administer chemotherapy, and citing the active accreditation of facilities treating patients with chemotherapy drugs through inspection by health ministry regulators, using checklists to inspect handling and management of cytotoxic drugs.[15] Current international literature reflects more positive and supportive international attention to improving cancer care in Africa (Ngwa et al., 2022a) while health system challenges are not regarded internationally as an impediment to expanding access to medication.

Furthermore, challenges of oncology drug management at the health facility level constitute a curious argument to deploy against local manufacture of these medicines. Indeed, this argument could be turned on its head. A manufacturing firm establishing oncology drugs production would have a strong incentive to work with oncologists, oncology nurses and other health experts to ensure that shared challenges such as keeping staff safe, avoiding cross-contamination, and managing waste disposal were applied right along the supply chain from producer to patient, since this would affect their accreditation and regulatory status. Such a firm would develop the technological and linkage capabilities to assist and support users in upgrading their knowledge and proficiencies while simultaneously learning from their users.

While the health system challenges are undoubtedly considerable, so are the potential benefits of local production. Manufacturers are aware that their employment and their own procurement of inputs feed back into and support the wider economy (Chapter 7). There are common skills to be developed along the entire supply chain in handling and using these medicines. Technology transfer can support manufacture, logistics handling, quality assurance and appropriate use right along the chain. Building the capability of one segment of the supply chain can feed back into and strengthen capabilities in another segment.

As the Indian evidence suggests, however, interventions are needed to consolidate demand and procurement and ensure procurement is used to manage the market. These interventions require collaboration between government and health system stakeholders, both public and private. In Tanzania, the National Health Insurance Fund covers cancer treatment and actively negotiates medicines prices with local pharmacies, achieving price reductions of around 25%.[16] Collaboration such as the Kenyan forum to create the essential medicines list and treatment guidelines that brought together public and private sectors can be further built on to develop market intelligence for investors. Procurement commitments, to buy for a number of years ahead, and consolidated procurement for regional markets require government initiative. Indeed cytotoxic cancer products are perfect candidates for public pool procurement initiatives, along the lines of the Tanzanian Medical Stores Department's lead role in the SADC pooled procurement initiative (Chapter 7). Health policy makers could also collaborate with manufacturers to refine a working list of the most appropriate medications for manufacturers' consideration: one interviewee, for example, suggested a small set of medicines widely used for the most prevalent conditions such as breast and cervical cancer. Oncology medicines production is a good example of the scope and imperative, discussed in Chapter 7, to raise industrial ambitions, including identifying local firms' potential markets as regional and international within and outside Africa.

Conclusion

In the context of continuing and rapidly increasing need and demand for cancer medicines, the emergence of local manufacturers could help improve access, price and supply chain stability. The lessons from India identify scope for competitive production and pricing within currently high-priced and fragmented international markets. Indian experience also illustrates the scale of pricing benefits to be gained from organised larger scale procurement, even in relation to market prices in the Indian market. Scaling up procurement, however, requires collaboration between public, non-profit and private sector users, and between national governments, in order to increase orders and exert more market leverage on prices. The pricing benefits will then be felt region-wide. Philanthropic supply offers, welcome in the short term, should be carefully scrutinised for medium-term impact and against the building up over time of local manufacturing capability.

Regulatory regimes can be scrutinised for impediments to rapid registration of imports where desirable, and clarity on technical requirements. Production of generic oncology medication can build effectively on the existing technological capabilities of local firms, creating skills that can also feed into health system capabilities. Major new plant investments are required for cytotoxic medicines production in secure high-quality production systems, and this will require active government support at the start and appropriate regulatory frameworks. This is a policy field where incremental and collaborative innovation between health, industrial, regulatory and research actors can generate large benefits for patients and the broader industrial economy. There is an interest coalition that can be built locally to raise the local manufacturing ambition in oncology.

Notes

1. Figures for each country are from the most recent national household budget surveys, see references. Sources for exchange rates for stated dates: Bank of Tanzania historical rates, https://www.bot.go.tz/ExchangeRate/previous_rates; Central Bank of Kenya

historical exchange rates, https://www.centralbank.go.ke/rates/forex-exchange-rates/, both consulted 16/08/22.
2. https://www.aspenapi.com/api-portfolio/ last consulted 04/10/2023
3. https://aspenshare.co.za/v/rl9I0xCKbcwJig4Frgag last consulted 04/10/2023
4. https://www.aspenpharma.com/high-potency-cytotoxics/ consulted 14/07/2022.
5. https://comtrade.un.org/.
6. 6-digit classification 300,490; major product groups such as penicillin (300,410), other antibiotics (300,420), anti-malarials (300,460) are listed separately.
7. Author's personal experience.
8. Author's calculation (Chaudhuri) from DGCI&S data base, https://tradedx.cmie.com/, June 2021.
9. Calculated from the DGCI&S database (from: https://tradedx.cmie.com/, June 2022).
10. https://ec.europa.eu/commission/presscorner/detail/en/QANDA_21_521.
11. https://ec.europa.eu/commission/presscorner/detail/en/QANDA_21_521 last consulted 20/02/2023
12. https://www.gov.za/speeches/media-statement-commissioner-investigation-manufacturers-cancer-drugs-13-jun-2017-0000 consulted 15/08/2022
13. https://www.clintonhealthaccess.org/chai-and-acs-announce-agreement-to-expand-cancer-access-partnership/.
14. Details of the initiative, including prices charged, amounts actually ordered and received to date, and the incentives for firms to sustain delivery, were not found to be available at the time of writing.
15. It was also noted that radiotherapy cannot be given without permission from the national regulator: the Tanzania Atomic Energy Commission.
16. Author's personal knowledge (Ngoma).

PART IV

Industrial Innovation and Industrial Policy

Findings from the ICCA project and Covid-19 pandemic experience accentuated the importance of often underrated dynamics and intricate linkages across local production, local innovation capabilities, business models, policy, entrepreneurship and local health security. This section identifies the practical scope for improving these linkages to enhance production and health benefits from medical devices and diagnostics, biologics and morphine manufacture.

Chapter 9 shows that in the medical devices and diagnostics sector in India, early stage financial support from Indian government schemes, financial institutions, universities and venture capital is instrumental in supporting entrepreneurship. However, firms struggle to capture value in later stages of technology commercialisation because of lack of last-mile investment, medical culture and barriers to accessing the public healthcare market. Implications are drawn for industrial support in African contexts.

Chapter 10 argues for the need to transition local production capabilities to biologics. Biologics offer a broader portfolio of therapies. Biologics such as monoclonal antibodies are an incremental innovation for current vaccine manufacturers and have lower learning and transition costs compared to chemical drugs. However, biologics production is not only a technological project, but is also political and economic, feeding into geo-politics debates.

Chapter 11 identifies the benefits of industrial policy clarity and simplification for improving access to morphine palliation in India. The argument is that some societies need no new science or manufacturing to solve health challenges, yet problems persist as a result of institutional gaps between industrial and health policies. Resolution of these institutional gaps is important for removing uncertainty facing public and private firms that need to invest in technological capabilities and have clear pathways to market for their products.

CHAPTER 9

Emerging Business Models in Cancer Diagnostic Startups in India and Lessons for African Countries

Dinar Kale, Smita Srinivas, and Geoffrey Banda

Introduction

India has a dynamic and innovative MedTech (medical technology) sector that has been growing despite an economic environment characterised by policy vacuum, regulatory lags and a low-value market for their outputs. So how are the firms driving this growth, and what are the supporting ecosystems for entrepreneurship and progressing innovations to the market?

D. Kale (✉)
The Open University, Milton Keynes, UK
e-mail: dinar.kale@open.ac.uk

S. Srinivas
Bengaluru, India

G. Banda
University of Edinburgh, Edinburgh, UK

G. Banda et al. (eds.), *Cancer Care in Pandemic Times: Building Inclusive Local Health Security in Africa and India*, International Political Economy Series,
https://doi.org/10.1007/978-3-031-44123-3_9

Over the last two decades, the Indian healthcare sector has made a gradual epidemiological transition, driven by a shift in disease burden from communicable to non-communicable diseases (NCDs). Among NCDs, cancer has emerged as a wicked problem due to the high cost of treatment, difficulty in early diagnosis and lack of comprehensive cancer control strategies. The mortality rate in India due to cancer increased by 6% between 2012 and 2014, while incidence from cancer registry data does not show an alarming rise relative to high-income countries (IARC, 2020). This emerging focus on NCDs and cancer has created a demand for affordable diagnostic technologies to detect and monitor cancer. The rising income levels among the Indian middle class, ageing population and private sector investment in healthcare have generated a significant demand for MedTech startups for technologies and services that improve access to cancer detection and monitoring services. The startups bridge the gap between need and effective availability.

However, the emergence of dynamic tech startups raises questions about the policy environment driving the growth of the Indian diagnostics sector. From an economic development standpoint, the role of learning in diagnostics firms has not been well understood compared to a mature body of scholarship on Indian pharmaceuticals and vaccines (Kale & Wield, 2018; Srinivas & Kale, 2022). This chapter focuses on business models adopted by emerging Indian innovative medical devices and diagnostic startups operating in cancer care. A business model mediates between the choice of technology and firm performance; as such, the selection and development of the right technology is a matter of a business model decision regarding openness and user engagement. This understanding of the business model provides an appropriate construct to explore Indian innovative startups' strategies to survive and succeed in a policy vacuum, low-value high-volume market and resource-constrained environment.

Cancer diagnosis and treatment are challenging issues for LIMCs. In India, between 1990 and 2016, the number of cancer deaths increased by 112% and disease incidence increased by 48.7% (GBD, 2017). In 2018, India had 2.25 million cancer patients and recorded more than 750 000 deaths due to cancer. It is suggested that every year, over 1.15 million people are diagnosed with cancer and close to 10% of Indians are at risk of developing cancer before they reach 75 (Kashyap, 2019). According to the Indian Council of Medical Research (ICMR), breast, cervical, oral and lung cancers constitute 41% of the cancer burden (Mathur et al., 2020).

It is also observed that India has a lower incidence of cancer than the US and several European countries. Still, mortality is much higher due to poor early diagnosis and late treatment (Verma, 2014). This need for early cancer diagnosis in India has fuelled the emergence of MedTech startups focused on creating access to cancer diagnosis and access. However, the policy- and market-constrained environment also makes it imperative for these startups to develop an appropriate business model for survival and growth whilst navigating local resource constraints.

From 2010 onwards, India witnessed a significant increase in medical devices and diagnostic startups developing innovative solutions to create access to appropriate cancer care for local populations. The emergence of this dynamic sector raises questions about how Indian startups are driving the growth of the medical diagnostic industry in an economic environment dominated by policy vacuum, regulatory lags and a low-value market. We engaged with the question by focusing on the business models adopted by the innovative Indian startups in this sector. This chapter employs case studies of three cancer diagnostic firms to explore their business models and their relevance for startups operating in other LIMCs. Primary data was collected through detailed open-ended semi-structured interviews with medical device and diagnostic firms in India, including interviewing the founders of the two startups that are part of this study. Our research highlights the importance of the state as an 'informal' provider of venture capital and international collaborations to plug the finance and knowledge gaps, respectively. This chapter concludes with a discussion on what business models are relevant and effective for firms operating in resource-constrained environments of LMICs.

MedTech Startups in Developing Countries and Systemic Scarcities

MedTech covers a wide range of medical devices, equipment, software and diagnostics companies, forming a significant and critical segment of the healthcare technology industry. MedTech is a focus sector for startups in India. A study of technology incubators in India showed that over 25% of incubated startups were in MedTech, the second largest industry after IT (Mukherjee, 2022). There are numerous examples of scientists, engineers or clinicians starting a venture by identifying an unmet clinical need based on their domain knowledge and understanding of the market gap. Several steps are involved in moving from identifying a need to a market launch, each of which requires considerable expertise and resources.

In high-income countries, what drove the rise of MedTech startups is the financial capacity to pay for innovations, ageing populations that create demand for sophisticated medical technologies, and more organised procurement systems that facilitate rapid adoption of innovative products into health systems (Kale & Wield, 2018). However, LMICs provide a different challenge. Innovation is a context-driven process; innovations and technologies solving a problem elsewhere may not be best for a different situation. LMICs' markets present growth opportunities, but governments and consumers have limited financial ability to afford innovative but expensive products sold with high margins by emerging startups in high-income countries. The constrained markets, limitation of medical professionals and lack of basic infrastructure create a need for a solution more appropriate to local conditions. Srinivas and Sutz (2008, p. 130) elaborate on systemic scarcity observed in LMICs markets by pointing out that "scarcity conditions include problems at the level of infrastructure that is missing or is not up to date, of access to materials and equipment of the required quality or accuracy, of institutional support for the building of endogenous capacities, of enough people with appropriate skills to run projects or discuss ideas, and of money to rely on well-known solutions". Within this context, healthcare technology firms developing technology without considering these systemic scarcities will struggle to make a desirable impact.

This discussion highlights that the institutional environment of LMICs is characterised by systemic institutional scarcities. In contrast, traditionally observed resource gaps are incidental scarcities that may be filled by funding (Srinivas & Sutz, 2008). The broader set of systemic scarcities makes collaborative action complex in medical diagnostics (Kale, 2019b). Within this context, our focus is on the emerging business models adopted and continuing institutional gaps faced by Indian startups in cancer care. Building on that, we further investigate what business models are relevant and effective for firms operating in the resource-constrained environments of LMICs.

The Business Model in Context

In many industries and sectors, there is growing awareness that for technological innovation to be successful, the business model must be an integral part of the process. Indeed, the business model concept is so vital that it can be argued that "a mediocre technology pursued within a great business model may be more valuable than a great technology exploited via a mediocre business model" (Chesbrough, 2010, p. 354). The business model is defined as a system that solves the problem of identifying who is (or are) the customer(s), engaging with their needs, delivering satisfaction and monetising the value (Baden-Fuller & Haefliger, 2013). A business model can be viewed as the logic of the company; how it operates to create and extract value for its stakeholders (Casadesus-Masanell & Ricart, 2010).

Hwang and Christensen (2008) point out value proposition, processes, resources and profit formula as four critical components of the business model. The value proposition, an affordable product or service that helps a customer perform a particular job effectively, represents a starting point for a business model. Firms bring together required resources such as people, equipment, finance, raw materials and so on to deliver the value proposition. Hwang and Christensen (2008) further suggest that firms create organisational processes and practices to create an efficient way of making these resources work together repeatedly. These routines are then ingrained in the business model. They further point out that a profit formula emerges based on the costing of resources and processes required to deliver the value proposition, profit margins, volumes and pricing.

Building on these four components, Winterhalter et al. (2017a) highlight value proposition, creation and capture as three interlinked tenets of the business model. The value proposition refers to critical attributes of a product or service that resolves specific or multiple needs of a customer in an affordable way. In contrast, value is created by identifying an innovative way to develop, manufacture, or deliver the product to the customer. The value created is then captured by product sales—apart from invaluable marketing effects (Table 9.1).

In the healthcare industry, the business model must consider the unique characteristics of the healthcare market, such as the absence of a retail market for products and intense regulatory demands on products and services. These characteristics result in multiple business models that

Table 9.1 Key tenets of the business model for healthcare innovations in LMICs

Value Proposition	Value creation	Value capture
Affordability and access to healthcare at low costs Patients do not have to travel to remote hospitals. Easy to use Efficiency gains for the healthcare system Low maintenance and repair Undiagnosed need or new to the market	Radical/Incremental/ architectural innovation through: Engineering Use and sourcing of materials and Production sites Reaching target market	Product sales, service subscription or both Cost reduction for patients, health system and business firms

Source Modified by the authors from (Winterhalter et al., 2017b, p. 7)

coexist with each other. These include a service model involving institutions that diagnose and solve the problem (hospitals), a product model involving firms transforming input resources into products of greater value and a hybrid model where a product and service model are delivered together through user networks (Hwang & Christensen, 2008).

In LMIC contexts, healthcare firms adopt business models with a primary focus on creating value in low-income environments dominated by the weak institutional environment and missing infrastructure (Hoskisson et al., 2013; Landau et al., 2016). These challenges and constraints force firms to adopt business models that create value for the business, people and social environment (London et al., 2010). As a result, in resource-constrained settings, business models serve their target customers and improve the entire healthcare system in the respective target market.

Table 9.2 Startups under study

Startup	*Year established*	*Nature of equipment*	*Key cancer areas*	*Market*
Sascan	2015	OralScan using imaging technology	Oral cancer	Product and service
AiNDRA	2012	AiNDRA point of care based on AI	Cervical cancer	Product
Panacea	1999	Bhabhatron-II, an Advanced Digital radiotherapy Telecobalt machine	All types of cancer	Product

Within the Indian context, the rising significance of data, the launch of the digitalisation initiative by the Indian government and the increasing per capita income have accelerated the emergence of startups focused on creating affordable diagnostics. Moreover, the launch of a range of new R&D subsidies, early-stage grants by the Indian government and the availability of both Indian and foreign private investment underscore the need to evaluate business models in India.

Case Studies

This section presents three case studies of cancer diagnostics devices developed by Indian startups. All devices were developed by scientists or engineers using a diverse set of technologies targeting different types of low-resource context challenges (Table 9.1). The information was collected from secondary sources and semi-structured interviews with the founders of two firms (Table 9.2).

Sascan

Oralscan, developed by Sascan, is an innovative diagnostic device that uses imaging technology to diagnose oral cancer in resource-constrained urban and rural areas. Sascan adopted a business model comprising product and service aspects to capture the value.

Sascan was founded in 2015 by Dr Subhash Narayanan, a physicist with expertise in laser technology and Dr Ruhi Agarwala, who was a public health expert. The startup was incubated at the Technology

Business Incubator (TiMED) wing of Sree Chitra Tirunal Institute for Medical Sciences & Technology (SCTIMST), a leading medical diagnostic centre and device development institute in India. Startup financial support came from government investment schemes; the Biotechnology Industry Research Assistance Council (BIRAC) based at the Department of Science & Technology (DST), the National Initiative for Developing and Harnessing Innovations (NIDHI) and Kerala StartUp Mission. In later years, Sascan also received investment from Unicorn India ventures. One of the founders commented:

> I was already doing work in that area [medical diagnostics] and had publications to show; it was easier for me to get a fellowship under the BIRAC grant, and once I got that, it was mandatory that we start an entity to get the funding, so we started a company with some of my colleagues from the same (author interview, 2019)

Sascan focused on the detection of oral cancer. The diagnostic technique used for oral screening was unreliable, and oral potentially malignant lesions (OPMLs) would often go undetected in the early stages (Kashyap, 2019). The existing clinical practice involves the detection of oral cancer via visual inspection of the oral cavity by a clinician using torchlight. If required, it is followed by biopsy-guided histopathological analysis. It was also observed that clinicians find it difficult to locate the optimal site for a biopsy based on conventional oral examination. Sascan identified this need in the market and focused on developing a handheld imaging device to screen and detect OPMLs. This need shaped the key value proposition for the firm and the main driving force for the development of Oralscan. One of the founders highlights that the device's novelty comes from using the intraoral camera to capture oral malignant cells. Oralscan combines the use of a highly sensitive intraoral camera with a fluorescence technique to get a correct diagnosis of oral cancer. This was the novelty of the product, and it received a patent in India. The proprietary software helps to identify the most appropriate site for taking a biopsy, thereby assisting in the diagnosis of malignancy and reducing patient discomfort that might result from inaccurate biopsy-taking procedures.

Sascan has received the ISO 13485 and CE certification for the Oralscan, and the device has undergone multi-centric trials covering six hospitals across the country. However, one of the founders acknowledges significant challenges, such as patient recruitment, doctors' attitudes and local culture in conducting clinical studies to validate the device. He pointed out:

> Again, the problem was getting patients. Oral cancer, per se, is a poor man's disease. Even though some rich people get it; so those kinds of patients were hard to get. We did the study for nearly 3-4 months, and we couldn't get many numbers, so we had to stop the study there and had to go for some other studies, which could give us better numbers. People are reluctant to go for cancer screening. That is a bigger problem for us. (author interview, 2019)

These challenges in patient recruitment and doctors' attitudes towards the device have implications for the market acceptance of the product. One of the critical obstacles observed was the attitude of doctors to the use of the device. It became evident during the clinical trials that some doctors were not keen as they felt that they could spot malignant sites without the help of the device and conduct a biopsy based on their experience in the field. One of the founders commented:

> Nobody realises that the mortality rates of oral cancer are more than 50% in the country. Why? People should admit to their deficiencies—doctors may never admit that they took a wrong biopsy. That is their fallacy. I don't know how to address this issue. When we start the sales, we may have resistance like this—we feel that over a period of time, we will be able to make it successful. (author interview, 2019)

Sascan is overcoming these market challenges and capturing value from innovation by employing a business model that combines social concern with profitability. One of the founders explained:

> Both have to work simultaneously - social concern and profitability. With that in mind, we have different types of business plans and schemes. One is to sell the device directly to the hospitals for biopsy guidance. We feel that the direct sales model can work. But we also plan to have a pay-per-use model – where we would give the device at a much lower cost on a pay-per-use for each screen; they give us some money in return. That is long-term revenue. We have for NGOs that want to use the device for programmes and screening camps – we give it on a monthly rental basis. These different models take care of different categories. (author interview, 2019)

Sascan frames the broad value proposition from a social concern and profitability perspective with utility accruing to the physicians/clinicians, hospitals and ultimately the patient. Given the cost barriers, Sascan proposed a business model innovation: the pay-per-use model. This model overcomes the need to spend significant money (capital expenditure) upfront, especially for small-sized health facilities in urban and rural areas. With this model, these health facilities do not incur huge costs to acquire the equipment and only need to manage operating expenditures. For the entrepreneur, the value capture comes from the use of their equipment by many small and medium-sized facilities and a steady income from their equipment. Thus, the value proposition to the clinician or health facility is access to expensive machines with no huge upfront investment, plus patients accessing care. The entrepreneur captures value through a steady revenue stream from a pay-per-use arrangement.

AiNDRA

The AiNDRA system, developed by AiNDRA, is an innovative diagnostic system that employs artificial intelligence (AI) technologies to facilitate early, affordable and accurate cervical cancer diagnosis in a clinical setting. It provides an alternative to the existing gold standard method of cervical cancer diagnosis and helps overcome the need for a trained pathologist.

AiNDRA was founded in 2012 by Adarsh Natarajan (CEO) and Abhishek Mishra to develop an innovative diagnostic device that facilitates the screening and detection of cervical cancer in women at an affordable cost. AiNDRA received funding from the Karnataka government and some private philanthropic foundations. One of the founder's commented:

> We have been supported by the government of Karnataka as well—one of the early grantees of the ELEVATE 100 program. We were also incubated out of the Bangalore bio-innovation centre (BBC), which is directly supported by the government of Karnataka. (author interview, 2019)

Building on this initial financial support, AiNDRA received further funding from Villgro Innovations Foundation, Indo-US Science and Technology Forum and Millennium Alliance, which helped them develop computational pathology tools for the early detection of cervical cancer.

In India, the screening and detection of cervical cancer is a complicated and costly process. It has been suggested that it takes around 4–6 weeks in India and costs approximately INR 2000 (about USD 26.54) for the entire process from pap smear sample collection to report delivery, depending on the sample collection location (Balaji, 2019). The main hindrance is the limited availability of trained pathologists. It creates a significant challenge for early diagnosis of cervical cancer, resulting in approximately 74, 000 deaths annually, accounting for 1/3rd of the burden of cervical cancer deaths globally (Diamond, 2018). Early detection and treatment are vital for those diagnosed with cervical cancer. It is certainly possible to reduce the number of deaths from cervical cancer as the early detection of cancerous cells can result in a positive outcome with an effective and low-cost treatment. AiNDRA sensed an opportunity to develop an AI-based platform that can provide an accessible and quick point-of-care diagnosis for cervical cancer. CEO Adarsh Natarajan was reported as commenting:

> Given the hype that technologies like AI and CRISPR have generated over the last couple of years, we see an increased awareness of the potential these technologies hold in the domain of oncology. This awareness has resulted in an easier adoption cycle for products that use this technology and solve the problem effectively. (Cheema, 2020)

AiNDRA collaborated with researchers at the Indian Institute of Technology Mandi (IIT M) to develop AI-based algorithms that enable the point-of-care device to undertake automatic screening for cervical cancer. The conventional system of diagnosing cervical cancer involves a 'pap smear test' in which cells are removed from the cervix are examined by a pathologist under the microscope. While this test has been the gold standard in screening for cervical cancer detection all over the world and has helped early detection, it also involves subjective analysis and interpretation. This test has therefore been associated with risks of the wrong diagnosis, and few studies have shown the accuracy of the Pap smear test to range between 60% and 85% (Balaji, 2019). It also involves patients travelling to the hospitals to take the tests, which is challenging for women living in rural areas or geographically distant regions that lack testing facilities. This creates barriers to testing and further delaying the results. In contrast, AiNDRA's point-of-care system is portable and removes the subjectivity in pap smear tests for diagnosis.

In the system, biological samples are stained by an autostainer, converted into a digital image and then analysed by AI algorithms to differentiate between cancerous cells and healthy cells (Diamond, 2018).

AiNDRA's collaborator analysed the Pap smear images provided by the startup and characterised them as "normal" and "potentially cancerous". They developed a computer programme that could differentiate between the two. One of the collaborators was reported explaining:

> We could demonstrate performance improvements over some of the contemporary methods, with relatively simpler and arguably more efficient methods. (Pharmabiz, 2019)

The developed algorithm is based on the deep learning paradigm of artificial intelligence and can be used to deal with a large amount and variability in data. The platform can sift through large numbers of samples and only escalate high-risk cases. In a country with a high patient-to-pathologist ratio, this has the potential to increase workflow efficiency, reduce costs and save lives (Diamond, 2018). One of the collaborators added:

> Given the shortage of pathologists in India, these algorithms will help in automating the process of screening Pap -Smear images. Thus, there will be a significant reduction in time spent by the pathologist, thereby reducing cost and improving the screening accuracy. (Pharmabiz, 2019)

The value proposition from the quote and example above is the utility of the technology, its efficacy and, more importantly, its portability. This approach reduces the cost per sample, has higher accuracy (reducing subjectivity) and shorter time for the patient to get their results (1–2 hours) instead of 5–6 weeks. Thus, the value proposition is at three levels: the health facility benefits, the clinicians benefit in using a more accurate and portable technology, and the patient accesses their results within a very short time, which enhances the patient experience and reduces their costs on transportation if they live far away from the health centre.

Further, this screening can be done on-site at a clinic, eliminating the need for the tedious process of manual staining and the transport of large batches of samples to distant laboratories. As a result, a patient is told if they have cancerous lesions within 1–2 hours instead of 5–6 weeks (Balaji, 2019). The collaborator highlighted the practical advantages:

> The difference between a conventional system and Aindra's point-of-care system is that the latter is portable and can be taken to potential patients. In the conventional system, the people have to visit the pathology laboratory to get themselves screened. (Pharmabiz, 2019)

AiNDRA applied for an international patent for the device and algorithm in 2016. The device prototypes have undergone clinical testing at some leading hospitals in Southern India and were found to be 88% accurate. AiNDRA has launched the product in the Indian market focusing on multi-component products and service offerings. But there have been significant challenges in realising the potential. One of the founders' commented:

> After initial seeding, which helps startups develop a proof of concept but from the proof of concept to the product actually being used by beneficiaries or customers - there is a long journey that these startups are required to traverse through. What many of us felt is that there are not enough linkages in the ecosystem for entrepreneurs to get from point A to Z. There is no concerted way to fast-track the innovations that they themselves have spent money on and they have found in their own healthcare systems network. We have noticed that it is difficult after that point for us to actually see things happening in terms of us getting a pilot that can become a precursor to a larger role – nothing of the sort exists as mechanized. (author interview, 2019)

Stressing the need for a stronger government role in screening for cervical cancer, one of the founders explained,

> So far, from what we have seen in our space in cervical cancer, it is largely not an effort that has been driven by the government healthcare system. It has mostly been NGOs who are trying to reach out to the larger section of society to get them to screen for breast cancer or cervical cancer, or any of the preventive conditions. It need not be necessarily driven by the government healthcare system, but it can be nudged through the private sectors as well. (author interview, 2019)

AiNDRA's value proposition is to create a diagnostic product that provides a significantly improved alternative in terms of accuracy, cost and time compared to the existing method of detection of cervical cancer in India. The firm has created value by employing AI and machine learning tools using local collaborators and research institutes to develop the devices. However, the firm is struggling to capture the value due to entry barriers in the market and a lack of government support in driving screening and detection initiatives.

Panacea Medical Technologies

Bhabhatron-II, an Advanced Digital radiotherapy Telecobalt machine developed and manufactured by Panacea Medical Technologies in India, improves automation, removes uncertainties and overcomes the need for trained manpower to operate it.

Panacea Medical technologies was founded in 1999 by a senior scientist and technocrat Mr G V Subrahmanyam, along with a group of technocrats with the aim of creating access to radiotherapy. Mr Subrahmanyam had a strong connection with IIT Madras, and that proved a critical breeding ground for developing ideas for developing technologically superior solutions to improve cancer care. The startup received financial support from a US-based venture capital fund called 'New Enterprise Association' from the early stage. Mr Subrahmanyam explained the motivation for entering the challenging area of radiotherapy,

> One single item that has inspired me and another two colleagues who started this is about making more access to radiotherapy. This is about 20 years back when we started this venture. We understand that at that point of time, we were India focused because India was having a lot of inaccessibility to radiotherapy and cancer therapy in general. (ICCA India podcast series, 2021)

Radiotherapy treatment machines are expensive and need extensive maintenance. Further, it requires trained professionals who know how to handle these machines and also understand the impact of radiation on cancerous cells. India and other LIMCs suffer from a lack of resources and trained manpower to operate the equipment. Panacea prioritised engaging with these two issues by developing a machine that is affordable and reduces the need for trained manpower to operate the machines. Mr Subramanyam explained that:

> India and LIMCs do not have the capex [capital expenditure resources] as well as the opex [operational expenditure resources] money to manufacture such a complicated machine. Most of these countries neither have trained

> manpower. These three items that you have to look at when you want to make access to radiotherapy to every person across in their domestic environment. (ICCA India podcast series, 2021)

The company faced some key challenges in their efforts to emerge as the only Asian company making radiology and radiotherapy equipment. Sweden's Elekta and Varian Medical Systems of the US are the leading two companies that dominate the $10 billion sectors of radiology and radiotherapy. The first product developed by the company was a radiation device based on brachytherapy, invasive radiation therapy for treating cancer. However, the company had to shelve the product four months after the launch as the radioactive isotopes, which were designed for those machines, were removed from medical use by regulators across the world. It was a big setback and resulted in two co-founders leaving the startup.

Despite these setbacks, the company started working with India's leading atomic research centre, the Bhabha Atomic Research Centre (BARC) and Society for Applied Microwave Electronic Engineering and Research (SAMEER) to design the tele-cobalt radiotherapy unit and linear accelerator. The collaboration focused on developing a machine that can be used in resource-constrained conditions without trained manpower. Mr Subramanyam explained that,

> The cancer patient is in many situations in these countries which have been our focus area has not able to travel to the metro city, and therefore the treatment is not even started for such people, and that is what is the basis on which we have looked at innovations on how we can work this machine to deliver in conditions of where is no manpower. (ICCA India podcast series, 2021)

Panacea invested in identifying ways to improve automation, remove uncertainties and make every delivery the same irrespective of the skills sets of people that will operate these machines in urban and rural centres. In 2006, Bhabhatron-II, an Advanced Digital radiotherapy Telecobalt machine, was commercialised. The company took six years to design, develop, manufacture and get regulatory approval to develop the product. This device managed to strike a balance between precisely targeted radiation therapy and the peaceful use of atomic energy. Mr Subramanyam highlighted the value proposition associated with Panacea's business model:

> There's nothing like we have brought in a solution which is out of the world but what we are confident is we have brought in a solution which is actually relevant to countries like India or LMICs from the initiation of any project idea or any product idea we take into consideration what the difference between what we will deliver versus what already exists in the market. (ICCA India podcast series, 2021)

By 2020, Panacea had installed this machine in more than 50 Indian hospitals, and the company is seeking to expand to the LMICs market. Mr Subramanyam explained the relevance of products for the LMIC market,

> We have a globally relevant solution today, and that solution is also more focused on affordability. This has made it possible to deliver a solution to LMICs. This has been a focus for the company in the last 20 years, and we continue with that. (ICCA India podcast series, 2021)

The Panacea case represents a significant adaptation of innovation to the local context. Distinguishing the policy menus that support such innovation matters, especially because the industrial policies to support such deepening or diversification of capabilities are not straightforward (Srinivas, 2006).

Analysis and Discussion

This section discusses the factors that catalyse the growth of Indian startups and highlights the issues that create gridlocks for their further development. It also reveals key value-creating attributes associated with their business models and innovative products. Finally, it points out the key implications for other LMICs.

Catalysts and Gridlocks in Indian MedTech Startups

Availability of finance, an ecosystem of incubation and technology institutions, and proximity of entrepreneurs and hospital systems for clinical trials has been critical for catalysing the growth of Indian MedTech startups. At the same time, there are challenges in translational pathways; taking the product to market and navigating dysfunctional public health procurement. This creates gridlocks for seamless development.

The evidence suggests the availability of adequate funding support from the government, venture capitalist and educational institutes. These funding sources have created and supported a vibrant innovation and entrepreneurship culture that led to the rise of dynamic startups in the medical diagnostic sector. Multiple government agencies such as BIRAC C-CCMP (Centre for Cellular and Molecular Platforms), Nidhi Prayas with DST run several funding schemes to support entrepreneurs. It is supplemented by external funders such as Indo-US collaboration funding and international venture capital firms, and internally by industry association schemes, state government schemes and private venture capitalists.

An ecosystem of incubation and technology institutions supported scientists and engineers to turn into entrepreneurs and convert their ideas into prototypes. The premier Indian technical institutes and public research laboratories stimulate the startup culture through funding schemes, inviting successful entrepreneurs on campus and facilitating linkages and collaborations with local industries. The development of prototypes is aided by the proximity of entrepreneurs and the Indian hospital systems. This facilitates user involvement in product development and clinical trials.

However, there is a need for more venture capital institutions, including the private sector, that cover funding for later stages of technology development and launch onto the market. Further, policy and institutional support needed to reduce market entry barriers and avoid the "valley of death" has been missing. The "valley of death" refers to the period where startups are yet to generate revenue and rely on investor funds. This lack of support towards the later end of the commercialisation chain is proving challenging for startups that need to reach a larger market and grow.

The lack of well-functioning health systems and dysfunctional procurement policies create a significant hurdle for startups in scaling up their businesses. One of the entrepreneurs elaborated,

> I was clear that selling to the government is not the first thing that has to happen, but it has to happen at some time if companies have to scale or be able to demonstrate the complete impact of what they are doing. (author interview, 2019)

This highlights the need for support and modification of existing procurement rules that can accelerate access to the market. The absence of an appropriate procurement policy and lack of well-functioning health systems creates significant hurdles for the long-term sustainability of startups. Scarcity-induced innovation recognises that among different types of innovative solutions, only some are best suited to their specific socioeconomic and institutional environment. The government may be indispensable for startups but not always the primary buyer. Lack of procurement agility has resulted in firms that received supportive public funding failing to effectively sell their products into the public health system.

The local healthcare systems need to be primed to buy local medical devices, and purposive policies should be implemented to support local entrepreneurs innovating to meet local market constraints. Innovative procurement by the healthcare sector can serve as an active industry policy to shape the local production of MedTech.

Business Models: Evaluating Value Proposition, Creation and Capture

The evidence highlights value creation based on key facets such as affordability, automation and high processing capabilities, early detection and quick turnaround for results, pay-per-use model—reducing CAPEX for resource-constrained hospitals and lower maintenance needs for cancer treatment machines. We adopt Winterhalter et al. (2017a) value framework (Table 9.1) to categorise these different facets associated with the business model adopted by the firms under study (Tables 9.2 and 9.3).

Each of these firms has a combination of different value propositions associated with its business model. Affordability was the critical value proposition associated with the business model adopted by each firm, but they also combined it with other value propositions. For example, in the case of diagnostic firms, early and accurate detection emerged as a significant value proposition. For example, one of the founders of Sascan explained their value proposition associated with Oralscan as follows:

> Early detection is a key component of reducing the cancer burden in the country. If a device can do that, it is a boon for the doctors and much more for the patient. For the hospital, this may generate less revenue, but for the patient, it is a big support. (author interview, 2019)

Table 9.3 Value proposition, creation and capture

MedTech startups	*Value proposition*	*Engineering*	*Value creation* *Use of sourcing and resourcing*	*Production sites*	*Reaching target market*	*Value capture* *Income*
Sascan	New to market Easy to use Efficiency gains	Reconfiguration of established technologies	Low-cost raw materials in India and China	India	Institutional and individual customers in urban and rural areas in India	Product sales Pay per use
AiNDRA	New to market efficiency gains	Using existing AI technology to develop software-based product for new purpose	Local produc-tion in India	India	Institutional and individual customers in urban and rural areas in India	Pay per use software as service
Panacea	Affordability efficiency gains	Cost saving through using existing technology	Low-cost raw materials In India	India	Institutional customers in urban and rural areas in India and African countries	Product sales

The Oral scan can also guide a clinician to the correct site to take a biopsy. In some cases, the visual impressions are not correct, and it creates a need for the right biopsy to be taken. This biopsy guidance has emerged as the key value proposition for using the oral scan device in urban clinical areas. Panacea combined affordability with efficiency gains through lower maintenance, increasing automation and high procession capabilities.

To achieve these ambitious value propositions, the firms have been creative in their value creation activities. For example, these firms manufactured locally and started creating local suppliers for high-tech components. Mr Subramanyam from Panacea explained:

> We have been focused on all development and manufacturing that happens in Bangalore, but as has been our vision, we have to make things which will work in a very difficult condition. (ICCA India podcast series, 2021)

The value created by the firms was captured mostly by reducing expenses by minimising manufacturing and R&D costs and adopting a creative sales model. Mr Subramanyam suggests,

> One more part which works is there's a bit of planning on how the treatment has to be delivered. If this can be done outside these remote locations, it can be centralised outside the tier 2 city, then it actually delivers the same kind of delivery as received by patients in a metro. If that can be achieved, then it actually means a lot. (ICCA India Podcast, 2021)

These firms are trying to adopt a mix of different sales models that can aid the value capture. For example, one model includes a consortium of providers running a government-approved programme where consortium members own different healthcare initiatives. These different partners then charge for their services on an OPEX model.

However, these firms are facing significant constraints in realising the value captured through sales due to a lack of government procurement. For example, a few of these startups can list their products for public health procurement due to archaic rules about the minimum size of the firms. Despite recent reforms (L1 reforms) in procurement policies, it remains a risky process for small and medium firms, thereby creating an issue of long-term viability.

Implications for Startups in LMICs

The Indian model highlights the influential role of the state, universities and research institutes in funding and support for entrepreneurs in transforming ideas into significant products. The situation with medical device startup companies in Sub-Saharan Africa, though, is characterised by a policy vacuum, a dearth of early-stage funding, incubation hubs and technological upgrading support, difficulty putting new products on the market and having to rely on European governance institutions, which increases regulatory costs.

We interviewed a startup medical devices company based in South Africa, a country with relatively better innovation ecosystem support capabilities. However, the entrepreneur, a surgeon, chronicled the challenges they had trying to access funds from financial institutions. They eventually resorted to raising funds from other surgeons and private funders. Even after raising funds, they struggled to get local sources of medical-grade plastic to use for their device. They eventually collaborated with a local company and incurred the learning costs for the plastics firm acquiring knowledge of the new technologies and importing new equipment. However, their value proposition to the plastics firm was that they were helping them broaden their product offering hence new revenue streams. The plastics company agreed and promised to produce the technology for the medical device at a preferential cost because the medical devices had funded the upgrading to the new technology. Accessing the clinical setting was not difficult for the innovator, given their professional networks and understanding of how to bring surgical-related devices into the hospital. One of their most significant challenges came from having to rely on notified bodies in Europe. The local regulator could inspect their premises and they needed the local standards body to certify their product. However, the local standards body is not a notified body. Thus, the firm had to send their devices to Europe for certification at high cost and considerable delays in terms of getting the product on the market.

Thus, the case studies from India highlight many learning points from the perspective of building an enabling set of agents, institutions and infrastructures required to support technological change and entrepreneurial activity in the medical devices sector and its proportionate and adaptive governance that allows clinicians and health care organisations to deliver better diagnostics and medical devices for the benefit of the patient. In the case of African countries, there has been clear evidence that some startups operating in the fintech sector receive overseas investment and get a valuation of over US$1bn without any financial support from the state (Pilling, 2021).

It has been suggested that the region is ripe for innovation in health and booming with entrepreneurial raw energy but it is let down by the overcautiousness of local financial institutions and the shortage of African venture capital (Pilling, 2021). African policymakers and financial institutions must focus on understanding and supporting new technologies and innovation, even if that means taking risks and confronting vested interests. For instance, working outside the big cities may create logistical hurdles, but the customisation of service delivery may be an essential starting point for innovation. African policymakers and venture capital firms should ensure that entrepreneurs are supported throughout different stages of the product life cycle and not just in the early stages of development. It also shows that African entrepreneurs should focus on ideas rooted in domestic healthcare systems and that can work with local resource constraints.

Conclusions

This chapter demonstrates that Indian startups operating in the MedTech sector have significantly benefitted from financial support offered by government schemes, financial institutions, universities and private venture capitalists. However, these firms are facing significant challenges in capturing value from their innovations due to a diverse set of issues that range from lack of last mile investment, medical culture and entry barriers for accessing the public healthcare market.

The business model framework helps to explain the value proposition, value creation and value capture strategies adopted by Indian startups. India is a unique, fertile ground for firms engaging in different types of innovations. By and large, the firms focusing on developing innovations closer to Indian problems are vibrant and technically proficient, and most are deeply committed to the cause of better diagnostics and outcomes in cancer.

Some of these innovations are adaptations of solutions that already exist in high-income countries but are not available in LMICs. At the same time, other types include innovations for problems mainly posed in LMICs and developed locally. However, only some of these business models are situated in the 'sweet spot' of long-term viability, and few currently have direct access to public health procurement which is an uncertain, risky process for small and medium firms. Unless these startups and innovations grow, LMICs will continuously adapt to the problems framed and solved elsewhere, predominantly in high-income economies.

Similarly, Indian business models—suited to their context—may eventually act in ways that are not always suited to highly diverse African contexts. As of now, Indian firms may have more answers for Kenya and Tanzania than firms from the US, UK, or Europe. As Chapter 6 has also discussed, specific industrial choices must be made to decide what is best suited for the 'Cupboard Full' situation. This is especially critical because emerging business models respond to procurement initiatives or become divorced from public health policy priorities and the need for patient-centric and service-responsive business models (including location, timeliness, specificity and the vagaries of existing electricity, water, roads or other infrastructure availability).

There are clear implications for African policymakers and financial institutions. There is no shortage of entrepreneurial energy and innovative ideas in African countries. Still, the lack of strategic sector funding for innovation and entrepreneurship, linkage with procurement policies and provision of the last-mile support, are issues that need to be resolved if a vibrant medtech sector is to emerge.

CHAPTER 10

Realistic Ambitions: Technology Transfer for Biologics Platform Technologies

Geoffrey Banda, Cecilia Wanjala, Veronica Manduku, and Dinar Kale

Introduction

Covid-19 disrupted vaccine, drugs and diagnostics supply chains and exposed African countries' epidemic and pandemic unpreparedness (Chapter 2). These events called for new sociotechnical imaginaries of local production to improve local health security and cumulatively assure global health security. This in turn requires collaboration between the state, technocrats, advocacy actors and the public to generate and sustain

G. Banda (✉)
University of Edinburgh, Edinburgh, UK
e-mail: Geoffrey.Banda@ed.ac.uk

C. Wanjala · V. Manduku
Kenya Medical Research Institute (KEMRI), Nairobi, Kenya

D. Kale
The Open University, Milton Keynes, UK
e-mail: dinar.kale@open.ac.uk

G. Banda et al. (eds.), *Cancer Care in Pandemic Times: Building Inclusive Local Health Security in Africa and India*, International Political Economy Series,
https://doi.org/10.1007/978-3-031-44123-3_10

long-term legitimacy, agency and urgency for resource allocation to the local health-industry complex development.

Building on existing technological capabilities in the local industry is an important first step to enhancing local health industries, including local production of oncology drugs in East Africa (Chapters 7 and 8). The next step is local production of more complex cancer therapies such as monoclonal antibodies (MAbs), which entails building a vibrant biologics industry. We take a contrarian position to choruses of "Africa should focus on the low-tech therapies" that we have heard in workshops and conferences, and ask why should African entrepreneurs not advance and compete internationally? There is an urgent need to build a robust local biopharmaceutical manufacturing ecosystem and to create advanced local health-industry complexes that generate better health outcomes for cancer and other patients. Production of advanced therapies is not the sole preserve of high-income countries. Covid-19 showed us the folly of such technology and innovation expertise exceptionalism for certain regions of the world.

We liken Covid-19 to a volcano: a *fast moving disaster* which creates an immediate crisis and quickly galvanises political agency and urgency to change public policy. However, there are also *slow moving but hugely impactful disasters* analogous to a glacier. Cancer and other non-communicable diseases affect many people on the continent and deserve the same urgent response and action as infectious diseases. Announcing technology transfer for mRNA vaccines to six African countries the WHO Director General said, "The best way to address health emergencies and reach universal health coverage is to significantly increase the capacity of all regions to manufacture the health products they need."[1]

This vision of an Africa with an advanced local health–industry complex also emerged from interviews with African industrialists and healthcare respondents. Biologics including regenerative medicine, gene therapy and MAbs are still expensive to produce and to procure for healthcare systems even in wealthy countries. However, with the right investment in technological capabilities, sustained learning and market formation they can be localised in Africa. In this chapter, we focus on biosimilars for MAbs because a significant number of them have fallen off-patent. The "generic" versions of biologics are called biosimilars. They provide an opportunity for technological capability upgrading and learning. For current drug manufacturers on the continent, biosimilars are a disruptive innovation, bringing significant discontinuities in production, quality assurance, distribution, industry-clinical linkages and regulatory processes.

Employing the concepts of disruptive and incremental innovation, we argue that technology transfer for MAbs is not insurmountable. For vaccine manufacturers, biologics are an incremental innovation because they already possess relevant sets of skills and capabilities. However, for regulators conversant with chemical drugs, biologics will be a disruptive innovation. Health system financing and procurement will need to be designed to adequately compensate local biologics (MAbs) manufacturers in a way that ensures business profitability and sustainability; this is the remit of innovative procurement (Chataway et al., 2016).

Why are Biologics, Especially MAbs, Important for African Countries?

We proffer three reasons why biologics and particularly MAbs are important for African countries: they open up international business opportunities, broaden technology choices and offer opportunities for value chain and technological capabilities upgrading.

Biopharmaceuticals are big business, and African entrepreneurs should participate in that market. Global expenditure on biopharmaceuticals was USD 277 billion in 2017 and is forecast to reach USD452 billion by 2022 (Cun et al., 2021). MAbs are expected to generate revenues of USD 300 billion by 2025 driven by their utility in immune-diagnosis and immunotherapy (El Abd et al., 2022). The sector is set to expand because it holds immense promise for many currently "undruggable" diseases. Biologics, specifically MAbs and RNA (ribonucleic acid) therapeutics are expected to address diseases caused by a broad range of pathogens that include group A and B *Streptococcus*, parasites such as *Taxoplasma gondii*, bacterial infections, cancer (colon carcinoma and melanoma) and passive vaccination (Blakney et al., 2021). It is these yet unrealised business promises of a vibrant emerging sector that have generated heated debates on strict observance of IP (intellectual property) even during the Covid-19 pandemic. When developing countries tried to reverse engineer mRNA vaccines, there was active resistance from incumbent firms. The recent refusal by innovator companies to share Covid19 mRNA vaccines technology openly with developing countries[2] (UNAIDS, 2021), which has caused outrage (Malpani & Maitland, 2021) may be premised on their fear of losing future lucrative oncology biopharmaceutical markets. Hence, the aggressive strategies to protect the first mover's advantage, driven by the blockbuster business model, even in the face of humanitarian need in African countries during Covid19.

Strong local health security is the foundation for robust global health security (Chapter 1). Localising biologics manufacture reduces current concentration risks. It contributes to enhanced global redistributed manufacturing systems for healthcare, by moving production facilities closer to point of care and embedding better demand signalling. The result should be better health outcomes.

Biological therapeutics play an important role in cancer therapies, and compared to chemical drugs, are reputed to have reduced side effects. Morrow and Felcone (2004) broadly categorise biologic agents as hormones (growth hormone, insulin or parathyroid hormone), interleukins, interferons, MAb, Growth Factors, proteins, polypeptides and vaccines. MAbs have grown as an important cancer therapy targeting particular types of cancers (Table 10.1). Recently regenerative medicine (especially immunotherapies) has emerged as a promising cancer therapy. Biologics technology transfer could drastically improve health outcomes for cancer patients by reducing treatment cost in the medium term, improving supply response and making the therapies more available. The Covid19 crisis triggered important questioning of conventional wisdom of dependency on global health supply chains especially during pandemics. Endemic and non-communicable disease are causing havoc and deserve the same urgency and agency to solve them as the pandemic effort.

Table 10.1 Monoclonal antibody therapies and targeted cancers

Monoclonal antibody	*Targeted cancer(s)*
Ipilimumab	Melanoma
Trastuzumab	Breast cancer
Panitumumab	Colon and rectal cancer
Alemtuzumab	Lymphocytic leukaemia
Cetuximab	Colon and rectal cancer; Head and neck cancer
Rituximab	Non-Hodgkinson's lymphoma

Source Compiled by authors from secondary sources

RNA-based therapeutics are another class of promising remedies for cancer and other infectious diseases. Current clinical trials of RNA therapeutics reveal application across a broad range of diseases including cystic fibrosis, neuroendocrine tumours, glaucoma, age-related macular degeneration, hepatic fibrosis, idiopathic pulmonary fibrosis and chronic hepatitis B viral infection (Dammes & Peer, 2020). Another class of biologics with great potential but still in infancy are cell therapies. Even for these, the business models, process technologies and regulatory systems are still in development in high-income economies (Banda et al., 2018, 2019). However, there is no reason why LMICs could not develop these therapeutics through more cost-effective manufacturing and delivery methods. The foundational technology and skills for these emerging technologies are similar to those found in the vaccine manufacturing sector, research institutions and universities.

Incremental Versus Disruptive Innovation and Impact on Business Models

Chapter 7 distinguished product innovations, which include physical artefacts or services that are new or possess significant improvements, from process innovations such as improved production techniques or delivery methods. Product innovations, including enhanced sub-units or components, software or attributes that embody better functionalities may be new to the world or, more usually, new to a certain place. The OECD[3] also identifies marketing innovations, such as better product design, product promotion or pricing and organisational innovations that enhance performance.

Process and product innovations can be disruptive or incremental in given industrial contexts. Tait et al., (2018) applied these concepts to new-to-the-world innovations that included cell therapies, financial technologies (FinTech) and synthetic biology. Their disruptive/incremental distinction is based on the impact of the innovation on business models, ability to generate competitive advantage, impact on the environment, how they relate to pre-existing regulatory frameworks, and whether they lead to sectoral transformations thereby generating stakeholder/ citizen concerns. Disruptive innovations are characterised by discontinuities in innovation pathways, requiring new areas of R&D and creating new modes of production and markets. For example, FinTech such as mobile money in African countries brought about new business models.

Mobile telephony companies and not banks introduced mobile money, and because of automation and resultant reduction in transaction costs, mobile money attracted previously unbanked populations and eventually eroded the market base of traditional banks. However, countries struggled with regulating mobile money because the business model was embedded in mobile phone companies, which did not fall under the regulatory purview of the central banks. Thus, mobile money was a disruptive innovation for traditional banks and the regulator. Disruptive innovations thus cause sectoral transformations and establish new sectors. These may have no regulatory precedent, hence the regulatory challenges described above. Such disruptive innovations may need new production or delivery modes, which necessitate the creation of new value chains.

Incremental innovations on the other hand are characterised by small improvements in products and processes, and consequently fit well with a firm's current business model(s). They usually lead to competitive advantages but align well with pre-existing regulatory frameworks. Therefore, incremental innovations do not usually generate sectoral transformations or cause significant stakeholder/citizen concerns or oppositions (ibid). Slow-release drugs were an incremental innovation over ordinary drugs. The methods of production, quality control and storage and distribution were essentially the same. Thus, incumbent companies could easily shift to new production lines as the skills, equipment and processes were similar. Table 10.2 describes the different impact of disruptive and incremental innovation on innovation pathways, research and development (R&D), competitive advantage generation, applicability of existing value chains or the need to develop new ones, and impact on regulatory capabilities and frameworks under which they fall.

Local manufacturing of MAbs in countries without vaccine manufacturing capabilities will be a disruptive innovation. There are, however, African countries in North Africa that already produce MAbs. Technology was successfully transferred from Israel and Russia amongst others. For current non-vaccine manufacturers the disruption emanates from the different skills sets, biological nature of starting materials, subsequent idiosyncrasies of production and distribution processes, quality assurance as well as regulatory and governance systems. For vaccine manufacturers the converse is true, and they are the best starting point for MAbs technology transfer. However, technology transfer is not an easy process, given current technological, infrastructural and institutional realities. In spite of this, countries can systematically build and broaden

Table 10.2 Impact of disruptive and incremental innovation on business models, value chains and processes

Disruptive innovation	*Incremental innovation*
Discontinuities in innovation pathways	Small incremental changes in innovation pathways
Requires new areas of R&D	Builds on existing R&D capabilities and skills
Creates new methods of production and markets	Generates competitive advantage by more efficient approaches to production and markets
May require new value chains or new roles in existing value chains	Likely to easily modify existing value chains and actors involved
Can create entirely new sectors with societal and economic benefits	Likely to build on existing sectors with the possibility of economic and societal benefit
Given the factors above—likely to lead to sectoral transformation and displacement of incumbent actors	Not likely to lead to sectoral transformation given the abovementioned factors
No regulatory precedence to govern potential human and environmental risk and safety issues	Likely to be covered by existing regulatory systems
Could lead to stakeholder concerns given no obvious regulatory system with a track record of success	Unlikely to lead to stakeholder concerns given there is an existing regulatory system with a track record of application
There may be a need to create a new business model if the innovation and technology and pathways to market do not exist	Existing business models are capable of incorporating the new innovation or technology

Source Compiled by authors from Tait et al. (2018)

industrial and technological bases coupled with systematic support for entrepreneurship. Incremental innovation provides a conceptual framework for constructing pragmatic technological, policy and practice interventions that can support the development of the biologics sector. The attraction of the incremental innovation framework is its ability to explain why it has been possible to transfer rapidly Covid19 vaccine technology to current African vaccine manufacturing entities. The framework provides a basis for arguing for resource allocation, and extension of long-term technology transfer, to emerging biologics such as RNA therapeutics for oncology needs and other currently "undruggable" diseases.

African Vaccine Manufacturing Footprint—Where are We Starting from?

Vaccine manufacturing is not a new phenomenon on the continent. Currently four countries have vaccine manufacturing capabilities; Egypt, Tunisia, Senegal and South Africa (Chapter 1; details in Table 10.3). Vacsera in Egypt was originally set up as a small government laboratory in 1897. It produces Tetanus Toxoid, Diphtheria and Tetanus Toxoid, Diphtheria, Tetanus and Pertussis, Meningococcal, Cholera and Typhoid vaccines. Demonstrating the incremental nature of vaccines, by February 2022, Vacsera was reported[4] to be producing over 30 million doses of the Sinovac/Vacsera Covid-19 vaccine. Sinovac Biotech transferred the mRNA technology to Vacsera. Egypt, Tunisia, Kenya, Nigeria, Senegal and South Africa are part of the WHO consortium that will engage in mRNA vaccine technology transfer.[5]

In Tunisia, Institut Pasteur de Tunis was established in 1893 and it produces the BCG and rabies vaccines. Senegal's Institut Pasteur de Dakar established in 1896 is one of four WHO-pre-qualified manufacturers of yellow fever vaccine (Ampofo, 2021). In July 2021, the Republic of Senegal working with Team Europe agreed to build a Covid19 and other endemic disease vaccine manufacturing plant in Senegal.[6] In addition, the Institut Pasteur de Dakar will host the regional manufacturing hub. The main hub funder is Team Europe, which with the Senegalese government will co-fund the plant's establishment. Team Europe is comprised of EU institutions including the European Investment Bank, the EU, its member states, and the European Bank for Reconstruction and Development (EBRD) (Keijzer et al., 2021).

South Africa has made huge strides in biologics manufacture. Institutions involved in biologics manufacture date back to the 1950s, although Aspen began in the 1850s in other drug businesses. Prominent companies on the biologics terrain include Afrigen Biologics, Biovac, Aspen and Cape Biopharms amongst others (Table 10.3).

Vaccine manufacturing plants in Senegal, Tunisia and Egypt are state owned, and South Africa has a public–private partnership, Biovac, plus CapeBiopharm, Aspen and Afrigen Biologics, which are private companies. Although Ethiopia, Nigeria, Zimbabwe and Ghana do not at the time of writing have vaccine manufacturing plants, they have long had an interest in establishing local vaccine production as members of the

Table 10.3 Vaccine and biologics manufacturers and the products manufactured locally as at 2022

Country	*Organisation*	*Established*	*Vaccines manufactured*
Egypt	Vacsera The only producer of vaccines and sera and one of the main blood banks	1897	• Tetanus Toxoid Vaccine • Diphtheria and Tetanus Toxoid Vaccine [paediatric and adult use] • Diphtheria, Tetanus and Pertussis • Meningococcal Vaccine • Cholera Vaccine • Typhoid Vaccine Produces Sinovac vaccines. Technology transfer between China's Sinovac and Vacsera A new vaccine facility outside Cairo will have capacity for 1 billion doses per annum Egypt is a participant on the WHO programme to transfer mRNA vaccine technology
Senegal	Institut Pasteur de Dakar "A non-profit association for public utility"[7] with over 80 years of vaccine production	1896	• Yellow Fever—since 1930s One of four WHO approved manufactures of Yellow Fever vaccine in the world
South Africa	Aspen	1850 went public in 1997[8]	• Johnson and Johnson Covid-19 Vaccine. First Covid vaccines manufactured on the continent. (Fill and Finish)

(continued)

Table 10.3 (continued)

Country	*Organisation*	*Established*	*Vaccines manufactured*
	Biovac	2003 as a PPP but has long links to previous vaccine manufacturing initiatives in South Africa	• BCG for TB • Measles Vaccine • Pneumococcal Conjugate Vaccine • Hepatitis B Vaccine • Hexavalent Vaccine for *Diphteria, Tetanus, Pertussi, Poliomyelitis, Haemophilus influenza B and Hepatitis B* • Tetanus Toxoid Vaccine Agreement to produce Pfizer Covid19 vaccine [Fill and Finish] Group B Streptococcus (GBS) Vaccine Development
	Cape Biopharms. Spun-off from The University of Cape Town's Biopharm Research Unit	2018	Production of recombinant proteins in tobacco plants Plant-based transient expression Molecular pharming (recombinant expression of pharmaceutically useful proteins in plants as bioreactors) (Marsian and Lomonossof, 2016)
	Afrigen Biologics	2014	Encapsulation technologies Vaccine adjuvants
Tunisia	Institut Pasteur de Tunis	1893-commissioning of establishment	• BCG Vaccines—Intradermal BCG and fresh BCG for Immunotherapy [bladder tumours] Under development—rabies vaccines for human and veterinary use and bacterial vaccines for veterinary use (mixed anthrax and enterotoxemia)

Source Compiled from Banda et al. (2022)

African Vaccine Manufacturing Initiative. Kenya has established Biovax, using KEMRI Production Unit as its stepping-stone (Chapter 2).

Underscoring the incremental innovation argument and technological readiness, Vacsera successfully transferred technology from China to produce Sinovac Covid vaccines, whilst Aspen in South Africa quickly transferred technology for Johnson and Johnson's Covid19 vaccines. Biovac agreed to fill-finish the Pfizer Covid19 vaccine. Morocco was already producing 3 million doses of the Chinese anti-Covid Sinopharm vaccine as at January 2022. This is evidence that new biologics are an incremental innovation for existing vaccine manufacturers, and technology transfer is possible. Contrary to this clear demonstration of technology transfer, some commentators in interviews, workshops and conferences argued that these technologies are too complex, requiring advanced processing technology and technical skills, and therefore technology transfer to developing countries is too difficult. They argue that African countries should either procure finished products or engage in fill and finish operations based on modular designs exported from incumbents. We argue to the contrary, that the requisite skills and capabilities exist for technology transfer and accept that more technological learning is required.

African countries, in conjunction with the WHO, have ignored these negative arguments and reverse engineered the mRNA vaccine technology in South Africa, using freely available information and solidarity from international scientists. The initiative involved using current vaccine manufacturers as centres for technology transfer. The consortium consists of Afrigen Biologics, Biovac with support from WHO, Medicine Patent Pool, South African Medical Research Council and African Centres for Disease Control. It is a component of the broader African Vaccine Manufacturing project set up in April 2021 at the height of vaccine nationalism. In January 2022 the South African company, Afrigen Biologics successfully reverse engineered Moderna's Covid19 vaccine, "both the mRNA and the formulation" and was at the time of writing optimising cheaper formulations that do not require refrigeration (Davies, 2022). Davies (2022) reports that these efforts were being undermined, and alternatives proposed were that modular-based mRNA factories from BioNTech be shipped to African countries. These would be staffed with staff from that company, which also proposed a new regulatory process whereby the EMA (European Medicines Agency) certifies the container factories. This proposition was seen as "paternalistic and unworkable" (Davies, 2022)) and in our view rather colonial. The pan-African WHO initiative has a vision to ramp up production of vaccines from a currently meagre 1% up to 60% by 2040, using the centre of excellence approach.

Planned and New Vaccine Plants Triggered by Covid19 Vaccine Nationalism

Covid-19 accelerated urgency for local manufacture of vaccines. Ghana, Morocco, Senegal, South Africa, Uganda and Kenya amongst others announced plans to establish new manufacturing plants (Table 10.4). South Africa broke ground for a new vaccine manufacturing plant for NantSA raising the number of local vaccine manufactures to three. Previously, government responses to support the sector had been rather lethargic. The African Vaccine Manufacturing Initiative (AVMI), an industry association had been lobbying governments for years without much progress. Covid19 vaccine intervention failures suddenly focused attention on the urgency of the calls.

The technologies under consideration include mRNA vaccines and therapies for HIV, TB, oncology and other coronaviruses (Table 10.4). These are huge projects with some forecast to cost USD 500 million, and actors involved include the private and public sectors and public–private partnerships.

These new developments are welcome. However, public policy decision-making during crises can obfuscate issues. Developing sustainable value chains, optimising production processes and securing the technological capabilities take time and effort, and require social capital to build relationships of trust. Creating markets for the vaccines was ignored in all the flurry to establish local plants. Table 10.4 shows some of the announced new investments, and sources of funds are from USA and Europe as well as governments. This produces tension from two perspectives: the threat of dependency and the risk of hegemonic behaviour given the drive for profit maximisation and repatriation.

However, another way to consider this strategy towards biologics would be to focus on capitalising on every opportunity for technology transfer, technological learning and structural change of the industry. The technology transfers in biologics are not only from USA and Europe. Countries in North Africa for example have engaged in technology transfer from Russia, Israel and China. Outside the biologics sub-sector, an executive for an East African pharmaceutical firm described dynamics

Table 10.4 Expressed interests in new investments in Covid19 vaccine manufacturing on the continent in 2022

Country	*Investor/collaborators*	*Investment*	*Products/technology*
Potential candidates- South Africa, Rwanda or Senegal	[9]Moderna	USD 500 million	mRNA vaccines API manufacturing, bottling and packaging capabilities
South Africa, Cape Town	Transfer technology NantWorks in USA. NantWorks SA works in collaboration with CSIR (Council for Scientific and Industrial Research Council), SA MRC (Medical Research Council) and SA universities	ZAR 3 billion	Covid Vaccines and vaccines targeting cancer, TB and HIV
Senegal	Team Europe, EU, European Investment Bank, France and Germany. Institut Pasteur de Dakar will host the regional manufacturing hub	Team Europe—Euro 6.75 million. BMZ supporting the manufacturing hub with Euro 20 million[10]	Vaccines
Ghana	Recent talks with BioNTech	Government of Ghana seed funding of USD 25 million	Vaccines

(continued)

Table 10.4 (continued)

Country	*Investor/collaborators*	*Investment*	*Products/technology*
Morocco	Senyso Pharmatech in partnership with Swedish company Recipharm	Euro 400–500 million required	API for more than 20 vaccines; 3 against coronavirus with anticipated coverage of 70% of Morocco's needs and 60% of Africa's needs[11]
Kenya	Already set up Kenya Biovax Institute Limited. Initial plans were to set up a PPP, but Covid19 accelerated local manufacturing plans and the government has funded everything to date	Sh 2.5 billlion	Covid and other vaccines

Source Compiled by authors from various sources,[12,13]

where expatriates from India transferred technology and left when locals were running the plant. So significant were the efficiencies in that local plant that the parent company in India would send staff to learn from it.

However, the source of funds being foreign is concerning. It seems there is still need for a radical change in the science paradigm on the continent. Long-term patient funding for these kind of technological projects needs to come from local sources. The risk that projects fail and the need to create markets for the new products is an area that governments can shape. Innovative procurement can be used as active industry policy to signal to the industrialists and private financiers that a product will have a market (Chataway et al., 2016) thereby creating risk appetite for funders.

Biologics as an Incremental Innovation on Vaccines and Molecular Biology Techniques

Although the biologics manufacturing footprint on the continent is small, it can be expanded. This will entail government investment in infrastructure, policy and institutional support to encourage technological learning.

Afrigen Biologics demonstrated that skills for reverse engineering and technology transfer exist on the continent. Biologics manufacturing is not a new phenomenon for research institutions and biologics manufacturers. With the right investments, science, industry and health policies, technology transfer is possible. However, there is a need to change pervasive colonial science systems in many countries which focused on establishment of local health and agricultural research centres (Clarke, 2013, 2018), for settlement and supporting trade with empire (Hodge, 2011; Worboys & Petitjean, 1996). Therefore, science systems and economic development imperatives need to be decolonised in order to establish institutions and infrastructures for high-tech value chains. National governments need to invest in creating innovation ecosystems for biologicals manufacture, including revision of the university curriculum to support appropriate education and training of professionals for industrial innovation.

Biologics technology complexity compared to chemical synthesis production methods for small molecules (drugs) makes it harder to adapt for current drug manufacturers. The sector deals with living entities and requires different skills sets, types of technology, production processes, approaches to quality assurance and distribution logistics. Hence, whilst biologics are a disruptive innovation for drug manufacturers, they are an incremental innovation for biologics (vaccine) manufacturers. Expanding biologics manufacture to RNA therapeutics would be easier for African universities, vaccine manufacturers, specialist research institutions such as KEMRI in Nairobi Kenya and biologics companies in for example South Africa. These organisations possess the requisite skills in cell and molecular biology, biotechnology, microbiology, virology and immunology. Transition to more complex technologies will require active learning and knowledge upgrading. Technological knowledge tends to be localised, embodied in people and technology and is embedded in routines and linkages between organisations. Thus, knowledge upgrading requires an interactionist approach (Lundvall, 2007, p. 107).

Table 10.5 shows the increasing complexity of technological capabilities with transition from whole cell to nucleic acid-based vaccines. However, most of the typical production processes are based on fermentation and cell culture techniques. Nucleic acid therapies leverage genome sequencing capabilities to chemically synthesise cDNA (Copy DNA) which can be inserted into commercially available or in-house developed vectors. These are used in fermentation or other processes to produce the required antigens. Genomic sequencing, cDNA synthesis and insertion of the required gene into a vector are commonplace activities in research and innovation communities in universities, research institutions and public and private research institutions. On-boarding these activities for biologics production should not be an onerous task given the incremental innovation nature and the opportunities to learn routines and linkages amongst different actors in the ecosystem using the interactionist approach (Lundvall, 2007).

The incremental/disruptive innovation concepts also apply to regulatory processes. One of the challenges faced by regenerative medicine arose when regulators tried to panel-beat the drugs regulatory system to fit that of living entities (Mittra et al., 2015). They argue that life science processes are a disruptive innovation for chemical synthesis regulatory processes. Regenerative medicine, they argued, may have been better served by the blood and blood product regulatory systems, since the processes display greater similarity. So for the regulators, shifting from regulating blood and blood products would be an incremental innovation.

In conversations with vaccine manufacturers on the African continent, the manufacturers reported regulatory approval challenges. According to industrial interviewees, inspections of premises for cGMP compliance were not a major hurdle. Challenges arose on quality assurance processes. The interviewees highlighted the fact that the "process is the product", unlike in chemical drug synthesis where you can characterise aspects such as chemical purity of raw materials and can subject the end-products to analytical tests. Biologics quality assurance depends on carefully following the production process to ensure that products are similar. Another challenge is that living organisms have inherent variability. The quality assurance process needs to consider this. We found the same phenomenon with regenerative medicine in the UK. This is one of the first challenges regulators experienced with chemical drugs will face when transitioning to biologics regulation.

In previous work on regenerative medicine (Banda et al., 2018) we discussed the "fellow traveller concept". Regulators in the UK admitted that they had to learn from the innovators on the specific idiosyncrasies of regenerative medicine, just as the innovators also learnt about the regulatory systems from the regulators. The fellow traveller concept is aligned with Lundvall's (1992) learning-by-doing and learning-by-searching concepts, and what is fascinating in this instance is the active

Table 10.5 The incremental innovation nature of vaccines types, antigen, production process and skills for incumbent players

Vaccine Type	*Technological complexity*	*Antigen*	*Typical Production Process*	*Skills Required*
Nucleic Acid Vaccines		Plasmid DNA (pDNA)	Fermentation	Microbiology and process engineering
		Messenger RNA (mRNA)	Chemical synthesis	Biotechnology techniques of sequencing, copy DNA (cDNA) production and introduction into a vector
		Recombinant vector vaccines	Cell culture	Cell and molecular biology and process engineering
Recombinant Vaccines		Recombinant protein Recombinant virus	Cell culture	Cell and molecular biology and process engineering
Sub-unit Vaccines		Recombinant protein	Cell culture (mammalian/insect)	Cell and molecular biology
		Polysaccharides and Peptides conjugates	Fermentation -(bacterial/yeast)	Microbiology and process engineering
Bacterial toxoids		Toxoid proteins	Fermentation	Microbiology and process engineering
Whole Cell Vaccines		Live Attenuated Virus	Mammalian cell culture	Cell and molecular biology Biotechnology techniques
		Live attenuated bacteria	Microbial cell culture	
		Inactivated virus	Egg-based or mammalian cell culture	Cell biology or biology
		Inactivated bacteria	Microbial cell culture	Microbiology

Source Adapted by authors from https://www.pall.co.uk/uk/en/biotech/vaccine-production.html, and Blakney et al., (2021)

learning processes between regulators and innovators, a relationship that sometimes can be adversarial.

As the African continent gears up to on-board biologics it may be beneficial that the fellow traveller concept is adopted by industrialists/innovators and regulators, but at the same time still leaving the distance required for objective governance. This is critical as regulating the biologics industry will bring both elements of radical and incremental innovation for the regulators depending on the field they are coming from. If the regulator is coming from the biologics industry, then the science and logic of the production process will be an incremental innovation. However if the regulator has experience with drugs and they are transitioning to biologics then this becomes a disruptive innovation for them. Signs coming from regulatory circles are encouraging, however. For example, the Zimbabwean regulator MCAZ (Medicines Control Authority of Zimbabwe) in February 2022 ran coaching clinics on regulating biologics.

The second challenge that regulators need to watch out for is regulatory ratcheting which leads to gold plating of standards. This phenomenon is usually driven by companies that are first on the market that engage in needless gold plating of standards as a competition tool to make it difficult for technology followers to get regulatory approval (Banda et al., 2018, Tait & Banda, 2016). We have previously argued that in instances where a new-to-the-world technology or innovation is being regulated, then it is important that the principles of proportionality and adaptive governance be applied.[14]

No single country possesses the critical mass of biologics regulatory skills. It will take time to develop these skills and in the early days it is likely that the revolving door notion of poaching skills between regulatory and industry as well as between companies may be common. Thus, it is imperative that skills retention be carefully looked at, and in addition, in the early days, that regulatory collaborations and coalitions such as ZAZIBONA be leveraged to efficiently regulate new plants. ZAZIBONA is an innovative organisational arrangement where experienced and emerging regulators are matched for training. The programme involves Zambia, Zimbabwe, Botswana and Namibia (ZAZIBONA), but lately membership has expanded.

The Market Challenges to Successful Technology Transfer

We have up to now discussed the feasibility of technology transfer and argued that because it is an incremental innovation for vaccine manufacturers, it is possible for biologics to be manufactured locally. We have also discussed how the regulatory systems can be shaped. However, one issue that remains unresolved is market formation for biologics and vaccines. In as much as governments and development organisations have all exhibited tremendous urgency and allocated resources to the establishment of new plants and expansion of existing ones, there has been no clear policy direction on, first, who will buy the products locally and where the resources will come from, and second, which international markets to target to ensure business sustainability.

We have previously argued that enhanced procurement of locally made drugs by public health systems can be used as active industrial policy to shape industrial development (Mackintosh et al., 2016). The challenge of low local procurement is not peculiar to the drug sector. Vaccine manufacturers over the last five or more years have pointed out that local procurement of vaccines is a huge challenge. Many African countries depend on GAVI (Global Alliance for Vaccines and Immunisations) for funding for procurement of essential vaccines. As of 2020, there were at least 33 out of 55 African countries that depended on GAVI for vaccines. GAVI selects countries based on GNI per capita. Countries that fall at or below the GNI per capita of USD1580 over the previous three years qualify for GAVI support. If African countries cannot procure the local vaccines and biologics then procurement cannot be used as a market-shaping tool. However as countries move up into middle-income status, as Kenya is doing, they acquire more responsibility for their own vaccine procurement and scope for innovative local procurement.

Market formation underpinned by strategic local procurement is likely in our opinion to be the Achilles hill for technology transfer and localisation at least for vaccines. The other biologics may have a different trajectory, but this will depend on the vibrancy of both public and private health insurance schemes in the countries. If biosimilars for example lead to better health outcomes at a more affordable cost, then it is possible for patients groups to call for their inclusion on oncology therapy regimes.

We are cognisant of the fact that biopharmaceutical manufacture is not only a technological project. It is also political and feeds into geopolitics debates. It is also a commercial project that generates hegemonic behaviour by commercial incumbents, which is not a new phenomenon. It occurred when Asian countries for example Bangladeshi, Sri Lanka and India began the journey to local manufacturing of drugs (Lall & Bibile, 1978; Reich, 1994) (Chapter 2). The heated issues are driven at macro level by national competitiveness and at micro level by immense commercial competition. Davies (2022) highlights the competition aspects by reporting that Pfizer and BioNTech have argued that sharing technology would not lead to high vaccine manufacturing at the moment because there would be stiff competition for raw materials from current mRNA vaccine manufacturers. These are clearly commercial self-interests at play. In the next section, we explore how Cipla acquired biologicals manufacturing capabilities through acquisition of biologicals firms—a possible avenue for rapid technology transfer for cash rich firms. We further discuss what went wrong with their biologics technology transfer efforts in South Africa- and the lessons for policy.

Technology Transfer can be Difficult—The Cipla Biologics Case Study

Cipla was established in 1935 by Dr. A. K. Hamied with the aim of making India self-sufficient in healthcare needs. It emerged as a technology leader in Indian pharma in the 1970s because of its ability to reverse engineer many internationally patented molecules and successfully launch low priced generic versions in the Indian domestic market. Over the last five decades, Cipla developed extensive capabilities in process R&D and emerged as a supplier of cheap generic drugs around the world. Cipla's international generics strategy received a big boost in 2001 with the launch of antiretroviral drugs (ARVs) in emerging country markets at extremely low prices. By 2012 Cipla was credited with transforming the global HIV-AIDS treatment landscape and emerged as one of the most successful Indian firms with an average annual growth rate of more than 20%.

Over the years, Cipla focused on emerging as a main supplier of APIs (Active Pharmaceutical Ingredients) to other MNCs and selling cheap generic version of drugs. However, the transformation of the Indian domestic market due to the strengthening of the Indian patent act in 2005 and increased competition from global generic manufacturers, created new challenges for Cipla's business model. In 2000, these challenges forced Cipla to embrace biosimilars as a key area of future growth. However, Cipla faced major hurdles in R&D and manufacturing capabilities. Reflecting the argument that this is disruptive innovation, Cipla had no previous experience of biotech R&D or innovative drug discovery R&D and lacked a manufacturing presence outside of India.

To accelerate biosimilar development in 2004 Cipla created Avesta Biologicals Ltd, a new biotech company in partnership with Avesthagen, an Indian biotech company. Avesthagen was responsible for biosimilar R&D whilst Cipla's role was to scale-up manufacturing and manage sales and distribution in domestic and international markets. In 2007, Avesta Biological acquired Siegfried Biologicals, a biotech company based in Germany, to access biological R&D expertise. Siegfried was a contract-manufacturing company with extensive experience in the development of biologicals including cell line generation, upstream process development and scale-up of manufacturing processes that comply with cGMP. However, in 2009 Cipla decided to dissolve Avesta Biologicals and Therapeutics due to lack of progress on the development of biosimilars.

To overcome this failure, in 2010 Cipla acquired a 25% stake in MabPharm, an India-based biotech firm. In 2011, Cipla helped MabPharma set up a state-of-the-art biotechnology manufacturing facility in India and, in 2014, Cipla gained full ownership of the manufacturing plant by acquiring the remaining 75% share. In parallel to the MabPharm acquisition, Cipla invested $65 million to acquire a 40% stake in Bio Mabs, a Shanghai-based biotech firm aimed at developing ten MAb drugs and fusion proteins against rheumatoid arthritis, cancers and asthma for marketing in India and China.

To complement these acquisitions, Cipla decided to build a biosimilar product portfolio through in-licensing. In 2013, Cipla launched its first biosimilar product, Etanercept, through in-licensing from China-based Shanghai CP Guojian Pharmaceutical Co, remarkably at a 30% reduced price compared to any other competitor brands. In 2014, Cipla in-licensed a second biosimilar, "Darbepoetin alfa", by entering a co-marketing deal with Hetero Drugs, an Indian biotech company. On completion of this deal Dr Jaideep Gogtay, Chief Medical Officer, Cipla explained,

> We look forward to partner with companies in India and around the world to bring wider access of biosimilar products to patients in need. We have been recognised as the partner of choice because of our expertise in specialist therapies and efficient supply and distribution. Therefore, we anticipate more number of deals across therapy areas in the near future. (Express Pharma, 2013)

In 2018, Roche and Cipla entered into an agreement for the promotion and distribution of Tocilizumab (Actemra) and other products. In 2020, it was further expanded to include Roche's highly successful trademark oncology drugs Trastuzumab (Herclon), Bevacizumab (Avastin) and Rituximab (Ristova) to address the unmet needs of cancer patients in India. Cipla used acquisition of firms with specific biologicals skills it did not have as well as entering distribution agreements with external firms.

Cipla in South Africa: A Lesson for Policy

Over the years, Cipla created partnerships in manufacturing, sales and marketing with firms all over the world. In 2012, a new management team initiated a strategy to convert these partnerships into subsidiaries and joint ventures to bolster complimentary capabilities. In 2013, Cipla acquired its distribution partner in South Africa, Cipla Medpro South Africa, for US$512 million and followed that by increasing its stake in a Uganda-based joint venture, Quality Chemical Industries Ltd (QCIL) from 14.5% to 51.05% for $15 million (Economic times, 2013; The Hindu Business Line, 2017). By 2021, Cipla emerged as the third largest market player in South Africa, with 7% market share of the South African private market.

Based on this progress, in 2016, Cipla announced plans to build a manufacturing facility in Durban, South Africa to produce biosimilar drugs, and invested $88m in the facility through its biotechnology subsidiary, Cipla BioTech. However, declines in profit and a 42% drop in earnings before interest, taxes, depreciation and amortization (EBIDTA) led to major restructuring aimed at cutting costs and improving profitability. In 2018, Cipla embarked on an in-licensing strategy to develop a biosimilar portfolio of products for distribution in India and other countries. This change in direction resulted in halting of biosimilar production plans in India and South Africa. Umang Vohra, Managing Director and Global Chief Executive Officer of Cipla commented that,

> We realised that manufacturing (of biotech drugs) is not important. There are enough efficiencies in the biotech system outside of our own. (Pilla, 2018)

This is a clear lesson for policy. Depending on commercial initiatives is problematic because of the profit motive. When huge projects are launched, they may run at a loss for a number of years before turning over a profit. Such projects, therefore, need patient investors. Commercial interests as is illustrated in the Cipla case, can easily cut off projects that are not immediately contributing to the bottom line or do not, for example, fit the strategy of new leaders.

Cipla dropped the local manufacturing project and emerged as the first company to launch Filgrastim Teva for oncology and haematology patients in South Africa in 2018. Post 2018, Cipla used the partnerships and strategic collaboration route to expand its biosimilar product portfolio and oncology products in Africa and other international markets. For example, in 2020, Cipla entered an exclusive partnership with Alvotech headquartered in Iceland, a leading biotechnology firm for the commercialisation of five biosimilar candidates in the immunology and oncology space. Alvotech will oversee the development and supply of the products and Cipla will be responsible for commercialization and regulatory registration (Alvotech, 2020). Building on that, Cipla set up a strategic collaboration with Alvogen in USA for four oncology products in 2021. Cipla followed up these collaborations with partnership agreements with the global biotechnology company mAbxience in March 2022 with an aim to provide essential oncology and respiratory-related biosimilars in South Africa (mABxience, 2022).

In the biosimilar market, Cipla is creating a product portfolio through in-licensing and investing in expanding its international presence by converting its existing partnerships into company-owned subsidiaries. This indicates that the company is using its cash rich status, strong complementary capabilities in sales and distribution infrastructure and leveraging partnerships and acquisitions for creating a biosimilar portfolio.

Conclusion

We have argued that it is feasible to engage in technology transfer for manufacturing of biologics on the African continent. The basis was that biologics are an incremental innovation for the vaccine manufacturing sector in terms of the platform technologies, production processes, quality assurance and regulatory systems. The skills in cell and molecular biology, microbiology, biotechnology and fermentation technology already exist in African universities, specialist research institutions and the private sector. Thus, the foundational base for technology, slim though it might be, actually exists on the continent. This base can be supported with concerted efforts that carefully nurture biologicals innovation ecosystems. Cipla used a faster approach through acquisitions; however, it changed its mind to in-licensing. The acquisition approach requires access to a huge chest of funds. Given the financial limitations of most existing generics firms in African countries, this approach may not be available to many except for companies such as Aspen. The Cipla South Africa local manufacturing failure is an important lesson for policy. Dependence on external commercial interests and funding for technology transfer in high-value manufacturing sectors can be problematic if strategy at the parent company changes and leads to divesture from particular technologies or ventures.

The fellow traveller concept is one of the approaches that can be used to develop regulatory capabilities and scale, and in addition whilst applying the principles of proportionality and adaptation. Solving the politico-technological aspects of the projects is only part of the journey. Markets, market formation and demand structuring are important. Until the procurement of drugs, biologicals and especially vaccine is resolved and based on local resources, sustainability may be compromised. However, we still argue that biologicals manufacture on the continent is feasible and this can significantly improve cancer care and pandemic preparedness.

Notes

1. https://www.who.int/news/item/18-02-2022-who-announces-first-technology-recipients-of-mrna-vaccine-hub-with-strong-support-from-african-and-european-partners.
2. https://www.unaids.org/en/resources/presscentre/featurestories/2021/october/20211021_dose-of-reality.

3. http://www.oecd.org/site/innovationstrategy/defininginnovation.htm.
4. https://www.egypttoday.com/Article/1/113073/Egypt-produces-over-30M-doses-of-Sinovac-VACSERA-COVID-19.
5. https://twitter.com/i/broadcasts/1OwxWzqXnlRJQ.
6. https://ec.europa.eu/commission/presscorner/detail/en/ip_21_3562.
7. https://www.pasteur.sn/fr.
8. https://www.aspenpharma.com/history/.
9. https://www.reuters.com/world/africa/moderna-plans-mrna-vaccine-factory-africa-2021-10-07/.
10. https://ec.europa.eu/commission/presscorner/detail/en/IP_21_3562.
11. https://www.france24.com/en/live-news/20220127-morocco-starts-construction-of-anti-covid-vaccine-plant.
12. https://twitter.com/i/broadcasts/1OwxWzqXnlRJQ.
13. https://ec.europa.eu/commission/presscorner/detail/en/ip_21_3562.
14. For a more detailed description of proportionate and adaptive governance of innovative technologies, please see Tait and Banda (2016).

CHAPTER 11

Palliation Economics: The Industrial Organisation of Morphine in India

Smita Srinivas, Ojasvi Ghai, and Lekhaabra Rajadhyaksha

Introduction: From Health Policy to Industrial Policy

Some societies need no new science or manufacturing to solve persistent health problems. Yet these problems persist because institutional gaps between health and industrial policies can create uncertainty for firms in both public and private sectors.

Institutions are the norms, customs, guidelines, standards, regulations or other laws by which societies function or fragment. Institutional gaps can be thought of as the continuing fragmented rule-book even

S. Srinivas (✉)
Bengaluru, India
e-mail: researchtclab@duck.com

O. Ghai
Dehradun, India

L. Rajadhyaksha
Deloitte India, Mumbai, India

G. Banda et al. (eds.), *Cancer Care in Pandemic Times: Building Inclusive Local Health Security in Africa and India*, International Political Economy Series,
https://doi.org/10.1007/978-3-031-44123-3_11

in societies that in principle have the technical capabilities to solve the problem, or have tried to solve the problem but generate more complex and conflicting rules. Identifying and prioritising such institutional gaps, especially in countries that have robust industry, is exercising a problem-solving muscle for development and planning capacity (Srinivas, 2016). The hypothesis at the start of the study was that a series of institutional gaps—especially in regulation—prevents the existing technologies and industrial capabilities from being focused on solving the palliation problem. This chapter looks at the practical economics of palliation, by focusing on how morphine availability is an outcome not of price barriers but of persisting institutional gaps in the morphine supply chain, and a lack of joint goal-setting and execution between health policy and industrial production. A lack of cohesion between national priorities to solve the problem and a focused plan with viable administrative and stakeholder processes can collide with global health policies and recommendations which often lack a discussion on technological capabilities. Policy autonomy and policy clarity go together.

The chapter uses data collected by a part of the ICCA India team. The study includes an extensive secondary data review of Indian and global health literature on palliation delivery, costs of opioids in cancer or other palliation, and opioid trafficking or abuse. The study's primary data was structured to include 6 detailed individual or team interviews (including one repeated interview) with experts in palliation and/or narcotics control. The interviews were conducted as in-person or group virtual meetings before and during Covid-19, with additional queries followed up by phone and emails. One interview with a multilateral agency was conducted outside India. The experts represented extensive experience with public sector and community health, public manufacturing, private sector manufacturing, and multilateral coordination. Each interview lasted approximately 45 minutes to an hour.

Our research found the initial hypothesis on persisting and conflicting institutional gaps to be valid. Furthermore, generalised LMIC analyses focusing on costs of morphine and other opioids are found to be unhelpful, even misleading in the case of India. Morphine availability requires neither new science nor a sizable technological shift in production capability, but is mired in at least four types of persistent institutional gaps: conflicting norms, technical guidelines, legal requirements, and industrial regulations. These various, conflicting, complex institutions emerge from a lack of clarity about how and why morphine is being produced in India, certainly a gap in its reliable production in the quantity needed for palliation. Furthermore, our findings suggest that the exercise of national policy autonomy in India and other countries should shift away from global health perspectives to long-term clarity on deepening of national industrial capabilities including the reliability of the why and how of morphine production. Our study also pushes towards the need for a multidisciplinary approach beyond medical expertise to set out clear palliation goals with special attention to industrial policies and domestic technological capabilities since morphine formulations are simple to produce.[1] Although medical retraining is certainly needed as the chapter shows, the focus should be on an integrated joint system of administration between health and industrial policies, with iterative planning refinements of opioid production and its availability.

Provision of Palliative Morphine

The life experience of people is shaped by their experience of pain, often even before they are officially diagnosed and designated as cancer patients. Palliative care as a rehabilitative strategy is also an essential part of treatment guidelines, even when the patient survives cancer. It involves not only the morphine that is administered to manage pain generated by cancer, but "psychological, social and spiritual suffering" of the patient and family members.[2]

The Lancet Commission's recommendation for access to palliative care and pain relief is to alleviate "serious health-related suffering". Palliative morphine is part of a wider regimen of palliative care.

> Palliative care is required as soon as suffering starts. Sometimes, suffering starts even before the diagnosis. Sometimes, even after the person's demise, their family suffers and requires palliative care. (Interview with palliative care expert, India)

Palliative morphine is used during palliative care to improve the quality of life of patients and their families (Knaul et al., 2018). In this sense, it is an essential medicine, required for pain and symptom management. 55% of patients report pain during anti-cancer treatment (van den Beuken-van Everdingen et al., 2016). However, considered a strong opioid, morphine is listed in Schedule 1 of the Single Convention on Narcotic Drugs, 1961, as amended by the 1972 Protocol (United Nations, n.d). It is subjected to control and is prescribed under strict monitoring. The World Health Organisation's analgesic ladder mentions that morphine can be used when it is not possible to control pain by non-opioid drugs, adjuvant medication or despite the addition of weak opioids (Harris et al., 2003).

India is a signatory to the three international conventions which form the basis of the international drug control regime. The three international conventions are: The Single Convention on Narcotic Drugs, 1961, as amended by the 1972 Protocol; Convention on Psychotropic Substances, 1971; and the United Nations Convention against Illicit Traffic in Narcotic Drugs and Psychotropic Substances, 1988 (International Narcotics Control Board, 2012). The Narcotic Drugs and Psychotropic Substances Act of 1985 which consolidates and amends narcotics law in India, and subsequent amendments to the Act have been in accordance with the three international conventions.

Resolution 53/4 adopted at the 53rd session of the Commission on Narcotic Drugs, promotes adequate availability of internationally controlled licit drugs for medical and scientific purposes and seeks to prevent their diversion and abuse (United Nations Office on Drugs and Crime, 2011). However, despite international guidelines promoting adequate availability of internationally controlled licit drugs for medical and scientific purposes, morphine is inaccessible to most low-income patients. According to INCB estimates, countries where 17% of the world population live consume 92% of the morphine used worldwide. These countries are primarily United States of America, Canada, New Zealand, Western Europe and Australia (International Narcotics Control Board, 2015). On the other hand, in 2018, people in low-income and low-middle-income countries, forming 79% of the world population consumed only 13% of the total amount of morphine used in pain management (International Narcotics Control Board, 2019). Similarly, inconsistency also arises when countries in South America like Brazil and Colombia with relatively high levels of consumption of opioids for pain management have low provision of palliative care, indicating consumption to be concentrated in certain areas (International Narcotics Control Board, 2015). Thus, even when opioid analgesics are available, the existence of adequate palliative care services in countries is required to prescribe and dispense those substances (International Narcotics Control Board, 2015).

Despite morphine being inexpensive, the amount of morphine-equivalent opioids distributed in mg/patient in low-income and lower–middle-income countries is quite low in comparison to wealthier countries and a high estimated percentage of their need for morphine is unmet during serious health-related suffering (Knaul et al., 2018). The Lancet Commission report's expert panel has developed an Essential Package of Palliative Care and Pain Relief Health Services for countries that includes a list of essential medicines and equipment that can be administered or safely prescribed in a primary care setting. Unfortunately, the per capita cost of this essential package is lower for richer countries as opposed to low-income and lower-middle-income countries which would pay additional costs in ensuring safe supply chain and training. The report states that access to best international prices could reduce the prices that low- and lower-middle-income countries would pay for the essential package of palliative care and pain relief health services (Knaul et al., 2018).

An Industrial Organsation Approach: Moving Beyond Price and Availability

However, our research shows that while price and availability are often debated together as part of global health inequities, the focus is misplaced. Pricing and availability of morphine to patients are a function of specific industrial organisation and national decisions on policy priority. Furthermore, countries with some technological capabilities may have more trouble exercising autonomy and establishing development priorities than those that are forced to import, precisely because coordinating multiple conflicting spheres of institutions is not easy (Srinivas, 2012).

Our research thus moves the debate to the *industrial organisation* of morphine as a critical aspect of morphine access. Furthermore, countries are differentiated by their *technological capabilities* in order to boost production and regulation of the morphine supply chain. Some countries possess technological and supply chain capabilities where palliative economics should focus because it reveals persistent institutional gaps even in "best case" scenarios.

The structure of the chapter is as follows. First, it reviews some of the health policy hurdles. Health policy hurdles directly affect industrial policy since medical professionals convey the demand for medical morphine to industry. Regulatory design shapes the norms and laws of morphine use, which has an impact on demand. The second part of the chapter dives into several aspects of this industrial organization and technology.

Differentiating Countries by Industrial Capabilities

Hurdles in industrial organisation affect the procurement and availability of various formulations of morphine even in recognised medical institutions.

Although a disproportionately high availability of opioid use today for pain management is evident in countries like the United States, Canada, Australia and some countries in Western Europe, it is a reflection in part of the industrial organisation of health and the social minimums and maximums for possible consumption based on production at home or suitable imports. The high consumption of opioids in these countries can be seen in S-DDD[3] per million inhabitants per day (International Narcotics Control Board, 2015) and high consumption of morphine in mg/capita for pain management (Connor, 2020) This can be contrasted with the disproportionately low availability of opioids in S-DDD per million inhabitants per day (International Narcotics Control Board, 2015) and low consumption of morphine in mg/capita for pain management in parts of Asia and most of Africa, despite some countries having industrial capabilities.

We argue that countries with disproportionately high and disproportionately low levels of consumption exhibit different industrial supply gaps of opioids and morphine manufacturing, whether they produce such opioids at home or have to import them. Thus, income and pricing may not explain the full issue, but industrial capabilities for morphine do. India is one such country with the technological capability across the supply chain of morphine. The annual Indian need for morphine for people going through severe pain during cancer is estimated to be 36,500 kg (Rajagopal and Joranson, 2007; Rajagopal, 2018). Yet in 2014, the consumption of morphine was 278 kg in India, which is sufficient to adequately treat only 40,000 patients (Jacob and Mathew, 2017). Persisting low consumption and high unmet requirement for morphine for medical purposes can be attributed to industrial supply gaps and health policy issues. Low morphine use in mg per capita in India calls for a focus on industrial policy to address these industrial supply gaps and reduced levels of consumption despite known patient needs and clinical demand. Fundamentally, despite easily manufacturing morphine formulations, India and other countries still lack access to pain relief and have reduced palliative care provision.

Insufficient Health Policy Reform

Notably, regulatory hurdles, penalties faced by doctors in the use of opioids, and out-of-date medical education, all result in doctors being a part of the problem. In practice, doctors should be adequately trained and legally empowered to prescribe morphine so that by prescription, at least morphine that can be orally administered should be accessible at Community Health Centres (WHO, 2018a).

> If you ask me, what are the barriers to pain relief or cancer care, I would put up the doctor's perception of duty of care; the procedural barriers as the second one; the society's perception and awareness as the third one. (Interview with a medical expert, 2021)

However, interviews indicate doctors' unease about potential addictions, which are reflected in regulatory design of very strict procurement, stocking, clinical use, disposal, and supervision. The Single Convention on Narcotic Drugs, amended by the 1972 Protocol, set out certain principles which are required to be followed by countries while developing their policies. The first principle is that individuals should have a licence to dispense opioids. The second principle is that opioids should be transferred between authorised parties. The third principle is that a medical prescription is required to dispense morphine (Foley et al., 2006). In India, The Narcotic Substances and Psychotropic Substances (NDPS) Act, 1985 consolidated and amended the law relating to Narcotic Drugs. Due to the non-uniformity of state NDPS rules of 1985 in India, there was a hindrance in the movement of legitimate opioids for medical use (Vallath et al., 2017). Strict regulations like involving multiple rounds of approval to acquire licences made processes lengthier and led to reduction in the procurement and use of morphine across the country. The requirement of six licences for every consignment made stocking and prescribing morphine difficult for hospitals (Jacob and Mathew, 2017). Frequent regulatory procedures also made storage and dispensing of morphine formulations cumbersome, thus, limiting the supply of morphine and the availability of opiate medications in institutions that dispensed it (Vallath et al., 2017).

This regulatory impact is visible in different institutional spheres: the use of morphine for medical purposes reduced from 716 kg in 1995 to 18kg in 2012 after the introduction of the NDPS Act, 1995 (Jacob and Mathew, 2017). Provisions in the Narcotic Substances and Psychotropic Substances Act, 1985, led to institutional gaps pertaining to legal requirements, technical norms and industrial regulations and resulted in this drastic reduction in the use of palliative morphine by patients. In 1998, the Government of India instructed state governments to simplify their narcotic regulations (Khosla et al., 2012) but most states did not do so (WHO, 2016a). Consequently, the lack of availability of oral morphine and limited access to hospitals also resulted in a vicious cycle, including a lack of exposure of medical professionals to the routine use of morphine (Vallath et al., 2017).

After the amendment of NDPS Act in 2014, opioid medication licensing came under the purview of the central government. The amendment made procurement of morphine easier as it reduced the number of licences required to procure and dispense morphine to a single licence (Jacob and Mathew, 2017). It included morphine in the list of essential narcotic drugs and defined “Recognized Medical Institutions”, which are officially recognised by the state drug controller and can stock, purchase, and dispense essential narcotic drugs.

Producers recognise that the demand and delivery systems are crucial for fine-tuning.

> Every district should have an accessible cancer care centre. (Interview, India: Expectation of an established firm from the industry body/ government)

The presence of Recognized Medical Institutions reduced the need for multiple licences from different government agencies since their authorisation to stock and dispense opioids for three years could be renewed with the same agency (Vallath et al., 2017). However, despite restrictions being lifted, access to palliative care has persisted as a problem: the gap in consumption will take time to be closed (International Narcotics Control Board, 2015) and physicians and medical professionals in India possess insufficient clinical knowledge regarding opioid pain medications due to gaps in medical training.

Besides large Indian metropolises, smaller cities and towns (still, with millions of people in some cases) lack morphine availability and have a dearth of medical oncologists, further compounding consumption and training gaps. The government of India classifies cities into three tiers on the basis of population density and infrastructure facilities (Ranganathan et al., 2021). Tier-1 cities are considered the most densely populated with relatively good infrastructure facilities, followed by comparatively smaller Tier-2 and Tier-3 cities, with Tier-3 cities having the lowest population density and fewer infrastructure facilities (Nagpal et al., 2022).

> Medical oncologists are not available in Tier 2 and Tier 3 cities, due to which patients suffer. Hence, government should make policy wherein doctors should be able to serve compulsorily in certain Tier 2 and Tier 3 cities. (Interview, established firm, India)

The NDPS Act, 1985 had added to the negative attitude exhibited by professionals towards the use of opioids. Palliative care was first included in undergraduate medical and nursing curriculum by St. Johns National Academy of Health Sciences in 2001 (Velayudhan et al., 2004). Due to slow progress, training of medical professionals in pain evaluation and correct pain control methods has been limited and there have been misconceptions that cancer pain is inevitable and largely unmanageable. The fear of dependence on a particular drug, form or process has increased doctor's inhibition from prescribing morphine. Despite high requirements, the demand of patients is not being conveyed and even if it is conveyed, hospitals in Tier-2 and Tier-3 cities lack *morphine* stock and availability.

Given the worryingly low availability of palliative morphine over decades, policy makers have initiated promising changes with legal amendments in national policies, programs, and medical education (Box 1).

Box 1 Amendment of Law and Programs

2012 National program of palliative care
2017 Inclusion of palliative care in National Health Policy
2010 Acceptance of palliative medicine as a medicine speciality and announcement of postgraduate education in palliative care
2019 Inclusion of palliative care in undergraduate medical programs

To summarise, the persisting gap in consumption continues due to demand-side and supply-side issues. On the demand side, lack of exposure and appropriate knowledge among physicians and medical professionals arises because of exaggerated fears of addiction and restricted exposure to injectable opioids that are used in emergency situations (Vallath et al., 2017). This stems from strict regulations from the NDPS Act and inhibits the demand for palliative morphine from those patients who require it. Moreover, due to sociocultural factors, people consider pain medications as toxic (Jacob and Mathew, 2017). On the supply side, lack of governance to ensure consistent supply from the government manufacturer of morphine salts to the producers of oral morphine pose problems (Vallath et al., 2017). If all people who need morphine demand it, better estimates will be provided to the manufacturing industries and improvements in machinery and technology will prove to be beneficial. States that have implemented the amended NDPS Act have shown improvements in palliative care, and it is the duty of the state governments to ensure the implementation of the amended rules in order to reduce the supply gap (Rajagopal, 2015).

> At least 96% of India does not have access to opium. Less than 4% have it. Even if you give the hospitals morphine, they don't know what to do with it. (Interview with a medical expert on palliative care 2021)

The Kerala state model in India has been more successful than other states in terms of providing palliative care, especially through the voluntary involvement of community and community health workers. The Government of Kerala had declared a palliative care policy and integrated it into health care in 2008 (Rajagopal, 2015), resulting in more palliative care centres than in the rest of the country (Jacob and Mathew, 2017) and more than 170 organisations to stock and dispense oral morphine (WHO, 2016a). Micro-donations from the public supplemented by government support contributed to funding for pain and palliative care services (WHO, 2016a). It is a decentralized system through a network of community health workers who aid in delivering morphine (Rajagopal et al., 2017) and requires palliative care training among medical professionals as well as community workers. During 2012 to 2015, the consumption of morphine in Kerala increased by 27% (Rajagopal et al., 2017).

New decentralised networks for palliation are being built out across other Indian states based on Pallium India's experience. Yet, even in Kerala, the system relies on existing industrial supply chains and has struggled to improve. We turn to the industrial issues next.

Industrial Policy Gaps and Opportunities

As we saw earlier, the consumption of palliative morphine in India is lower than the amount of palliative morphine needed and demanded by people. Yet, India is one of the few countries which has in principle the entire supply chain under its control. It is one of the very few countries where the cultivation of opium is legally permitted and possesses the technological capability to produce opioids and manufacture morphine formulations. This indicates that there is a pressing requirement for an integrative system with an adequate focus on industrial policies, health policies and autonomy on regulatory design. While regulatory barriers, severe gaps in medical training and socio-economic factors are a part of *health policy*, the *industrial policy* is equally critical if not foundational. Its institutional gaps include several existing but poorly coordinated technological capabilities: supply chain management, procurement, dispersal and shop-floor and logistics of the manufacture of morphine formulations from raw opium.

Morphine salts can be extracted through opium gum or concentrate of poppy straw produced from opium poppy. India maintains the largest stocks of opium in the world. It accounted for 98% of the global production of opium in 2020 and continues to be the main producer and *only licit exporter* (International Narcotics Control Board, 2021) of raw opium. Legal cultivation of opium poppy takes place in tracts of the large states of Madhya Pradesh, Uttar Pradesh and Rajasthan in India. Opium can be converted to morphine salts in two ways. In the first method, after the cultivation of the Opium poppy plant (*Papaver somniferous*), opium gum is extracted by the cultivators through lancing. The poppy plant contains an important organ, known as the capsule, which provides raw opium. During lancing, skilled workers make an incision on the opium capsule and collect latex. The opium gum produced after solidification of the latex is dried and sent to the alkaloid plant for the production of alkaloids (Central Bureau of Narcotics, n.d) The second method of producing morphine is the Concentrate of Poppy Straw (CPS) process.

In this method, rather than extracting opium gum, the bulb is cut with 8" of the stalk and is processed entirely (Mishra et al., 2013).

India is authorised by the United Nations Single Convention on Narcotics Drugs (1961) to legally produce opium gum. It follows the first method to extract alkaloids. The whole process of cultivation of poppy; production of opium gum by the cultivators and the extraction of alkaloids is done by the government under strict supervision, involving stringent licensing and regulations. After the conversion of opium to alkaloids, morphine salts are sent to private manufacturers who convert them into morphine formulations, as tablets and injections (Jacob and Mathew, 2017). The Narcotics Commissioner allocates quotas to companies that manufacture formulations of morphine and supply them within India. The number of pharma companies that get manufacturing licences varies each year, depending on the availability of stocks. The effectiveness of this quota process procurement requires attention. The amount of morphine salts allocated to pharmaceutical companies is less than the annual need of morphine formulations for medical use.

From 2000–2004, the average annual quantity of morphine salts sold by the Government Opium and Alkaloid Factories to companies that manufacture various formulations of morphine was 142.32 kg (Rajagopal and Joranson, 2007). Between 2011–2012 and 2016–2017, the average domestic sales of morphine and its salts (including Dionine) from the Government Opium and Alkaloid Factories was 265.66 kg (see Table 11.1).

Table 11.1 Sales of Government Opium and Alkaloid Works (GOAW) in India (kg)

Year	*2011–2012*	*2012–2013*	*2013–2014*	*2014–2015*	*2015–2016*	*2016–2017*
Morphine and its salts (including diomine) (kg)	223	292	279	329	240	231

Source Sales of Government Opium and Alkaloid Works (GOAW) in India. Available at: https://www.indiastat.com/table/template/industries/sales-government-opium-alkaloid-works-goaw-india-2/1006491. Also available on Annual Reports, Ministry of Finance

Given that the estimated annual need of morphine in India is higher, there needs to be an increase in the manufacturing capacity and the availability of morphine formulations. Many medical institutions in India lack stock of morphine. According to a cross-sectional validated web-based survey conducted from November 2017 to April 2018, across 102 National Cancer Grid Cancer Centres, 72.5% out of all centres had generalist palliative care training, and the licence to dispense, store and procure morphine was available with 84.3% of the centres. Yet only 77.5% of the centres had an uninterrupted supply of oral morphine for patients (Damani et al., 2020). An increase in the average domestic sale from the Government Opium and Alkaloid Works has not been able to resolve the problem of access to opioids. This is partly because the amount of formulations of morphine being produced needs to be gradually increased. At 43 mg, India has only enough morphine-equivalent to satisfy 4% of the need of patients (Knaul et al., 2018).

Figure 11.1 displays recent data for the estimated demand for the top five narcotic drugs in India. There is a high possibility of capacity being reduced due to the impact of Covid-19 and the existence of a significant gap between demand and supply that pre-dated the pandemic.

The requirement for opioids is the highest for codeine and is followed by morphine (Fig. 11.1).

We can see from Fig. 11.2 that after a massive reduction in the production of opiate raw materials rich in morphine in 2016, there has been a rise in production in 2017, which is positive as compared to the previous two years. Overall, the production of opiate raw materials rich in morphine has seen drastic changes and has been lower in the second half of 2010s in comparison to the first half. Estimates for 2020 and 2021 due to Covid-19 will likely be significantly higher than actual production.

Historically, India has played an important role in exporting opium. Due to an increase in the morphine-producing capacity for export in traditional supply countries in years before 1979 and a resulting mismatch between global demand and supply, the Economic and Social Council of the United Nations had passed a resolution (E/RES/1979/8). It called upon importing countries to support and provide practical assistance to traditional supply countries by expanding imports through them. The resolution was passed to keep excess stocks under check and to restrict over-production (International Narcotics Control Board, 1979).

India along with Turkey were traditional suppliers of narcotic raw materials to the United States. Morphine has always been extracted from

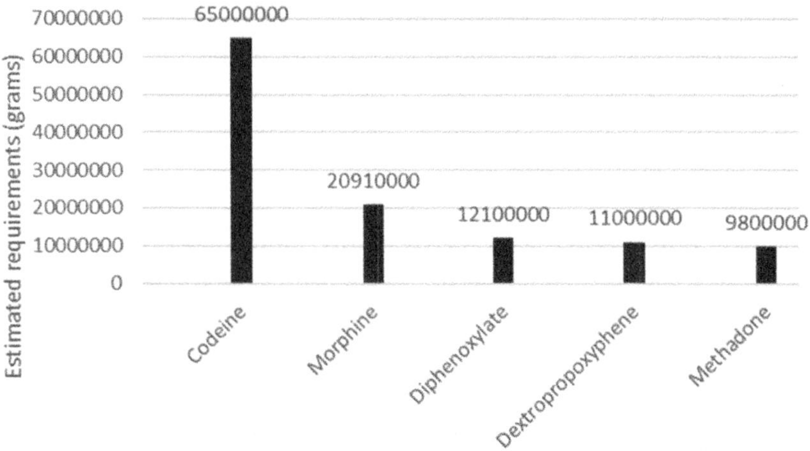

Fig. 11.1 Estimated Indian top 5 opioid requirements (grams) (May 2022) (*Source* Estimated world requirements for narcotic drugs in grams for 2022 (May 2022). Available at: https://www.incb.org/documents/Narcotic-Drugs/Status-of-Estimates/2022/EstMay22.pdf)

opium gum in India. Turkey shifted to extracting morphine through the Concentrate of Poppy Straw process in 1974 (International Narcotics Control Board, 1974). Over time there is declining international demand for opium gum produced in India (International Narcotics Control Board, 2020). In 2020, exports from India were at the lowest levels in twenty years (International Narcotics Control Board, 2021).

The United States, which was a major importer from India in the past, reduced imports significantly in 2015 and 2016. In 2019, Japan switched to importing concentrate of poppy straw and stopped importing raw opium which led to a further increase in stocks of opium in India (International Narcotics Control Board, 2021). Countries are responsible for keeping the amount of stocks of opium in check. Yet despite having large stocks of opium and availability of raw materials, formulations of morphine are still unavailable at many licensed Indian centres which dispense morphine. Increasing the availability of morphine requires greater production of morphine formulations from the extracted alkaloid. This will become fruitful if the translatory gap between the needs and

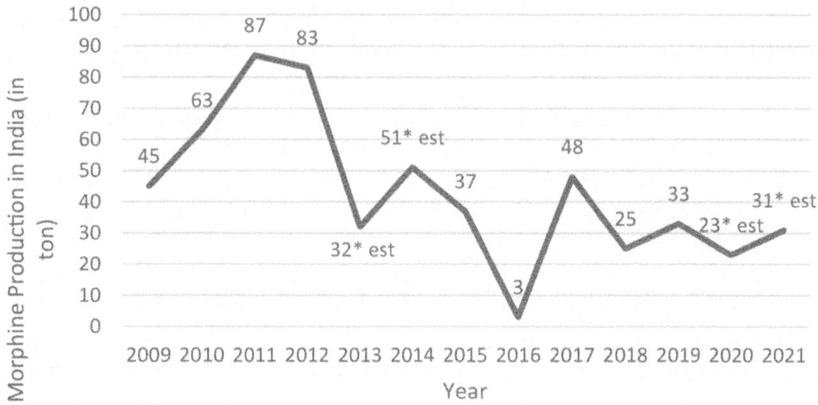

Fig. 11.2 Opiate raw materials rich in morphine: production in India (in ton) *Sources* International Narcotics Control Board, 2013. Supply for opiate raw materials and demand for opiates for medical and scientific purposes. Available at: https://www.incb.org/documents/Narcotic-Drugs/Technical-Publications/2013/Part_3_supply_E.pdf; International Narcotics Control Board, 2019. Supply for opiate raw materials and demand for opiates for medical and scientific purposes. Available at: International Narcotics Control Board, 2020. Supply for opiate raw materials and demand for opiates for medical and scientific purposes. Available at: Narcotic Drugs — Estimated World Requirements for 2021 — Statistics for 2019 (https://www.incb.org/documents/Narcotic-Drugs/Technical-Publications/2020/8_NAR_2020_Part_III_Supply_and_Demand_E.pdf); Note: A severe drop in the estimates of Morphine production in India was expected due to Covid-19.)

the demand for morphine in India is reduced (Interview with palliative expert, India).

Capacity Utilization and Technology Used

And now India faces some technology choices in processing to increase manufacturing capacity and the availability of morphine via investment in machinery and enhanced technology such as the Concentrate of Poppy Straw Technology. The existing process of lancing is labour intensive, especially when opium is harvested and requires skills, experience and knowledge (Booth, 1999, p.5). Only a fraction of alkaloid content gets utilised and the rest remains in the straw and capsules (Nordal, 1956).

Furthermore, extracting opium through lancing involves a greater chance of illicit diversion and therefore greater need for regular checks, reviewing and increasing the Minimum Qualifying Yield. On the other hand, the Concentrate of Poppy Straw process is less labour intensive and reduces the chances of diversion to illicit channels (United Nations Office on Drugs and Crime, 2005). Specific CPS variety seeds can be cultivated. However, shifting to CPS affects farmers currently producing poppy through lancing.

The government has begun providing licences to private manufacturers to produce alkaloids from Indian opium. Private manufacturers use CPS technology to produce the end product. Two private companies were given permission for trial cultivation for two years 2017–2018 and 2018–2019. According to the outcomes submitted, more extraction of alkaloids took place with CPS than with the opium gum method. However, firms faced legal inconveniences when it came to obtaining a possession licence from the state governments concerned (Dhoot, 2021).

Along with the establishment of the public–private partnership model that the Government of India is considering, the use of enhanced technology and the involvement of private manufacturers must not increase the overall price of the drug.

The increased manufacture of morphine formulations would be beneficial if the needs and requirements of people are met through measures like policy implementation of the NDPS Amendment Act across all states, healthcare professionals getting better training in palliative care, greater autonomy in regulatory designs and an increase in awareness.

Policy Priorities for India

Overall, therefore, a persistent fragmentation of institutions exists for morphine production, its network of delivery and consumption, and mixed messages and confusions of goals layered over these within regulation design. The fragmentation of the industrial organization is summarized in Table 11.2.

We return to the hypothesis that the major hurdles are in systemic institutional gaps that fail to acknowledge the central role of the industrial production capabilities of morphine: diffuse goals set for industrial production, complex industrial relationships of firms and other organisations to demand and delivery, major regulatory gaps in the intermediate services of management and dispersal of regulated substances. The stock

Table 11.2 Fragmentation of the industrial organization of palliation

Fragmentation	*Policy options*
Manufacturing capacity of the Government Opium and Alkaloid Factories utilized in less effective manner	Better utilisation of the manufacturing capacity of the Government Opium and Alkaloid Factories with the use of better technology and revamped machineries
Companies restrained from manufacturing formulations of morphine due to the licensing procedures and the low cost of the drug	Policies could promote the use of enhanced technologies and greater manufacture of the drug, without increasing the selling price of morphine
Reduced manufacturing of morphine, lack of availability in Recognized Medical Institutions and National Cancer Grids owing to interrupted supply, procurement and licensing issues	Given that India has the capability of manufacturing morphine, the lack of availability of palliative morphine to patients requires major focus on industrial regulation
Required implementation of NDPS Amendment	The number of licences required is reduced, however lack of implementation of the NDPS Act in all states continues

of opium and its supply is in principle not a problem in India. India has the cultivation-to-processing capacity and few technology transfer changes are needed. Concentrate of poppy straw processing could help, but even at current technological capabilities with opium gum, diversification of alkaloids is possible and the essential (and cheapest) forms of opioids could be dramatically increased in volume. According to a survey conducted with 26 established drug manufacturers, the key challenges they face are access to raw materials, regulatory or policy gaps and market reach.

Persistent bottlenecks to the production and consumption of morphine thus require policy clarity and no new science or urgent technology transfer. It requires greater focus on industrial policy and enhancing the supply chain capabilities within India for meeting domestic requirements and later if needed, encouraging exports to other LMICs.

As such, even were routine medical training to be improved, the lack of manufacture and availability of morphine formulations is a policy and administrative failure arising from a misunderstanding of the industrial foundations of health policy. Once fully acknowledged, in principle, persistent bottlenecks could be managed from start to finish with simple restructuring and regulatory oversight of a highly fragmented system struggling under regulatory stringency. This requires attention to iterative, intermediate tasks: dynamic consumption estimates, better procurement strategies, creating licensing, regulatory continuity and buying at attractive rates, and finally providing the drug for patients at subsidised rates. Hospitals, their procurement systems and state government oversight of procurement should manage the rest, as quite successful in other areas of both public and private healthcare. Moreover, India is in a unique position relative to most countries, industrialised or wealthier, of having its own agricultural lands for opium-related cultivation, and in principle, can restructure incentives for firms that wish to bid for the small profit margins but potentially high-volume business. Supplier countries with some technological capabilities in morphine must therefore define and exert greater national industrial autonomy to serve their health policies, and health policy designers must recognise the industrial foundations of palliation in order to fine tune its persistent domestic institutional gaps.

There is however one area where global health coordination may yet help such countries, but further research is required. Narcotics-funded terrorism is a parallel growing concern, shaping how future global and within-country industrial supply chains will be regulated from field to patient through the degree of controls over higher value-added synthetic pharmaceuticals. India in particular has an opportunity to exert more industrial autonomy precisely to separate regulation of the illegal drug trade from domestic medical use of opioids. It is positioned between the Golden Crescent, which includes Iran, Afghanistan and Pakistan and the Golden Triangle, which includes Burma, Thailand and Laos. Both, Golden Crescent and Golden Triangle are the two largest areas of illicit opium production in the world (United Nations Office on Drugs and Crime, 2005).[4] Consequently, India is increasingly targeted as a transit route for illegal drug exports from these regions as well as a destination of illegal drugs. Illicit drug trade, with trafficking from Turkey, Pakistan, and Afghanistan and being driven through India, is also creating more pressure on opioid regulation to attend to narcotics illegality rather than medical needs. Illicit cultivation of opium is also prevalent in certain regions like Manipur, India (Kipgen, 2019). While historically, stringent regulations aimed at preventing addiction and trafficking, the consequences of such regulatory design also affect the availability of morphine formulations for medical use. Given the dominance of Afghanistan production sites, and the Taliban's new ban on the cultivation of opium poppy, India saw a rise in illegal narcotics trade after Talibani takeover. Contours of their military expansion, spillover in Pakistan, and US departure from the region since, could lead to a further increase in the illegal narcotics trade.

India can exercise more autonomy over its demand and priorities such that regulatory policy does not hinder, but only enhances, the availability of palliative morphine in India. Despite destabilising geopolitics from overconsumption and trafficking and uncertainty of poppy-growing areas, India's industrial capabilities are well situated to meet domestic palliation consumption needs and growing export demand in the next decade.

Discussion and Conclusion

The economics of morphine for palliation in India is dependent not on cost and pricing of morphine but on recognising the institutional gaps in morphine production, including the reliability of its supply chain. Palliative economics requires policy clarity and industrial simplification, such as a clear clinical-industrial framework as discussed in Chapter 6 or priority analysis of the why and how of minimum Cupboard Full requirements. The morphine case illustrates that delivery and consumption domains face continued supply chain issues and regulatory bottlenecks, compounded by misinformation and clinical hesitation. The gaps can be seen as a result of norms and rules fragmentation and isolation of knowledge sub-systems within Indian healthcare from clinical training to manufacturing.

There is reason for optimism, however. The Choosing Wisely India study makes several practical recommendations such as opting for conventional radiotherapy instead of advanced radiotherapy techniques and a focus on symptom relief and palliative care rather than chemotherapy in specific advanced cancers, in the absence of strong evidence that survival or quality of life will be affected by the measure (Pramesh et al., 2019). A Choosing Wisely India guideline for opioids (Pramesh et al., 2020) and existing material from Pallium India, are building out alongside new palliative care medical training programmes, new networks in primary healthcare across the country, and improved procurement guidelines for national procurement reform. From a production standpoint, India has in principle full control over the entire supply chain for opium to manufacturing morphine formulations for medical use. Policies can therefore now focus more on whether the advantages of shifting to more efficient technologies like the CPS technology and incentivizing private manufacturers to produce morphine formulations can maintain low final prices and strict logistics regulations.

There are also newer geopolitical challenges. Policy priorities in production cannot ignore the challenge of higher-value opioids which are complicating a neat separation between medical incentives versus narcotics trafficking. More morphine rather than fentanyl should perhaps be considered as fentanyl is comparatively more expensive for patients and performs poorly in titration of dose. Methadone is an inexpensive alternative to morphine and fentanyl, however, it is available with its own challenges of danger of accumulation, requiring educational programs and safety measures on storage and dispensing (Rajagopal, 2018). While traditional economics and markets encourage product variety, without an overall health goal or industrial clarity, alternative opioids having higher price and trafficking potential are counterproductive to industrial, health, or national security policies.

Despite these challenges, policy tenacity in improving and stitching existing supply chain capabilities can positively influence the accessibility of morphine per patient, exports to other lower and lower-middle-income countries, and reduce the per capita price that those countries would pay. Within a two-to three-year timeline and with greater policy and administrative focus, India's integrated solutions to palliative morphine in cancer and other care are possible, and can also make fundamental contributions to global supply and availability.

Notes

1. The Cupboard Full, Cupboard Empty (CFCE) approach laid out in Chapter 6 is easily adapted to decide simple guidelines to *minimum* requirements of morphine stocking for every sizable Indian hospital or rural PHC. As an industrial problem, it is solvable in less than 2 years, but medical systems overhaul is slow.
2. "Palliative care is treatment of serious health-related suffering (SHS). It includes management of pain and other symptoms and addresses psychological, social and spiritual suffering of patients and their families" (Pallium India).
3. S-DDD: defined daily doses of opiate medication for statistical purposes.
4. From hashish to heroin, now more pharmaceutical trafficking including synthetic drugs, and in some cases illicit opium growing

and trafficking. News 18 Oct 14 2021 "With Rise of Taliban in AfPak, Narco-Terrorism a Visible Threat to India's Internal Security" https://www.news18.com/news/opinion/with-rise-of-taliban-in-afpak-narco-terrorism-a-visible-threat-to-indias-internal-security-4321139.html, last accessed 04–05-2020. Zee News. Aug 16 2020. "NCB busts Jharkhand based opium network; seizes Rs 20.8 lakh, 26 kg opium 6 kg opium in Uttar Pradesh's Hardoi", https://zeenews.india.com/india/ncb-busts-jharkhand-based-opium-network-seizes-rs-20-8-lakh-26-kg-opium-6-kg-opium-in-uttar-pradeshs-hardoi-2303156.html, last accessed 04–05-2020. See also WION "Drug trafficking a challenge to India's security" June 30 2017. https://www.wionews.com/south-asia/drug-trafficking-a-challenge-to-national-security-17448, last accessed 04–05-2022.

PART V

Tackling Institutional Gaps: Using Scenarios

In late 2018/early 2019, initial workshops in both Tanzania and Kenya brought together a wide range of stakeholders in cancer care and related policy, regulation and manufacturing with the ICCA project researchers. A shared commitment to finding practical ways to bridge the health-industrial divide to address major cancer care needs was carried through the project, despite pandemic impediments to face-to-face workshops.

This section explains and demonstrates the use of scenario-building to tackle complex inter-linked policy shifts needed to address institutional gaps. Chapters 12 and 13 mainly report a sustained collaborative effort to understand the roots of the undertreatment of severe cancer pain in Tanzania. Chapter 12 undertakes what scenario-builders call a "landscape analysis" of the context for the observed shortages of opioid medication required for treating severe pain in Tanzania. The chapter documents critical causal feedback loops generating undertreatment and identifies innovations that could turn this around.

Chapter 13 explains the use of scenarios as a practical tool for generating policy change. Scenario-building is highly participatory, relying on collaboration to envisage possible different futures and answer "what if" policy questions. The chapter explains how to build scenarios and describes two cancer care innovation case studies. The first describes collaborative findings on tackling pain management in Tanzania; the second documents collective envisaging in Kenya of how to improve access to essential cancer care commodities, needed to support dignity and ability to work, through local manufacturing.

In pulling the book's themes together in the conclusion, Chapter 14 emphasises as a key theme the scope for bringing together health, industrial development and innovation to build greater local health security, for cancer care and across the spectrum of health needs.

CHAPTER 12

Innovation and Policy in Cancer Pain Management: Systemic Interactions in Tanzania

Chux Daniels, Ine Steenmans, Fortunata Songora Makene, Richard Ngilangwa, Twalib Ngoma, Cristina Santos, and Maureen Mackintosh

Introduction

There is a well-documented, and devastating, gap between the need for palliation of severe physical pain, from cancer and other conditions such as sickle cell disease, and the availability of medication, in particular morphine and other opioids to treat such pain in African countries

C. Daniels (✉)
University of Sussex Business School, Brighton, UK
e-mail: C.U.Daniels@sussex.ac.uk

I. Steenmans
University College London, London, UK

F. S. Makene · R. Ngilangwa
Economic and Social Research Foundation (ESRF), Dar Es Salaam, Tanzania

G. Banda et al. (eds.), *Cancer Care in Pandemic Times: Building Inclusive Local Health Security in Africa and India*, International Political Economy Series,
https://doi.org/10.1007/978-3-031-44123-3_12

(Knaul et al., 2018). Interviews in Tanzania in 2019 with cancer patients and health professionals, and a workshop discussing early results of the research with local stakeholders, identified the undertreatment of pain as a major concern in the provision of cancer care in Tanzania. Opioid medication was identified as the key medication for the treatment of severe pain. Shortages were recorded of opioid medication when needed, just as in India (Chapter 11). However, in contrast to India, a lack of local production has led to complete reliance on imports of morphine and other opioids.

Subsequent discussions with policymakers and manufacturers seeking to explain the morphine shortage further made visible the complex multiple interacting health system and industrial supply factors currently contributing to the undertreatment of severe pain in Tanzania. These factors included pricing, accessibility challenges, supply chains difficulties, clinicians' perceptions of opioid medication, and skills and training challenges facing health professionals, regulators and policymakers. Globally, "pain is experienced by 55% of patients undergoing anti-cancer treatment and by 66% of patients who have advanced, metastatic, or terminal disease" (WHO, 2018d, p. 9). One objective of palliative care is to help reduce suffering by preventing or relieving pain. In the case of cancer patients, this could be pain relief or pain management for survivors and also for terminal cancer patients.

Pain management for cancer patients is one of the foremost targets in the treatment process (WHO, 2018d). In a majority of cancer cases, severe pain relief and management can be achieved by inexpensive oral morphine or other opioids (Chapter 11). However, the Tanzanian evidence presented in this chapter shows a widespread lack of access to oral morphine. The associated barriers explored here are mirrored in many low- and middle-income countries (LMICs), including reported gaps in policies and regulatory frameworks, weaknesses in the health systems,

---

T. Ngoma
Muhimbili University of Health and Allied Sciences (MUHAS), Dar Es Salaam, Tanzania

C. Santos · M. Mackintosh
The Open University, Milton Keynes, UK

deficiencies in palliative care, and inadequate pain management services (WHO, 2020).

This chapter and the next pick up from the central argument of Chapter 11: that improving access to effective pain medication requires tackling institutional gaps between clinical, regulatory and industrial domains. This chapter presents a Tanzanian case study of the systemic nature of the gap between need and availability of medication for severe pain, and the serious effects of that gap for late-stage cancer patients. It documents the extent of the gap between need and availability of medication for severe pain and creates one illustrative estimate of the size of the gap. The chapter also explores the potential for local manufacturing of morphine as a possible contributor to closing the identified gaps.

The chapter then sets out to identify why some of the policy efforts to date have had limited impact on the undertreatment of pain with morphine. It does so by tracing critical causal feedback relationships between procurement, prescription, palliative care, import licensing and industrial manufacturing. Analysis of these cross-sectoral relationships with causal loop diagrams (Wolstenholme, 2003), in collaboration with local stakeholders, revealed a fundamental pinch point of two opposing interactions between the processes that should drive increased demand for palliation medicine and the processes sustaining a highinertia, low level of accessibility of morphine.

This need-demand gap model was then used as a focal point for discussion with key industrial, health, regulatory and clinical stakeholders in Tanzania, both to validate the framework that identified the systemic challenges, as well as identify gaps in understanding of local palliation practices. This chapter uses evidence from secondary data, interviews and stakeholder discussions to identify ways forward, including a discussion of the local manufacturing of morphine as one potential contribution to closing the need-demand gap and tackling the deficits in cancer pain management.

Framing the Undertreatment of Pain in Cancer Care

Chapter 1 briefly documented Africa's "cancer explosion" and noted the "abyss" of pain management failure this has brought with it (Knaul et al., 2018). The barriers to cancer pain management are diverse world-wide, ranging from patients' acceptance and endurance of pain and patients' knowledge, to the neglect of pain management by health care providers and negative attitudes towards the effectiveness of analgesics, which include fear of addiction (Orujlu et al., 2022). A Kenyan study of barriers to cancer pain management among oncology nurses revealed a high level of undertreatment of severe pain. Up to 80% of cancer patients in Kenya were reported to suffer from untreated moderate to severe pain, with barriers resulting from factors such as lack of access to medication, restrictions resulting from dispensing guidelines, and fears related to opioid addiction (Onsongo, 2020).

Morphine and other opioids remain the mainstay for severe pain management world-wide. However, unavailability of morphine continues to pose major challenges to patients, especially in LMICs (Sung et al., 2021; WHO, 2020) (see also Chapter 11). Even in cases where morphine is available, access to these essential drugs often confronts significant barriers to cancer pain treatment and management in Africa. Many countries in Sub-Saharan Africa (SSA) are unable to address the enormous unmet need for cancer pain treatment, with evidence indicating that the situation has not been improving over the years. Access to pharmaceutical opioids in LMICs remains "a tiny fraction of the availability in high-income countries" (HRW, 2011; UNODC, 2021).

It is estimated that about 57% of all new cancer cases, globally, occur in LMICs, with the situation exacerbated by a lack of awareness, less attention to preventive strategies, and improvements in quality of life that are reflected in increased life expectancies. With respect to SSA, despite the mounting evidence on the rising incidence and mortality rates resulting from cancer, the disease has so far not received the desired level of attention in both research fields and health care services (Hamdi et al., 2021) as well as in policy and government circles, sometimes due to gaps in evidence to inform appropriate policies and policymaking (Nonvignon, 2021). Cancer pain management—prevention and alleviation of suffering and pain resulting from cancer—in SSA requires early identification and careful assessment of pain and other problems that manifest themselves in physical, psycho-social and spiritual forms (van der Plas et al., 2020) (see also Chapter 3).

In East Africa, there is increasing awareness of the huge need for better palliative care among many stakeholder groups including citizens, government ministries, healthcare leaders, and politicians (Fraser et al., 2018; Hartwig et al., 2014; Kamonyo, 2018). This is vital because as Kamonyo (2018) argues, access to pain relief medicines, a central part of palliative care, remains "a dream in most African countries" (p. 1). Greater awareness will help improve understanding of challenges related to establishing a robust palliative care agenda in countries within the region and support progress in cancer pain management. Although progress has been slow in the policy environment, within the region Kenya and Uganda are particularly recognised to have made progress in making palliative care and pain relief more accessible to their citizens (Kamonyo, 2018). The Ugandan case is discussed further below.

This chapter draws on interviews, workshops and focus groups in Tanzania in 2019 with cancer patients, health professionals, and many other stakeholders in cancer care (see Chapter 1). Early results from the research and engagement with stakeholders in Tanzania identified the undertreatment of pain as a major concern within cancer care. Although the interviews identified opioid medication as a key resource for the treatment of severe pain, the lack of local production of opioid medications implies reliance on imports. The evidence also made visible the complexity of interacting health system and industrial supply factors that could hinder or contribute to more effective pain management. These factors included the price of morphine, challenges related to access to cancer care, supply chains and regulatory difficulties, perceptions of opioid medication, and capability challenges related to the skills and training gaps facing health professionals and policymakers.

In this chapter we frame cancer pain management as a policy topic specifically in need of evidence-based contributions that can identify key innovations and institutional changes that can be considered by policymakers. Chapter 13 then builds on some of the evidence and ideas in this chapter and uses them to show how scenario building can be used as a policy tool to map critical interactions—both those that contribute to generating undertreatment and those that arise from innovations—and to identify areas where further information is required to complete the scenarios in a form that can be used by policymakers.

Specific to this chapter, we focus on the dimensions and scale of the undertreatment problem in Tanzania. In doing so, we demonstrate the importance of diagnosis of the underlying need-demand gap in line with the dimensions of cancer care and pain management. Pain management is a cross-sectoral, multi-level challenge, cutting across industrial, health care, societal and policy systems. We build on and develop the WHO domains for palliative care development. The WHO identifies three domains—health policy (also described as 'integration into national health

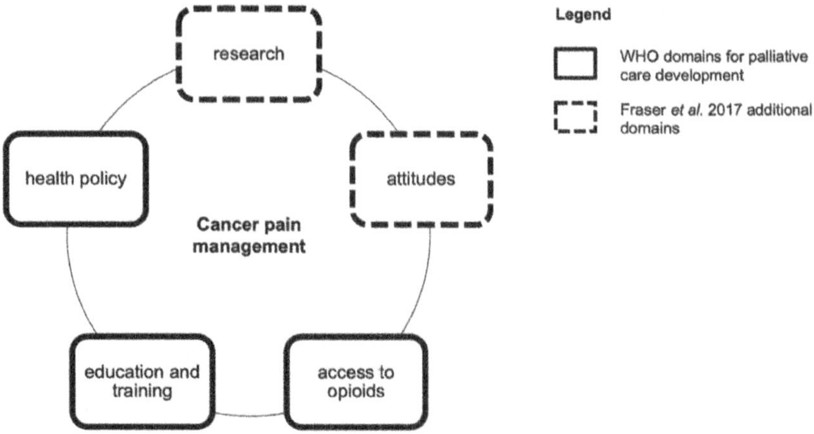

Fig. 12.1 Dimensions of cancer care and pain management (*Source* Authors)

systems'), education and training (of healthcare workers), and drug availability (often described with specific reference to opioids)—as critical to the development of palliative care (HRW, 2011, p. 1). Fraser et al. (2018) have expanded on these three domains to include cultural aspects (public and professional 'attitudes') and knowledge ('research'). Combined, these domains help to demonstrate that palliative care more broadly, like cancer pain management, is multi-dimensional, and requires coordination of actions across policy, industry, community, hospital management and other critical service sectors (Fig. 12.1).

Undertreatment of Cancer Pain in Tanzania

The evidence on the undertreatment of cancer pain in Tanzania draws on the experiences of 62 cancer patients; interviews with 22 health professionals in three regions including Dar es Salaam, and focus groups of health professionals, held in the Dar es Salaam specialist cancer hospital, Ocean Road Cancer Institute, and in two regional hospitals (Makene et al., 2022) (see also Chapter 1). A workshop in Dar es Salaam, followed by focus groups with a wide range of stakeholders including regulators, manufacturers, policymakers, clinicians and civil society actors including survivors' groups, provided further evidence and perspectives.

These stakeholders reaffirmed and deepened our understanding of pain management as an important challenge for cancer care in Tanzania.

Experiences of Pain

A majority of the Tanzanian patients interviewed (53 out of 62) described pain as a central feature of their symptoms. They described pain spreading through parts of their body, and escalating from just "pain" to "severe", "very severe" and over time "extreme" or "unbearable" pain. Back pain was described as spreading to the chest; vaginal pain to the abdomen; pelvic pain spreading through the back and abdomen and becoming "severe"; lower back pain spreading to the stomach and becoming "unstoppable"; stomach pain becoming "extreme" or "very severe" over time, and leg pain "unbearable". Pain was central to most interviewees' experience of cancer.

The interviews showed that people were struggling with high levels of pain, with several patients stating they felt better at the moment when the pain stopped. In the absence of morphine or other forms of opioids, many patients had resorted to repeated use of over-the-counter "pain killers": basic pain medication that is largely inadequate and ineffective at dealing with moderate to severe pain. Patients reported that rising levels of pain were not effectively managed by hospitals, resulting in low expectations of pain control by patients. Given the levels of pain described, it seems likely that pain as a potential symptom of cancer is often not picked up early, reflecting the evidence that in Tanzania, late diagnosis of cancer is widespread (Chapter 5).

Palliative Care Provision

Tanzanian research participants working at various levels of the health system—national, regional and district—identified the provision of palliation as central to cancer care, including pain relief and management, as well as mitigating side-effects of radiotherapy and blood transfusion. Approaches adopted by health professionals included cooperation with spiritual leaders (Chapter 3). The importance in palliative care among Tanzanian patients and healthcare professionals of strong personal faith, as a way of dealing with exceedingly difficult conditions, has also been documented in other studies (for example, Esmaili et al., 2018). Furthermore, participants stressed the value of other actions to mitigate social and physical pain including attempts to help patients in financial distress (see also Buhl, 2019; Hartwig et al., 2014). The views of health care professionals interviewed that are echoed elsewhere in the literature included the need for more dedicated palliative care teams to help manage high patient load (see also (Buhl, 2019; Esmaili et al., 2018), and the need to address patients' difficulties in accessing pain relief due to staff shortages (Kohi et al., 2019).

Access to Pain Medication

In Tanzania, the first line of pain relief was the purchase of over-the-counter painkillers, often repeatedly. Only two patients specifically mentioned being given morphine: one at a zonal Lutheran-supported hospital and one at Ocean Road Cancer Institute (ORCI) (the national cancer hospital). One patient mentioned that ORCI provided repeated pain relief as needed. However, many patients may have been unaware of which pain medication they were provided with. Most of the "pain killers", presumed to be non-opioids, mentioned in interviews were dispensed by drug shops, pharmacies, dispensaries, health centres and district hospitals.

Pain medicines mentioned by name were paracetamol and diclofenac, including mentions of their use for late-stage cancer. Provision of paracetamol for cancer pain was mentioned by several participants working at lower tiers of the health system. These health professionals did not have access to more appropriate pain relief and their patients were located at a great distance from ORCI. Reported interviews with staff treating paediatric cancer at Bugando Medical Centre (Esmaili et al., 2018) similarly indicated challenges in accessing morphine which meant that most staff reported the use of paracetamol or diclofenac for pain relief in terminal patients. At the time our research was conducted, morphine was almost entirely unavailable below the zonal hospital level in Tanzania. At the regional hospitals included in the study, morphine was either not available, or was irregularly available. Hospitals below the zonal were therefore not only unlikely to have opioids, but importantly also unlikely to expect to have them. An important implication of these expectations is that these hospitals may well not order opioids for future use: the implication of cumulative under-ordering in the health system is discussed further below.

The Need-Demand Gap for Severe Pain Relief

How has such a serious gap arisen between the need for morphine, a vital treatment for pain and pain management for cancer patients, on the one hand, and the supply of morphine and other opioids by the relevant authorities, on the other hand? A key element in the explanation is the gap between the extent of need, as expressed and acknowledged by patients and health professionals, and the national demand for opioid medication as expressed in ordering levels and licensing requests to the International Narcotics Control Board (INCB) for annual morphine imports.

The need for morphine and other opiate-based medication is defined here by the levels of severe physical pain that can be alleviated through medication. Since the import of opioid medication requires licensing, and distribution of controlled medication must be managed nationally, the national demand for the controlled medication is measured in practice by the requested levels of licensed imports. Those licensing levels, procurement based on the annual licence, and the distribution of opioid medication to hospitals, determine the availability of the medication across the country. When the availability of imported medication falls so far below need, a need-demand gap opens up, resulting in high levels of untreated severe pain.

Figure 12.2 illustrates this relationship visually: the demand for the imported medication, at national level, plus the decisions on its distribution within the health system, drive availability at hospital level. This availability, it is accepted, currently falls substantially below need, leaving many patients including those with late-stage cancer in high levels of pain.

Morphine Ordering and Distribution

Imports of controlled opioid medication require licencing from the INCB. INCB reports state that many LMICs, including African countries, consistently request an annual licence for morphine imports that is substantially lower than what is needed (International Narcotics Control Board, 2019) (see also Chapter 11). How is this low level of licensing request determined in Tanzania? Why is it so far below the requirements for meeting need?

Health professional staff interviewed at national and zonal hospital level explained that the Tanzanian public wholesaler, Medical Stores Department (MSD), is the sole institution licensed to import morphine

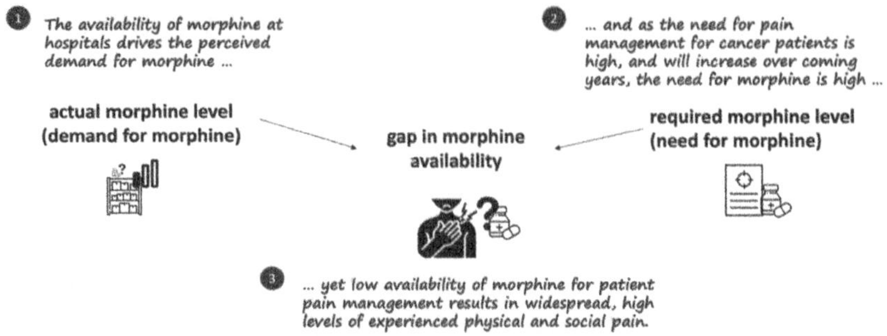

Fig. 12.2 Understanding the need-demand gap in morphine for cancer pain management (*Source* Authors)

and other opiate-based medication for Tanzania.[1] ORCI and the zonal hospitals order morphine through MSD. Regional hospitals could also acquire opioid medication directly from ORCI. The process of obtaining morphine was however described as "very difficult" by one regional hospital pharmacist, who also noted challenges with storing the drug, and the complex requirements that must be met before it could be prescribed to a patient.

A focus group discussion among staff at a regional hospital explored the problem from their perspective. Supplies of morphine at the hospital had run out at that time, and the hospital did not then have a permit in place to order more from ORCI. Cancer patients from the hospital were therefore sometimes referred from the regional level to ORCI to access morphine for severe pain. They or a relative would need to travel to Dar es Salaam to acquire it; otherwise, according to one senior clinician, patients might be treated with tramadol, pethidine or paracetamol if available.

According to Tanzania's palliative care operating procedures, patients or their relatives who have come from a long distance can be given morphine and/or other medicine for two weeks to one month, depending on how far they have travelled.[2] Hospitals in Tanzania use pethidine, another controlled medication, for pain control after surgery. Pethidine is much more widely available than morphine in the health system, for surgical use.

This low level of availability of morphine at regional hospital level and below feeds back into ordering and procurement at national level. Hospitals which are accustomed to low levels of availability may not push to order more. At regional level there are concerns to avoid diversion for illicit sale, which may constrain facilities from requesting supplies. One Regional Medical Officer interviewed commented on the need for close surveillance of morphine prescribing at lower levels of the health system:

> Morphine is a narcotic medicine. Therefore, it can't just be left for anyone to prescribe because it might be used for another purpose.

Given these tight constraints and fears of illicit use, lower-level health facilities will not translate their observed need for severe pain management into orders for morphine. Overstretched palliative care teams, and lack of training in severe pain management using morphine may also constrain efforts to increase the amounts of morphine ordered. Participants in a focus group at ORCI highlighted a lack of training in palliative care as an issue.

Procurement decisions at national level are generated from aggregation of stated requirements within the health system. The amounts requested may also be strongly influenced by amounts ordered in the previous year, since additional requests will need to be justified in a context of fears of illicit diversion. The national procurement totals for morphine may therefore suffer from institutional "stickiness" or inertia: they will be similar to previous years' procurement decisions unless health system stakeholders intervene to argue for a major change. Low procurement levels will then feed back into reinforcing low availability and a large and even increasing need-demand gap (Fig. 12.3).

Is Fiscal Constraint the Problem?

Public debate has suggested that the very sharp financial constraints faced by the Tanzanian health sector are at the root of recurrent shortages and prevalent under-ordering (Magubira, 2019). So is the cost of morphine a major constraint on MSD's demand for imports? A number of sources suggest not. Currently, pain medication appears to represent a very small portion of overall budgets for cancer treatment. An oncologist interviewed stated that the cancer medicines budget for ORCI, of approximately TZS 10 billion (USD 4.4 million), was largely ("95%") expended on chemotherapy, while pain medication was not currently a large cost. A regional hospital focus group reported that morphine costs

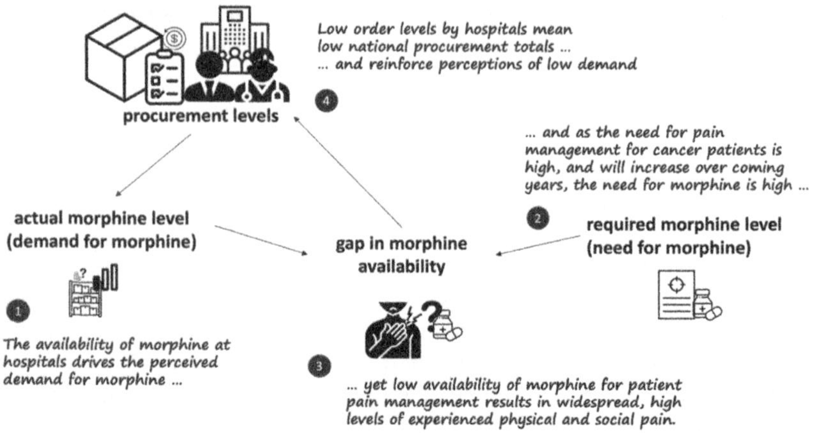

Fig. 12.3 Morphine: relationship between procurement and availability levels (*Source* Authors)

were not a significant barrier to access by patients: the problem was one of the availability of the medication.

There are however some contradictory accounts from the patients' and health professionals' perspectives. Esmaili et al. (2018) identify the cost of morphine, alongside other medicine and costs associated with hospitalisation, as a major impediment to paediatric cancer patients at Bugando Medical Centre (a faith-based zonal hospital) continuing to receive palliative treatment at the end of life. They also found that post-mortem fees that would be incurred should a patient die while in hospital were another significant reason why terminal patients were withdrawn from care including pain management. In 2018, one Tanzanian palliative care specialist argued that the omission of palliation from insurance packages meant that many patients could not afford morphine and were thus suffering severe pain (Qorro, 2019).

Up-to-date trade prices for morphine powder—the form in which morphine is imported—were not easy to obtain. The Lancet Palliative Care Commission (Knaul et al., 2018) used a figure of USD 0.01849 per milligram for sustained release morphine tablets or capsules, the import price cited by Rwanda for 2014.[3] The lowest international price found by the Commission would have reduced that in 2014 by 60%. No price was given for wholesale morphine powder import. The Lancet Commission costed the morphine in their essential package for palliative care at USD 20 per patient at Rwandan prices for 2014, and USD 8 per patient at the lowest international prices then available.

Trends in prices for medical opioids bought by LMICs are also not easy to track after 2015, when the International Medical Products Price Guide ceased annual publication. Before that date, the Guide (MSH, 2015 and previous years) registered prices for morphine in tablet form and other medical opioids including pethidine and tramadol. Figure 12.4 shows that median registered buyer prices in LMICs for morphine sulphate tablets varied but were on an apparently falling trend from 2010–2015, while median prices for morphine sulphate injectable ampoules were rising.

Median buyer prices for pethidine tablets meanwhile had been rising, while prices for pethidine and tramadol injectables were recorded in the MSH data as stable over the same period. In general, there was considerable variation around these median prices, with a number of LMICs paying substantially more than the lowest international prices registered in the Guide. We did not find data for buyer or seller prices for bulk morphine powder.

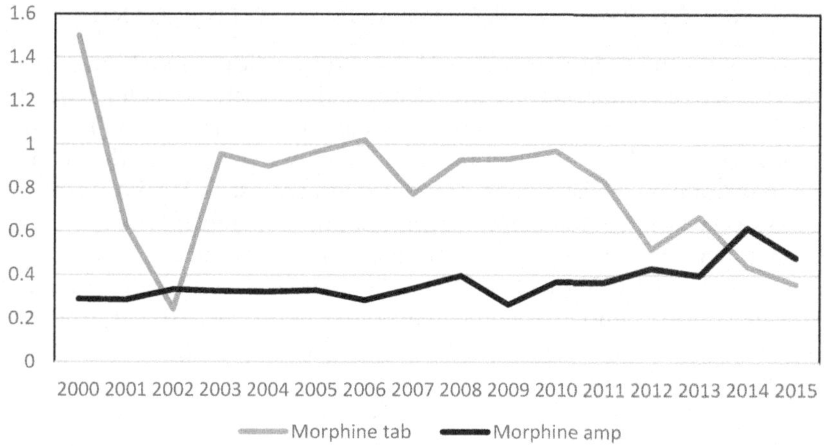

Fig. 12.4 Median buyers' prices: 2000–2015, morphine sulphate 30 mg tablet and morphine sulphate 15 mg/ml ampoule (USD) (*Source* Drawn by authors from MSH (2015) and previous years (online))

Relevant prices include wholesale import prices, and also prices for local distribution. The MSD catalogue at the time of the research (MSD, 2020) gave a sale price of TZS 12,300.00 for 10 ampoules of 10 mg/ml morphine injectable, the only morphine listed (USD 0.53 per ampoule). Pethidine 50mg/ml injectable was priced at TZS 9100.00 for 10 ampoules (USD 0.4 per ampoule). A news report in 2019 reported ORCI prices to hospitals for liquid morphine of 6000 TZS (USD 2.6) per litre and prices at outlying hospitals of 8–10,000 TZS including the markup for staff time and cost of travelling to obtain the medication in Dar es Salaam. That report stated the government was planning to subsidise the price (Magubira, 2019). For comparison, Hill et al. (2016) by contrast gave Indian retail prices (from the Indian maximum permitted price list for controlled prices) for a 30mg morphine tablet as USD 0.08, very considerably lower than the international prices shown in Fig. 12.4. The patchy recent data do therefore imply that Tanzanian prices along the supply chain to patients at the time of the research were substantially higher than those experienced in India.

Measuring the Need-Demand Gap for Morphine: A Comparison with Uganda

How large is the need-demand gap for opioid medication in Tanzania? In the absence of comprehensive prevalence and associated data for required medication for pain management, it is hard to estimate need. In order to develop some kind of quantitative estimate, we compare in this section the usage of pain medication in Tanzania with the use in Uganda. Uganda is a country facing comparable challenges, but with a history of successful development of low-cost access to morphine (Amandua et al., 2019; Fraser et al., 2018; Kamonyo, 2018). Uganda is also the highest-ranked African country among low-income countries in the 2015 Quality of Death index, and the second highest ranked in the group of African and Middle Eastern Countries.

Nevertheless, coverage of need is still patchy in Uganda. A statement published by civil society organisations in 2020[4] noted that the Ugandan government's Health Sector Development Plan 2015/16–2019/20 (MoH, 2015) showed that palliative care services were being offered in only 4.8% of the public hospitals in the country. Since 2015, the coverage seems to have expanded: Kamonyo (2018) stated that there were inpatient and home care programs in 90 of 112 health districts with at least one accredited health facility. Coverage of palliative care in Uganda depends heavily on non-governmental organisations providing hospice and outreach care at the community level. Morphine for palliative pain control is provided to patients free of charge in Uganda, and is included, as in Tanzania, in the national essential medicines list. Procurement of morphine powder and its constitution into liquid morphine was centralised in Uganda in a collaboration between the Ministry of Health and the NGO Hospice Africa Uganda (Fraser et al., 2018).

Amandua et al. (2019) showed that the "standalone" (NGO) providers of palliative care in Uganda were supported by two sources: 93% of financial running costs had come from donations over five recent years, while the government was providing in kind support in the form of medicines, training and payment (presumably waiver) of taxes. In recent years there has been no budget line for palliative care in the government health budget[5]; the most recent year for which this budget line was given was 2016/17, at Ugandan shillings 155 million (approximately USD 46,000). In general, the Ugandan health budget is very donor-dependent and also relies heavily on charging. Only around 13% of the total health budget is government-funded and the absolute total has been falling, as have payments by the government to non-profit private health providers in Uganda (Ssennyonjo et al., 2018).

Given the greater success in Uganda in extending access to severe pain medication, one illustrative estimate of the need-demand gap in Tanzania can be constructed by comparing imports into the two countries in relation to cancer incidence and population size. Table 12.1 shows the different levels of imports between the two countries, and estimates what would be involved in bringing Tanzanian imports up to Ugandan levels, given the different estimated cancer incidences.

To make this estimate, Table 12.1 compares data on morphine imports licence requests to the INCB for Uganda and Tanzania, taken from International Narcotics Control Board (2019). The prevalence and population data are the 2020 numbers from the WHO's Globocan global registry of cancer data. Table 12.1 shows that the morphine request for Tanzania for 2020 per estimated cancer case was much lower (at 0.14 grams) than it was for Uganda (0.8 grams).[6] To request morphine imports equivalent to the Ugandan order in terms of availability/case would have required Tanzania to order 58.6 kg. as compared to the 2020 order of 10.02 kg. Tanzania would therefore have needed to order an extra 48.6 kg or nearly 6 times its 2020 order to match Uganda's availability per case, according

Table 12.1 Estimates of the Tanzanian morphine ordering gap 2020, using a Uganda comparison

1	Estimated cancer prevalence **Tanzania** (cases, 2020)	73,303
2	**Tanzania** population	59,734,213
3	Case to population estimate **Tanzania** (1/2)	0.00123
4	Morphine requirements to purchase 2020 **Tanzania** (grams)	10,020
5	Morphine order per case estimate **Tanzania** (grams) (4/1)	0.14
6	Estimated cancer prevalence **Uganda** (cases, 2020)	62,548
7	**Uganda** population	45,741,000
8	Case to population estimate **Uganda** (6/7)	0.00137
9	Morphine requirements to purchase 2020 **Uganda** (grams)	50,000
10	Morphine order per case estimate **Uganda** (grams) (9/6)	0.80
11	Morphine required in Tanzania at Ugandan order/case (grams) (9*(1/6))	58,597
12	**Tanzania ordering gap estimate 2020 (grams) (11–4)**	48,577

Sources Lines 1, 2, 3: WHO/Globocan https://gco.iarc.fr/today/data/factsheets/populations/834-tanzania-united-republic-of-fact-sheets.pdf; Lines 6, 7, 8: WHO/Globocan https://gco.iarc.fr/today/data/factsheets/populations/800-uganda-fact-sheets.pdf; Lines 4, 9: INCB https://www.incb.org/documents/Narcotic-Drugs/Technical-Publications/2019/Narcotic_Drugs_Technical_Publication_2019_web.pdf

to INCB published data. We do not have import prices for morphine powder to allow a calculation of the total additional cost of those imports.

Tanzania's population is higher than Uganda's. However, Uganda's estimated cancer case/population ratio is higher than Tanzania's (Table 12.1). Cancer cases furthermore may be underestimated, given the many difficulties patients face in accessing diagnosis (Chapters 4 and 5). At Uganda's higher prevalence rate (line 8), Tanzania's larger population would imply an estimated 81,836 cases (lines 2*8) and a larger ordering gap of 55.5 kgs. This exercise provides just one indicative method of estimating the need-demand gap by volume for morphine in Tanzania, showing the scale of the gap based on higher Ugandan availability/case. Yet, as noted above, the Lancet Palliative Care Commission (Knaul et al., 2018) calculated that Uganda was itself far from achieving use adequate for need. In addition, there is necessarily a large training cost associated with widening access to morphine. In 2004 Uganda legalised the prescribing of oral morphine by clinical officers and nurses who had undertaken nine months palliative care training. This was a key step in widening access, allowing home and local use for palliative care. That training programme was based at Makerere University and run jointly with the NGO Hospice Africa Uganda. Uganda has undertaken quite widespread integration of palliative care into medical and nursing curricula, including a national palliative care training manual developed by the Ugandan Ministry of Health for health care providers at all levels of service delivery (Fraser et al., 2018). No costing of this training programme appears to be publicly available.

Addressing the Cancer Pain Management Deficit: Mutually Supportive Innovations

The research presented so far has identified a chain of interconnected factors operating in a systemic way across health care, training, procurement and supply chains to influence the pain management outcomes. Figure 12.5 adds more critical components of cancer pain management to Fig. 12.1, based on this evidence. Innovations in these areas can be linked up systematically to help to tackle the pain management challenges. This section draws on Tanzanian focus group discussions and workshops to outline how this might be done, to help to tackle the persistent gap in severe pain management in Tanzania. It includes the scope for local manufacturing of opiate pain medication to contribute to solutions.

Chapter 7 introduced the concept of an innovation eco-system: a network of local multi-sectoral institutions that reinforce learning, innovation and competence building. This framework can be applied to

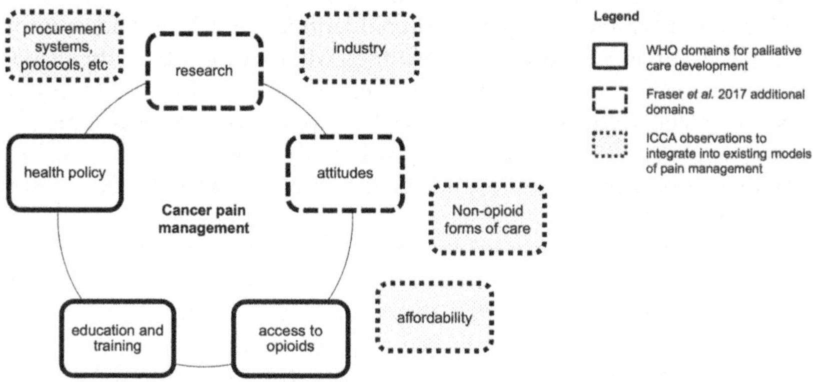

Fig. 12.5 Critical components of cancer pain management (*Source* Authors)

identifying routes to more effective and inclusive management of severe pain. The innovations required—in terms of product, process, social, organisational and marketing innovations, and innovations in policies and policymaking—necessarily involve highly varied actors and stakeholders such as government Ministries of Industry, Finance, Trade and Health; health professionals and manufacturers; researchers in the public and private sectors; and civil society organisations. Externally they include private overseas investors, development funders, and external institutions including the INCB.

The Scope for Local Manufacturing

At present, Tanzania imports all its opioid medication.[7] Discussion with local manufacturers confirmed that they have the technical capability to manufacture oral morphine and other opioid tablets. The main technical barriers identified were in the production of injectable morphine, since Tanzania at the time of the focus group discussions in 2021 did not have a manufacturing plant capable of producing sterile injectables. However, as Chapter 7 documented, the first sterile manufacturing plant in Tanzania began production in 2022. Tanzania is thus developing these upgraded industrial capabilities; in the wider region, Kenya, which already had injectables manufacturing capability, is also seeing further investment (Chapter 7).

The chief barriers to local morphine manufacturing identified were market access and information, and security. As for oncology drug production (Chapter 8), manufacturers identified a lack of market information for pain medication and questioned whether the size of the market was sufficient for a return on investment. The low level of morphine imports—so far below need—reinforced this perception of a small market. As for oncology medication, a policymaker also emphasised the need for a regional approach, and for pooled procurement, to support the viability of local production.

The problem of security in opioid manufacturing multiplies many of these challenges for manufacturers. First, it raises direct production costs. One manufacturer reported that they currently produced a single item, a cough medicine, with a controlled ingredient. The storage and logistics costs for this ingredient were high: USD 4000 per month for secure storage, and each secure transport from storage into the plant cost over USD 500 for a single trip. The security required, because of the danger of illicit diversion, therefore pushes up the price of any opioid medication, since the API has to be imported, stored and handled securely. However, the huge price gap noted above between Indian and African prices for morphine tablets suggests that despite the security costs there may nevertheless be scope for local manufacturing to be viable and still to lower prices to the health system.

Second, all the regulatory challenges facing exporters (Chapter 7) are multiplied for controlled medication, raising manufacturers' risk. One manufacturer explained that producing a controlled drug means that:

> It makes the matter even [more] complicated. …it will require so many controls which means you will add more risk. There is a risk of handling the material, that the materials are not distributed on the illicit pathway, and should you import, if the market is small, there is a risk of the material expiring before it is even used. (Focus group participant, 2021)

Given these risks, government support for manufacturers to find patient finance might be needed to start investment in local production.

The dangers of illicit use, in a context where there is already a problem of addiction, have to be taken very seriously. One participant argued that the government should explore the scope for local API production—while recognising the dangers of illicit diversion. It was noted that to make the regulatory challenge manageable for manufacturers, while sustaining stringent controls, necessarily requires collaboration among a number of authorities including the Tanzania Medicine and Medical Devices Authority (TMDA), the Drug Control Enforcement Authority (DCEA), the Medical Stores Department (MSD) for procurement, Ministry officials responsible for health, industrial, legal, regulatory and trade issues, the Pharmacy and Poisons Board (PPB) and still others. Regulatory stakeholders however strongly supported the need for such collaboration to increase access to much-needed controlled medication. One participant argued for the government to regard this as a strategic area:

> The government can intervene by applying for permits so that it can go into local production [of the API] on its own and term it as a strategic project. Another option is to give local production a special preferential status due to current demand. Because of the increasing number of people with cancer … we cannot continue to rely solely on imports. The next step is for the government to engage in production to cover that [the need-demand] gap (Focus group participant, 2021).

Skills, Training and Management of Medication by Health Workers

Focus group participants argued that skills, training, prescription and the culture of managing pain needed to change across the health, regulatory and industrial sectors. The documented need for more industrial pharmacists and industrial chemists (Wangwe et al., 2021) applies also in this field.

An oncologist noted that to raise procurement through the INCB, it is essential to first use each existing consignment within the health system fully. To ensure this, and to increase demand, attitudes needed to change, including prescribing behaviour. Doctors needed to be more aware of the benefits of morphine: they can lack confidence in managing the medication or fear prosecution. One clinician described their efforts to increase the use of pethidine, an opiate, for sickle cell pain and how that had benefitted patients, arguing that the same effort was required to benefit cancer patients. Enhanced training in morphine use is therefore needed within medical training. The fear of creating addiction, which appears to hold back prescribing, needs to be addressed so that patients requiring the medication, including those with terminal cancer, are not denied it.

The curriculum for nurses and clinical officers would also need to be enhanced, if controlled medication were to be handled at lower levels in the health sector. For example, as one participant noted, a specialist hospital cancer centre may prescribe pain medication, but the patient should be able to access it at a local hospital or through a pharmacy licensed to supply it. The Uganda case shows the scope for a much more active role for trained nurses in managing severe pain. Uganda also demonstrates the important role of civil society organisations in the palliative care field in supporting wider access to morphine according to need. Focus group participants noted that donor support for "training the trainers" could improve skills and awareness of severe pain management across the Tanzanian health system.

Wider use of licit morphine also requires training and organisational changes in managing security at lower levels of the health sector. The changes include processes for handling and reporting use of controlled medication. For methadone, used to support recovery from addiction, donors have supported costs of licensing and control. For licit morphine, local management and control requires collaboration between enforcement agencies, regulators, supply chain actors, clinicians, pharmacists and health facility management among others. This has been already occurring: the DCEA for example reported that they were providing short training courses, jointly with the TMDA and government chemistry laboratory agencies, teaching different service providers to manage controlled medication, including how to prescribe them and follow them. The training included supportive supervision. Several participants noted high levels of willingness across the system to make this work.

Conclusion: A Focus on Policies, Regulations, and Licensing

Improving pain management is one important element in Tanzania's commitment to make Tanzania "among countries with low cancer burden"(URT, n.d, p. 10). This chapter has identified the need-demand gap in Tanzania for access to severe pain medication and has noted that this is a widespread phenomenon across Sub-Saharan Africa. As an interview at the INCB also established, African countries including Tanzania can increase their imports of opioid medication at their request, so long as they are able to use the increased allocation. So when this chapter talks of "demand" we refer to the amount the country is annually licensed to import. In Tanzania, as across Sub-Saharan Africa, this is greatly below need.

We have traced the roots of this need-demand gap for severe pain management to a set of interlocking factors. We have argued that cost, while always important in low resource systems, is not the core constraint. Oral morphine is not an expensive medicine. Instead, the low demand is rooted in low *use*: a pattern of low prescribing and management of the medication constrained to a few specialist centres. This low use is aggregated nationally into low national demand, reinforcing the "abyss" of poor control of pain which is increasingly of international concern.

Stakeholder workshops and a brief comparison with Uganda's approach, have identified a series of interlocking areas where innovation could "unstick" the low demand, responding better to patients' needs, raising expressed requirements, growing aggregated demand, and generating a better supply of care for severe pain. They include training and regulatory changes, and potentially also local manufacturing of essential opioid medication. The comparison with India (Chapter 11), which already produces this medication, shows that although local manufacturing in itself does not ensure better access, it is vital to improving the situation and addressing the need-demand gap in SSA. Indeed, the Indian example also shows that, where demand increases and use becomes more confident and widespread, the capability of local manufacturers to respond is a major policy resource. In the case of SSA, innovation and policy can help steer progress in the right direction.

The next chapter builds on these insights to propose a policy tool—scenario building—that can help identify the key linkages and innovations needed within the health-industrial system.

Notes

1. A clinician in a major private hospital noted that the hospital sometimes also faced difficulties in ensuring access to morphine.
2. https://www.orci.or.tz/wp-content/uploads/2020/04/zz.pdf accessed 7/5/2022.
3. Source: online data appendix, *Lancet* Palliative Care Commission report https://www.mia.as.miami.edu/_assets/pdf/data-appendix-lcgapcpc-oct122017_xk-4-22-201.pdf accessed 4/5/22.
4. Statement by Civil Society Organizations in Uganda on Budget Allocation for Palliative Care Services for the Financial Year 2019/2020 submitted to The Deputy Speaker of Parliament / The Chairperson Committee on Health, written by Organisations working on Palliative Care, Human Rights and Budget Advocacy, Kampala December 2020 https://pcauganda.org/wp-content/uploads/2020/12/Civil-Society-Statmemt-on-National-Budget-Allocation-of-Palliative-Care-April-2019-1.pdf accessed 5 May 2022.
5. According to the Civil Societies' Organisations' statement, see previous note.
6. Tanzania also requested 30 kilos of codeine and 77 kilos of pethidine; these were also substantially lower than Uganda's request for 100 and 150 kilos respectively, despite a lower population (International Narcotics Control Board, 2019).
7. This is also the case in Kenya; one Kenyan manufacturer that previously produced opiate medication had ceased to do so.

CHAPTER 13

Using Scenarios to Support Innovation and Mutual Linkages

Ine Steenmans, Maimanah Idris, Joanna Chataway, Mercy Karimi Njeru, and Samuel Wangwe

Introduction

The strengthening of health systems through innovation is a continuous process that involves countless activities by a huge range of actors. Though we may refer at times in everyday conversation to healthcare innovation as if it were an easily locatable process, in practice we usually find it to be a fuzzier and harder to pin down phenomenon, distributed across multiple sectors, geographies, and, crucially, multiple timelines. Nor is health system innovation a process led by health sector actors

I. Steenmans (✉) · M. Idris · J. Chataway
University College London (UCL), London, UK
e-mail: ine.steenmans@ucl.ac.uk

M. K. Njeru
Kenya Medical Research Institute (KEMRI), Nairobi, Kenya

S. Wangwe
Economic and Social Research Foundation (ESRF), Dar Es Salaam, Tanzania

G. Banda et al. (eds.), *Cancer Care in Pandemic Times: Building Inclusive Local Health Security in Africa and India*, International Political Economy Series,
https://doi.org/10.1007/978-3-031-44123-3_13

alone. Health systems change because of the action of stakeholders across multiple sectors, ranging from education and hospital facility management to manufacturing and international logistics.

Our focus in this chapter is on the linkages between two sectors critical to cancer care innovation: industrial production and healthcare. These two emblematic sectors span the activities of diverse actors with wide-ranging day-to-day responsibilities and long-term agendas. They include pharmacists dispensing drugs to patients, hospital administrators managing staff rotas, doctors prescribing different treatments to patients, factory plant owners investing in a new production line, supply chain operators upgrading security infrastructure around a medical supplies distribution hub, drug regulators monitoring compliance with different licences, R&D institutions, policymakers health insurance systems, and family members saving for treatment.

The current realities, as well as the futures, of these actors are highly interlinked—even if the linkages are not necessarily always visible to everyone as they go about their work and social activities. The choices and planning by one group will unavoidably impact those of others. Changes made by one group can end up significantly enabling or constraining future outcomes for others. In upgrading of a manufacturing plant, an engineer's technical appraisal in favour of one cold storage option over another may, for example, constrain in future the local availability of medical supplies to a region. Similarly, a hospital records manager who complies with requirements to report only prescribed medication, rather than also estimated future needs, may distort the demand data used by an investor appraising the viability of localising manufacturing.

To enhance and coordinate the alignment of the behaviours of such diverse health and industrial sector stakeholders, we can benefit greatly from identifying where there might be a common 'direction' along which to steer future innovation pathways. Searching for and revealing such mutually desirable pathways needs tools with which health and industry actors can share and explore their respective visions, agendas and plans for the future. One locus of this knowledge about the future lies within the future sociotechnical 'imaginaries' held by health and industry actors (see Chapter 2 for an introduction to such imaginaries). Embedded within these imaginaries are values, ideas, and other knowledges that exist today and are likely to shape what the future may look like. Ultimately, a deeper understanding of the similarities and differences across future health and industry imaginaries can guide, and even coordinate, mutually supportive action and health system development—strengthening the likelihood of accessible, affordable, timely cancer care for patients both now and in the future.

Tools to Support Innovation and Health-Industry Linkages

In this chapter, we focus on a set of practical questions: how can stakeholders explore linkages across industrial production and health-care futures? What tools can aid health and industry actors in exploring different visions for future cancer care? And what lessons can be shared from recent experiences with these tools when examining systemic innovation in highly uncertain contexts?

We respond to some of the historical and current calls to bridge industrial production and health systems sectors. The health systems community has called for greater use of 'systems-based' tools to support cross-sectoral improvement of care (Greenhalgh & Papoutsi, 2018; Kwamie et al., 2021; UNU-EHS & UNDRR, 2022). Likewise, systemic innovation scholars argue that any efforts to co-create value across sectoral boundaries would benefit greatly from drawing more directly on the body of work on 'systems thinking' theory and practice from the past 50 years (Midgley & Lindhult, 2021). For those working towards better cancer care, we need practical examples of such 'systems-based' tools, how they work, when, and for whom, for the improvement of future healthcare.

Recent efforts have proposed new mechanisms for driving systemic innovation at policy and governance levels (UNU-EHS & UNDRR, 2022). These have focused on improving accessibility for industry and health leaders, researchers, and policymakers to participate in cross-sectoral events and processes. New health system governance structures, health-industry policy fora, and dedicated funding for research and innovation have been developed to support cross-sectoral collaboration (for example, the GAVI public–private vaccine partnership). Yet there are few available accounts of how dialogue is facilitated once these actors from different sectoral contexts, professions and backgrounds participate in these cross-sectoral spaces. For those wanting to improve cancer care, there are few publicly documented experiences with different tools to share the lessons learned on what works in facilitating cross-linkage conversations.

In the following sections, we propose the use of 'scenario tools' for exploring linkages that can shape innovation to be mutually beneficial for health and industry sectors. We briefly introduce: what scenarios are; what they can be used for; how they can be developed and used; and to what extent they are used already in health. We then share two experiences where scenario tools were used to take a systems-based approach to developing future cancer care innovation imaginaries in Tanzania and Kenya (see Chapter 1 for background on data and research). We hope not only to demystify scenarios for readers, but also to share our experiences in using them to facilitate systemic innovation dialogues. A final section summarises some key principles for using scenarios.

A Practical Tool: Scenarios

Scenarios are coherent descriptions about hypothetical futures (van Notten, 2006). At the heart of scenarios are 'what if …?' questions about how future events might unfold. Such what-if narratives might explore, for example, how a national election in a high-income country might lead to very different health policy priorities, which in the longer term might change the need for international health infrastructure finance. Other what-if scenario questions might instead explore more local and operational health issues, exploring how a new disease might increase district hospital visits and simultaneously result in an increase of staff illness and absence. Such 'what if …?' scenario narratives all explore how hypothetical actions can potentially lead to different future outcomes. Scenarios are thus not tools for predicting what *will* happen, but rather for learning from what *might* happen.

The flexible and open nature of scenarios means they are used for a wide range of purposes. A common scenario use is to convene stakeholders and elicit their hopes, fears, and ideas about possible futures (Wilkinson et al., 2013). This 'visioning' use of scenarios asks: 'what future would be possible, and what future would be preferred?' (Gordon, 2011). A second common use of scenarios is for exploring action and innovation pathways that might increase the likelihood of specific futures being realised (Sarpong & Maclean, 2011). When used in this way, scenarios become tools for comparing and appraising options for action through their simulation of possible future stakeholder interactions and outcomes. This 'planning' use of scenarios serves as a basis for action and asks: 'how could a target future be achieved?' (Börjeson et al., 2006).

The strength of scenarios lies in their hypothetical 'what-if' simulations. This supports learning about potential opportunities and risks without experimenting with those actions in the real world (Pruyt, 2011). Scenarios force us to reflect on causal linkages and understand how systems can change, thus helping their users avoid the pitfalls of simplistic prediction (Wright & Goodwin, 2009).

Validity and quality in scenario construction and use are not determined by whether a scenario is 'right'. Instead, value and quality emerge when 'scenario thinking' supports different stakeholders in gaining new insights and deeper understanding of innovation in the past, present, and future (Sarpong & Maclean, 2011).

For those unfamiliar with scenarios, it can be mystifying as to where scenarios derive this power for learning, meaning-making and inference. As Ramirez and Wilkinson explain, their analytical power is contributed by their users. Scenario construction and use are typically highly participatory processes since the analysis and interpretation of scenario insights rely firmly on 'the inherent human capacity for imagining futures to better understand the present situation' (Ramirez & Wilkinson, 2016, p. 1). Figure 13.1 summarises this way in which participatory multi-stakeholder processes can construct alternative 'what-if' scenarios that explore different causal linkages, facilitating shared learning about what could happen in different future imaginaries.

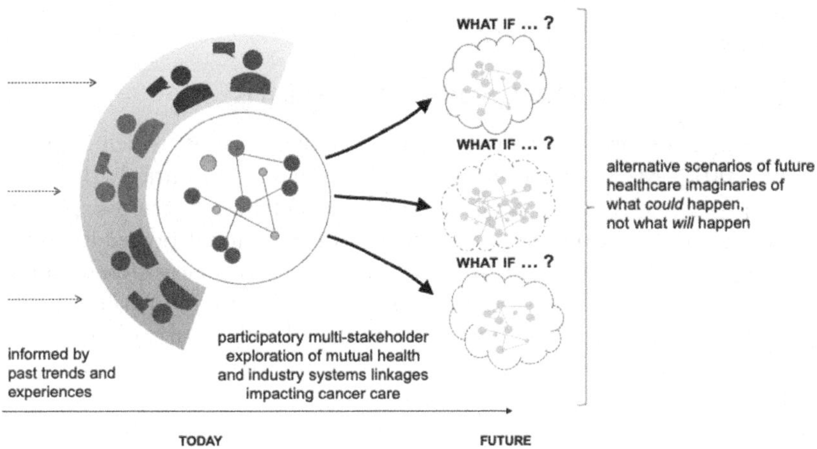

Fig. 13.1 Scenarios are tools for exploring how mutual health-industry linkages can shape a wide range of possible health innovation futures (*Source* Authors)

Scenarios in Health Policy

The primary use of scenarios in the health sector has been for local healthcare provision and resource planning. Typical uses of scenarios have been: to explore future hospital needs (e.g. (Haghdoost et al., 2017); modelling of future health workforce availability challenges (e.g. (Hayhoe et al., 2018); resource and asset management of, for example, bed availability in different future scenarios (e.g. (Mackay & Lee, 2005); or emergency planning for disasters (e.g. Amorim-Lopes et al., 2021).

Far less shared and discussed is the use of scenarios for strategic health system innovation management, despite calls for their more widespread use (De Savigny et al., 2017). Fourie (2007) noted that scenarios bring the critical long-term view needed to 'galvanise political will and action across the African continent and beyond' on health issues. It is likely that the absence of widespread visible experiences with scenarios in health systems policy development constrains the confidence that is needed in experimenting with them. Vollmar suggests that 'with greater transparency, the scenario method could become an excellent tool for … strategic decision-making in public health' (Vollmar, 2017, p. 209). To help bridge this 'scenarios transparency gap', we share an account of how scenarios were used in two health policy cases in Tanzania and Kenya, and reflect on what was useful in meeting different purposes across different contexts.

Developing Scenarios

How scenarios are constructed and developed varies widely (Bishop et al., 2007). Methods and tools used can range from entirely dialogue-based processes, to using pen and paper for sketches, to photos, physical speculative design objects, or the use of computational power for simulation models that produce quantitative descriptions of different future outcomes. In terms of who is involved in scenario construction and use, this too can vary, ranging from individual reflection to large group engagement, often at different times and even different locations.

Irrespective of the many variations between scenario development methods, the historically typical approach begins by identifying a small set of specific variables believed both important and highly uncertain in their likely influence on the behaviour of a future system.[1] Such 'top-down' scenario development approaches might take variables such as, for example, population growth and affordability of healthcare, and explore how changes in their future levels might impact other future outcomes such as the level of demand for hospital healthcare.

In a strategic innovation context there are many interrelated uncertainties that are likely to influence future healthcare innovation outcomes. Examples include future education demand, structure of international supply chains, models of manufacturing investment and technological advances in cancer diagnostics and treatment for better cancer care. Scenario builders may therefore prefer not only to consider multiple uncertainties, but also to allow for the later inclusion of additional causal influences of interest. In such contexts, we can adopt a more open and exploratory approach to scenario construction. While there is no single best approach for doing this, open and exploratory approaches typically begin with initial exploration and 'mapping' of system issues that make explicit the causal linkages between them (Wright et al., 2013). Some of the typical 'systems mapping' methods include 'cognitive mapping', 'causal loop diagrams', and 'issue mapping' (Barbrook-Johnson & A. S. Penn, 2022; Sterman, 2000).

Three-Stage Process for Health System Scenarios

We suggest a three-stage scenario process to explore the complex linkages between industrial and healthcare innovation. Prior to any in-depth development of any scenario, the intended uses of scenario building must be identified and the selection of overall scenario topic and subject focus justified. This is essential for managing the overall scope of the work in what are often highly participatory processes. It also informs subsequent choices in the design of bespoke processes suitably aligned to meet the hopes and expectations of intended users. This process is adaptable for a broad range of analytical needs and healthcare innovation contexts.

Stage 1: 'What?' landscape analysis

The first stage elicits descriptive knowledge in response to 'what?' questions about the problem context. This includes questions such as: What do we know about the issues faced and why they exist? What are key trends, patterns, and underlying drivers of change? Who are different stakeholder groups influencing change, and what are their needs and interests? What is known about the dependencies between activities in healthcare and industrial production systems? What are the key uncertainties faced? What are known knowledge gaps? As this stage aims to produce a 'whole system view' that situates the policy issue of interest within its associated sector and policy contexts, it is sometimes also termed a 'landscape' analysis of the evidence. Inputs are typically mixed empirical data sources—for example, patient experience reports; industrial capability forecasts; research on policy barriers and historical imports data. Collaborative, multi-stakeholder processes are common for collecting and combining these different knowledges, and exploring what challenges faced in one sector might be linked to those faced in another.

Stage 2: 'What if?' and 'so what?' scenario construction

A second scenario stage uses the preceding foundation of descriptive, contextual knowledge and asks 'what if?' questions to construct scenarios. It also asks 'so what?' questions to generate interpretative knowledge with both stakeholders and scenario builders about the possible implications of different future outcomes. This requires exploration of possible actions and events sequences and their impacts on different groups in society. This stage also makes inferences about what causal mechanisms might generate very different future outcomes. It typically draws on discussion for exploring potential ideas and systematically investigates the sequential 'what-if' chains of influence.

Stage 3: 'Now what?' scenario recommendations

A third and final reflection stage asks 'now what?' questions to identify and propose potential areas for action. This explores what actions in the short term could support longer-term planning or policy and strategy development.

Following the scenario analysis, construction and exploration stages, the insights and evidence generated about the innovation and policy issues of interest, can be summarised, and shared with their users and wider communities of interest with summary notes, briefs, reports, etc. Additionally, we encourage recording reflections and lessons learnt about the building and use of scenarios for health systems. Table 13.1 provides an overview.

Two Scenario Case Studies for Cancer Care Innovation

Over a year-long period in 2020–2021, ICCA research developed several scenarios for different uses. To contribute to the reduction of the 'scenarios transparency gap' in the health systems innovation context, this

Table 13.1 1 Health systems scenarios process overview

Stage	*Purpose*	*Guiding questions addressed*
Preparation	Scenario topic identification	What are the critical issues of interest for investigation?
	Scenario use identification	What evidence and/or learning is needed, who will use it, and when is it required?
Stage 1	Landscape analysis	'What' do we know about the issues and problem context? What linkages exist between different systems and sectors?
Stage 2	Scenario construction	'What if' we imagined different future events and activities? Which of the possible innovations do we want to explore in greater dep'So what' would need to happen for the innovation scenario to be possible? th with a more detailed scenario?
Stage 3	Scenario recommendations	'Now what' does this mean for our actions today?
Follow-up	Lessons capture	What was learnt from this scenario construction and exploration?

chapter shares details of activities used to scope, develop, and interpret scenarios.

Experiences from two scenario case studies are described. The first case study describes the development of a scenario about a future with greater access to medication for management of severe pain including the scope for localised pain medication manufacturing capability in Tanzania. This scenario description builds on the pain management case study in Chapter 12. The second case study shares experiences with initial scenario development activities about a future with greater access to essential cancer care commodities and consumables in Kenya including scope for local manufacturing, picking up from some evidence in Chapter 7. Combined, these two cases reflect two distinctive but complementary uses of scenarios in healthcare policy innovation. The first case study illustrates the use of scenarios for exploration of pathways for action. The second case study illustrates the use of scenarios for more aspirational and collective visioning of what a preferred future might look like to identify possible areas for further work.

Exploring Innovation Pathways Using Scenarios: A Tanzania Cancer Care Case Study

A striking and unexpected experience of the ICCA project was the emphasis that emerged from early project workshops in Tanzania and Kenya foregrounding issues of care, palliation, dignity, and ability to work. These wider aspects of cancer care are considered more fully in Chapter 3. When the multidisciplinary ICCA teams discussed what potential topics could benefit from further investigation with the use of relatively unfamiliar scenario-based methodologies, the Tanzanian team selected this problem topic as its scenario analysis focus: pain management.

The aim of using a scenarios-led methodology in this case was to engage local researchers and stakeholders across the industrial and health sectors in a systematic but flexible collaborative process exploring pain management issues and linkages. This section narrates the scenario building process in Tanzania—despite pandemic constraints—and its interim outcomes.

Stage 1: 'What?' Landscape Analysis

By the time the Tanzanian and UK researchers agreed the pain management focus, and could come together to work on it, the pandemic was underway. The research teams therefore worked online to develop an initial 'landscape analysis' of the potential pain management issues to be considered.

As a way of mapping the team's diverse insights, a visual 'systems map' was constructed depicting an overview of the multiple sectoral and cross-sectoral linkages generating the problem structure of pain management in Tanzania and internationally. The researcher leading the scenarios development undertook real-time 'system mapping'[2] while listening to research team members' presentations and discussions of their current understanding of critical issues impacting pain management. Their possible interdependencies and relationships of influence were noted. Issues were captured as individual notes on the online Kumu relationship mapping software (Kumu, 2022), though other platforms and media can be used. Systems mapping can also be done using post-it notes, or pen and paper. Where a relationship of influence was described between two issues (for example, where high travel costs for patients to access hospitals lead to reduced levels of patient trips for pain medication collection), this is depicted on the systems map with an arrow from the first driving issue to the second impacted one.

The resulting systems map was validated through a group-based review of the areas of significant cross-sector linkages that emerged across the map. Figure 13.2 shows an extract of the overall systems map produced. Cancer pain, it was noted, not only severely reduces patients' quality of life but also limits their ability to participate in daily social and economic activities (Chapter 3; marked on Fig. 13.2 as 'work and social participation of patients'). The most effective and important form of severe pain management for cancer care involves opioid derivatives which were and are undersupplied, and not manufactured, in East Africa (Chapters 11 and 12; marked on Fig. 13.2 as 'local opioid production capacity'). The whole map can be accessed using the link in Endnote 2.

It was agreed that more in-depth landscape analysis specific to key trends, issues and drivers of change affecting the undersupply of opioids for cancer care in Tanzania would corroborate and provide helpful empirical detail of the mutual sector linkage areas identified with the systems mapping discussions. The output of this follow-up analysis was a working paper summarising the landscape analysis of crucial issues and linkages framing the pain management problem and key uncertainties. This working paper informed the next step in scenario planning; it also forms the basis, in reworked form for Chapter 12 in this book. In brief, this working paper considered that the undersupply of critical pain medication appeared to arise from a set of interlinked issues including: healthcare worker education and training, hospital purchasing practices, inventory forecasting methods, reporting requirements, prescription norms, policy priorities, local manufacturing capability, and wider awareness of the significance of pain management in cancer care (Chapter 12).

Stage 2: 'What If?' and 'so What?' Scenario Development

For the second scenario stage, a hybrid online and in-person full-day workshop with the researchers and high-level local stakeholders was organised by the Tanzanian team. Participants included officials from relevant Ministries; professional pharmaceutical and clinical associations; regulatory and procurement bodies; leading clinical oncology centres; local pharmaceutical manufacturers; as well as local healthcare professionals. The range of participants illustrates the level of local concern and importance given to this issue at this stage. As preparation for this workshop, participants received the working paper on the landscape analysis of pain management issues, from Stage 1, and heard presentations summarising early findings evidencing the significance of industrial-health linkages.

The workshop aimed to explore possible future options for improving pain management in cancer care and involved two key activities. First, the group explored possible areas of innovation by exploring different future events and activities different from today. The group's exploration

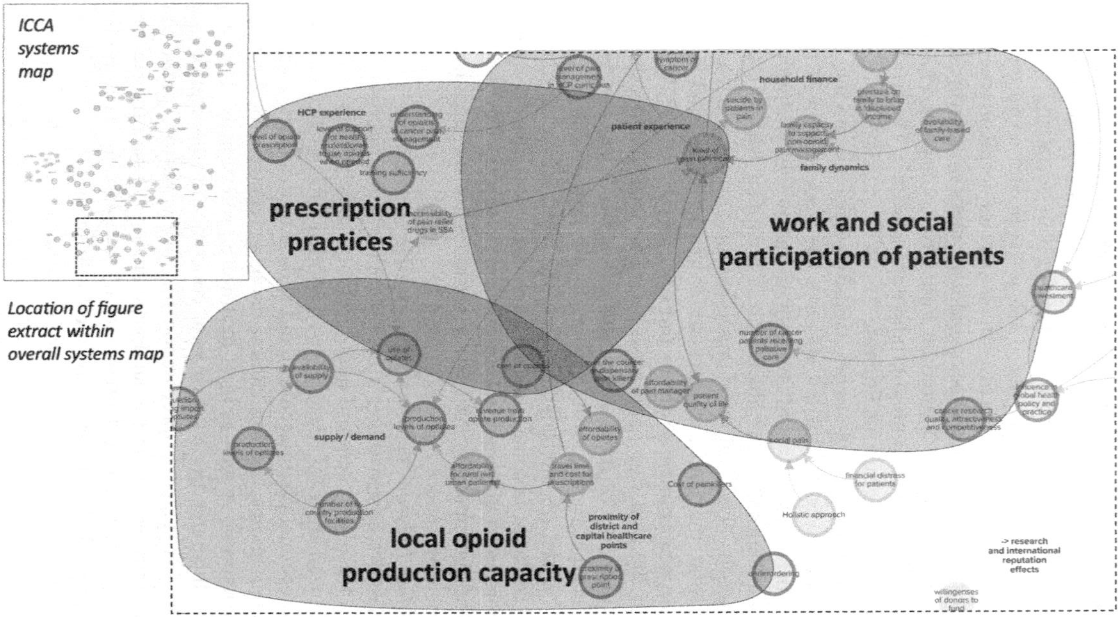

Fig. 13.2 A partial view of the systems map of the systemic problem of systemic cancer care pain management and opioid undersupply. It highlights three sub-themes across the driving health-industry linkages discussed

of different future innovations was facilitated by inviting participants to suggest 'what-if ...?' questions that could describe an eventual, better cancer care future. Participants were encouraged to share ideas that might improve pain management, regardless of their perceived plausibility. Contributed ideas ranged across sectors from ideas for education ("what if… health care practitioner education significantly enhanced palliative care curricula?"), to alternative medical protocols ("what if cannabis was provided for terminally ill patients?"), to manufacturing innovations ("what if there was local manufacture of opioid medication?"). All 'what-if' ideas and discussion points were captured by the facilitator on a shared online whiteboard (Miro, 2022). This process aimed to support participants in recalling and reflecting on ideas shared, as well as identifying topics potentially not yet suggested.

As the second key activity, the group discussed what different innovations might be imagined, and what possible sequences of events might be involved in achieving them. The facilitator used a set of 'so what?' questions. These included questions of what inputs would be required to initiate essential activities, what results would be expected, what outcomes might be observed, what eventual impacts would be anticipated, who might benefit in what way, and what undesirable consequences and uncertainties are faced (some readers may recognise these as common questions used in evaluation techniques such as 'logic models', or 'theories of change').

At this point, the discussions had generated a rich set of ideas for innovation, as well as insights into possible activities and sequences of events that could result in the imagined outcomes. In order to provide a reference point to support the group in synthesising some of these ideas about future innovations and possibilities, a visual scenario of a possible chain of future events was sketched to summarise some of the key discussion points. One particular innovation, the localisation of opioid medication production was selected for this visualised scenario. The tidied post-workshop version is depicted in Fig. 13.3. It imagines a future scenario where investment in Tanzania-based opioid production facilities will result in increased procurement of pain medication, leading to greater opioid prescription across national and local levels. The direct anticipated effect is a major reduction in patients' pain, with further direct and indirect effects of reducing future costs of care, as well as also enabling patients with reduced pain to return to work and social activities.

Even though this scenario focuses on only one of the multiple innovations discussed, the discussion highlighted the group's strong belief that this future scenario of improvement of pain management was dependent

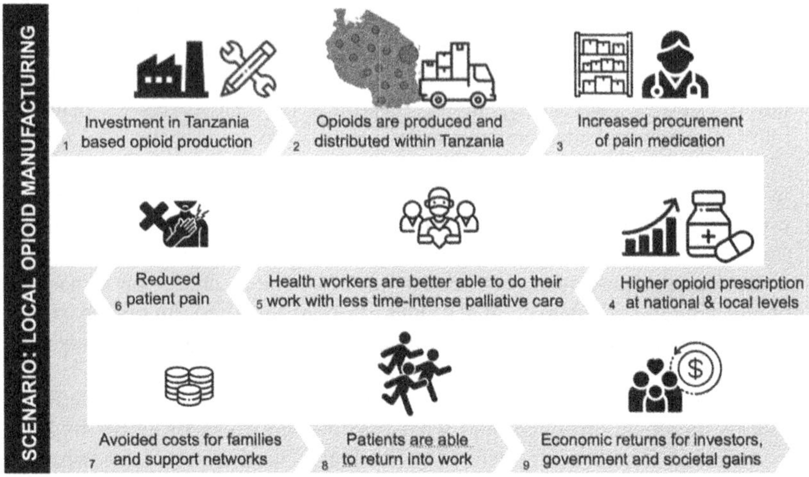

Fig. 13.3 Scenario of localised opioid manufacturing

on an integrated approach that actively addressed linkages between production and other systems. For example, greater localised production and distribution of opioids within Tanzania (step 2 in Fig. 13.3), will only have the increased prescription and pain management effects (step 4–6 in Fig. 13.3) if other issues such as hospital procurement of opioid medication is supported by changed ordering protocols in order to raise system demand, and if education and professional development systems provide the requisite training to support professionals working at more local levels of health systems in prescribing morphine.

Stage 3: 'Now What?' Future Insights for Industry-Health Linkages

As a final stage in validating the assumed scenario insights about possible future cancer care innovations and developing possible propositions for action, the team organised two focus groups with key stakeholders in cancer pain management, opioid supply chains, and local manufacturing capabilities. These focus groups included participants from the major Tanzanian cancer hospitals, regional pharmaceutical manufacturers, Ministry of Health, Drug Control and Enforcement Authority, national Palliative Care Association, Tanzania Medicines & Medical Devices Authority and Ministry of Trade and Investment. Table 13.2 presents the primary discussion questions used for this continuing evaluation of innovation ideas.

Table 13.2 Focus group questions for scenario validation and 'now what?' propositions

Scenario evaluation focus	*Questions*
Inputs for Tanzania-based opioid production	What is the critical pre-existing capacity of pharmaceutical manufacturers in the region? What are the major upfront costs? What cannot be done locally?
Activities of Tanzania-produced opioid distribution	What pricing is needed? Upper, lower limits? What is the level of technology challenge? What is the critical demand for skills? What barriers are faced? What do ministries need clarity about?
Outputs of Tanzania-produced opioid distribution	What is needed to estimate demand? What are the limits on likely markets
Outcomes and impacts	What if there are no government purchase/procurement guarantees? What other benefits to manufacturers? What are the risks to manufacturers? What are the benefits and risks to patients? What are the benefits and risks to hospitals?
Now what?	What are important areas for near-term action?

Some outcomes of these focus group discussions are summarised in Chapter 12. Focus groups participants argued that the need-demand gap for access to opioid medication faced in Tanzania critically requires 'linked up' innovation that recognises the linkages between training, health facility management, regulatory changes, and local manufacturing development.

Reflections on Practice

This Tanzania case study demonstrated that scenario development can support knowledge sharing across research teams and identify themes and interconnections between research insights across traditionally siloed areas of work, such as industrial manufacturing capabilities and hospital patient care practices. Crucially, it demonstrated how the process of building a future innovation scenario can not only elicit a rich range of ideas for change, but also provide a process by which stakeholders are actively supported in making sense of the complex linkages. At each stage of the final local production scenario development, both researchers and stakeholders observed the need for mutually reinforcing innovations—a complex but crucial message to agree.

The research team also reflected that the use of a scenario-led methodology facilitated the safeguarding of time for exploratory conversations about potential future problems, rather than early on identification of a single 'preferred' or 'right' innovation pathway to pursue. This increased the team's opportunities for evaluating and learning about health-industry linkages and ultimately led to more clearly bounded research and evidence outputs for policy.

Collective Visioning with Scenarios: A Kenya Cancer Care Innovation Case Study

As noted above, early workshops with stakeholders in both Tanzania and Kenya foregrounded perceived relative neglect of issues of survivorship, dignity, and palliation within cancer care. The Kenyan researchers particularly noted the complaints by patients and carers about lack of access to, and high costs of, basic commodities such as colostomy bags: items that supported dignity and ability to work and socialise. Industrial interviewing confirmed that despite the strengths of the Kenyan industrial sector, none of these essential items were manufactured locally (Chapter 7). Surprised, even shocked, the research team subsequently identified improved local manufacturing of commodities as local priority issue for cancer care and selected it as a second scenario case topic.

The broad purpose of this local commodities manufacturing scenarios work was to provide the research team with an ambitious but evidence-grounded approach to collaboratively identifying cross-sectoral areas with innovation potential in the Kenyan context. The longer term intended use of this exploratory exercise was to be able to better engage health, industry, and policy stakeholders in more focussed discussion of such innovative health-industry possibilities in later project stages. A scenario-based methodology has strengths for this purpose, as scenarios can draw on current evidence for envisaging actions significantly different from status quo processes.

Stage 1: 'What?' Landscape Analysis

To develop a shared overview of the possible challenges faced in improving commodities access, a half-day workshop with the research team shared initial summary presentations and discussion of key findings from the primary research and earlier workshops. These discussions explored possible key issues and reflections on the extant evidence base about the wider 'landscape' of issues that should be considered. Importantly, this evidence base included primary analysis of the experience of patients experiencing social and psychological distress as a consequence of lacking prostheses, slings, colostomy bags, etc. (Chapter 3) and interviews with relevant industrialists (Chapter 7). The discussions concluded that at least two significant systemic challenges, both similarly encountered in the previous pain management scenario case, frame the future availability of cancer care commodities: first, an important gap between need and demand; and second, a lack of local production capability.

Stage 2: 'What If?' and 'So What?' Scenario Development

The next stage of work sought to elicit insights and possible ideas for disrupting the status quo. The team needed to find a way to draw on their valuable knowledge about the challenges currently faced, and yet not get constrained into describing what *is* currently experienced in access to cancer care commodities rather than what *could* be experienced instead. This type of ideation of possible, even preferred ideas for the future that contrast with experiences today can be challenging for researchers who are often judged on the 'realism' of their analysis. A typical practical challenge therefore encountered when participating in 'what if' discussions is that the pressures for 'realism' or 'realistic ideas' often silence hope for radically different and better futures, leading to subconscious suppression by participants of thoughts and ideas that have genuine potential for desired and disruptive innovation.

The moderator therefore performed a key role during the discussion of 'what if' ideas to explore potential future innovation areas. They supported this by continuously encouraging participants to imagine creative possibilities and offering reassurance that preferability rather than plausibility should be used as the criterion for appraisal of ideas. As a prompt to help participants engage with ideas of preference rather than plausibility, the moderator asked participants to draw on their emotive understanding of the challenges faced; that is, to articulate their hopes and visions, as well as their fears and reservations about the potential challenges faced in realising these imagined future cancer care commodities futures in Kenya.

Individuals often also benefit from private time for reflection to develop innovative ideas without concerns for appearing 'realistic' in the perceptions of others. A post-workshop questionnaire capturing hopes, fears, visions for cancer commodities was therefore circulated to capture anonymous researchers' ideas and concerns. Respondents were encouraged to include any aspect they believed interesting, from a range of patient, policy, local and international perspectives. They took an average half an hour to complete the questionnaire with highly qualitative contributions. An illustrative example of a typical 'what if' imagination response was:

> I see a scenario where the critical requirements [for commodities] are being sustainably met. These include an adequate supply of commodities and that they are accessible, affordable and safe to use. The sustainability is being driven by various technological, trade and industrial solutions which include local manufacturing of these commodities in established firms or reconverted firms dealing in plastics, presence of capital and technologies to foster context specific innovations for instance, skin colour matching breast prostheses.
>
> The final responses resulted in a range of different innovation ideas embedded within participants' individual visioning scenarios, as follows.

In a future with improved local manufacturing of cancer care commodities in Kenya:

- There are breast prostheses, colostomy bags, catheters, and other essential commodities available and affordable for those who need them, in appropriate sizes and colours.
- The sources of cancer care commodities for patients, carers and survivors include health facilities and local chemists or pharmacies, and can be bought with cash or insurance, just like medicine.
- Affordability is supported by lower prices and inclusion in the National Health Insurance fund (NHIF).
- Health workers are aware of the needs and requirements for prostheses and other requirements and able to supply in health facilities; patients and carers are made aware early of what they will need and involved in specifying what they need.
- Local industry is aware of and responsive to needs and potential demand, able to custom-make items and developing regional exports.
- Government has a role in sharing market information, procurement of the commodities and incentivising local manufacturers to respond.

Stage 3: 'Now What?' Future Insights for Industry-Health Linkages

The final scenario use stage engaged stakeholders in identifying areas of interest for further work to support commodities manufacturing innovation. A final half-day workshop convened participants from relevant ministries, representative bodies and industry experts in discussion of key sectoral and cross-sectoral issues.

The discussion needed a way to access the ideas generated by the team's preceding landscape and 'what if' analyses. It would not have been appropriate at this stage, however, to present the research team's analysis of possible future innovations as a single, coherent account of sequenced events. A visual 'rich picture' technique was therefore used to summarise some of the distinctive ideas into a single future scenario, as presented in Fig. 13.4. This rich picture scenario visualisation intentionally avoids the implication of a necessary structure or order of ideas, nor specifies particular causal pathways to achieve identified innovations and outcomes. This approach to presenting future scenarios has strengths in being able to quickly make visible key ideas, while leaving space and opportunity for new participants to explore their own ideas for what might happen. A weakness of this approach is that the single visual scenario representation did not relay all of ideas and insights previously shared by the research team in the workshop. These had to be shared verbally and revisited instead.

Following discussion and clarifications of underpinning assumptions, the group aimed to identify tangible areas for follow-up action. The discussions had highlighted multiple cross-cutting linkages across health and

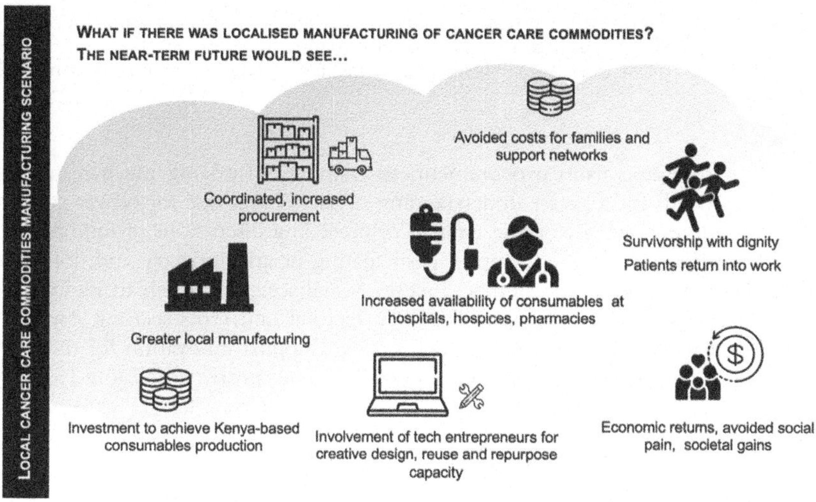

Fig. 13.4 A future scenario for local manufacturing of cancer care commodities in Kenya

Table 13.3 Key sectoral and cross-sectoral issues for localised production of commodities

Key user	*Questions to guide further work*
Industry	Are manufacturers prepared to supply initially small markets? How can local industrialists access capital for the required infrastructure and technology to manufacture cancer care commodities? What infrastructure investment is needed to produce locally acceptable colostomy bags and breast prosthesis? Are local materials available? How can industry be given confidence that products will be bought? Why is there an industry perception of low demand for consumables?
Health	What data can health workers share to help understand and quantify the need representing potential commodities market size? What patients have similar needs for these commodities outside of cancer? How can health professionals feasibly participate in research and development to develop products that suit patient needs? How can we shift the mindset from commodity import to local manufacturing? How can we ensure that greater availability results in greater access?
Patients	How can patients and carers be included in commodity development? What are the needs to inform product design? What would be the impact overall of earlier diagnosis on patient demand?
Policy	What evidence is needed to increase political confidence and support for localised commodity manufacturing? How can affordability of locally manufactured commodities be achieved?

industry ranging from procurement, to training, to pricing mechanisms, to data needs for a better understanding of the market size for cancer care commodities. In the working context of preceding discussions of multiple, cross-cutting issues, the group of participating health, industry and policy leaders repeatedly used references to the visual scenario sketch to identify mutual areas of interest, as well as key sectoral and cross-sectoral issues they believed in the need for further work to support innovation for more localised production of commodities. These are summarised in Table 13.3.

Reflections on Practice

This Kenya case of scenario use was a first attempt at using scenarios to engage partners in identification and prioritisation of innovation ideas. Despite serious logistical pandemic limitations on mechanisms for team exchange of evidence and discussion, the team's experiences illustrate how scenarios can be used to shift research focus from probabilities premised in an understanding of the status quo, towards possibilities of novel future innovations. The case study further demonstrates the utility of scenario development in providing a tool for transparently identify what knowledge uncertainties are of mutual interest between diverse stakeholder groups for further work and investigation. As an outcome of this scenario work, local production of commodities was included in a policy brief on opportunities for strengthening Kenyan cancer care (Manduku et al., 2022) Furthermore, the exercise provided a space within a broader research process to take time to imagine positive change, and to develop empathy with future health and innovation stakeholders. The researchers reported benefits in clarifying areas that future work could build on, and also a hopeful experience in increasing motivation for targeting research outputs towards related policy issues in the near-term.

The Strengths of Scenarios for Cross-Sectoral Innovation Support

Drawing on the experiences in developing the above scenarios, we reflect here on the distinctive strengths of scenario tools when looking to better support linkages between health, industry, and policy for cancer care innovation in Africa.

A Whole System View

First, those working to understand and strengthen mutual linkages between health, industry and policy need to consider the needs and experiences of a wide range of groups, including patients and carers. A holistic view that transcends historical, sectoral, and professional boundaries is needed. Often the methods and tools we use to analyse issues employ a particular and typically partial perspective that focuses on specific processes or incomplete consideration of system developments.

Scenarios tools are open and flexible in terms of the sectors, processes or types of outcomes considered. Their what-if explorations can cut across systems, as they do not follow domain-specific events but look instead to describe and explain how event sequences might unfold—even where these involve causal linkages across domains. We note that even with scenarios and other systems-based methods absolute comprehensiveness remains lacking. No methodology can ever definitively cover all potential dimensions and details of a system. The strength of systems-based scenarios, however, is that they explicitly support a multi-dimensional and whole systems view of issues as faced by stakeholders.

Synthesis Across Sectors and Professions

In a multi-stakeholder context, a whole systems view needs to bring together diverse contributions. The process combining diverse evidence contributions to generate additional learning from these evidence inputs is known as synthesis. Various practical challenges faced in achieving synthesis arise from standard data and research practices. Groups across different sectors often collect and store evidence using different data types and formats. Some professionals may use spreadsheets of projected demand levels, while others have lived experience in working with patients, and other have tacit knowledge of comparative strengths and weaknesses of different manufacturing machinery. Each of these evidence types useful for systemic innovation learning uses different norms, assumptions and logics, also known as epistemological boundaries.

Scenarios provide those working in cross-linkage cancer innovation with tools that can rapidly establish a common reference frame for synthesising diverse quantitative, qualitative, social, economic, political knowledges across groups. Using visions of the future, as in the Kenyan local commodities case, scenarios can draw out the connection of one profession's issue to another profession's interests (Gregório et al., 2014). Scenarios thereby often combine and synthesise qualitative, quantitative evidence and transcend disciplinary and epistemological boundaries (Ramirez & Wilkinson, 2016).

Usefulness in Research and Evidence

One pitfall often encountered by research and knowledge synthesis efforts aiming to support innovation is a lack of evidence that is action-oriented. That is, while the rigour and quality of research outputs are high, they can find themselves more heavily weighted towards descriptions of, for example, the state of access to drugs, and interpretative evidence about implications for care, rather than propositional and reflective evidence needed for action by policymakers, industry leaders, and healthcare leaders. This has sometimes been described as the gap between 'research about practice' and 'research for practice' (Rein & Schön, 2013).

Scenarios anticipate futures needs, issues, as well as potential opportunities, risks, mechanisms for change and the consequences of action. Wright et al. (2009) emphasise that through understanding the connections, causal processes and logical sequences which determine how events may unfold to create different futures, scenarios challenge conventional thinking and improve current organisational decision-making. They are also able to explore ideas that are radically different from the status quo, which is essential for exploring innovation options. Innovation needs exploration of the possible, more so than the probable. In exploring 'what-if' questions, scenarios challenge conventional thinking, and subsequently reframe perspectives of what can be achieved. Scenario techniques can within a single methodology translate speculative, propositional analysis into actionable evidence for decision-making.

Uncertainty and the Absence of Empirical Data

Innovative action and change can potentially incur high costs, and multiple risks. A typical precondition for investment and support for change in healthcare or industrial production is the availability of evidence charting what is possible and likely. In a context where prediction is impossible, scenarios explore potential significance and impacts of innovative future measures without bearing actual risk. Unlike many other methods familiar to medical researchers, economists, social researchers, and others working in health and industry, the validity and usefulness of scenario analysis is not dependent on observation or comparison with real-world events.

Inclusive and Accessible Tools

A final strength of scenarios is the wide accessibility of their narrative-based approach to developing collective visioning and exploring future pathways. Effective engagement and synthesis tools are those that capture the experiences and contributions of diverse stakeholders. A collaboratively developed, shared evidence base is essential to inform mutually supportive action across different stakeholder groups (Innes & Booher, 2010). Through their basis of 'what-if' questions, they can involve a wide range of stakeholders through story-telling, even potentially stakeholder groups who were not directly involved in the scenario building activities themselves.

In terms of their set up, scenarios can be developed and used, as shown here, without computer models, mathematical formula, or complicated setups. They can use flexibly visuals, objects and even enactment to help participants share and engage with each other's contributions. They are adaptable to the typically time-pressurised and resource-constrained context of health innovation work, and can be used with minimal set up, yet while still contributing insights within short time frames, with reusable outputs for different evidence collection and dissemination activities.

Using Scenarios to Build Cross-Sector Innovation Capability

For those readers wanting to make use of scenario tools in the context of their own mutual linkage policy problem, but potentially with little existing experience with them, we conclude with five principles for using scenarios when building cross-cutting innovation capability. These principles combine extant recommendations from wider scenario theories and practices, as well as lessons learned in using scenarios to support innovation for cancer care in Africa.

1. **Dispel the idea of a 'right' way to use scenarios**. Purpose determines whether scenarios are used to vision, anticipate future outcomes, or learn for action. The scope, duration, inputs, methods, and output formats of scenario use can all be adapted to a user's needs and constraints.
2. **Derive validity from usefulness, not accuracy**. No scenario can accurately predict the future. Prioritise provision of time and space for achieving the value and validity that come out of discussions about, and learning from, coherent future 'what-if' narratives.
3. **Discuss different future scenarios to uncover mutual linkages**. Encourage discussion of a wide range of future outcomes, events, and actions between diverse stakeholders to reveal critical linkages between parts of the health innovation system.

4. **Include diverse stakeholders with mixed tools.** Use a range of visual, numeric, descriptive, or other tools to facilitate scenario discussions. People differentially find it easier or harder to synthesise information as well as contribute their ideas using visual, written, or oral modes of engagement.
5. **Explore what could be possible, beyond what might be probable.** Innovation capability is strengthened by learning from ideas and insights that go beyond what is already well-known or widely practised. Improbable future scenarios are likely to reveal influential yet uncertain assumptions framing the current understanding of mechanisms of change—and the real-world opportunities and constraints that shape their future outcomes.

Notes

1. A popular method for such top-down, deductive scenario construction generates a '2 × 2' matrix that combines opposing future levels of two uncertain key variables leading to four resultant scenarios. This approach was made popular by the early scenario planning work of Royal/Dutch Shell in the energy sector in the 1970s (see Schwarz, 2012).
2. There are several variants of 'systems mapping', such as 'cognitive mapping', 'issue mapping', 'causal loop diagramming'. Crucially, they all make explicit mental models of critical issues shaping the behaviour of a systems of interest, and relationships of influence between these issues. Readers interested in further detail of the systems mapping for the ICCA project can access the whole map and details of process on visiting https://www.ucl.ac.uk/steapp/research/21st-century-decision-making/icca-innovation-cancer-care-africa. For a recent overview of some common systems mapping methods see Barbrook-Johnson and Penn (2022).

CHAPTER 14

Conclusion: Better Cancer Care and Greater Local Health Security: Lessons, Opportunities and Ways Forward

Geoffrey Banda, Maureen Mackintosh, Mercy Karimi Njeru, Smita Srinivas, Joanna Chataway, and Fortunata Songora Makene

Core Themes

There are (at least) five core themes within this research-based book.

First, there is a growing recognition of the rising healthcare challenges for non-communicable diseases exemplified by cancer in this book. Non-communicable diseases require urgent policy and practice attention, at the

G. Banda (✉)
University of Edinburgh, Edinburgh, UK
e-mail: Geoffrey.Banda@ed.ac.uk

M. Mackintosh
The Open University, Milton Keynes, UK

M. K. Njeru
Kenya Medical Research Institute (KEMRI), Nairobi, Kenya

G. Banda et al. (eds.), *Cancer Care in Pandemic Times: Building Inclusive Local Health Security in Africa and India*, International Political Economy Series,
https://doi.org/10.1007/978-3-031-44123-3_14

level of public policy urgency and agency demonstrated during the Covid-19 pandemic. Structuring responses to non-communicable diseases entails careful consideration of aspects of health system organisation, as well as the types and costs of diagnostic tools, medical devices and therapies and the role of local production.

Second, building better cancer care in Africa and India implies identifying and tackling the huge gaps between needs for care, and the extent of available, affordable care. Listening to patients, carers and cancer survivors is, as we learned, the essential starting point for understanding their needs and priorities, finding the gaps inherent in the system, and seeking ways to address those gaps.

Third, inter-linking health care with industrial development, via many "bridging" institutions that include research centres, regulators, professional and industrial associations, and a wide range of policy actors, is an essential way forward to better care and greater local health security. It can be done, and can serve to strengthen the impact of moves towards universal health coverage (UHC).

Fourth, the Covid-19 pandemic has transformed the political, technological and innovation space for building stronger local health security in lower resource contexts including African countries and India, and space for demonstrating trust in local technological capabilities. Sustaining that social, political and technological space and using it to accelerate development of broad industrial capabilities for local health benefit and broader development, is a major opportunity and challenge. Health industrial projects are technological and political projects. Their promotion will generate resistance from incumbents, as such national governments need to be prepared for an international backlash, as well as local political and economic contestations.

And fifth, solving the rising non-communicable and current infectious disease challenges requires collective socio-technical visions of the

S. Srinivas
Bengaluru, India

J. Chataway
University College London, London, UK

F. S. Makene
Economic and Social Research Foundation (ESRF), Dar Es Salaam, Tanzania

future that involve governments, industrialists and other stakeholders in the health care field. Framing these socio-technical imaginaries can be supported by methodological approaches such as scenario-building, as presented in the previous chapter of this book.

As cancer care rises up global and local health priorities, its difficult challenges help to identify routes to improvement that have wider implications across the healthcare spectrum in low-and middle-income countries. And as the immediate pandemic crisis recedes, this book shows ways to learn from and build upon the cross-sectoral collaborations and innovations achieved in the worst of the crisis years.

This final chapter briefly summarises and reflects on themes and lessons in the book. We argue for policy reframing, using interdisciplinary frameworks and methodologies that can break open the policy and intellectual "silos" of health and of industry and generate cross-sectoral understanding and collaboration for local health security.

Local Health Security: Pandemic Lessons

This book aims to widen and rework current international understandings of how to build local health security. Health security is often understood, in definition and practice, to refer to national responses to health emergencies arising from infectious disease (Brown et al., 2022). Current work also recognises the importance of health system strengthening as underpinning pandemic preparedness (Brown et al., 2022; WHO, 2021a). This book greatly widens this frame of reference, arguing that building local health security in low- and middle-income countries, and specifically in Africa, requires the integration of broader industrial and economic developments with health outcome improvements (Chapters 1 and 2). Consequently, public policy is an important factor for achieving these goals.

This argument is supported by the pandemic experience of collapsing global supply chains (Chapter 2). As had been widely predicted, African countries found themselves at the back of the queue, not just for vaccines—the current global focus—but for the full range of essential medicines, equipment and commodities required to tackle the epidemic. At the same time, local responses demonstrated how much could be achieved in such a crisis by countries with greater depth of industrial and technological capabilities.

Local health security must therefore be understood in a broader political economy framework. There are major developmental advantages to be drawn from geographical and relational proximity: they include shared knowledge, common resource pools, short supply lines, shared culture, and feedback from economic spillovers from local upskilling and knowledge development (Chapter 2). These are the historic roots of local economic development across the world, and they form the groundwork for building local health security. They help to build the synergies and linkages between industrial investment and innovation, regulatory changes and adaptability, research, market creation and shaping through consolidating health system demand and procurement, and interactions with health system organisation. At the same time positionality—the locus of power, agency and responsibility—generates specific local priorities and contextualised interventions that are likely to differ systematically from high-income countries' focus.

The authors of Chapter 2 argue that achieving these developmental benefits allied to health care improvement requires not only better cross-sectoral linkages and dialogue, but also a sharp leap of imagination. What is needed are new "socio-technical imaginaries" about what is desirable and possible: envisaging technological futures and generating the local agency and legitimacy to work towards them over the medium term, including the legitimation of channelling of public funds to these long-term technical projects. Later chapters develop this theme of new imaginaries in practical terms for Eastern and Southern African contexts, including routes to greater industrial ambition in the local health industries (Chapter 7), and the exploitation of the momentum in local vaccine development to extend African capabilities in the biotechnology platforms (Chapter 10).

Crises disrupt conventional traditions, paradigms and wisdom (Nohrstedt & Weible, 2010) and they force a re-thinking of the status quo. The Covid-19 pandemic opened up political, policy, technological and institutional spaces for innovation and technological developments. Many authors of this book and their professional networks became deeply involved in building these linkages and innovations under acute pressure in both India (Chapter 6) and East Africa (Chapter 7). Maintaining this momentum is now a major challenge for governments and industrial and health system stakeholders, in the face of exhaustion, backlogs and continuing crises.

This book explores in depth how the lessons about what is possible—learned or reinforced during the pandemic—can be taken forward to build not just greater preparedness for the next pandemic, but greater local health-related capability and security in addressing the range of health challenges faced. In this effort, renewed momentum towards UHC can be supported by strengthened and shortened supply chains and improved broader local industrial capabilities. Cancer care improvement—one of the most difficult challenges among the rising tide of non-communicable disease burdens—provides us with a powerful "lens" to study how to take these lessons forward.

Need, Demand, Supply, Access: Tackling Institutional Gaps in Cancer Care

The cancer "explosion" in African countries (Ngwa et al., 2022b) is increasingly well documented in the international literature, and concern to tackle the crisis in cancer care has been rising up the international agenda (Boyle et al., 2019) (Chapter 1). This book aims to contribute to further understanding of the nature of that crisis, and to situate the scope for achieving improvements within a broad understanding of cross-sectoral linkages between health and industrial change.

Interviews with over 450 cancer patients and survivors in East Africa generated new understandings of their perspectives and experiences. The research team learned, first, the importance participants gave to issues perceived to be under-valued: issues of dignity, survivorship, palliative care, family cohesion, addressing stigma, and support for continuing social and economic activity (Chapter 3). The interviews and discussions also with carers, activists and health professionals broadened our understanding of need, and charted the social pain generated by cancer for all those involved, including communities, families and individuals, carers and health professionals. Improving access to diagnosis and treatment were relocated as very important elements within a broader spectrum of response to cancer care needs.

Participants shared experiences of a health sector in Tanzania and Kenya which, while trying hard to improve cancer care, still presented a maze-like face to people seeking help (Chapter 4). The aim of describing these experiences of navigating a maze largely unaided—and providing examples of where maps and guides had helped to smooth patients' pathways—is to improve understanding of the current health systems as encountered by patients. It also helped to identify affordable approaches that could reduce pain and delay.

Evidence from these experiences about reasons for delayed diagnosis—and hence the risk of poorer outcomes—showed that most recorded delay occurred after these patients went to facilities with worrying symptoms. Caution is needed therefore before framing the cancer challenge as one of late presentation by patients to the health system, a framing that tends to foist responsibility for delay largely on the patient. Rather, these patients' experiences identified multiple interconnected health system factors contributing to the scourge of late-stage cancer diagnosis, including a lack of diagnostic capabilities at lower levels of the health system and the need for a concerted improvement in referral processes. Analysing these experiences can support professionals and policymakers to prioritise specific improvements (Chapter 5).

Through all these documented experiences, lack of access to essential medicines, diagnostics and treatments was a recurrent theme. These gaps between established needs and access to requirements occur not only in East Africa, where most required cancer supplies are imported, but also in India, where most essentials can be and are locally produced (Chapters 6, 11). A huge range of uncertainties—about what is needed for inclusive health care in general, and cancer in particular, and therefore what should be produced and supplied—were exposed and mapped during the Covid-19 crisis. This research fed into improving health-industrial communication, mutual understanding and joint activity, aiming to shrink some of these "institutional gaps" (Chapters 6, 11).

The institutional nature of the gaps between industrial decision making, procurement and supply decisions and health care needs is well documented in this book for the case of cancer care requirements. While financial constraint is often central to explaining lack of access to essential supplies, this is by no means always the case. Essential basic commodities such as colostomy bags and prostheses were hard to find in the Kenyan private market, were available only as expensive imports, and were not covered by insurance nor widely supplied through public procurement (Chapters 3, 7, 12). Yet industrial capabilities existed locally to produce these items, and industrialists stated that they were unaware of demand.

This need-demand gap, resulting from a failure of market consolidation and organisation, was found to extend in Kenya and Tanzania far beyond these basic commodities. The local supply gaps for items that were well within local industrial capabilities to produce included bandages and swabs, diagnostic kits, IV fluids, basic equipment and a range of medication including antibiotics and pain medication (Chapters 7, 8, 12). These gaps were thrown into relief by the pandemic, and some efforts to tackle them were underway at the time of writing (Chapter 7). Consolidating demand to respond to identified needs, through improved public procurement, public–private collaboration and regional market integration, offers routes to generate affordable improvements in supply and access to essential cancer care, including less expensive oncology medication (Chapter 8).

Scope for Investment in Local Manufacture of Drugs, Vaccines, Biologics and Medical Technologies

This book extends our previous arguments that there is a need to consider the political economy of industrialising for local health, and that local production of medicines is a critical component for enhancing local health security (Mackintosh et al., 2016). As discussed in Chapters 2, and 7–10, there is great scope for investment in local manufacture of drugs, vaccines, diagnostics and medical devices. However, there are contextual and innovation ecosystem hurdles or opportunities that need to be considered.

Investment in building broad industrial capabilities is a long-term venture that requires patient capital especially in the nascent stages of developing or localising new technologies. Chapter 9 demonstrates how the state, other funders and a constellation of science, technology and innovation institutes collaborated to support an innovative medical devices and diagnostic sector in India. However, this innovative Indian MedTech (medical technology) sector still faces a policy vacuum, regulatory lag and small market for low-value products. The scope for investment in local manufacture should structure the policy environment that supports entrepreneurship, faster pathways to market and innovative procurement regimes that actively use health policy as active industry development policy.

The book highlights the need to leverage market and non-market relationships that encompass supplier—buyer linkage capabilities, procurement agencies actively pursuing innovative procurement, active guidance of search and knowledge transfer for emerging technologies that purposively links research institutes and innovators, and bridging institutions in the innovation ecosystem.

Incremental innovation offers a faster pathway for technology upgrading. In the drugs sector the Indian pharmaceutical sector developed through backwards linkages as distributors turned to production. We argue that it is easier for current vaccine manufacturers than for chemical drug manufacturers to transition to biologics production in Africa. They have similar production and quality assurance processes as well as the skills sets. For a more rapid technology transfer route, countries can actively pursue joint ventures for transition to radical innovations embodied in manufacturing more complex technologies. Achieving these transitions requires strategic interlinkages between health policy and industrial policy, as well as industrial organisation.

Evidence from India suggests that the emergence of entrepreneurship, technology development and business model options are driven by funding and policy infrastructures that shape the sectoral innovation ecosystem. However, last mile challenges for MedTech still need to be resolved.

Turning to biologics manufacture on the continent, Chapter 10 argued that local production of biologics therapies for oncology is feasible. This is important because future diagnosis and treatment of cancer will most likely be based on exploitation of a range of platform technologies (Bargahi et al., 2022; Klinghoffer et al., 2015; Ohannesian et al., 2020), some of which will be based on biotechnology. A number of African countries possess the foundational technological capabilities in research institutions, the private sector and universities to enhance local production of biologics. Building these capabilities will require concomitant building of capabilities in biologics regulation.

Interlinking Health Care and Industrial Development: Reframing Policy

As the discussion of socio-technical imaginaries and the identification of institutional gaps suggests, exploiting the potential synergies between industrial development and better health care starts from an exercise in reframing policy. The intellectual and institutional "silos" of industrial policy and health policy are hard wired, locally and internationally. The pandemic forced onto the policy agenda the need to address collapsing supply chains and resolve mutual incomprehension between industry and health actors (Chapters 2, 6). The implied need to align broad industrial development much more closely to public health goals was strongly argued to the G20 in 2021 (Srinivas, 2021a). Yet even now, recent international work on local health security, cited above, does not address the organisation of the health industries. And what international attention is currently given to localisation of industrial production for health needs within African countries is limited to vaccine production.

Policy reframing is therefore a key requirement for building local health security. The understanding of institutions in this book is evolutionary: different industrial, health and other key institutions develop within their own trajectories and policy frames (Chapter 6). To generate the innovations in products and processes needed to deepen and upgrade local manufacturing, supporting networks of actors are required, sometimes called an innovation ecosystem (Chapter 7). The relevant actors include industrial and health service producers, regulators, standard setting bodies, policy makers, researchers and civil society organisations.

One analytical framing used here builds on the large literature on national systems of innovation (NIS) (Chapter 7). Over the last three decades, NIS has been influential as a conceptual framework for understanding the relationship between innovation, policy and institutional environments. Conjoined analysis of health systems with industrial structures using this framework reveals opportunities for industrial deepening and backward linkages in the drugs, vaccines, biologics, medical devices and diagnostic value chains. A wide range of industrial sectors link to healthcare, encompassing, among many others, metals and plastics fabrication, metrology, precision manufacturing, poppy plant growth and extraction of morphine, chemical synthesis, and biological drug substance production using fermentation and other techniques.

Lundvall's (1992) NIS framework has three building blocks, namely sources of innovation, non-market institutions and types of innovation. We use this framework as a foundation to distinguish between incremental and disruptive (radical) innovations (Chapter 10). Incremental innovations are less disruptive to business models, production processes and regulatory pathways (Tait & Wield, 2021). Thus, biologics production in African contexts can build incrementally on vaccine manufacturing capabilities, however, biologics are a disruptive innovation in the wider health-industrial innovation ecosystem, demanding sharp changes in regulatory rules and processes and new capabilities in local standards bodies

(Chapter 10). NIS literature has typically used retrospective analysis to capture insights into ways in which national contexts, institutions, organisations and policies have shaped how innovation occurs or does not in specific environments.

However, a growing strand of NIS literature has sought to look forward, at ways to reshape innovation and innovative environments to directly address social challenges (Arocena & Sutz, 2014; Chataway et al., 2014). This trend is associated with more recent demands to aim innovation and innovation policy directly at creating more inclusive and equal societies (transformative innovation). Rather than assuming that the benefits of innovation will automatically lead to progress of various kinds, there is a need to steer innovation to address head-on pressing social, institutional and environmental problems.

For this purpose, scenarios, as a tool and an approach to policy and problem framing, build effectively on the strengths and integrity of NIS analysis of specific contexts as they evolve. Scenario creation starts from this type of landscape mapping (Chapter 12). It then offers a practical way to look forward and deal explicitly with uncertainty (Chapter 13). Looking forward aims to generate directionality in steering innovation across sectors. That requires in turn uncovering mutually desirable directions among the diverse sectors and institutions mapped and invited.

Scenario building then provides tools with which health and industrial actors can share and explore their respective visions, policy frames, agendas and plans for the future. Using scenarios frameworks and techniques has the advantage that the focus is very much on agency and on the complex dynamics associated with agendas for change and policy interventions. Chapter 13 provides two examples—developed collaboratively within tight pandemic constraints—and aims to illustrate the scope for scenario building to help to tackle cross-sectoral innovation and problem solving for cancer care and for wider health security.

Concluding Reflection

The project in which this book is rooted set out to study cancer care in East Africa and India—and the researchers then found themselves embroiled in pandemic demands. The pandemic experience was both highly stressful, and also deeply illuminating in intellectual and policy terms. This book has set out to capture both the lessons from the research on cancer care, and also the unforeseen lessons learned while studying that "wicked problem" (Chapter 1) in the midst of the pandemic. In so many ways, these lessons formed a coherent whole. We had started out, based on past work, to embed our research and understanding of cancer care within the broader political economy of healthcare and industrial development in two East African countries and in India. The pandemic hugely reinforced for us the importance of that broad developmental view.

Cancer care is a crisis that local policies aim to tackle within the context, in India, Tanzania and Kenya as elsewhere, of moves towards universal health coverage to generate more inclusive health systems. The pandemic years undermined progress on cancer care and UHC. However, the pandemic has also helped illuminate the possibilities for legitimating active public policy to allocate resources to support systemic improvement, investment in local manufacturing capabilities and promotion of strategic inter-sectoral interlinkages that drive local health security. The findings on improving cancer care align with the longer-term requirements of building local health security, which we have argued earlier are the precursor and foundation for global health security.

Achieving local health security entails purposive structuring of health-industrial linkages. This requires a legitimate role for public policy during non-pandemic times in resource mobilisation to stimulate knowledge development and diffusion, entrepreneurship and market formation. Public action is also needed to legitimate new technologies and create markets through innovative procurement, and to counter local and international institutional resistance by engaging in political and economic contestations with incumbents.

We argue in this book that health industry development projects are not only technical projects, but by virtue of international economic competitiveness contestations and global production value chain power asymmetries, also embody political and economic aspects. They are political-technical projects. It is conceivable that local production arguments will be met with counter arguments for dependence on global pharmaceutical value chains based on scale, efficiency, intellectual property rights as well as patient safety. These arguments are long standing: India, Bangladesh, Sri Lanka (Lall & Bibile, 1978; Reich, 1994) and China faced them.

The urgency of dealing with rising non-communicable diseases exemplified with cancer in this book cannot be over-emphasised. Most of the therapies required are off-patent and global production systems may de-emphasise them because of low profit margins. Consequently, this calls for public policy to be bold in solving local health challenges in order to build robust local health security. The Covid-19 pandemic amply demonstrated the risk of not having broad local industrial capabilities (Banda et al., 2022). Broad industrial capabilities are important for solving current local health challenges and generating future pandemic preparedness and agility.

References

Alvotech. (2020). *Alvotech and Cipla partner to ensure access to biosimilars in South Africa*. https://www.alvotech.com/newsroom/alvotech-and-cipla-partner-to-ensure-access-to-biosimilars

Amandua, J., Kimaro, M. S., Mwebesa, E., Taremwa, I. M., & Atuhairwe, C. (2019). The financing of stand-alone palliative Care Services in Uganda: Analysis of the implications for sustainability. *BMC Palliative Care, 18*(1), 48.

Amorim-Lopes, M., Oliveira, M., Raposo, M., Cardoso-Grilo, T., Alvarenga, A., Barbas, M., Alves, M., Vieira, A., & Barbosa-Póvoa, A. (2021). Enhancing optimization planning models for health human resources management with foresight. *Omega, 103*. https://doi.org/10.1016/j.omega.2020.102384

Andrews, M. A., Areekal, B., Rajesh, K. R., Krishnan, J., Suryakala, R., Krishnan, B., Muraly, C. P., & Santhosh, P. V. (2020). First confirmed case of COVID-19 infection in India: A case report. *Indian Journal of Medical Research, 151*(5), 490–492.

Ariga, E. S., & Mujinja, P. G. M. (2017). Family role and causes of delay in seeking treatment by cervical cancer patients after diagnosis in Dar es Salaam, Tanzania. *Journal of International Academic Research for Multidisciplinary, 5*(5), 80–89.

Arocena, R., & Sutz, J. (2014). Innovation and democratisation of knowledge as a contribution to inclusive development, in The Latin American Experience. In *National innovation systems, social inclusion and development*.

Baden-Fuller, C., & Haefliger, S. (2013). Business models and technological innovation. *Long Range Planning*, *46*(6), 419–426. https://doi.org/10.1016/j.lrp.2013.08.023

G. Banda et al. (eds.), *Cancer Care in Pandemic Times: Building Inclusive Local Health Security in Africa and India*, International Political Economy Series,
https://doi.org/10.1007/978-3-031-44123-3

Bahati, F., English, M., Sayed, S., Horton, S., Odhiambo, O. A., Samatar, A. A., & Mcknight, J. (2021). Information asymmetry in the Kenyan medical laboratory sector. *Global Health Action, 14*(1), 1964172.

Balaji, R. (2019). *This Bengaluru startup's low-cost device is using AI to detect cervical cancer in rural Karnataka* [Online].

Banda, G., Mugwagwa, J., Kale, D., & Ndomondo-Sigonda, M. (2016a). Pharmaceutical standards in Africa: The road to improvement and their role in technological capability upgrading. In M. Mackintosh, G. Banda, P. Tibandebage, & W. Wamae (Eds.), *Making medicines in Africa* (pp. 224–242). Palgrave Macmillan.

Banda, G., Wangwe, S., & Mackintosh, M. (2016b). Making medicines in Africa: An historical political economy overview. In M. Mackintosh, G. Banda, P. Tibandebage, & W. Wamae (Eds.), *Making medicines in Africa* (pp. 7–24). Palgrave Macmillan.

Banda, G., Tait, J., & Mittra, J. (2018). Evolution of business models in regenerative medicine: Effects of a disruptive innovation on the innovation ecosystem. *Clinical Therapeutics, 40*(7), 1084–1094.

Banda, G., Tait, E., & Mittra, J. (2019a). Regenerative medicine as a disruptive technology: Implications for manufacturing and clinical adoption. *Cell and Gene Therapy Insights, 5*(10), 1287–1303.

Banda, G., Mittra, J., Tait, J., Watkins, A., & Omidvar, O. (2019b). Understanding the emergence and evolution of new business models in the UK regenerative medicine sector. *Technology Analysis & Strategic Management, 33*(3), 320–333.

Banda, G., Kale, D., Mackintosh, M., & Mugwagwa, J. (2021a). *Local manufacturing for health in Africa in the time of Covid-19: Experience and lessons for policy*. DEGRP Webinar 2021 ONLINE. Development and Economic Growth Research Programme (DEGRP). https://webarchive.nationalarchives.gov.uk/ukgwa/20211030172136/https://degrp.odi.org/publication/webinar-report-local-manufacturing-for-health-africa-covid19/

Banda, G., Mugwagwa, J., Wanjala, C., Mackintosh, M., & Kale, D. (2021b). Local manufacturing, local supply chains and health security in Africa: Lessons from COVID-19. *BMJ Global Health, 6*(6), e006362.

Banda, G., Mackintosh, M., Mugwagwa, J., & Mukwashi, A. (2022). *Localisation of medical manufacturing in Africa*. Johannesburg South Africa, Institute of Economic Justice (IEJ).

Barasa, E., Kazungu, J., Orangi, S., Kabia, E., Ogero, M., & Kasera, K. (2021). Indirect health effects of the COVID-19 pandemic in Kenya: A mixed methods assessment. *BMC Health Services Research, 21*, 1–16.

Barbrook-Johnson, P., & Penn, A. S. (2022). *Systems mapping: How to build and use causal models of systems*. Palgrave Macmillan.

Bargahi, N., Ghasemali, S., Jahandar-Lashaki, S., & Nazari, A. (2022). Recent advances for cancer detection and treatment by microfluidic technology, review and update. *Biological Procedures Online, 24*(1), 5.

Bishop, P., Hines, A., & Collins, T. (2007). The current state of scenario development: An overview of techniques. *Foresight, 9*(1), 5–25.

Blakney, A. K., Ip, S., & Geall, A. J. (2021). An update on self-amplifying mRNA vaccine development. *Vaccines (Basel), 9*(2), 97.

Booth, M. (1999). *Opium—A history*. St. Martin Griffin.

Börjeson, L., Höjer, M., Dreborg, K.-H., Ekvall, T., & Finnveden, G. (2006). Scenario types and techniques: Towards a user's guide. *Futures, 38*(7), 723–739.

Boyle, P., Ngoma, T., Sullivan, R., & Brawley, O. (2019). Cancer in Africa: The way forward. *Ecancermedicalscience, 13*, 953.

Brand, N. R., Qu, L. G., Chao, A., & Ilbawi, A. M. (2019). Delays and barriers to cancer care in low- and middle-income countries: A systematic review. *The Oncologist, 24*(12), e1371–e1380.

Brown, G. W., Bridge, G., Martini, J., Um, J., Williams, O. D., Choupe, L. B. T., Rhodes, N., Ho, Z. J. M., Chungong, S., & Kandel, N. (2022). The role of health systems for health security: A scoping review revealing the need for improved conceptual and practical linkages. *Globalization and Health, 18*(1), 51.

Buhl, A. (2019). Transfiguration(s) of palliative care: The moral economy of end-of-life care in a Tanzanian cancer hospital. In J. Kehr, H. Dilger, & P. van Eeuwijk (Eds.), *Zeitschrift für Ethnologie* (143). Special Issue—Transfigurations of health and the moral economy of medicine: Subjectivities, materialities, values (Vol. 143, pp. 85–104). Reimer Verlag.

Burke, N. J., Armin, J., & Eichelberger, L. (2019). Introduction: Framing cancer and structural vulnerability. In N. J. Burke, J. Armin, & L. Eichelberger (Eds.), *Negotiating structural vulnerability in cancer control* (pp. 1–20). University of New Mexico Press.

Carvalho, T., Krammer, F., & Iwasaki, A. (2021). The first 12 months of COVID-19: A timeline of immunological insights. *Nature Reviews Immunology, 21*(4), 245–256.

Casadesus-Masanell, R., & Ricart, J. E. (2010). From strategy to business models and onto tactics. *Long Range Planning, 43*(2), 195–215.

Central Bureau of Narcotics. (n.d.). *Opium cultivation: Licit cultivation of opium poppy* [Online]. http://cbn.nic.in/en/opium/overview/

Chataway, J., Hanlin, R., & Kaplinsky, R. (2014). Inclusive innovation: An architecture for policy development. *Innovation and Development, 4*(1), 33–54.

Chataway, J., Banda, G., & Cochrane, G., & Manville, C. (2016). Innovative procurement for health and industrial development. In M. Mackintosh, G.

Banda, P. Tibandebage, & W. Wamae (Eds.), *Making medicines in Africa: The political economy of industrializing for local health* (pp. 243–260). Palgrave Macmillan.

Chatterjee, P. (2020). Indian pharma threatened by COVID-19 shutdowns in China. *Lancet, 395*(10225), 675.

Chaudhuri, S. (2016). Can foreign firms promote local production of pharmaceuticals in Africa? In M. Mackintosh, G. Banda, P. Tibandebage, & W. Wamae (Eds.), *Making medicines in Africa: The political economy of industrializing for local health*. Palgrave Macmillan.

Chaudhuri, S. (2019a). *Are medicine prices high and unaffordable after TRIPS? Evidence from pharmaceutical industry in India* [Online]. Centre for Development Studies.

Chaudhuri, S. (2019b). *How effective has been government measures to control prices of anti-cancer medicines in India?* (Working Paper 490). Thiruvananthapuram, Kerala, India Centre for Development Studies.

Chaudhuri, S. (2021). *Product patent protection, the TRIPS LDC exemption and the Bangladesh pharmaceutical industry*. Penang, Malaysia, Third World Network.

Chaudhuri, S., Mackintosh, M., & Mujinja, M. (2010). Indian generics producers, access to essential medicines and local production in Africa: An argument with reference to Tanzania. *The European Journal of Development Research, 22*(4), 451–468.

Cheema, K. (2020). *World cancer day: India's healthtech startups fight the battle* [Online]. https://inc42.com/features/world-cancer-day-2020-india-healthtech-oncology-startups-fight-the-battle/

Chesbrough, H. (2010). Business model innovation: Opportunities and barriers. *Long Range Planning, 43*(2–3), 354–363.

Clarke, S. (2013). The research council system and the politics of medical and agricultural research for the British Colonial Empire, 1940-52. *Medical History, 57*(3), 338–358.

Clarke, S. (2018). Scientific research and colonial development after 1940. In *Science at the end of empire* (pp. 49–75). Manchester University Press.

Connor, S. R. (2020). *Global Atlas of palliative care* (2nd ed.). Worldwide Hospice Palliative Care Alliance.

Cun, D., Zhang, C., Bera, H., & Yang, M. (2021). Particle engineering principles and technologies for pharmaceutical biologics. *Advanced Drug Delivery Reviews, 174*, 140–167.

Cuomo, R., Seidman, R., & Mackey, T. (2017). Country and regional variations in purchase prices for essential cancer medications. *BMC Cancer, 17*(1), 1–10.

Damani, A., Salins, N., Ghoshal, A., Chowdhury, J., Muckaden, M. A., Deodhar, J., & Pramesh, C. S. (2020). Provision of palliative care in National Cancer

Grid treatment centres in India: A cross-sectional gap analysis survey. *BMJ Support Palliat Care*.

Dammes, N., & Peer, D. (2020). Paving the road for RNA therapeutics. *Trends in Pharmacological Sciences, 41*(10), 755–775.

Davies, M. (2022). Covid-19: WHO efforts to bring vaccine manufacturing to Africa are undermined by the drug industry, documents show. *BMJ, 376*, o304.

De Martel, C., Georges, D., Bray, F., Ferlay, J., & Clifford, G. M. (2020). Global burden of cancer attributable to infections in 2018: A worldwide incidence analysis. *The Lancet Global Health, 8*(2), e180–e190.

De Savigny, D., Blanchet, K., & Adam, T. (2017). *Applied systems thinking for health systems research: A methodological handbook*. McGraw-Hill Education

Dhoot, V. (2021, April 7). Govt. to reboot dated opium strategy. *The Hindu*.

Diamond, M. (2018). *Powerful predictors: Diagnosing cancer in India using AI* [Online]. https://digital.hbs.edu/artificial-intelligence-machine-learning/powerful-predictors-diagnosing-cancer-in-india-using-ai/

Duggan, C., Trapani, D., Ilbawi, A. M., Fidarova, E., Laversanne, M., Curigliano, G., Bray, F., & Anderson, B. O. (2021). National health system characteristics, breast cancer stage at diagnosis, and breast cancer mortality: A population-based analysis. *The Lancet Oncology, 22*(11), 1632–1642.

Dyer, O. (2017). Pfizer and Cipla plan to make cancer drugs affordable in Africa. *BMJ, 359*, j4848.

Economic Times. (2013). *Cipla completes buyout of Cipla Medpro for Rs 2,707 crore*. https://economictimes.indiatimes.com/industry/healthcare/biotech/pharmaceuticals/cipla-completes-buyout-of-cipla-medpro-for-rs-2707-crore/articleshow/21102931.cms?utm_source=contentofinterest&utm_medium=text&utm_campaign=cppst

El Abd, Y., Tabll, A., Smolic, R., & Smolic, M. (2022). Mini-review: The market growth of diagnostic and therapeutic monoclonal antibodies—SARS CoV-2 as an example. *Human Antibodies, 30*(1), 15–24.

Elmore, S. N. C., Polo, A., Bourque, J. M., Pynda, Y., Van Der Merwe, D., Grover, S., Hopkins, K., Zubizarreta, E., & Abdel-Wahab, M. (2021). Radiotherapy resources in Africa: An international atomic energy agency update and analysis of projected needs. *The Lancet Oncology, 22*(9), e391–e399.

Esmaili, B. E., Stewart, K. A., Masalu, N. A., & Schroeder, K. M. (2018). Qualitative analysis of palliative care for pediatric patients with cancer at Bugando Medical Center: An evaluation of barriers to providing end-of-life care in a resource-limited setting. *Journal of Global Oncology, 4*(1), 1–10.

Espina, C., Mckenzie, F., & Dos-Santos-Silva, I. (2017). Delayed presentation and diagnosis of breast cancer in African women: A systematic review. *Annals of Epidemiology, 27*(10), 659–671.

European Patients Forum. (2016). *Defining and measuring access to healthcare: The patients' perspective: Position statement*. European Patients Forum.

Federation of German Industries. (2020). Export controls and export bans over the course of the Covid-19 pandemic. In S. A. Mildner, F. Esser, N. Keßels, L. Jansen, A. Kantrup, K. Tepper, J. Muck, & G. Popzyk (Eds.), *Position. Foreign Trade Policy. COVID-19: Document number: D 1169*. ONLINE.

Fleming, K. A., Horton, S., Wilson, M. L., Atun, R., Destigter, K., Flanigan, J., Sayed, S., Adam, P., Aguilar, B., Andronikou, S., Boehme, C., Cherniak, W., Cheung, A. N., Dahn, B., Donoso-Bach, L., Douglas, T., Garcia, P., Hussain, S., Iyer, H. S., … Walia, K. (2021). The Lancet Commission on diagnostics: Transforming access to diagnostics. *Lancet, 398*(10315), 1997–2050.

Foley, K., Wagner, J., Joranson, D., & Gelband, H. (2006). Chapter 52: Pain control for people with cancer and AIDS. In D. T. Jamison, J. G. Breman, & A. R. Measham (Eds.), *Disease control priorities in developing countries* (2nd ed.). The International Bank for Reconstruction and Development/ The World Bank.

Fourie, P. (2007). The future of AIDS in Africa: Lessons from two scenario projects. *African Journal of AIDS Research, 6*(2), 97–107.

Fransen, L., Nkengason, J., Srinivas, S., & Vella, S. (2021). *Boosting equitable access and production of diagnostics, therapeutics and vaccines to confront COVID-19 on a global footing: Policy Brief*. T20 Task Force 1 Global Health and COVID-19.

Fraser, B. A., Powell, R. A., Mwangi-Powell, F. N., Namisango, E., Hannon, B., Zimmermann, C., & Rodin, G. (2018). Palliative care development in Africa: Lessons from Uganda and Kenya. *Journal of Global Oncology, 4*, 1–10.

Gelband, H., Sankaranarayanan, R., Gauvreau, C. L., Horton, S., Anderson, B. O., Bray, F., Cleary, J., Dare, A. J., Denny, L., Gospodarowicz, M. K., Gupta, S., Howard, S. C., Jaffray, D. A., Knaul, F., Levin, C., Rabeneck, L., Rajaraman, P., Sullivan, T., Trimble, E. L., & Jha, P. (2016). Costs, affordability, and feasibility of an essential package of cancer control interventions in low-income and middle-income countries: Key messages from disease control priorities (3rd ed.). *Lancet, 387*(10033), 2133–2144.

Gerhold, L., & Brandes, E. (2021). Sociotechnical imaginaries of a secure future. *European Journal of Futures Research, 9*(1), 7.

Gesink, M. P., Chamberlain, R. M., Mwaiselage, J., Kahesa, C., Jackson, K., Mueller, W., Meza, J. L., & Soliman, A. S. (2020). Quantifying the underestimation of cervical cancer in remote regions of Tanzania. *BMC Cancer, 20*(1), 939.

Global Burden of Disease Study (GBD). (2017). *Findings from the Global Burden of Disease Study 2017*. Seattle, United States: Institute for Health Metrics and Evaluation (IHME). https://www.healthdata.org/research-analysis/gbd

Globocan. (2020a). *Africa Fact-Sheet* [Online]. International Agency for Research on Cancer (IARC)/World Health Organization. https://gco.iarc.fr/today/data/factsheets/populations/903-africa-fact-sheets.pdf

Globocan. (2020b). *India Fact-Sheet* [Online]. Geneva International Agency for Research on Cancer (IARC)/World Health Organization. https://gco.iarc.fr/today/data/factsheets/populations/356-india-fact-sheets.pdf

Gopichandran, V., & Chetlapalli, S. K. (2013). Dimensions and determinants of trust in health care in resource poor settings—A qualitative exploration. *PLoS ONE, 8*(7), e69170.

Gordon, A. (2011). The uses and limits of visionary scenarios: Learning from the African experience. *Foresight, 13*(4), 64–81.

Greenhalgh, T., & Papoutsi, C. (2018). Studying complexity in health services research: Desperately seeking an overdue paradigm shift. *BMC Medicine, 16*(1), 95.

Gregório, J., Cavaco, A., & Velez Lapão, L. (2014). A scenario-planning approach to human resources for health: The case of community pharmacists in Portugal. *Human Resources for Health, 12*(1), 58.

Hack, B., Piddock, K., Stanway, S., Balachandran, K., Board, R., Chopra, N., Okonji, D., Sirohi, B., Sullivan, R., & Wakeham, K. (2019). Cancer control in low- and middle-income countries: Time for action. *Journal of the Royal Society of Medicine, 112*(6), 213–217.

Haghdoost, A., Pourhosseini, S. S., Emami, M., Dehnavieh, R., Barfeh, T., & Mehrolhassani, M. H. (2017). Foresight in health sciences using Causal Layered Analysis method. *MJIRI, 31*(1), 492–499.

Hamdi, Y., Abdeljaoued-Tej, I., Zatchi, A. A., Abdelhak, S., Boubaker, S., Brown, J. S., & Benkahla, A. (2021). Cancer in Africa: The untold story. *Frontiers in Oncology, 11*, 650117.

Harris, J. T., Kumar, K. S., & Rajagopal, M. R. (2003). Intravenous morphine for rapid control of severe cancer pain. *Palliative Medicine, 17*(3), 248–256.

Hartwig, K., Dean, M., Hartwig, K., Mmbando, P. Z., Sayed, A., & De Vries, E. (2014). Where there is no morphine: The challenge and hope of palliative care delivery in Tanzania. *African Journal of Primary Health Care & Family Medicine, 6*(1), E1-8.

Hayhoe, B., Cowling, T. E., Pillutla, V., Garg, P., Majeed, A., & Harris, M. (2018). Integrating a nationally scaled workforce of community health workers in primary care: A modelling study. *Journal of the Royal Society of Medicine, 111*(12), 453–461.

Hill, A., Gotham, D., Fortunak, J., Meldrum, J., Erbacher, I., Martin, M., Shoman, H., Levi, J., Powderly, W. G., & Bower, M. (2016). Target prices for mass production of tyrosine kinase inhibitors for global cancer treatment. *BMJ Open*.

Hodge, J. M. (2011). The hybridity of colonial knowledge: British tropical agricultural science and African farming practices at the end of empire. In B. M. Bennet & J. M. Hodge (Eds.), *Science and empire—Knowledge and networks of science across the British Empire, 1800–1970*. Palgrave Macmillan.

Hodgson, G. M. (2007). An institutional and evolutionary perspective on health economics. *Cambridge Journal of Economics, 32*(2), 235–256.

Horton, S., Sullivan, R., Flanigan, J., Fleming, K. A., Kuti, M. A., Looi, L. M., Pai, S. A., & Lawler, M. (2018). Delivering modern, high-quality, affordable pathology and laboratory medicine to low-income and middle-income countries: A call to action. *Lancet, 391*(10133), 1953–1964.

Hoskisson, R. E., Wright, M., Filatotchev, I., & Peng, M. W. (2013). Emerging multinationals from mid-range economies: The influence of institutions and factor markets. *Journal of Management Studies, 50*(7), 1295–1321.

HRW. (2011). *Global state of pain treatment: Access to palliative care as a human right*. Human Rights Watch.

Hudd, T., & Moscovitch, D. A. (2021). Social pain and the role of imagined social consequences: Why personal adverse experiences elicit social pain, with or without explicit relational devaluation. *Journal of Experimental Social Psychology, 95*, 104121.

Hwang, J., & Christensen, C. M. (2008). Disruptive innovation in health care delivery: A framework for business-model innovation. *Health Aff (millwood), 27*(5), 1329–1335.

IARC. (2020). *World cancer report: Cancer research for cancer prevention*. Lyon France, International Agency for Research on Cancer.

ICCA India Podcast Series. (2021). *Significance of medical devices and diagnostics in cancer care* [Online]. https://www.youtube.com/watch?v=03T3pFKufHQ

India Brand Equity Fountation. (2022). *Pharmaceutical industry report* [Online]. https://www.ibef.org/industry/pharmaceutical-india

Innes, J. E., & Booher, D. E. (2010). *Planning with complexity: An introduction to collaborative rationality for public policy*. Routledge.

International Narcotics Control Board. (1974). *Report of the international narcotics control board for 1974*. International Narcotic Board.

International Narcotics Control Board. (1979). *Report of the international narcotics control board for 1979*. International Narcotics Control Board.

International Narcotics Control Board. (2012). 'Guide on Estimating Requirements for Substances under International Control: Developed by the International Narcotics Control Board and the World Health Organisation for use by Competent National Authorities'. United Nations. Available at: https://www.incb.org/documents/Narcotic-Drugs/Guidelines/estimating_requirements/NAR_Guide_on_Estimating_EN_Ebook.pdf

International Narcotics Control Board. (2015). *Availability of internationally controlled drugs: Ensuring adequate access for medical and scientific purpose international narcotics control board.*
International Narcotics Control Board. (2016). *Estimated world requirements for 2017.* Statistics for 2015 International Narcotics Control Board.
International Narcotics Control Board. (2019). *Estimated world requirements for 2020.* Statistics for 2018 International Narcotics Control Board.
International Narcotics Control Board. (2020). *Estimated world requirements for 2021.* Statistics for 2019 International Narcotics Control Board.
International Narcotics Control Board. (2021). *Estimated world requirements for 2022.* Statistics for 2020 International Narcotics Control Board.
Irwin, A. (2021). How COVID spurred Africa to plot a vaccines revolution. *Nature.*
Jacob, A., & Mathew, A. (2017). End-of-life care and opioid use in India: Challenges and opportunities. *Journal of Global Oncology, 3*(6), 683–686.
James, T. C., Kumar, D., & Chawla, D. (2021). *Public policy and economic development case study of Indian pharmaceutical industry.* Research and Information System for Developing Countries (RIS).
Jasanoff, S., & Kim, S. (2013). Sociotechnical imaginaries and national energy policies. *Science as Culture, 22,* 189–196.
Jasanoff, S., & Kim, S. (2015). *Dreamscapes of modernity: Sociotechnical imaginaries and the fabrication of power.* University of Chicago Press.
Jedy-Agba, E., Joko, W. Y., Liu, B., Buziba, N. G., Borok, M., Korir, A., Masamba, L., Manraj, S. S., Finesse, A., Wabinga, H., Somdyala, N., & Parkin, D. M. (2020). Trends in cervical cancer incidence in sub-Saharan Africa. *British Journal of Cancer, 123*(1), 148–154.
Joko-Fru, W. Y., Jedy-Agba, E., Korir, A., Ogunbiyi, O., Dzamalala, C. P., Chokunonga, E., Wabinga, H., Manraj, S., Finesse, A., Somdyala, N., Liu, B., Mcgale, P., Jemal, A., Bray, F., & Parkin, D. M. (2020). The evolving epidemic of breast cancer in sub-Saharan Africa: Results from the African Cancer Registry Network. *International Journal of Cancer, 147*(8), 2131–2141.
Juma, C. (2016). *Innovation and its enemies: Why people resist new technologies.* Oxford University Press.
Kale, D. (2019a). From small molecule generics to biosimilars: Technological upgrading and patterns of distinctive learning processes in the Indian pharmaceutical industry. *Technological Forecasting and Social Change, 145*(1), 370–383.
Kale, D. (2019b). Mind the gap: Investigating the role of collective action in the evolution of Indian medical device regulation. *Technology in Society, 59,* 101121.

Kale, D., & Wield, D. (2018). In search of the missing hand of 'collaborative action': Evidence from the Indian medical device industry. *Innovation and Development, 9*, 1–23.

Kale, D., Watkins, A., Papaioannou, T., & Mugwagwa, J. (2015). Why industry associations matter for healthcare industries in emerging countries: Evidence from the Indian biotechnology and medical device industries. In *13th Globelics international conference*. Havana, Cuba.

Kamonyo, E. S. (2018). The palliative care journey in Kenya and Uganda. *Journal of Pain and Symptom Management, 55*(2), S46–S54.

Kanté, A. M., Exavery, A., Phillips, J. F., & Jackson, E. F. (2016). Why women bypass front-line health facility services in pursuit of obstetric care provided elsewhere: A case study in three rural districts of Tanzania. *Tropical Medicine & International Health, 21*(4), 504–514.

Kashyap, S. (2019). *9 startups working to make cancer diagnosis and care easy and convenient* [Online]. https://yourstory.com/2019/09/startups-cancer-diagnosis-care-easy/amp

Kassaman, D., Mushani, T., Kiraithe, P., Brownie, S., & Barton-Burke, M. (2022). Fear, faith and finances: Health literacy experiences of English and Swahili speaking women newly diagnosed with breast and cervical cancer. *Ecancermedicalscience, 16*, 1350–1350.

Keijzer, N., Burni, A., Erforth, B., & Friesen, I. (2021). *The rise of team Europe approach in EU development cooperation. A moving target* (Discussion Paper). German Development Institute. https://doi.org/10.23661/dp22.2021

Khosla, D., Patel, F. D., & Sharma, S. C. (2012). Palliative care in India: Current progress and future needs. *Indian Journal of Palliative Care, 18*(3), 149–154.

Kipgen, N. (2019). Why are farmers in Manipur cultivating Poppy? *Economic and Political Weekly, 54*(46).

Kizub, D. A., Naik, S., Abogan, A. A., Pain, D., Sammut, S., Shulman, L. N., & Martei, Y. M. (2022). Access to and affordability of world health organization essential medicines for cancer in sub-Saharan Africa: Examples from Kenya, Rwanda, and Uganda. *The Oncologist, 27*(11), 958–970.

Kleinman, A. (1997). "Everything that really matters": Social suffering, subjectivity, and the remaking of human experience in a disordering world. *The Harvard Theological Review, 90*(3), 315–335.

Klinghoffer, R. A., Bahrami, S. B., Hatton, B. A., Frazier, J. P., Moreno-Gonzalez, A., Strand, A. D., Kerwin, W. S., Casalini, J. R., Thirstrup, D. J., You, S., Morris, S. M., Watts, K. L., Veiseh, M., Grenley, M. O., Tretyak, I., Dey, J., Carleton, M., Beirne, E., Pedro, K. D., … Olson, J. M. (2015). A technology platform to assess multiple cancer agents simultaneously within a patient's tumor. *Science Translational Medicine, 7*(284), 284ra258.

Knaul, F. M., Farmer, P. E., Krakauer, E. L., De Lima, L., Bhadelia, A., Jiang Kwete, X., Arreola-Ornelas, H., Gómez-Dantés, O., Rodriguez, N. M.,

Alleyne, G. A., Connor, S. R., Hunter, D. J., Lohman, D., Radbruch, L., Del Rocío Sáenz Madrigal, M., Atun, R., Foley, K. M., Frenk, J., Jamison, D. T., & Rajagopal, M. R. (2018). Alleviating the access abyss in palliative care and pain relief-an imperative of universal health coverage: The Lancet Commission report. *Lancet, 391*(10128), 1391–1454.

KNBS. (2018). *Basic report on well-being in Kenya: Based on the 2015/16 Kenya Integrated Household Budget Survey (KIHBS).* Kenya National Bureau os Statistics.

Kohi, T. W., Von Essen, L., Masika, G. M., Gottvall, M., & Dol, J. (2019). Cancer-related concerns and needs among young adults and children on cancer treatment in Tanzania: A qualitative study. *BMC Cancer, 19*(1), 82.

Kumu. (2022). *Kumu relationship mapping software* [Online]. https://kumu.io. Accessed 27 Jan 2023

Kwamie, A., Ha, S., & Ghaffar, A. (2021). Applied systems thinking: Unlocking theory, evidence and practice for health policy and systems research. *Health Policy and Planning, 36*(10), 1715–1717.

Lall, S. (1992). Technological capabilities and industrialization. *World Development, 20*(2), 165–186.

Lall, S., & Bibile, S. (1978). The political economy of controlling transnationals: The pharmaceutical industry in Sri Lanka, 1972–1976. *International Journal of Health Services, 8*(2), 299–328.

Lancet Oncology Editorial. (2017). Cancer control in Africa: Infrastructure, not philanthropy. *Lancet Oncology, 18*.

Landau, C., Karna, A., & Sailer, M. (2016). Business model adaptation for emerging markets: A case study of a German automobile manufacturer in India. *R&D Management, 46*(3), 480–503.

Lehmann, J., Machira, Y. W., Schneidman, M., & Chuma, J. (2020). *Economic and social consequences of cancer in Kenya*. World Bank.

Levesque, J. F., Harris, M. F., & Russell, G. (2013). Patient-centred access to health care: Conceptualising access at the interface of health systems and populations. *International Journal for Equity in Health, 12*(1), 18.

Livingston, J. (2012). *Improvising medicine: An African oncology ward in an emerging cancer epidemic*. Duke University Press.

London, T., Anupindi, R., & Sheth, S. (2010). Creating mutual value: Lessons learned from ventures serving base of the pyramid producers. *Journal of Business Research, 63*(6), 582–594.

Lundvall, B. Å. (1992). *National systems of innovation: Towards a theory of innovation and interactive learning*. Pinter Publishers.

Lundvall, B.-Å. (2007). National innovation systems—Analytical concept and development tool. *Industry & Innovation, 14*, 95–119.

Lundvall, B.-Å. (2016). *The learning economy and the economics of hope*. Anthem Press.

Mabxience. (2022). *Cipla enters a partnership to provide affordable oncology biosimilars to South Africa* [Online]. https://www.mabxience.com/cipla-enters-partnership-to-provide-affordable-oncology-biosimilars-to-south-africa/

Mackay, M., & Lee, M. (2005). Choice of models for the analysis and forecasting of hospital beds. *Health Care Management Science, 8*(3), 221–230.

Mackintosh, M., & Tibandebage, P. (2016). *Health as a productive sector: Integrating health and industrial policy*. THDR 2017: Background Paper No 8. Dar es Salaam: Economic and Social Research Foundation. https://esrf.or.tz/wp-content/uploads/2021/06/THDR-2017-BP-8.pdf

Mackintosh, M., Banda, G., Tibandebage, P., & Wamae, W. (2016). *Making medicines in Africa: The political economy of industrializing for local health*. Palgrave Macmillan Open.

Mackintosh, M., Mugwagwa, J., Banda, G., & Tunguhole, J. (2017). *Local production of pharmaceuticals and health system strengthening in Africa: An evidence brief*. German Health Practice Collection, BMZ.

Mackintosh, M., Mugwagwa, J., Banda, G., Tibandebage, P., Tunguhole, J., Wangwe, S., & Karimi Njeru, M. (2018a). Health-industry linkages for local health: Reframing policies for African health system strengthening. *Health Policy and Planning, 33*(4), 602–610.

Mackintosh, M., Tibandebage, P., Karimi Njeru, M., Kariuki Kungu, J., Israel, C., & Mujinja, P. G. M. (2018b). Rethinking health sector procurement as developmental linkages in East Africa. *Social Science and Medicine, 200*, 182–189.

Mager, A., & Katzenbach, C. (2021). Future imaginaries in the making and governing of digital technology: Multiple, contested, commodified. *New Media & Society, 23*(2), 223–236.

Magubira, P. (2019, April 20). Morphine is coming around again to Tanzania. *The East African*.

Makau-Barasa, L. K., Greene, S. B., Othieno-Abinya, N. A., Wheeler, S., Skinner, A., & Bennett, A. V. (2018). Improving access to cancer testing and treatment in Kenya. *Journal of Glob Oncology, 4*, 1–8.

Makene, F. S., Ngilangwa, R., Santos, C., Cross, C., Ngoma, T., Mujinja, P. G. M., Wuyts, M., & Mackintosh, M. (2022). Patients' pathways to cancer care in Tanzania: Documenting and addressing social inequalities in reaching a cancer diagnosis. *BMC Health Services Research, 22*(1), 189.

Malerba, F. (2002). Sectoral systems of innovation and production. *Research Policy, 31*(2), 247–264.

Mallath, M. K., Taylor, D. G., Badwe, R. A., Rath, G. K., Shanta, V., Pramesh, C. S., Digumarti, R., Sebastian, P., Borthakur, B. B., Kalwar, A., Kapoor, S., Kumar, S., Gill, J. L., Kuriakose, M. A., Malhotra, H., Sharma, S. C., Shukla, S., Viswanath, L., Chacko, R. T., ... Sullivan, R. (2014). The growing burden of cancer in India: Epidemiology and social context. *The Lancet Oncology, 15*(6), e205-212.

Malpani, R., & Maitland, A. (2021). *Dose of reality: How rich countries and pharmaceutical corporations are breaking their vaccine promises*. https://webassets.oxfamamerica.org/media/documents/A_Dose_of_Reality-Briefing_Note_kOW1yUs.pdf

Manduku, V., Wanjala, C., Njeru, M., Mokua, S., Nyandieka, L., & Mackintosh, M. (2022). Strengthening Kenyan industrial development to improve cancer care *KEMRI Policy Brief* [Online]. https://www.kemri.go.ke/wp-content/uploads/2022/07/ICCA-Project-Policy-Brief-Revised-Strengthening-Kenyan-industrial-development-to-improve-cancer-care-policy-29th-June-2022-2.pdf. Accessed 2 Nov 2022.

Martei, Y. M., Rick, T. J., Fadelu, T., Ezzi, M. S., Hammad, N., Quadri, N. S., Rodrigues, B., Simonds, H., Grover, S., Incrocci, L., & Vanderpuye, V. (2021). Impact of COVID-19 on cancer care delivery in Africa: A cross-sectional survey of oncology providers in Africa. *JCO Global Oncology, 7*, 368–377.

Martins, B., & Mawdsley, J. (2021). Sociotechnical imaginaries of EU defence: The past and the future in the European Defence Fund. *JCMS: Journal of Common Market Studies, 59*(6), 1458–1474.

Mathieu, E., Ritchie, H., Ortiz-Ospina, E., Roser, M., Hasell, J., Appel, C., Giattino, C., & Rodés-Guirao, L. (2021). A global database of COVID-19 vaccinations. *Nature Human Behaviour, 5*(7), 947–953.

Mathur, P., Sathishkumar, K., Chaturvedi, M., Das, P., Sudarshan, K. L., Santhappan, S., Nallasamy, V., John, A., Narasimhan, S., & Roselind, F. S. (2020). Cancer statistics, 2020: Report from national cancer registry programme, India. *JCO Global Oncology, 6*, 1063–1075.

Mattila, P. O., Babar, Z.-U.-D., & Suleman, F. (2021). Assessing the prices and affordability of oncology medicines for three common cancers within the private sector of South Africa. *BMC Health Services Research, 21*(1), 661.

Medicines and Healthcare Products Regulatory Agency. (2017). *International strategy; Item 10* [Online]. MHRA. https://assets.publishing.service.gov.uk/government/uploads/system/uploads/attachment_data/file/609425/Item_10__2017-OB-05__International_Strategy.pdf

Midgley, G., & Lindhult, E. (2021). A systems perspective on systemic innovation. *Systems Research and Behavioral Science, 38*(5), 635–670.

Ministry of Chemicals and Fertilizers. (2021). *Production Linked Incentive Scheme (PLI) for pharmaceuticals*. In Department of Pharmaceuticals (Ed.). Department of Pharmaceuticals, Government of India.

Ministry of Finance and Planning. (2016). *National five year development plan 2016/17–2020/21*. United Republic of Tanzania.

Ministry of Health. (2017). *National cancer control strategy 2017–2022*. Ministry of Health Kenya.

Ministry of Health and Social Services. (2013). *National cancer control strategy 2013–2022*. In Ministry of Health and Social Services (Ed.). United Republic of Tanzania.

Ministry of Industry Trade and Cooperatives. (2017). *Buy Kenya, Build Kenya Strategy*. Nairobi. https://www.trade.go.ke/sites/default/files/BUY_KENYA_BUILD_KENYA_STRATEGY_v2_1.pdf

Miro. (2022). *Miro online whiteboard (no version provided)* [Online]. RealTimeBoard, Inc. www.miro.com. Accessed 27 Jan 2023.

Mishra, B. K., Anu, R., Ameena, S., Mrinalini, S., Nidhi, V., Rawli, P., Naresh Chandra, S., & Sudhir, S. (2013). Opium poppy: Genetic upgradation through intervention of plant breeding techniques. In A. Sven Bode (Ed.), *Plant breeding from laboratories to fields* (Ch. 8). IntechOpen.

Mittra, J., Tait, J., Mastroeni, M., Turner, M. L., Mountford, J. C., & Bruce, K. (2015). Identifying viable regulatory and innovation pathways for regenerative medicine: A case study of cultured red blood cells. *New Biotechnology, 32*(1), 180–190.

Mkwashi, A. S. (2020). *Medical device regulations, industrial capabilities, and affordable healthcare technology development: Case studies from the United Kingdom and South Africa*. The Open University.

Mkwashi, A., & Brass, I. (2022). *The future of medical device regulation and standards: Dealing with critical challenges for connected, intelligent medical devices* [White Paper]. https://petras-iot.org/wp-content/uploads/2021/06/White-Paper-The-Future-of-Medical-Device-Regulation-and-Standards.pdf

Mlange, R., Matovelo, D., Rambau, P., & Kidenya, B. (2016). Patient and disease characteristics associated with late tumour stage at presentation of cervical cancer in northwestern Tanzania. *BMC Women's Health, 16*(1), 5.

MoFP-PED, & NBS. (2019). *Tanzania mainland household budget survey 2017–18, key indicators report*. United Republic of Tanzania.

MOH. (2015). *Health sector development plan, 2015/16–2019/20*. Ministry of Health of the Republic of Uganda.

MOH. (2017). *National cancer control strategy 2017–2022*. Ministry of Health, Nairobi, Kenya.

MOH. (2019). *Kenya national cancer treatment protocols*. Ministry of Health, Nairobi, Kenya.

Moodley, J., Cairncross, L., Naiker, T., & Constant, D. (2018). From symptom discovery to treatment—Women's pathways to breast cancer care: A cross-sectional study. *BMC Cancer, 18*(1), 312.

Morrow, T., & Felcone, L. H. (2004). Defining the difference: What makes biologics unique. *Biotechnology Healthcare, 1*(4), 24–29.

MSD. (2020). *Price catalogue 2019 2020*. Medical Stores Department.

MSH. (2015). *International medical products price guide management sciences for health*. https://msh.org/wp-content/uploads/2020/03/msh-2015-international-medical-products-price-guide.pdf

Mukherjee, S. (2022). *MedTech startups in India* [Online]. https://innohealthmagazine.com/2021/persona/medtech-startups-in-india/

Mulemi, B. A. (2010). *Coping with cancer and adversity: Hospital ethnography in Kenya*. African Studies Centre.

Mutebi, M. (2021). Global cancer control: Choosing the road less travelled. *The Lancet Oncology, 22*(9), 1209–1211.

Mwaka, A. D., Walter, F. M., Scott, S., Harries, J., Wabinga, H., & Moodley, J. (2021). Symptom appraisal, help-seeking and perceived barriers to health-care seeking in Uganda: An exploratory study among women with potential symptoms of breast and cervical cancer. *British Medical Journal Open, 11*(2), e041365.

Nagpal, R., Mehrotra, D., Sehgal, R., Srivastava, G., & Lin, J. C.-W. (2022). Overcoming smart city barriers using multi-modal interpretive structural modeling. *Journal of Signal Processing Systems*.

Natarajan, A., Mehra, N., & Rajkumar, T. (2020). Economic perspective of cancer treatment in India. *Medical Oncology, 37*(11), 101.

Ngoma, T., Mandeli, J., & Holland, J. F. (2015). Downstaging cancer in rural Africa. *International Journal of Cancer, 136*(12), 2875–2879.

Nguyen, V. K. (2010). *Republic of therapy: Triage and sovereignty in West Africa's time of AIDS*. Duke University Press.

Ngwa, W., Addai, B. W., Adewole, I., Ainsworth, V., Alaro, J., Alatise, O. I., Ali, Z., Anderson, B. O., Anorlu, R., Avery, S., Barango, P., Bih, N., Booth, C. M., Brawley, O. W., Dangou, J. M., Denny, L., Dent, J., Elmore, S. N. C., Elzawawy, A., ... Kerr, D. (2022). Cancer in sub-Saharan Africa: A Lancet Oncology commission. *The Lancet Oncology, 23*(6), e251–e312.

Nkengasong, J. N., Ndembi, N., Tshangela, A., & Raji, T. (2020). COVID-19 vaccines: How to ensure Africa has access. *Nature, 586*(7828), 197–199.

Nnaji, C. A., & Moodley, J. (2021). Impact of the COVID-19 pandemic on cancer diagnosis, treatment and research in African health systems: A review of current evidence and contextual perspectives. *Ecancermedicalscience, 15*, 1170.

Nnaji, C. A., Ezenwankwo, E. F., Kuodi, P., Walter, F. M., & Moodley, J. (2022). Timeliness of diagnosis of breast and cervical cancers and associated factors in low-income and middle-income countries: A scoping review. *British Medical Journal Open, 12*(2), e057685.

Nohrstedt, D., & Weible, C. M. (2010). The logic of policy change after crisis: Proximity and subsystem interaction. *Risk, Hazards & Crisis in Public Policy, 1*(2), 1–32.

Nonvignon, J. (2021). Promoting evidence-informed cancer treatment policy making in sub-Saharan Africa. *The Lancet Global Health, 9*(9), e1193–e1194.

Nordal, A. (1956). *Natural and synthetic drugs with morphine—Like effects considered from a pharmacognostic point of view*. United Nations Office on Drugs and Crime.

Ohannesian, N., Gunawardhana, L., Misbah, I., Rakhshandehroo, M., Lin, S. H., & Shih, W.-C. (2020). Commercial and emerging technologies for cancer diagnosis and prognosis based on circulating tumor exosomes. *Journal of Physics: Photonics, 2*(3), 032002.

Olson, A. C., Afyusisye, F., Egger, J., Noyd, D., Likonda, B., Masalu, N., Suneja, G., Chao, N., Zullig, L. L., & Schroeder, K. (2020). Cancer incidence and treatment utilization patterns at a regional cancer center in Tanzania from 2008–2016: Initial report of 2,772 cases. *Cancer Epidemiol, 67*, 101772.

Onsongo, L. N. (2020). Barriers to cancer pain management among nurses in Kenya: A focused ethnography. *Pain Management Nursing, 21*(3), 283–289.

Orujlu, S., Hassankhani, H., Rahmani, A., Sanaat, Z., Dadashzadeh, A., & Allahbakhshian, A. (2022). Barriers to cancer pain management from the perspective of patients: A qualitative study. *Nursing Open, 9*(1), 541–549.

Pharmabiz. (2019). *IIT Mandi researchers aid development of a portable device to screen cervical cancer*.

Pilla. (2018). *Cipla puts biosimilar business on backburner as part of business rationalisation*. https://www.moneycontrol.com/news/business/companies/cipla-puts-biosimilar-business-on-backburner-as-part-of-business-rationalisation-2289369.html

Pilling, D. (2021). African startups attract international investors—But need local ones too. *Financial Times*.

Poli, U., Bidinger, P., & Gowrishankar, S. (2015). Visual inspection with acetic acid (via) screening program: 7 years experience in early detection of cervical cancer and pre-cancers in rural South India. *Indian Journal of Community Medicine: Official Publication of Indian Association of Preventive & Social Medicine, 40*, 203–207.

Pramesh, C. S., Badwe, R. A., Borthakur, B. B., Chandra, M., Raj, E. H., Kannan, T., Kalwar, A., Kapoor, S., Malhotra, H., Nayak, S., Rath, G. K., Sagar, T. G., Sebastian, P., Sarin, R., Shanta, V., Sharma, S. C., Shukla, S., Vijayakumar, M., Vijaykumar, D. K., … Sullivan, R. (2014). Delivery of affordable and equitable cancer care in India. *The Lancet Oncology, 15*(6), e223-233.

Pramesh, C. S., Chaturvedi, H., Reddy, V. A., Saikia, T., Ghoshal, S., Pandit, M., Babu, K. G., Ganpathy, K. V., Savant, D., Mitera, G., Sullivan, R., & Booth, C. M. (2019). Choosing Wisely India: Ten low-value or harmful practices that should be avoided in cancer care. *The Lancet Oncology, 20*(4), e218–e223.

Pramesh, C. S., Chaturvedi, H., Reddy, V. A., Saikia, T., Ghoshal, S., Pandit, M., Govind Babu, K., Ganpathy, K. V., Savant, D., Mitera, G., Sullivan, R., & Booth, C. M. (2020). "Choosing Wisely" for cancer care in India. *Indian Journal of Surgical Oncology, 11*(1), 4–6.

Prince, R. J., & Otieno, P. (2014). In the shadowlands of global health: Observations from health workers in Kenya. *Global Public Health, 9*(8), 927–945.

Pruyt, E. (2013). *Small system dynamics models for big issues: Triple jump towards real-world complexity*. TU Delft Library. ISBN/EAN: 978-94-6186-195-5.

Qorro, E. (2019, February 9). Make health insurance available for palliative care patients in Tz. *The Guardian*.

Qu, L. G., Brand, N. R., Chao, A., & Ilbawi, A. M. (2020). Interventions addressing barriers to delayed cancer diagnosis in low- and middle-income countries: A systematic review. *The Oncologist, 25*(9), e1382–e1395.

Quesada, J. (2019). *Afterword: Revealing erasures, configuring silences: Structural vulnerability in cancer prevention, treatment, and research*. University of New Mexico Press.

Rajagopal, M. R. (2015). The current status of palliative care in India. *Cancer Control*.

Rajagopal, M. R. (2018). Methadone is now available in India: Is the long battle over? *Indian Journal of Palliative Care, 24*(Suppl 1), S1-s3.

Rajagopal, M. R., & Joranson, D. E. (2007). India: Opioid availability—An update. *Journal of Pain and Symptom Management, 33*(5), 615–622.

Rajagopal, M. R., Karim, S., & Booth, C. M. (2017). Oral morphine use in South India: A population-based study. *Journal of Global Oncology, 3*(6), 720–727.

Ramirez, R., & Wilkinson, A. (2016). *Strategic reframing: The Oxford scenario planning approach*. Oxford University Press.

Ranganathan, P., Sengar, M., Chinnaswamy, G., Agrawal, G., Arumugham, R., Bhatt, R., Bilimagga, R., Chakrabarti, J., Chandrasekharan, A., Chaturvedi, H. K., Choudhrie, R., Dandekar, M., Das, A., Goel, V., Harris, C., Hegde, S. K., Hulikal, N., Joseph, D., Kantharia, R., … Pramesh, C. S. (2021). Impact of COVID-19 on cancer care in India: A cohort study. *The Lancet Oncology, 22*(7), 970–976.

Reich, M. R. (1994). Bangladesh pharmaceutical policy and politics. *Health Policy and Planning, 9*(2), 130–143.

Rein, M., & Schön, D. (2013). Reframing policy discourse. In *The argumentative turn in policy analysis and planning*. Duke University Press.

Rubagumya, F., Mitera, G., Ka, S., Manirakiza, A., Decuir, P., Msadabwe, S. C., Adani Ifè, S., Nwachukwu, E., Ohene Oti, N., Borges, H., Mutebi, M., Abuidris, D., Vanderpuye, V., Booth, C. M., & Hammad, N. (2020).

Choosing wisely Africa: Ten low-value or harmful practices that should be avoided in cancer care. *JCO Global Oncology, 6*, 1192–1199.

Samiei, M. (2013). Challenges of making radiotherapy accessible in developing countries. *Cancer Care in Emerging Health Systems*, 87–96.

Sarpong, D., & Maclean, M. (2011). Scenario thinking: A practice-based approach for the identification of opportunities for innovation. *Futures, 43*(10), 1154–1163.

Schön, D. A. (1979). Generative metaphor: A perspective on problem-setting in social policy. In A. Ortony (Ed.), *Metaphor and thoughts* (2nd ed., pp. 137–163). Cambridge University Press.

Schroeder, K., Saxton, A., Mcdade, J., Chao, C., Masalu, N., Chao, C., Wechsler, D. S., Likonda, B., & Chao, N. (2018). Pediatric cancer in Northern Tanzania: Evaluation of diagnosis, treatment, and outcomes. *Journal of Global Oncology, 4*, 1–10.

Seraphin, T. P., Joko-Fru, W. Y., Kamaté, B., Chokunonga, E., Wabinga, H., Somdyala, N. I. M., Manraj, S. S., Ogunbiyi, O. J., Dzamalala, C. P., Finesse, A., Korir, A., N'da, G., Lorenzoni, C., Liu, B., Kantelhardt, E. J., & Parkin, D. M. (2021). Rising prostate cancer incidence in Sub-Saharan Africa: A trend analysis of data from the African cancer registry network. *Cancer Epidemiology, Biomarkers & Prevention, 30*(1), 158–165.

Severance, T. S., Njuguna, F., Olbara, G., Kugo, M., Langat, S., Mostert, S., Klootwijk, L., Skiles, J., Coven, S. L., Overholt, K. M., Kaspers, G., & Vik, T. A. (2022). An evaluation of the disparities affecting the underdiagnosis of pediatric cancer in Western Kenya. *Pediatric Blood & Cancer, 69*(10), e29768.

Shengelia, B., Murray, C. J., & Adams, O. B. (2003). *Beyond access and utilization: Defining and measuring health system coverage*. World Health Organization.

Sirohi, B., Chalkidou, K., Pramesh, C. S., Anderson, B. O., Loeher, P., El Dewachi, O., Shamieh, O., Shrikhande, S. V., Venkataramanan, R., Parham, G., Mwanahamuntu, M., Eden, T., Tsunoda, A., Purushotham, A., Stanway, S., Rath, G. K., & Sullivan, R. (2018). Developing institutions for cancer care in low-income and middle-income countries: From cancer units to comprehensive cancer centres. *The Lancet Oncology, 19*(8), e395–e406.

Smith, R. D., & Mallath, M. K. (2019). History of the growing burden of cancer in India: From antiquity to the 21st century. *Journal of Global Oncology, 5*, 1–15.

Srinivas, S. (2006). Industrial development and innovation: Some lessons from vaccine procurement. *World Development, 34*(10), 1742–176.

Srinivas, S. (2012). *Market menagerie: Health and development in late industrial states*. Stanford University Press.

Srinivas, S. (2016). Healthy industries, unhealthy populations: Lessons from Indian problem-solving. In M. Mackintosh, G. Banda, W. Wamae, & P.

Tibandebage (Eds.), *Making medicines in Africa: The political economy of industrializing for local health*. Palgrave Macmillan.

Srinivas, S. (2020). Institutional variety and the future of economics. *Review of Evolutionary Political Economy, 1*(1), 13–35.

Srinivas, S. (2021a). Industrial policies for health: The G20 must act now. *IAI Commentaries*.

Srinivas, S. (2021b). Updating the economics of the "War on Cancer": False metaphor and faulty economics. *Cancer Control*, 28–31.

Srinivas, S., & Kale, D. (2022). New approaches to learning and regulation in medical devices and diagnostics: Insights from Indian cancer care. *Innovation and Development*, 1–24.

Srinivas, S., Prasad, R., & Rao, P. (2020). *The clinical foreground and industrial background: Customizing national strategy for COVID-19 testing* (IKD Working Paper No. 87). Online: Open University. https://www.open.ac.uk/ikd/publications/working-papers/87

Srinivas, S., & Sutz, J. (2008). Developing countries and innovation: Searching for a new analytical approach (prior Harvard working paper attached, Economic Development and Innovation: Problem-solving in Scarcity Conditions). *Technology in Society, 30*, 129–140.

Ssennyonjo, A., Namakula, J., Kasyaba, R., Orach, S., Bennett, S., & Ssengooba, F. (2018). Government resource contributions to the private-not-for-profit sector in Uganda: Evolution, adaptations and implications for universal health coverage. *International Journal for Equity in Health, 17*(1), 130.

Stefan, D. C., Masalu, N., Ngendahayo, L., Amadori, D., Botteghi, M., Mendy, M., Othieno-Aabinya, N. A., Ngoma, T., Asirwa, F., Balogun, O., Ngwa, W., Vuhahula, E., & Adesina, A. (2015). Pathology and oncology in Africa: Education and training for the future in cancer research—East African Regional Meeting. *Infectious Agents and Cancer, 10*, 48.

Stein, F., Perry, M., Banda, G., Woolhouse, M., & Mutapi, F. (2020). Oxygen provision to fight COVID-19 in sub-Saharan Africa. *BMJ Global Health, 5*, e002786.

Sterman, J. (2000). *Business dynamics: Systems thinking and modeling for a complex world*. Irwin/McGraw-Hill.

Sullivan, N. (2012). Enacting spaces of inequality: Placing global/state governance within a Tanzanian hospital. *Space and Culture, 15*(1), 57–67.

Sullivan, R., Pramesh, C. S., & Booth, C. M. (2017). Look beyond technology in cancer care. *Nature, 549*(7672), 325–328.

Sung, H., Ferlay, J., Siegel, R. L., Laversanne, M., Soerjomataram, I., Jemal, A., & Bray, F. (2021). Global cancer statistics 2020: GLOBOCAN estimates of incidence and mortality worldwide for 36 cancers in 185 countries. *CA: A Cancer Journal for Clinicians, 71*(3), 209–249.

Tait, J., & Banda, G. (2016). *Proportionate and adaptive governance of innovative technologies Financial Technologies (FinTech), Cell Therapies and Synthetic Biology: The role of regulations, guidelines and standards*. BSI (British Standards Institution).

Tait, J., Banda, G., & Watkins, A. (2018). *Proportionate and adaptive governance of innovative technologies (PAGIT): A framework to guide policy and regulatory decision making*. British Standards Institution (BSI).

Tait, J., & Wield, D. (2021). Policy support for disruptive innovation in the life sciences. *Technology Analysis & Strategic Management, 33*(3), 307–319.

The Hindu Business Line. (2017). *Cipla increases stake in Uganda company*. https://www.thehindubusinessline.com/companies/Cipla-increases-stake-in-Uganda-company/article20691436.ece

UNAIDS. (2021). *A dose of reality: How rich countries and pharmaceutical corporations are breaking their vaccine promises* [Online]. https://www.unaids.org/en/resources/presscentre/featurestories/2021/october/20211021_dose-of-reality

UNAIDS. (2022). *The impact of the COVID-19 response on the supply chain, availability and cost of generic antiretroviral medicines for HIV in low- and middle-income countries* [Online]. https://www.unaids.org/sites/default/files/media_asset/covid19-supply-chain-availability-cost-generic-arv_en.pdf

UNIDO. (2019). *Pharmaceutical industry in sub-Saharan Africa: A guide for promoting pharmaceutical production in Africa*. United Nations Industrial Development Organization.

United Nations. (n. d.). 'Single Convention on Narcotic Drugs, 1961. As amended by the 1962 Protocol amending the Single Convention on Narcotic Drugs, 1961'. United Nations. Available at: https://www.unodc.org/pdf/convention_1961_en.pdf

United Nations Office on Drugs and Crime. (UNODC) (2005). *South Asia regional profile*. United Nations Office on Drugs and Crime.

United Nations Office on Drugs and Crime. (UNODC) (2011). *The non-medical use of prescription drugs* [Policy direction issues]. United Nations Office on Drugs and Crime.

United National Office on Drugs and Crime. (UNODC) (2021). *World drug report: Executive summary policy implications*. United Nations.

UNU-EHS & UNDRR. (2022). *Rethinking risks in times of COVID-19* [Online]. https://www.undrr.org/rethinking-risk-times-covid-19. Accessed 22 Aug 2022.

Urias, E. (2019). The potential synergies between industrial and health policies for access to medicines: Insights from the Brazilian policy of universal access to HIV/AIDS treatment. *Innovation and Development, 9*(2), 245–260.

URT. (2017). *Tanzania breast health care assessment 2017*. Ministry of Health, Community Development, Gender, Elderly and Children (MHCDGEC), United Republic of Tanzania.

URT. (n.d.). *National Cancer Control Strategy (NCCS) 2013–2022*. Ministry of Health and Social Welfare, United Republic of Tanzania.

Vallath, N., Rajagopal, M. R., & Tandon, T. (2017). *Guidelines for stocking and dispensing essential narcotic drugs in medical institutions national cancer grid*.

Van Den Beuken-Van Everdingen, M. H., Hochstenbach, L. M., Joosten, E. A., Tjan-Heijnen, V. C., & Janssen, D. J. (2016). Update on prevalence of pain in patients with cancer: Systematic review and meta-analysis. *Journal of Pain and Symptom Management, 51*(6), 1070-1090.e1079.

Van Der Plas, W. Y., Benjamens, S., & Kruijff, S. (2020). The increased need for palliative cancer care in Sub-Saharan Africa. *European Journal of Surgical Oncology, 46*(7), 1373–1376.

Van Notten, P. W. F. (2006). Scenario development: A typology of approaches. In: OECD (Ed.), *Think scenarios, rethink education*. OECD Publishing.

Velayudhan, Y., Ollapally, M., Upadhyaya, V., Nair, S., & Aldo, M. (2004). Introduction of palliative care into undergraduate medical and nursing education in India: A critical evaluation. *Indian Journal of Palliative Care, 10*.

Verma, S. (2014). Cancer survival rate in India among the lowest in the world *Healthworld.Com*.

Vollmar. (2017). Scenario technique: A tool for simulating and reflecting on alternative solutions. In D. De Savigny, K. Blanchet, & T. Adam (Eds.), *Applied systems thinking for health systems research: A methodological handbook*. McGraw-Hill Education.

Wang, T., Molassiotis, A., Chung, B. P. M., & Tan, J. Y. (2018). Unmet care needs of advanced cancer patients and their informal caregivers: A systematic review. *BMC Palliative Care, 17*(1), 96.

Wangwe, S. M., Simonetti, R., Tibandebage, P., Mackintosh, M., Israel, C., & Mujinja, P. (2021). Upgrading under globalization in health-related industries in Tanzania: The case for dynamic industrial deepening. *Innovation and Development, 12*, 479–496.

Watkins, A., Papaioannou, T., Mugwagwa, J., & Kale, D. (2015). National innovation systems and the intermediary role of industry associations in building institutional capacities for innovation in developing countries: A critical review of the literature. *Research Policy, 44*, 1407–1418.

WHO. (2016a). *Planning and implementing palliative care services: A guide for programme managers*. World Health Organization.

WHO. (2016b). *Towards improving access to medical devices through local production: Phase II: Report of a case study in four sub-Saharan countries*. World Health Organization.

WHO. (2017). *China policies to promote local production of pharmaceutical products and protect public health*. World Health Organization.

WHO. (2018a). *Integrating palliative care and symptom relief into primary health care: A WHO guide for planners, implementers and managers*. World Health Organisation.

WHO. (2018b). *Pricing of cancer medicines and its impacts technical report*. World Health Organization.

WHO. (2018c). *Technical report: Pricing of cancer medicines and its impacts: A comprehensive technical report for the World Health Assembly Resolution 70.12: Operative paragraph 2.9 on pricing approaches and their impacts on availability and affordability of medicines for the prevention and treatment of cancer*. World Health Organization.

WHO. (2018d). *WHO guidelines for the pharmacological and radiotherapeutic management of cancer pain in adults and adolescents*. WHO.

WHO. (2020). *WHO report on cancer: Setting priorities, investing wisely and providing care for all*. World Health Organization.

WHO. (2021a). *Health systems for health security: A framework for developing capacities for international health regulations, and components in health systems and other sectors that work in synergy to meet the demands imposed by health emergencies*. World Health Organization.

WHO. (2021b). *World Health Organization model list of essential medicines—22nd List, 2021*. World Health Organization.

WHO. (2021c). *World Local Production Forum: Enhancing access to medicines and other health technologies, report of the first WLPF*. World Health Organization.

Wilkinson, A., Kupers, R., & Mangalagiu, D. (2013). How plausibility-based scenario practices are grappling with complexity to appreciate and address 21st century challenges. *Technological Forecasting and Social Change, 80*(4), 699–710.

Winterhalter, S., Zeschky, M., Neumann, L., & Gassmann, O. (2017a). Business models for frugal innovation in emerging markets: The case of the medical device and laboratory equipment industry. *Technovation*, 66–67.

Winterhalter, S., Zeschky, M., Neumann, L., & Gassmann, O. (2017b). Business models for frugal innovation in emerging markets: The case of the medical device and laboratory equipment industry. *Technovation, 66*(6–7), 3–13.

Wolstenholme, E. F. (2003). Towards the definition and use of a core set of archetypal structures in system dynamics. *System Dynamics Review, 19*(1), 7–26.

Worboys, M., & Petitjean, P. (1996). British Colonial Science Policy, 1918–1939. In *Les Sciences Coloniales: Figures and institutions* (pp. 99–112). ORSTOM.

Wright, G., Bradfield, R., & Cairns, G. (2013). Does the intuitive logics method—And its recent enhancements—Produce 'effective' scenarios? *Technological Forecasting and Social Change, 80*, 631–642.

Wright, G., & Goodwin, P. (2009). Decision making and planning under low levels of predictability: Enhancing the scenario method. *International Journal of Forecasting, 25*(4), 813–825.

Index

Note: The page numbers followed by 'b', 'f' and 't' represents box, figure and table

A

access to cancer care, case studies, 70b, 75b, 77b, 83–84b
access to medicines
  morphine, 243–249, 268–273, 278
  oncology, 63, 80–82
active pharmaceutical ingredients (APIs), 12, 28, 31, 39
addiction to morphine, 247, 250, 283, 284
affordability of treatment, 82–88, 163–166
African manufacturing
  active pharmaceutical ingredients (APIs), 12, 28
  antibiotics, 148
  biologics, 40, 217–218, 220–228
  challenges, 41, 108, 149–151, 179–186
  current capabilities, 10–12, 11f, 175–179
  government policy, 9, 183, 155–156, 185
  health security, 5, 29, 30, 317–319, 322–324, 325
  innovation, 39–40, 140–141, 146–149, 305–308
  investment in, 151–152, 158–159, 227–228, 301–302
  opioids, 282, 199
  pandemic innovation, 26, 139–141, 146–149, 305–308
  see also specific countries
African Vaccine Manufacturing Initiative (AVMI), 225, 226
Afrigen, 224t, 225, 229
AIDS. *See* HIV/AIDS
AINDRA, 197t, 200–204, 209t
alkaloid production, 251–252, 256
antibiotic production, 148
anti-retrovirals (ARVs), 33, 234

G. Banda et al. (eds.), *Cancer Care in Pandemic Times: Building Inclusive Local Health Security in Africa and India*, International Political Economy Series,
https://doi.org/10.1007/978-3-031-44123-3

APIs. *See* active pharmaceutical ingredients (APIs)
artificial intelligence (AI), 200–204
ARVs. *See* anti-retrovirals (ARVs)
Aspen, 167, 171, 175, 223t, 225
Avesta Biologicals Ltd, 235
AVMI. *See* African Vaccine Manufacturing Initiative (AVMI)

B

bank loans, 152
Bill and Melinda Gates Foundation (BMGF), 151
biologics
  cancer treatment, 218–219
  Cipla, 234–238
  incremental vs disruptive innovation, 219–221, 228–234, 322–323
  mRNA vaccines, 32, 217, 222–228, 231t
Biovac, 224t
blood transfusions, 81
BMGF. *See* Bill and Melinda Gates Foundation (BMGF)
breast cancer, 7–8, 49–51, 75b, 100
business models, 192–197, 208–210, 219–221

C

Cancer Access Initiative, 178
cancer centres, 9, 18, 80, 156, 253
cancer rates, 7–8, 193, 200, 268, 279
cancer research focus, 4, 5–9, 14–19, 315–317
caregivers, impact, 49–51, 55–57, 59–63
cDNA (copy DNA), 229
cell therapies, 219
cervical cancer, 7, 54, 55, 83–84b, 96–98, 200–204
CFCE. *See* 'Cupboard Full, Cupboard Empty' (CFCE) framework
chemotherapy, 85, 163, 165, 166
China, 12–13, 27, 31, 39
Choosing Wisely India initiative, 134, 259–260
'churning', 74, 99
Cipla, 234–238
clean room technology, Kenya, 149–151
collaboration, international, 175, 183
colon cancer, 70b
competitive pricing, medicines, 171–179
Concentrate of Poppy Straw (CPS) process, 251, 254–256
copy DNA. *See* cDNA (copy DNA)
coronavirus. *See* Covid-19
costs for patients
  diagnosis, 105–110
  medical insurance, 85–88, 90
  travel, 77–79, 80, 85
  treatment, 69, 82–88, 164–166, 179
counselling, 81
Covid-19
  innovation, 39–40, 140–141, 146–149
  local health security, 317–319
  mRNA vaccines, 32, 217, 220–228, 231t
  need and demand, 123–128
  policy changes, 36, 41–44, 315, 322–323
  supply chains, 28–32, 33
CPS. *See* Concentrate of Poppy Straw (CPS) process
cross-sectoral collaboration, 291–296, 298–313, 317, 318. *See also* health-industry collaboration

'Cupboard Full, Cupboard Empty' (CFCE) framework, 119, 128–136

D

deaths, 7–8, 192, 201
delays in diagnosis
  affordability of treatment, 82–88, 163–166
  fear of cancer, 52–53, 57–58, 109, 198
  lack of pathology, 103–105
  late-stage presentation, 93–97
  'maze' of cancer care, 69–75, 79–82, 89–91
  referrals, 74, 99–103, 107
diagnostic devices, 12, 43–44, 197–206, 211
digital technologies. *See* artificial intelligence (AI)
dignity and rehabilitation products, 63–64, 144, 304
disruptive vs incremental innovation, 219–221, 228–234, 322, 323
doctors. *See* health professionals
downstaging cancer, 8
drug controls, 244, 258–259, 274, 282, 283
drugs. *See* morphine; oncology medicines

E

early detection of cancer, 12, 96–99, 144, 197–206, 208
Economic and Social Council (UN), 253
education and training, 154–155, 159, 270
Egypt, vaccines, 222
emotional impact, 50, 52–55, 56–59
employment, impact, 49–51, 64
essential medicines, 144, 167–169, 171, 245, 248
Essential Package of Palliative Care and Pain Relief Health Services, 245
exports
  from China, 12, 31–32
  from India, 10, 169–170, 172–175, 253–255
  pandemic supply chains, 28–30
  see also imports

F

faith-based support, 59–63, 65–66
family and friends, 49–51, 55–57
fear of cancer, 52–53, 57–58, 109, 198
'fellow traveller' concept, 233, 239
financial impact, 49–51, 55, 59–63, 87–88, 107
foreign investment in Africa, 151–154, 183–186
free health care
  National Health Insurance Fund (NHIF), 86–87, 106, 110, 165
  Universal Health Coverage (UHC), 155, 157, 325
friends and family. *See* family and friends
friends and family, impact, 49–51, 55–57, 59–63
funding
  bank loans, 152
  international, 151–152
  public health, 19, 144, 156–157
  startups, 198, 211

G

GAVI. *See* Global Alliance for Vaccines and Immunisations (GAVI)

generic medicines. *See* oncology medicines
Ghana, vaccines, 227t
Global Alliance for Vaccines and Immunisations (GAVI), 233
global supply chains, Covid-19, 28–32, 33
government policy
  Africa, 9, 155–156, 183, 184
  India, 9, 32, 38–39, 118, 120
  procurement, 40
  regulations, 247–249, 256–260, 278–281
  sociotechnical imaginaries, 36

H

hand sanitizer production, 140
health-industry collaboration
  East Africa, 155–159, 306–308
  reframing policy, 322–324
  scenarios, 294, 309–313
  South Africa, 43–44, 211
health professionals
  failures, 53–55, 99–102, 198–200
  shortages, 97, 103–104
  support for reforms, 116, 184
  training, 248, 249, 284–285
health security. *See* local health security
HIV/AIDS
  anti-retrovirals (ARVs), 33, 234
  compared to cancer, 57, 59–60, 63
hospitals, 74, 258, 276
household income, 60–63, 88, 108, 192

I

ICCA. *See* Innovation for Cancer Care in Africa (ICCA)
ICDC. *See* Industrial and Commercial Development Corporation (ICDC)
illicit drugs. *See* drug controls
imports
  Africa, 12–13, 29–32, 142, 147, 166–170, 279
  India, 31, 33
  taxes and duties, 158
  see also exports
incremental vs disruptive innovation, 219–221, 228–234, 322, 323
India
  cancer care challenges, 8, 116
  Choosing Wisely India initiative, 134, 259–260
  Cipla, 234–238
  'Cupboard Full, Cupboard Empty' (CFCE) framework, 119, 128–136
  exports, 10, 30, 169–170, 172–175, 253–255
  Kerala state model, 250
  morphine, 243–249, 251–260
  National Cancer Grid, 9
  pandemic, 32–34, 124
  pharmaceutical sector, 30
  startups, 191–193, 197–206, 206–210
Industrial and Commercial Development Corporation (ICDC), 153
industrial organization challenges, 245–251, 256–259
industrial policy
  Covid-19, 43–44, 124–128
  India, 119–120, 128–136, 251–255
  see also health-industry collaboration
innovation
  Africa, 39–40, 140–141, 146–149, 305–308

incremental vs disruptive, 219–221, 228–234, 231t, 322
national systems of innovation (NIS), 323–324
pandemic, 39–40
scenarios, 294–296, 298–309
startups, 191–193, 197–206, 206–210
Innovation for Cancer Care in Africa (ICCA), 3–5, 14–19, 296, 298, 300f
institutional variety (IV), 121, 124, 125, 128, 132
Institut Pasteur de Dakar, 222, 223t
Institut Pasteur de Tunis, 222, 224t
insurance, medical, 85–87, 90, 106, 110, 165, 276
international collaboration, 175, 185
investment in Africa, 151–152, 158–159, 227–228t, 301
IV. *See* institutional variety (IV)
IV fluids, 147, 149

K
KEMRI. *See* Kenyan Medical Research Institute (KEMRI)
KEMSA. *See* Kenyan Medical Supplies Authority (KEMSA)
Kenya
access to cancer care, 49–51, 69–75, 89–91, 96–103
health system organisation, 19
innovation scenarios, 304–309
investment in, 151–154, 228
local manufacturing, 39–40, 139–141, 228t, 306–308
National Health Insurance Fund (NHIF), 86–87, 106, 110, 165
procurement, 145–146, 157–158
sterile technology, 149, 150
vaccines, 40, 225
Kenyan Essential Medicines List, 166
Kenyan Medical Research Institute (KEMRI), 39–40
Kenyan Medical Supplies Authority (KEMSA), 143
Kerala state model, 250

L
laboratory capabilities, 103–105
Lancet Palliative Care Commission, 243, 245, 276
late-stage diagnosis, 93–97, 108–110, 111
licensing
Cipla, 238
morphine, 254, 258, 273–275, 284
linkages. *See* health-industry collaboration
LMICs. *See* low and middle-income countries (LMICs), challenges
loans, bank, 152
local facilities, lack of, 76–79, 98
local health security, 5, 29–31, 317–319, 323, 325. *See also* sociotechnical imaginaries
local manufacturing in India, 10, 30, 34
lockdowns. *See* Covid-19
low and middle-income countries (LMICs), challenges, 7–9, 13, 193–197, 210–213, 243–249

M
MAbs. *See* monoclonal antibodies (MAbs)
machine learning, 203
Maneno case study, 49–51
manufacturing incentives, 39, 145–146, 161
mapping systems, 295, 300f
market consolidation, 144, 158

'maze' of cancer care, 69–75, 79–82, 89–91
medical insurance, 85–87, 90, 105–107, 110, 165, 276. *See also* out-of-pocket (OP) payments
Medical Stores Department (MSD), 145, 283
medical technology (MedTech) sector
  African manufacturing, 12–13, 42, 305–308
  diagnostic devices, 12, 43–44, 197–206, 211
  need-demand gaps, 141, 144
  pathology, 103–105
medicines. *See* morphine; oncology medicines
MEDS. *See* Mission for Essential Drugs & Supplies (MEDS)
MedTech. *See* medical technology (MedTech) sector
men, prostate cancer, 7, 77b, 104, 107
messenger ribonucleic acid. *See* mRNA (messenger ribonucleic acid) vaccines
misinformation, cancer, 50, 52–55, 57
Mission for Essential Drugs & Supplies (MEDS), 143
monoclonal antibodies (MAbs), 216–219, 220
Morocco, vaccines, 225, 228t
morphine, 247–249
  access to, 243–249, 268–273, 278
  addiction, 247, 250, 283, 284
  controls and regulations, 258–259, 273, 283, 284
  India, 251–259
  need-demand gap, 278–281
  pricing, 276–278, 282–283
  Tanzania, 270–278, 282, 298–303
  training staff, 284
mortality rates, 7–8, 192, 193, 199
mRNA (messenger ribonucleic acid) vaccines, 32, 217, 222–228, 231t
MSD. *See* Medical Stores Department (MSD)

N

narco-terrorism, 258–259. *See also* drug controls
Narcotic Drugs and Psychotropic Substances Act (NDPS), 247–249
National Cancer Grid, India, 9, 253
National Health Insurance Fund (NHIF), 86–87, 106, 110, 165
national systems of innovation (NIS), 323–324. *See also* health-industry collaboration
NCDs. *See* non-communicable diseases (NCDs)
NDPS. *See* Narcotic Drugs and Psychotropic Substances Act (NDPS)
need-demand gap, morphine
  India, 251–255
  Tanzania, 269, 273–275, 278–281
NGOs. *See* non-governmental organizations (NGOs)
NHIF. *See* National Health Insurance Fund (NHIF)
non-communicable diseases (NCDs), 5, 192
non-governmental organizations (NGOs), 98
North Africa, vaccines, 11, 11f, 220–224
nucleic acid therapies. *See* RNA (ribonucleic acid)
nurses, training, 284

O

Ocean Road Cancer Institute (ORCI), 272, 274

oncology medicines
access to, 63, 80–82
affordability, 82–88, 163–166
African manufacturing, 10–12, 11f, 26, 146–149, 175–179
chemotherapy, 85, 164–166
essential list, 144, 167–169, 171, 245, 248
imports/exports, 12, 28–32, 169–170
pricing, 171–175, 276–278, 283
radiotherapy, 134, 204–206
toxicity, 180, 250
opioids/opiates, 255f, 260, 284. *See also* morphine
oral cancer device, 197–200
ORCI. *See* Ocean Road Cancer Institute (ORCI)
out-of-pocket (OP) payments, 88. *See also* medical insurance

P
packaging production, 148
painkillers, 272
palliative care
East Africa, 265–273, 278–281, 302–303
Essential Package of Palliative Care and Pain Relief Health Services, 245
experiences of pain, 271
importance of, 243–244
India, 135f, 249, 251
see also morphine
Panacea Medical Technologies, 197t, 204–206, 209–210, 209t
pandemic. *See* Covid-19
pap smears, 201, 202. *See also* cervical cancer
paracetamol, 272
pathology capabilities, 103–105
pethidine, 284
pharmaceutical industry, current capabilities
Africa, 10–13, 34, 175–179
India, 10, 30–34, 37–39
PLI. *See* Production Linked Incentive (PLI) Scheme
policy frameworks, India
Choosing Wisely India Initiative, 134, 259–260
'Cupboard Full, Cupboard Empty' (CFCE), 119, 128–136
post-mortem fees, 276
poverty, 52, 82–84, 108
prices of medicines, 28, 172–179, 276–278, 283
Primary Health Centre (PHC), 129–131
private health care, 18–19, 72, 75b, 76, 86, 105
procurement
Africa, 143–146, 157–158, 167, 233, 248, 278–279
India, 174–175, 208
Production Linked Incentive (PLI) Scheme, 32
prostate cancer, 8, 77b, 104, 107
psychological impact, 55
public health care, 17, 72, 76, 86, 105

Q
quality control, 154

R
R&D. *See* research and development (R&D)
radiotherapy, 134, 204–206
reagents, 105
Recognized Medical Institutions, India, 248
referrals, 74, 99–103, 107

regenerative medicine, 218, 230
regulatory systems
  incremental vs disruptive innovation, 228–234
  medical equipment, 42, 186
  morphine, 247–249, 251–252, 258–259, 282–283
rehabilitation and dignity products, 63–64, 144, 304
research and development (R&D), 159, 160, 310–311
research focus, cancer, 4, 5–9, 14–19, 315–317
retail prices of medicines, 171–175, 278
RNA (ribonucleic acid), 217, 219, 222–228, 231t

S

SARS-CoV-2. *See* Covid-19
Sascan, 197–200, 197t, 208, 209t
scenarios for innovation, 294–296, 298–309
screening, 8, 96–99, 144, 198–206
self-funding treatment, 77
self-referrals, 74, 101–103, 108
Senegal, vaccines, 222, 223t, 227t
shortages, 80, 97, 103–104, 105, 141, 142
side effects of treatment, 54, 57, 63–64
Single Convention of Narcotic Drugs (UN), 243, 244
social pain of cancer, 14, 49–60, 62–66
socioeconomic challenges. *See* poverty
sociotechnical imaginaries, 34–37, 292–296, 298–309, 317, 318
South Africa
  active pharmaceutical ingredients (APIs), 12, 168
  Cipla, 236–237
  health-industry collaboration, 43–44, 211
  vaccines, 11f, 40, 222, 223t, 227
South African Competition Commission, 175
spiritual support, 65–66
stakeholder views, 285, 292, 299–302, 311
startups
  Africa, 211
  India, 191–193, 197–206, 206–210
sterile technology, 149, 150, 180
stigma of cancer, 51, 56–59, 61, 62–63
supply chains, 28–32, 33, 140, 156, 251, 323
support for patients, 58–60, 64–66
survivors, cancer, 63–64

T

Taliban, opium ban, 258
Tamil Nadu Medical Services Corporation (TNMSC), 174–175
Tanzania
  access to cancer care, 18–19, 75, 96–103
  investment in, 143–146, 152, 301
  National Health Insurance Fund (NHIF), 105–107
  opioid manufacturing, 273–281, 282, 299, 301–303
  palliative care, 267, 269–273, 298–303
  procurement, 145–146, 157–158
  sterile technology, 149
  travel costs, 108–110
taxes and duties on imports, 158
Team Europe, 222
technology transfer
  Africa, 151–156, 183, 225, 229
  biologics, 221, 228–237, 229

TNMSC. *See* Tamil Nadu Medical Services Corporation (TNMSC)
toxicity of medicines, 250
Trade-Related Intellectual Property Rights (TRIPS), 38
traditional medicine, 95
training and education, 154–155, 159, 270
travel costs, 78, 80, 85, 108–110
treatment for cancer
  affordability, 82–88, 163–166
  biologics, 218–219
  blood transfusions, 81
  chemotherapy, 85, 163, 165, 166
  downstaging, 8
  radiotherapy, 134, 204–206
  side effects, 54, 57, 63–64
  traditional medicine, 95
  see also morphine
triad of health care, 121–123, 125, 129, 132, 133, 135
TRIPS. *See* Trade-Related Intellectual Property Rights (TRIPS)
tumour boards, 100
Tunisia, vaccines, 222, 224t

U
Uganda, 278–281, 284
UHC. *See* Universal Health Coverage (UHC)
United Nations (UN), 244, 253
United States (US), 178, 254
Universal Health Coverage (UHC), 155, 157, 325

V
vaccines
  Africa, 11f, 12, 40, 217–219, 222–228
  GAVI, 233
  India, 32, 33
Vacsera, 222–224
ventilators, regulations, 42
visual inspection with acetic acid (VIA), 97–98. *See also* cervical cancer

W
waiting times, 73
WHO. *See* World Health Organization (WHO)
witchcraft, as cause, 53, 95
women
  breast cancer, 7–8, 49–51, 75b, 96–98, 100
  cervical cancer, 7, 54, 83–84b, 200–204
  stigma, 51
work, impact, 49–51, 61, 64
World Health Organization (WHO), 111, 183, 269–270

Y
young people, and cancer, 64

Z
ZAZIBONA collaboration, 232

The manufacturer's authorised representative in the EU is Springer Nature Customer Service Centre GmbH, Europaplatz 3, 69115 Heidelberg, Germany. If you have any concerns regarding our products, please contact ProductSafety@springernature.com

Printed and bound by CPI Group (UK) Ltd, Croydon, CR0 4YY
28/09/2026
02224060-0003